CISTERCIAN STUDIES SERIES: NUMBER NINETY–EIGHT

ERUDITION AT GOD'S SERVICE

CISTERCIAN STUDIES SERIES: NUMBER NINETY–EIGHT

ERUDITION AT GOD'S SERVICE

STUDIES IN MEDIEVAL CISTERCIAN HISTORY, XI

Edited by
John R. Sommerfeldt

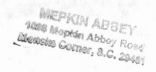

Cistercian Publications Inc.
1987

© Copyright, Cistercian Publications Inc., 1987

The work of Cistercian Publications is made
possible in part by support from Western Michigan
University to the Institute of Cistercian Studies.

Available in Britain and Europe from
A.R. Mowbray & Co Ltd
St Thomas House Becket Street
Oxford OX 1 1SJ

Available elsewhere (including Canada) from

Cistercian Publications
WMU Station
Kalamazoo, Michigan 49008

Typeset by the Carmelites of Indianapolis

Library of Congress Cataloging-in-Publication Data

Erudition in God's Service
(Studies in medieval Cistercian history; 11)
(Cisterican studies series; no. 98)
Papers from the 1985 and 1986 Cistercian Studies
Conferences, organized by the Institute of Cistercian
Studies of Western Michigan University, and held in
conjunction with the 20th and 21st International
Congress of Medieval Studies in Kalamazoo, Michigan,
on May 9–12, 1985 and May 8–11, 1986.
1. Cistercians—Europe—History—Congresses.
2. Spirituality—Catholic Church—History of
doctrines—Middle Ages, 600–1500—Congresses
3. Catholic Church—Europe—History—Congresses.
4. Europe—Church history—Middle Ages, 600–1500—
Congresses. I. Sommerfeldt, John R. II. Cistercian
Studies Conference (1985: Western Michigan University)
III. Cistercian Studies Conference (1986: Western
Michigan University) IV. Western Michigan University.
Institute of Cistercian Studies. V. Series.
VI. Series: Cistercian studies series; no. 98.
BX3415.E78 1987   271'.12   87–6380
ISBN 0-87907-898-7

This volume is gratefully dedicated to

CORNELIUS LOEW,

President and Chairman of the Board

of

Cistercian Publications,

whose unfailing and resolute
support of the Institute of
Cistercian Studies and the
Medieval Institute of Western
Michigan University have made
possible the Conferences and
Congresses at which these
papers were presented.

TABLE OF CONTENTS

PREFACE

The International Congress on Medieval Studies met for the twentieth and twenty-first times on May 9–12, 1985, and May 8–11, 1986, at Western Michigan University in Kalamazoo, Michigan. The undefatigible Director or the Medieval Institute, Professor Otto Gründler, served once more as our gracious host. And once more he encouraged the Institute of Cistercian Studies of Western Michigan University to hold its 1985 and 1986 Cistercian Studies Conferences in conjunction with the Congress.

Professor E. Rozanne Elder, Director of the Institute of Cistercian Studies and Editorial Director of Cistercian Publications, was the convener and hostess of these Conferences within Congresses. She assembled scholars from Austria, Canada, France, Germany, the Netherlands, as well as the United States, for the two Conferences. These scholars read some sixty excellent papers in nineteen full and profitable sessions during the meetings. I join this distinguished group in expressing our deep gratitude to Professor Elder for herculean labors and unmatched graciousness as our hostess.

The title of this collection derives from that of one of its papers, the second by Professor Kienzle on Hélinand of Froidmont. Curiously enough, this is the second time that Professor Kienzle has supplied the title for a volume of *Studies in Medieval Cistercian History*. Professor Kienzle's ability to turn a happy phrase is a boon to an editor hard-pressed to identify a common theme in papers ranging chronologically from the sixth to the sixteenth century and topically from eucharistic spirituality to the patronage of Burgundian knights. The erudition of Bernard and William and Aelred is surely of a different sort than that of Hélinand, but both were deliberately—indeed passionately—put to God's service. And I trust the erudition displayed by the contributors to this volume will contribute to the same end.

J. R. S.

The University of Dallas

EAT, DRINK, AND BE MERRY:
THE EUCHARISTIC SPIRITUALITY
OF THE CISTERCIAN FATHERS

Marsha L. Dutton

WILLIAM OF ST THIERRY says:

> The sight for seeing God . . . is charity. There are, how-
> ever, two eyes in this sight, always throbbing by a sort of
> natural intensity to look toward the light that is God: love
> and reason. . . . One of them—reason—cannot see God ex-
> cept in what he is not, but love cannot bring itself to rest ex-
> cept in what he is. . . . Reason . . . seems to advance through
> what God is not toward what God is. Love, putting aside
> what God is not, rejoices to lose itself in what he is.[1]

With these two eyes the Cistercian Fathers look into the Eucharist for the sight of God, attempting with the eye of reason to understand the presence of Christ's body and blood in the bread and
wine—to see God in what he is not—and with the eye of love to
rest in union with him, to lose themselves in what he is. This attempt to do two things at once, to understand God rationally and
love him intimately, results for them in an understanding that is
love, a transformation of the two eyes into a single vision of God's
face, a contemplation that manifests itself in a spirituality centered
in the sacred humanity of Christ.

The real presence of Christ in the Eucharist, of the substance of
his body and blood in the sacrament, increasingly occupied twelfth-
century Christians anxious to ascertain the way in which he was
present there, the relationship between the *res*—the substance of
the Eucharist—and the *sacramentum*—the species of bread and

wine. As such questions ramified, the Cistercian Fathers began seriously to explore them. If the Eucharist was the food of salvation, they needed to understand what it was and what were its effects. The eye of reason had plenty of work to do.[2]

At the same time the Fathers longed to know God now, in this life, to love him and join with him in mutual embrace. While his presence in the Eucharist ensured that embrace, their rational hesitance to relax into a solution theologically but not emotionally satisfying restrained them from easily acquiescing to it. Their unsatisfied longing to know and love God led the Cistercians of the twelfth century finally to a new way of understanding him and to intimate love shaped by that understanding. So they created a eucharistic and incarnational spirituality, one that was within a century to turn medieval Christianity toward the humanity of Christ and so to direct the attention of western Christianity from that time on to the incarnate God, Jesus of Nazareth.

Three of the early Cistercians, William of St Thierry, Baldwin of Ford, and Isaac of Stella, wrote theological treatises on the Eucharist.[3] But as the Fathers were not men of the schools, their inquiry into eucharistic theology emerged not by and large in theological treatises but in their affective works, treatises and sermons concerned with knowing God through love. At the same time they were intellectual men, insisting that reason, however alienated from God, must seek him out and understand him before the heart can love him. William so defines the route to God and the Cistercian inquiry into the Eucharist, urging: "Therefore let us strive as far as possible to see, by seeing to understand, and by understanding to love, so that by loving we may possess."[4]

The Cistercian Fathers' approach to the Eucharist begins, then, in two places with two different questions, one rational, the other affective. From them two lines of inquiry develop, but as the one engenders the other and exists for its sake, the two cannot long stay separate. They overlap and intertwine almost at once, uniting in one spirituality centered in Jesus. Although William, for example, allows them to be distinct for a time, he suggests that at last: "Love gives life to reason and reason gives light to love; thus their gaze becomes simple as the dove's in contemplation and prudent in circumspection."[5]

This paper attempts to keep the two strands separate, to speak of the Fathers' approach to the Eucharist through reason and through love, but the distinction is artificial and nonsustainable. I here first establish the framework for a complete study of the Cistercians and the Eucharist, then examine the questions asked of the Eucharist by reason and the Cistercian responses to them. The other half of the scheme, which emerges from the questions asked by love, will be developed separately (see "Intimacy and Imitation", below).

THE EYE OF REASON

Three large questions shape the Cistercians' rational exploration of the Eucharist: (1) Which body of Christ is found in the species of bread and wine? (2) What in this life is the significance of finding that body? and (3) What in the life to come is the effect of the Eucharist?

While the three great Cistercian Fathers, Bernard of Clairvaux, William of St Thierry, and Aelred of Rievaulx, agree in finding the answers to these questions and related ones in the sacred humanity of Christ, the differences among the three, especially between Bernard and William on the one hand and Aelred on the other, reveal an idea in the process of being shaped, a new attitude emerging and culminating in Jesus as the center of Christain devotion. Between Bernard, who urges love toward the infant and crucified lord as a means to the spiritual love of God, insisting on "that other love that does not know the Word as flesh so much as the Word as wisdom, as justice, truth, holiness, loyalty, strength,"[6] and Aelred, who marvels that "He who fills heaven and earth is enclosed in a manger; he who owns the earth and the fullness thereof has no room in an inn,"[7] a new element has entered Christian spirituality.

THE EYE OF LOVE

The eye of love, like the eye of reason, begins its inquiry with the Eucharist. It is concerned not with rational questions about the nature and effects of the Eucharist, but rather with one much more immediate:"Who can love what he does not see? How can that be lovable that is not in some way visible?"[8] William asks that question in the person of Moses, longing to see God's face, and Moses' sight of God's back answers William's question as well: both are able to love the God whom they are allowed to see in the flesh, the incarnate God.

The question addressed to the Eucharist by the Cistercians is the same: "Given that I cannot see Christ in the sacrament, how can I love him there?" The inevitable answer to the question for them as for all Christians is "You cannot." And from the evidence of the Incarnation, they infer that God agrees: in the fullness of time he became man and dwelt among men.

But after the Ascension Jesus, who had showed God to man because humans cannot love what they cannot see, was no longer visible to human sight. Aelred asks: "What then are we to say, Brothers, for he is not physically present on earth and we are not able to receive him physically: must we then despair of his coming?"[9] Unwilling finally either to accept that hopelessness or to attempt to love by faith alone, the Cistercians found an answer in what they could see and physically receive, the sacrament of Christ's body and blood. Aelred explains in the words of Paschasius Radbert: "An impatient love considers difficulty only an excuse and does not yield before impossibility."[10]

The humanity of Christ, already discovered by the eye of reason, solves the central question of the eye of love as the Cistercian Fathers come to see that they can love God by loving the man they meet in the Eucharist and that by loving him in his humanity they can come to union with him in this life and the next. Further, they provide the method, declaring that by imitating those who once lived in intimacy with Jesus, men and women may be intimate with him even now in his crucifixion, his body and blood.

While the meeting with Jesus may be accomplished by meditation or in metaphor, it is, the Cistercians, insist, certain in the Eucharist. So the Cistercian Fathers bring their new knowledge of and love for God as man full circle, again to its natural end in the Eucharist, where it is not necessary to imagine or allegorize, but merely to eat and drink of Jesus' body and blood, in *sacramentum* and in *res*.

THE SINGLE EYE OF CHARITY

When the communicant has eaten of the sacrament and received its substance, when both eyes have seen the man whose body and blood constitute the sacrament, the yearning soul has become one with him. The eyes at last are one, "illumined by grace" and "of great mutual assistance," as William promised all along, transformed in love "into a certain spiritual and divine understanding that transcends and absorbs all reason."[11] It is no longer necessary to inquire or even to receive in blindness, unable to understand the God who lay in the manger and on the cross and lies now on the altar, for love itself is understanding.

WHICH BODY?

For the Cistercians the first question prompting reason's search into the Eucharist concerned the presence of Christ within it: "Which body of Christ is present in the Eucharist?" Medieval theologians agreed by and large that Christ was truly present in the Eucharist in his body—but precisely which body that was, was a greater problem. Was it the body born of Mary and hung on the cross, or the body glorified and sitting at the right hand of God? Or was it perhaps the body of the Church itself? Such questions led the Cistercians toward a new concern with Jesus, born of Mary and crucified under Pontius Pilate.

This concern of Jesus had of course formed the life and kerygma of Christianity, but in the post-biblical writings of the early Church Jesus is hidden in the manger, more significant in what he is to become than what he is, a human baby.[12] With the Cistercians, however, that baby began slowly to make himself known.

Bernard, the first of the Cistercian Fathers, is often credited with originating the medieval devotion to the humanity of Christ and the affective piety that accompanied it. W. R. Inge wrote in 1899: "[Bernard's] great achievement was to recall devout and loving contemplation to the image of the crucified Christ, and to found that worship of our Saviour as the 'Bridegroom of the Soul,' which in the next centuries inspired so much fervid devotion and lyrical sacred poetry."[13] In 1927 Pierre Pourrat agreed, saying that Bernard "excelled in bringing into relief the touching aspects of the lives of the Saviour and of the blessed Virgin . . . . he contributed more than anyone to the giving of an affective character to the piety of the Middle Ages.''[14]

The eucharistic ground of Bernard's devotion to the humanity of Christ appears in any reading of his works. Eating and drinking appear throughout his sermons and spiritual treatises as the central metaphor for coming to the understanding of God. In the first of his sermons on the *Song of Songs* he presents God as he who is seen in the breaking of the bread and who himself breaks it, biblical language for understanding the Eucharist itself.[15] Defining the *Song of Songs* as a loaf of "splendid and delicious bread," he asks:

> But who is going to divide this loaf? The Master of the house is present; it is the Lord you must see in the breaking of the bread. For who else could more fittingly do it? . . . For I myself am one of the seekers, one who begs along with you for the food of my soul, the nourishment of my spirit. . . . O God most kind, break your bread for this hungering flock.[16]

Bernard again speaks in *Sermon Twelve* of the Lord known in the breaking of bread, but more concretely, with more attention to the question of the body of Christ present in the bread and wine. Here Bernard addresses, though without resolving, the difficulty of distinguishing between the two bodies of Christ, that born at Bethlehem and crucified at Golgotha, and that which is the church, his bride:

> It will thus be clear that you abound with the best ointments, that you have undertaken to care not only for the head or feet of the Lord, but, as far as in you lies, for his whole body which is the Church. It was perhaps for this reason that the Lord Jesus would not allow the mixture of spices to be used on his dead body: he wished to reserve it for his living body. For that Church which eats the living bread which has come down from heaven is alive: she is the more precious Body of Christ that was not to taste death's bitterness, whereas every Christian knows that his other body did suffer death.[17]

In another sermon Bernard speaks explicitly of eating and drinking of the crucified Jesus, now with no mention of the sacrament:
"They pierced his hands and his feet, they gored his side with a
lance, and through these fissures I can suck honey from the rock
and oil from the flinty stone—I can taste and see that the Lord is
good."[18] In this abstract and allegorical eating of Jesus' flesh the
combination of the words from Dt 32:13 with those from the
Gospel narrative of the Passion insists on the human—and crucified—Jesus tasted in the Eucharist, responding to reason's question: "Which body?"

Although Bernard repeatedly shows that it is Jesus, the son of
Mary, who is present in the Eucharist, he usually presents him not
historically but symbolically, liturgically, and spiritually, as the
bread of heaven, the fruit of salvation. Explaining Sg 2:3—"As an
apple-tree among the trees of the wood, so is my beloved among
the sons"—he says:

> Justly "as an apple tree," since after the manner of a fruit-
> bearing tree he casts a refreshing shadow and yields excellent
> fruit. . . . Christ alone, the Wisdom of God, is the tree of
> life, he alone the living bread which comes down from
> heaven and gives life to the world. . . . His shadow is his
> flesh; his shadow is faith. The flesh of her own Son over-
> shadowed Mary; faith in the Lord overshadows me. And
> yet why should his flesh not overshadow me too, as I eat
> him in the sacrament?[19]

While Bernard, then, finds and loves the Jesus present in the
Eucharist, he is always less concerned with the man than with
what his flesh provides, in this life faith—the evidence of things not
seen—and in the next salvation.

Like Bernard, William writes of Jesus with less attention to his
humanity than to its significance and the salvific effects of his
crucifixion. He too finds in the Eucharist the body of Christ, and
in that crucified body he finds the sacrament: "Open to us your
body's side, that those who long to see the secrets of your Son
may enter in and may receive the sacraments that flow therefrom,
even the price of their redemption."[20]

Further, William defines this sacrament as that through which the communicant remembers both Jesus' redemptive deed and his command so to remember:

> This is what happens when we eat and drink the deathless banquet of your body and your blood. As your clean beasts, we there regurgitate the sweet things stored within our memory and chew them in our mouths like cud for the renewed and ceaseless work of our slavation. That done, we put away again in that same memory what you have done, what you have suffered for our sake.[21]

But for William Jesus is more often allegorically or dogmatically conceived—as the bridegroom who feeds his bride or as the second person of the Trinity, the Son of the Father, more nearly half God and half man than wholly God and wholly man: "Let me . . . pour [the perfume] out upon your head, whose head is God, and upon your feet, whose lower part is our humble nature."[22]

In fact William sees the humanity of Christ in the Eucharist as the door to the reality of God, but not as essentially important in itself. He sometimes, even while specifying that the species of the Eucharist are indeed Jesus' flesh and blood, denies their importance there: "To those fretting about the sacramental mystery of his Body and Blood he says: It is the Spirit who gives life; the flesh, however, does not profit anyone."[23]

In the writings of Aelred, however, the humanity of Jesus discovered in the Eucharist by Bernard and William is fully developed and welcomed. In Aelred's sermons and contemplative works the humanity of Jesus emerges from inquiry into the Eucharist, but for him Jesus is rarely the Logos or an allegorically conceived bridegroom; rather is he wholly man, a man of flesh and blood. And not only does Aelred not hasten to distinguish between the man Jesus and the Godhead in this life, he understands even beatitude in terms of Jesus, there indeed glorified, sitting to judge the quick and the dead, but showing the same face to the blessed as to his friends during his human life: "Jesus' face shines upon them, not terrible but lovable, not bitter but sweet, not frightening but caressing."[24] In his writings Aelred progresses from a tentative attention to Christ's humanity like that he has met in Bernard and William to a fully developed devotion to the man Jesus.

Like his predecessors, Aelred explicitly associates the humanity of Christ with the Eucharist, sometimes in language full of the symbolic and eucharistic significance of the infant Jesus. He says in *On Jesus as a Boy of Twelve* that God led him to a city that "abounds in bread and is called the House of Bread, Bethlehem . . . . You have filled [the hungry soul] with that bread indeed which came down from heaven and was laid in the manger to become the food of spiritual animals."[25] He continues, explaining not only the Nativity but the Incarnation itself in the language of the Eucharist:

> For bread made from fine wheaten flour is pure, clean, without ashes, without leaven, without husks—"In the beginning was the Word, and the Word was with God, and the Word was God." But who is capable of assimilating this? It is the bread of angels, whose palate has not been dulled by tasting sour grapes. Therefore they taste and see fully and perfectly that the Lord is sweet. But in order that men might eat the bread of angels, the Bread of Angels became man, taking upon him the husks of our poverty, the ashes of our mortality, the leaven of our infirmity. He who is great became a little child.[26]

Aelred writes again in *On Reclusion*[27] of the body of Christ as the food of those who love him, allowing to the Eucharistic symbols the literal and physical reality of the Crucifixion. When the soldier pierces Jesus' side, Aelred urges the contemplative: "Hasten, linger not, eat the honeycomb with your honey, drink your wine with your milk. The blood is changed into wine to inebriate you, the water into milk to nourish you."[28] In this passage the wine of the Eucharist is certainly Jesus' blood: the recipient drinks of Jesus himself. It is not, Aelred suggests, that the substance of the wine is changed into blood during the Mass, but that it was blood in the first place.

Immediately after receiving Jesus' blood, the contemplative enters the wound in his side to become one with him in his flesh. Within the wound the blood is not wine, but blood, and she is to kiss it until her lips are stained with it, "become like a scarlet ribbon." As she then helps to carry Jesus to the tomb she is to "gather up carefully the drops of the precious blood as they fall one by one."[29] The blood becomes wine for her who will drink of it, but it remains primarily and always Jesus' precious blood.

Although all three of the Fathers describe the sacraments as flowing from Jesus' side, Aelred here is the most explicit of them in identifying the eucharistic wine with Christ's blood, concretely and visually substantiating eucharistic doctrine, like contemporary paintings of the Passion with angels receiving directly into chalices the blood that pours from Jesus' wounds.

His explanation that at the crucifixion the blood and water are transformed into wine and milk to inebriate and nourish the lover of Christ may also be regarded as a response to one of the continuing eucharistic questions, the relationship between the accidents and the substance of the eucharistic species, between the *sacramentum*, the bread and wine, and the *res sacramenti*, Christ's body and blood. For centuries the church had struggled to explain why and how in the Mass, at the prayer of consecration, the bread and wine are transformed in substance into body and blood, why the sensible characteristics, their accidents, remain those of bread and wine, and why when one eats Christ's body it looks like, smells like, and tastes like bread.

From the time of Ambrose the church had explained that the accidents persist "so that there shall be no horror of the blood" (*horror cruoris*).[30] That is, the body and blood retain the appearance of bread and wine as a comfort to the sensibilities of the communicants, and through these accidents the species indeed both nourish and inebriate. When Aelred argues that the true transformation took place once for all at the Crucifixion,[31] turning body and blood into bread and wine to nourish, inebriate, and moreover, comfort through avoidance of the *horror cruoris*, he echoes the Church's various explanations for the fact of and the reason for the concurrent presence in the Eucharist of substance and species.

Having emerged from the Eucharist, risen in the flesh from the manger, the cross, the tomb, and the altar, Jesus for Aelred is always fully human, fully flesh, but at the same time he is also always divine, his humanity always sacred. In *On Reclusion* the infant Jesus is no longer the bread of spiritual animals, but has be-

come a real child to be caressed and loved in all humanity. Aelred
says to the contemplative:

> When the infant is laid in the little manger break out into
> words of exultant joy together with Isaiah and cry: "A child
> has been born to us, a son is given to us." Embrace that
> sweet manger, let love overcome your reluctance, affection
> drive out fear. Put your lips to those most sacred feet, kiss
> them again and again.

Again he asks, "Do you not think you will gain some devotion by
contemplating him at Nazareth as a boy among boys, obedient to
his mother and helping his foster-father with his work?"[32]

This emphasis on Jesus' human body and work culminates for
Aelred at the Passion, when the contemplative is to "lick the dust
from his feet" in the Garden of Gethsemane and on the road to
the tomb.[33] The new devotion to the God-man budding in the
spirituality of Bernard and flowering in William has come to fruit
in Aelred's dusty-footed Jesus.

WHAT DOES IT SIGNIFY?

Neither the Nativity nor the Crucifixion is self-explanatory, and
their mystery becomes for the Fathers identical with the mystery
of the Eucharist. Just as they look into the manger to find the infant Lord and into the Crucifixion to find the God who hangs
there dead, so they search with the eye of reason into the Eucharist to pierce beyond the *sacramentum* and find out the *res*, the humanity of Christ, and would go yet beyond, to the divinity with
the humanity. For as the significance of the Nativity and Crucifixion is within, not apparent to the onlooker, so too is that of the
Eucharist. What for this life is the significance of the Eucharist
and, specifically, of the humanity of Christ discovered there?

This is the second of the great questions raised for the Fathers by
the search of the eye of reason into the Eucharist, for when it has
found the sacred humanity of Christ, what then? If they find there
only Jesus, a man bleeding and dead, then surely they have found
nothing. Is it possible in the man they have found in the Eucharist
to reach God as well, to know Christ's divinity with his humanity?

Or is it true that as the communicant cannot with bodily senses see or taste the bread and wine as other than bread and wine, so the eye of reason cannot find out the divinity within the dead Lord?

On this question too Bernard, William, and Aelred's positions present an overlapping development, culminating in Aelred's greater incarnationalism and fuller, more confident, devotion to Jesus. As for both Bernard and William the humanity of Christ leads the Christian onward past him to the Godhead, for them concentration on his humanity endangers the Christian, for he may in his fallen state rest there, in carnal love, never continuing to Christ's divinity.

For both William and Aelred, however, it is possible sometimes even in this life to know the divinity of Christ, though only through his humanity. Where all three of the Fathers understand the sacrament to emerge from Jesus' wounds, only these two allow the worshipper to enter the wound itself. For them the risk is not only worth the reward but the only way to it. In fact, Aelred sees little risk in loving Jesus; for him Jesus is always God as well as man, man as well as God, and while one would linger in loving him if one could, "in this wretched life nothing is stable, nothing eternal."[34] The risk is slight because impossible; the Christian needs more often to be urged to overcome timidity, reluctance, and fear than to be restrained and warned.

The Fathers' exploration of this second question sometimes seems to leave the Eucharist far behind, as for all three of them the question and the answer arise in the midst of meditation on Christ's humanity, not in eucharistic commentary. But as his humanity is comprehended by the Crucifixion, in the breaking of his body and the spilling of his blood, they are unable long to contemplate that humanity without coming again to the body and blood. The humanity emerges for them in the first place from the Eucharist and coexists with the Eucharist, so for them to meditate on Christ's humanity is to contemplate the Eucharist.

Bernard is most unwilling to rest for any time in contemplation of Jesus. For him, the Eucharist is in this life to be eaten primarily in faith and to produce faith. While the eucharistic feast is made up of the body and blood of Jesus, Bernard's attention is rather on the feast and its salvific benefits than on Jesus himself. Bernard eats of Jesus' flesh in order to be overshadowed with faith in his divinity. For him devotion to Jesus and his human activity is always somewhat suspect, certainly only an intermediate stage, valuable in this life for drawing worshippers onward to love him spiritually:

> Notice that the love of our heart may be carnal when it has as its object the flesh of Christ; that which Christ did or taught in the flesh specially touches our human heart. The faithful soul ... meditates on nothing more sweetly than the life of Christ.... To the Christian who prays the image presents itself of the God-man being born, fed with milk, or teaching, dying, rising from the dead or ascending to heaven.... For my part, I think that the chief reason which prompted the invisible God to become visible in the flesh and to hold converse with man was to lead carnal men, who are only able to love carnally, to the healthful love of his flesh and afterwards, little by little, to spiritual love.[35]

Bernard warns that even to the contemplative God does not appear in his humanity:

> For I believe that in this vision images of his flesh, or of the cross, or any other suggestions of physical fraility were not imprinted on [the bride's] imagination, since the Prophet tells us that under these forms he possessed neither beauty nor majesty. But as she now contemplates him, she declares him both beautiful and majestic, making it clear that her present vision transcended all others.... She must have glimpsed something of the beauty of his higher nature, something that wholly transcends our vision, that eludes our experience.[36]

For Bernard, as Dom Cuthbert Butler points out, "When the bride is the soul of the devout individual man, the Bridegroom is not Jesus Christ in His Humanity, but the Divine Word, the Logos, the Second Person of the Holy Trinity—in more than one place He is called 'the Bridegroom-Word,' 'Verbum Sponsus' (*Cant.* lxxiv. 3)."[37] Indeed Bernard will not allow his Bridegroom-Word to be understood as the human Jesus: "And when you consider the lovers themselves, think not of a man and a woman, but of the Word and the soul."[38]

Bernard understands meditation on the humanity of Christ rather than on the allegorically conceived bridegroom of the soul as essentially an aid to virtue, food for spiritual beginners:

> I have said that wisdom is to be found in meditating on these truths [of the "anxious hours and bitter experiences of my Lord"]. For me they are the source of perfect righteousness, of the fullness of knowledge, of the most efficacious graces, of abundant merits. . . . For anyone traveling on God's royal way, they provide safe guidance amid the joys and sorrows of life, warding off impending evils on every side. . . . This is my philosophy, one more refined and interior, to know Jesus and him crucified. . . . I do not ask where he rests at noon, for I see him on the cross as my Savior. What [the bride] desired is the more sublime; what I experience is the more sweet. Her portion was bread that satisfies the hunger of children; mine is the milk that fills the breasts of mothers.[39]

For Bernard, then, Jesus illuminates the way to the Godhead but does not himself manifest the Godhead:

> Even now he appears to whom he pleases, but as he pleases, not as he is. Neither sage nor saint nor prophet can or could ever see him as he is, while still in this mortal body; but whoever is found worthy will be able to do so when the body becomes immortal. Hence, though he is seen here below, it is in the form that seems good to him, not as he is.[40]

William too sees Jesus as showing the way to God, frequently defining his humanity as a door to knowledge of God, but he is torn between a longing to enter that door, anxiety that it may be closed to him, and fear that once he has entered it will close behind him, trapping him there apart from the joy of salvation. William of the three Fathers is most aware of Paul's warning that he who partakes of the Eucharist without discerning the Body "eats and drinks judgment on himself,"[41] yet he fears that in discerning the Body one may know no more of Christ than that.

Repeatedly William insists that the crucified Jesus is necessary for the Christian, the only and efficacious door to God:

For he labors who would go up some other way, but he who enters by you, O Door, walks on the smooth ground and comes to the Father, to whom no one may come except by you.... In sweet meditation on the wonderful sacrament of your passion she muses on the good that you have wrought on our behalf, the good that is as great as you yourself are great, the good that is yourself. She seems to herself to see you face to face when you thus show her, in the cross and in the work of your salvation, the face of the ultimate Good. The cross itself becomes for her the face of a mind that is well-disposed toward God.[42]

But William sometimes finds himself stopped short of the fullness of God even when approaching him through that door, whether in meditation or in the sacrament:

But when in my eagerness I would approach him and ...like Thomas, that man of desires, I want to see and touch the whole of him and—what is more—to approach the most holy wound in his side, the portal of the ark that is there made, and not only to put my finger or my whole hand into it, but wholly enter into Jesus' very heart, into the holy of holies, the ark of the covenant, the golden urn, the soul of our humanity that holds within itself the manna of the Godhead—then, alas! I am told: "Touch me not!"[43]

Elsewhere, however, he offers more hope of finding God there:

Those unsearchable riches of your glory, Lord, were hidden in your secret place in heaven until the soldier's lance opened the side of your Son our Lord and Savior on the cross, and from it flowed the mysteries of our redemption. Now we may not only thrust our finger or our hand into his side, like Thomas, but through that open door may enter whole, O Jesus, even into your heart, the sure seat of your mercy, even into your holy soul that is filled with the fullness of God, full of grace and truth, full of our salvation and our consolation.[44]

William sometimes promises not only knowledge of Christ's humaity and divinity, but unity with him and the Father:

When you say to the longing soul, "Open your mouth wide
and I will fill it," and she tastes and sees your sweetness in
the great Sacrament that passes understanding, then she is
made that which she eats, bone of your bone and flesh or
your own flesh. Thus is fulfilled the prayer that you made to
your Father on the threshold of your passion. The Holy
Spirit effects in us here by grace that unity which is between
the Father and yourself, his Son, from all eternity by nature,
so that, as you are one, likewise we may be made one in
you.[45]

For William meditation on the humanity of Christ is in fact
equivalent to receipt of the sacrament; it effects a spiritual
knowledge of and union with the body and blood of the Lord. He
promises through it full possession of the spiritual presence of
Christ, the *res* of the sacrament, without necessary sacramental reception of the body and blood:

Anyone who has the mind of Christ knows also how profitable it is to Christain piety, how fitting and advantageous it
is to God's servant, the servant of Christ's redemption, to
devote at least one hour of the day to an attentive passing in
review of the benefits conferred by his Passion and the Redemption he wrought, in order to savor them in spirit and
store them away faithfully in the memory. This is spiritually
to eat the Body of the Lord and drink his Blood in remembrance of him who gave to all who believe in him the com-
mandment: "Do this in remembrance of me." . . .
    The sacrament without the substance brings death to the
communicant, but the substance of the sacrament, even
without the visible species, brings eternal life.
    Now if you wish, and if you truly desire it, this is at your
disposal in your cell at all hours both of day and of night. As
often as you stir up sentiments of piety and faith in recalling
to mind him who suffered for you, you eat his body and
drink his blood. As long as you remain in him through love
and he in you through the sanctity and justice he works in
you, you are reckoned as belonging to his Body and
counted as one of his members.[46]

While Aelred does not directly address William's question,

whether meditation on the humanity is equivalent to receipt of the Eucharist, he allows the contemplative full knowledge of and full union with the humanity and divinity of Jesus in meditation on his Passion, and he seldom speaks of the sacrament except through moments in the life of Jesus. The center of Aelred's theology is Jesus, not the Church or its sacraments.

However, like both Bernard and William, Aelred recognizes the danger of receipt of Christ's flesh without the spirit. In a sermon on the Assumption he comments of Mary and Martha that:

> These two women were blessed in receiving him physically, but much more blessed because they received him in spirit. Many in those days received him physically and ate and drank with him, but not having received him in the spirit, they remained in their misery.[47]

The Jesus who appears in Aelred's works is indeed true God and true man. Aelred consistently tells of a Jesus who is fleshly and human rather than allegorical or metaphorical, but who is also divine. He does not allow Jesus' divinity to be severed from his humanity, and his crucified Christ does not merely lead from earth to heaven, but links heaven and earth: "The Mediator of God and men hangs midway between heaven and earth, unites the depths with the heights and joins the things of heaven to the things of earth."[48]

For Aelred as for William Jesus' humanity appears in his feet, but for Aelred his divinity rests there as well. At Jesus' birth Aelred directs the contemplative to kiss "those most sacred feet,"[49] later she sees the paralytic let down "before his feet, where kindness and power came to meet one another,"[50] and finally she hears Jesus keep Mary Magdalene "at a distance from [his] most sacred and most desirable feet," but only for a time.[51] In Aelred's works Jesus' feet and head as well show forth both man and God in Christ, and both are to be adored by the Christian: "Break then the alabaster of your heart and whatever devotion you have, whatever love, whatever desire, whatever affection, pour it all out upon your bridegroom's head, while you adore the man in God and God in the man."[52]

Aelred argues, however, that one comes to the divinity through the humanity, kissing the feet in order to know their sacredness, loving the man and so discovering the love of God; in that he has no disagreement with his predecessors. He identifies Christ's two natures with milk and wine in his meditation on the Last Supper and indicates the order in which they are known: "If you are not capable of greater things, leave John to inebriate himself with the wine of gladness in the knowledge of the Godhead while you run to feed on the milk which flows from Christ's humanity."[53]

And when in meditation on the Crucifixion the contemplative is to receive the two combined, Aelred is careful again to explain them as distinct though indistinguishable: "Then one of the soldiers opened his side with a lance and there came forth blood and water. Hasten, linger not, eat the honeycomb with your honey, drink your wine with your milk. The blood is changed into wine to inebriate you, the water into milk to nourish you."[54]

Throughout his meditation on the humanity of Christ Aelred is more confident in assuring knowledge of Christ's divinity in union with Christ than either Bernard or William. Although he, like William, shows the risen Jesus sending Mary Magdalene away, saying "Do not touch me," for him these words do not suggest a barrier to knowledge of Christ's divinity in this life. Rather, Aelred allows Mary to engage in reasoned conversation with Jesus, to raise a theological question calling attention to his new state, and to receive an answer typically divine.

Mary asks Jesus: "Are you less gentle than usual because you are more glorious?" Jesus' answer, like God's to Job, is tangential, experiential, and affective rather than speculative, but it is the right one for Mary: "'Fear not, this boon is not refused you but kept until later.' . . . And notice, the boon is now given which had previously been kept until later, for they came close and clasped his feet."[55]

Aelred understands Christ's rejection of Mary to be temporary, not absolute, even in this life, and although Mary is sent away by the risen lord, he welcomes her back to physical embrace. She recognizes him, questions him, and finally with her companions is allowed once again, in his resurrection as in his life, to clasp his feet.

Aelred argues not only that one may know Christ's divinity in this life, but that one may come into physical and spiritual unity

with him here. He directs the contemplative to eat and drink of
his body, then to enter into the wound in his side, "in which, like
a dove, you may hide." In this union the worshipper becomes not
only physically one with her lord but like him, her lips stained
with his blood and her word sweet. Seeing her inability to stay
there, Aelred urges: "But wait yet awhile until that noble coun-
cilor comes to extract the nails and free his hands and feet."[56]
After Mary Magdalene is allowed to clasp the feet of the risen
Christ, he says again:

> Linger here as long as you can, virgin. Do not let these de-
> lights of yours be interrupted by sleep or disturbed by any
> tumult from without. However, since in this wretched life
> nothing is stable, nothing eternal, and man never remains in
> the same state, our soul must needs, while we live, be fed
> with a certain variety.[57]

Jesus is fully God and fully man, and the one who loves him is
spirit and flesh as well. Jesus both feeds and is fed by Mary and
Martha:

> If only Mary had been in that house, no one would have
> been there to feed the Lord, and if only Martha, no one
> would have been there to delight in the sermons and pre-
> sence of the Lord.... Mary signifies the rest that frees a
> man from bodily works that he may delight in the sweetness
> of God.[58]

Similarly, the contemplative both washes his feet and allows him
to wash hers, "because the man whom he does not wash will have
no part with him."[59] Thus the union with Christ in the sacrament
is for Aelred not merely physical ("We become part of Christ because we eat him"[60]), but spiritual as well: "The man who unites
himself with him becomes one spirit with him, passing into that
unity which is always the same and whose years do not come to
an end."[61] The union for Aelred in the meditation on Christ's humanity and in the Eucharist is real, present, and joyful.

For Aelred the body available to Christians is the same after the
resurrection as before; not only is the body received in the Eucharist both the body crucified and the body resurrected, but it may in

this life, however briefly, be known as the person of God himself. For Aelred one finds God in the divinity of Christ, whenever one finds his humanity, whether before the Crucifixion, in the Crucifixion, or in the Resurrection.

WHAT EFFECT?

The last of the great eucharistic questions asked by the Fathers is really only a variant of the second: what in the life to come is the effect of the Eucharist? Specifically, what is the relationship of the feast of Christ's body and blood to the heavenly banquet? Where the first question of the eye of reason discovered the humanity of Christ in time past and the second considered the experience of the worshipper in time present, the third inquires into the things to come in beatitude.[62]

In the twelfth century the salvific benefits of the Eucharist were a matter of general agreement, but as the Fathers emerged from their new and reasoned understanding of the humanity of Jesus they came to a new understanding of the Eucharist. No longer was receiving the species merely an act of faith, a blind tasting in unquestioning acceptance of what that tasting promised; now it meant feasting with both eyes open. Indeed, each of the Fathers came to see the Eucharist and its eternal benefits much as they saw the Jesus they had come to know there. As his flesh was the sacrament, it was not surprising that their new conception of him shaped their conception of the sacrament.

Thus, as Bernard and William see Christ's humanity as essentially a door to the Godhead and fear that lingering there will keep them from eternity, so they understand the Eucharist itself as an invitation, a foretaste, a transitory table at which one dare not linger. They see that God invites them to him through these gifts of his grace but argue that the one who considers those gifts the feast rather than the invitation will eat and drink to judgment. And as Aelred knows Jesus' humanity to be one with his divinity and encourages those who would know him to hasten to him and linger at his feet, so he considers the Eucharist itself a feast of delight, certainly a foretaste of what is to come, but no less an occasion of joy in this world.

At the same time, in this third step in understanding the Eucharist, the Fathers move again away from the humanity of Christ, into eating and drinking, banquets, milk, oil, bread, and wine. As the writers turn to the eucharistic banquet and to the foretaste it offers of the heavenly banquet to come, of salvation itself, they turn increasingly toward the face of God or the vision of Christ coming in glory. Jesus the man is now left far behind, become in the writings of the Fathers once again almost symbolic.

The Cistercian Fathers agree the goal of the pilgrim in this world to be beatitude, the heavenly Jerusalem, the eternal banquet of the vision of God: "Taste and see how sweet is the Lord."[63] Their regular repetition of these words, surely the biblical verse most frequent in the works of the Fathers, enforces the interrelated themes that God is to be tasted to be known and that one tastes in this world in order to dine in the world to come. As knowing leads to love, so tasting brings eternal vision.

This apparently mixed metaphor present in the Psalm and used by the Fathers exemplifies their common understanding of the effects of the Eucharist for all time, in time to come. That effect is the salvation of believers, the redemption of all who eat of the body and blood, restoration to the sight of God's face lost in the Fall. As Adam and Eve in eating of the tree of the knowledge of good and evil brought about expulsion from the Garden and hence from the sight of God, so those of their descendents who eat of God himself are restored eternally to his sight. It is not surprising that, for the Cistercians, eating brings vision, tasting allows one to see.

All three of the Fathers indicate this understanding of the Eucharist when they speak of Jesus in the words of *Genesis*: "The Lord God made trees spring from the ground, all trees pleasant to look at and good for food; and in the middle of the garden he set the tree of life and the tree of the knowledge of good and evil."[64]

Bernard enunciates the reversal of the Fall and the Christian's experience of the reversal in the Eucharist: "Christ alone, the Wisdom of God, is the tree of life, he alone the living bread which comes down from heaven and gives life to the world. . . . [He alone provides] a life-giving food . . . the enduring fruits of salvation."[65]

William too brings together man's Fall and restoration through eating of God:

For when of old in your paradise you created me, and gave

> me the tree of life for my possession, as of abiding right, you
> willed—or at least you allowed me to reach my hand out
> also for the fruit of the tree of the knowledge of good and
> evil. . . . I tasted of the fruit and saw not your sweetness but
> my own shame. . . . And now, Desire of my soul, my soul
> desires to wait on you a little space, and to taste and see
> how sweet you are, O Lord.[66]

Aelred too links taste and sight, Fall and Redemption, explaining humankind's loss of the enduring sight and taste of God
through Adam's eating in the Garden. For Aelred Jesus' life and
crucifixion are rectification of the Fall; when Christians next eat,
now of his body, they will at last taste of God and see him without
error. In a sermon on the Nativity he says that Jesus was born to
restore what Adam lost:

> [In creation man's] memory was like a thread of the soul, re-
> taining God without ever forgetting him; his reason was like
> a look which saw God without possibility of error; his love
> was a tasting of God in the interior of his heart, which made
> him desire no other.
>   O unhappy Adam! What more did you want? O ingrate!
> Here you are considering your crime: "No, I will be like
> God." O ingrate! . . . O intolerable pride! You were just
> made from clay and mud, and in your insolence you wish to
> be like God. It is very possible that the devil, seeing this
> foolish thought in your spirit, said, "I will show you a way:
> eat and you will be like the gods."[67]

For the Cistercian Fathers the Eucharist above all redeems the
fallen and restores to them what was lost in Adam's eating from
the tree, the vision of God in eternity. The feast of Christ's body is
at last the fruit of the tree of life for Adam's heirs, the food of salvation and of eternal life.

The Fathers differ, however, in their degree of emphasis on the
Eucharist as preliminary, partial, anticipatory. Of the three, Bernard most systematically uses the language of eating and drinking
to define the stages to the eternal vision of God: he insists that the
union with God in the sacrament, while real and substantial
enough, is incomplete, a help along the way to beatitude. Much as

he speaks of meditation on Christ's humanity as "safe guidance on God's royal way,"[68] he explains Jesus' words from John 14:6, "I am the way, the truth, and the life," as meaning finally "I am the food, the viaticum, to sustain you on the way."[69]

Bernard repeatedly defines the journey to God in three steps, at least three times in the eucharistic language of the *Song of Songs*: "Eat, my friends, and drink; be inebriated, my dearest ones."[70] He explains that although bread and wine are available at all stages along the way to God, beginners are restricted to the bread of sorrow and the wine of compunction. Elsewhere Bernard insists that the highest step, with the purest wine, is available only to the blessed, seated already at the heavenly banquet:

> Then at last, the soul is admitted to the wine-bowl of wisdom, of which it is said: "How good is my cup, it inebriates me!" . . . Eat before death, drink after death, be inebriated after the resurrection. It is right to call them dearest who are drunk with love; they are rightly inebriated who deserve to be admitted to the nuptials of the Lamb, eating and drinking at his table in his kingdom.[71]

The same scheme appears briefly in a sermon, where Bernard again defines the Eucharist as foretaste, saying that in this world and while "in the corruptible flesh" one eats what one will later drink, now eating in faith, later drinking in contemplating the face of the Lord, seeing him face to face.[72]

Repeatedly Bernard emphasizes that eating Jesus "in the memorial of his Passion" prepares one for salvation:

> In the meanwhile memory is sweet for those who seek and long for God's presence, not that they are satisfied but that they may hunger all the more for him that they might be satisfied. Thus he testifies that he himself is food: "Who eats me, will hunger for more." Whoever is nourished by him says: "I shall be satisfied when your glory appears."[73]

While Bernard consistently speaks of knowing God now only in anticipation and by faith, only as he wills to be known, William occasionally allows real unity with God in this life in the Eucharist, however briefly, promising that: "In the great Sacrament that

surpasses understanding . . . the Holy Spirit effects in us here by
grace that unity which is between the Father and yourself, his Son,
from all eternity by nature; so that, as you are one, likewise we
may be made one in you."[74]

Elsewhere, however, after quoting from Jesus' prayer in the
Garden—"I in them, and you in me, that they may be made
perfect in oneness"—he acknowledges that:

> This unity of course transcends the limits of our human
> nature, but falls short of the unity that belongs to the being
> of God. . . . Moreover, the likeness of God will be conferred
> on us by the sight of God, when we see not only that he is,
> but as he is; that is the likeness that will make us like to
> him.[75]

William argues finally that while unity with Christ is possible in
this life, it is rare and incomplete; real and enduring union with
the Father and the Son comes only in beatitude, and the Eucharist
is primarily an anticipation of that vision and that union rather
than an eternal verity:

> Then just as in the past the new sacraments of grace put an
> end to the old sacraments, so the Reality of all the sacra-
> ments [*res ipsa sacramentorum omnium*] will utterly put an
> end to all sacraments. In the sacraments of the New Testa-
> ment, it is true, the day of new grace began to break, but in
> that end of perfect consummation will come the full noon-
> day when glass and riddle and that which is in part shall be
> done away, but there shall be the vision face to face and the
> plenitude of the highest Good.[76]

Like Bernard, William writes frequently of the grace of God
that makes itself known in food and drink to beginners on the
road to God, but warns against accepting that grace as a stopping
place rather than as a help along the way:

> When [the soul], like a person raised in the country, nour-
> ished on and accustomed to country cooking, has begun to
> taste these affections of which we spoke, it is like her first
> entrance to a royal court. When she is ignominiously chased

away and violently thrown out, she can hardly consent to
return again to the house of her poverty. She returns time
after time to the door, importunate, persistent, and eager, as
one in need. As a beggar, hoping, sighing, she looks up to
see if anything is going to be offered to her whenever the
door is opened. And sometimes by her shamelessness and
importunity she has so overcome and overstepped all
hurdles that, leaping along in her desire even up to wisdom's
inmost table, she may impudently take a seat, a guest sure to
be turned out again, and may hear, "Eat, friends, drink!
Drink freely, my dearest friends!"

At this stage, unless one is on his guard, the grave hindrance of temptation occurs. . . . What one has received for
the journey from his dutiful Father, to prevent him from
succumbing on the way, he begins to consider adequate,
and setting up a milestone of his journey there, where he
fails to advance, he really begins to fail! . . .

The psalmist says: "The enemies of the Lord lied to him
and their time shall be forever. And he fed them with the
finest wheat and satisfied them with honey from the rock."
Notice: they are fed; yet notice: they are enemies! Notice:
they are satisfied; yet, notice: they are liars! Notice: not only with wheat but with the finest wheat, not just the rock
but honey from the rock, that is, the hidden and divine
grace of the sacraments. . . . Anyone who is satisfied seeks
no longer what he has received, for he is full; what he has is
enough for him.[77]

Like William, Aelred sees both the union with God in Christ
here and the Eucharist as promises of the fullness to come, but
while he agrees in regarding them both as temporary, his incarnational certainty renders them both less transitory, more satisfying
in themselves than is true for Bernard and William. Where Bernard repeatedly preaches that the wine that inebriates is to be
found only in beatitude, for Aelred the Christian may obtain it
here, from Jesus himself, and where both Bernard and William
argue that the Jesus one meets here is only the back of, the door
to, his Father, for Aelred he is true God, in whom the worshipper
may find union.

Aelred appears to see little risk that the worshipper may be
tempted to stay in the fleshly delights of either the embrace of

Jesus or the eucharistic banquet. One is at more risk by holding back, ashamed of "that insolent serving girl, my flesh"[78] or needing to be urged forward. Over and over in his meditation on Jesus' humanity Aelred says "Hasten, run!" or "Do not delay to claim for yourself some portion of this sweetness."[79]

So too the Last Supper described by Aelred is both a meal producing salvation and one of delights in itself. He says to the contemplative:

> Now then go up with him into the large upper room, furnished for supper, and rejoice to share the delights of the meal which brings us salvation. Let love overcome shyness, affection drive out fear, so that he may at least give you an alms from the crumbs of that table when you beg for something. Or stand at a distance and, like a poor man looking to a rich man, stretch out your hand to receive something, let your tears declare your hunger.[80]

This concrete and biblical variant on the parable told by William is for Aelred not followed by a warning against lingering there, but quite a different question: "Why are you in such a hurry to go out now? Wait a little while." And at once the contemplative is directed to see the disciple John receiving the wine of the knowledge of the Godhead and being inebriated by it, just as she herself is to do at the Crucifixion. For Aelred the Eucharist, like Jesus the God-man, is both a promise of things to come and complete in itself, to be eaten and enjoyed in assurance of what is to come but also as a present delight.

But Aelred too insists that this meal is primarily a foretaste, provided as an appetiser for what is to come:

> Love is the heart's palate for him who knows that you are sweet. . . . This is that abundance of your house, by which your lovers are inebriated, passing out of themselves that they may pass over into you. And how, Lord, unless in loving you? . . . I beg, Lord, that some small portion of this great sweetness of you may descend into my soul, by which the bread of its bitterness may become sweet. Let it experience in this little draught the foretaste of what it desires,

what it longs for, what it sighs for in this its pilgrimage. Let it have its foretaste in hungering, its drink in thirsting. For those who eat of you hunger still, and those who drink you thirst still. They will be sated, however, when your glory appears, when that great abundance of your sweetness is shown.[81]

He speaks similarly of "those gifts of God's goodness" known only to the contemplative, but suggests in using the word *debriauit* rather than his more usual *inebriauit* that for him as for Bernard the inebriation of the contemplative is different in quality from that experienced in beatitude:

With how glad a face Christ comes to meet one who renounces the world, with what delights he feeds her in her hunger, what riches of his compassion he shows her, what affections he arouses in her, with what a cup of charity he inebriates [*debriauit*] her. . . . How often he lifted up your mind from the things of earth and introduced it into the delights of heaven and the joys of Paradise.[82]

Aelred is less concerned than Bernard and William to warn against stopping short with the Eucharist, the taste of God's sweetness in this world, assuming apparently that the delights of the taste will be sufficient to draw one onward, but he is no less clear than the others that it is the heavenly banquet for which one longs, the joy of beatitude and of eternal sweetness. For while the Christian may delight in the food of the Eucharist or in meditation on the humanity of Christ, it is more common that he will eat his bread in the sweat of his face, like all the descendents of Adam.

The Fathers' shared understanding of the relationship between the things of this life and those to come appears in Aelred's conclusion to his meditations on things past, things present, and things to come:

Meditation will arouse the affections, the affections will give birth to desire, and desire will stir up tears, so that your tears may be bread for you day and night until you appear in his sight, are received by his embrace, and say to him what is written in the *Song of Songs*: "My Beloved is mine and I am his."[83]

The Cistercians agree finally that the Christian must wait in darkness, loneliness, and hunger for that day when he will come to "the sight, the knowledge and the love of the Creator" when "that lovable face, so longed for, upon which the angels yearn to gaze, will be seen."[84] Then he may rejoice with all those who are"glad with the ceaseless glory of the sight of [him], rid of all that could distract from feasting for ever on [his] face."[85]

For the Cistercian Fathers the eye of reason has moved from the bread and wine within which the body of Christ is hidden to that body of Christ itself and, finally, now in faith reformed through experience, back to the Eucharist, understood not as an end in itself, but as an anticipation, a foretaste of the vision of God to come in the heavenly Jerusalem.

The University of Michigan

NOTES

1. Nat am 3:21; PL 184:393; CF 30:77-78. Occasionally the translation in the text varies from the standard translation, as I have attempted to allow the common eucharistic vocabulary of the Fathers to appear in the English. Any unattributed translation is my own.

2. An excellent recent study of the Eucharist in the Middle Ages is Gary Macy's *The Theologies of the Eucharist in the Early Scholastic Period* (Oxford,1984). My brief summaries of the various eucharistic questions explored by the Cistercian Fathers are generally derived from Macy's thorough treatment. A valuable compendium of the development of eucharistic theology from the primitive church forward is Darwell Stone, *A History of the Doctrine of the Holy Eucharist* (New York and London, 2 vols., 1909). Chapters 5 and 6 of vol. 1 are those relevant to the medieval period.

3. William of St Thierry, *De sacramento altaris*, PL 180:341-66; Baldwin of Ford, *De sacramento altaris*, PL 204:641-774, ed. John Morson and trans. E. de Solms, *Baudouin de Ford. Le sacrement de l'autel*, SCh 93-94 (Paris, 1963); Baldwin, *Tractatus de sanctissimus sacramento eucharistiae*, PL 204:403-414; ed. and trans. R. Thomas, *Baudouin de Ford, Traités*, Pain de Citeaux 35-40 (Chimay, 1973-1975); Isaac of Stella, *Epistola ad Joannem Episcopum Pictaviensem de officio missae*, PL 194: 1889-96.

4. Ep frat II:194; SCh 223:302; CF 12:77.

5. Cant I:8.92; SCh 82:212; CF 6:74.

6. SC 20:8; SBOp 1:120; CF 4:154.

7. *S. in nativitate Domini*; ed. C. H. Talbot, *Sermones inediti beati Aelredi abbatis Rievallensis*, Series S. Ordinis Cisterciensis I (Rome, 1952), p.37.

8. Contemp 3; SCh 61:17; CF 3:40.

9. *S.in assumptione b. Mariae*, PL 195:303; trans. Anthony Storey, "The Castle of the Soul," *The Tablet*, 198 (1951) 91.

10. *S. in natale apostolorum Petri et Pauli*; ed. Talbot, p. 135. Charles Dumont, *Saint Aelred de Rievaulx* (Namur, Belgium, 1960), p. 135, attributes this sentence to Paschasius.

11. Cant I:8.92; SCh 82:212; CF 6:74.

12. In *Homily 24* on 1 Corinthians John Chrysostom, "Doctor Eucharistiae," had said: "This body even when lying in a manger the Magi reverenced. These heathen foreigners left home and country and went on a long journey, and came and worshipped him with fear and great trembling. We are citizens of heaven: let us imitate these foreigners. For they approached with great awe when they saw him in the manger and in the cell and saw him in no way such as you see him, not in a manger but on an altar, not with a woman holding him but with a priest standing before him, and the Spirit descending upon the offerings with great bounty." Stone, p. 55.

13. W. R. Inge, *Christian Mysticism* (London, 1899), p. 140, n. 2.

14. Pierre Pourrat, *Christian Spirituality*, trans. S. P. Jacques (Westminster, 1953), p. 20. First published 1927 as *La spiritualité chrétienne*. Pourrat here rejects the common assumption of Franciscan originality in such devotion, saying, "St Francis of Assisi was not the first to pour forth lamentations before the crucifix, nor to weep with pity when contemplating the infant God in the manger. Before him, St Bernard had let his grief burst forth while meditating on the passion of Christ, and was moved to tears when speaking of Christmas night."

15. See Lk 24:35.

16. SC 1:4; SBOp 1:4; CF 4:3.

17. SC 12:7; SBOp 1:65; CF 4:83.

18. SC 61:4; SBOp 2:150; CF 31:143.

19. SC 48:5-6; SBOp 2:70; CF 31:16-17.

20. Med 6:12; PL 180:226; CF 3:131.

21. Med 8:5; PL 180:230-31; CF 3:142.

22. Med 5:9; PL 180:221; CF 3:123.

23. Spec fid 60; SCh 301:126; CF 15:46.

24. Inst incl 33; CCCM I:679, 1444-46; CF 2:99. This is the only use of the name "Jesus" in Aelred's meditation on the future; elsewhere he is called judge (*iudex*), Christ, Son (*Filius*), or Lord (*Domine*).

25. Iesu 3; CCCM I:252, 82-87; CF 2:7.

26. Iesu 11-12; CCCM I:259, 26-36; CF 2:16.

27. Although this work, *De Institutione inclusarum*, is better known by its title in the CF 2 translation of M. P. Macpherson, O.C.S.O., *Rule of Life for a Recluse*, I here use a direct translation of the Latin title, which better defines the work.

28. Inst incl 31; CCCM I:671, 1188-90; CF 2:90. The language and eucharistic insistence of Aelred's Passion scene recalls Berengar's Oath at the Synod of Rome in 1079, the culmination of the great eucharistic controversy of the age: "The bread and wine which are placed on the altar . . . are changed substantially into the true and proper vivifying body and blood of Jesus Christ our Lord and after the consecration there are the true body of Christ which was born of the virgin . . . and the true blood of Christ which flowed from his side, not however through sign and in the power of the sacrament, but in their real nature and true substance." Macy, p. 37.

29. Inst incl 31; CCCM I:671, 672, 1194, 1202-203; CF 2:91.

30. *De sacramentis* iv.20; PL 16:443A.

31. Aelred here addresses another enduring eucharistic controversy, whether the sacrifice on the cross took place once for all (see Heb 10:10) or recurs in each Mass. His statement that the blood is changed to wine at the Crucifixion itself argues one sacrifice, not replicable but recallable.

32. Inst incl 29; CCCM I:663–64, 923–24, 952–55; CF 2:81, 82.
33. Inst incl 31; CCCM I:669, 672, 1109–110, 1203; CF 2:88, 90.
34. Inst incl 31; CCCM I:673, 1240; CF 2:92.
35. SC 20:6; SBOp 1:118; CF 4:152. The four references to Christ's flesh in this passage are all variants of *caro*.
36. SC 45:6, 10; SBOp 2:45; CF 7:236, 239.
37. Cuthbert Butler, *Western Mysticism* (London, 1922), p. 97.
38. SC 61:2; SBOp 2:47; CF 31:141.
39. Sc 43:4; SBOp 2:38; CF 7:222–23.
40. SC 31:2; SBOp 1:220; CF 7:125.
41. 1 Co 11:29.
42. Med 10:7; PL 180:236; CF 3:154.
43. Contemp 3; SCh 61:64; CF 3:38.
44. Med 6:11; PL 180:225–26; CF 3:131–32.
45. Med 8:5; PL 180:231; CF 3:142.
46. Ep frat 30:115, 117–19; SCh 223:234–38; CF 12:49–51.
47. *S. in assumptione b. Mariae*; PL 195:303; Storey, p. 91.
48. Inst incl 31; CCCM I:670, 1157–60; CF 2:89.
49. Inst incl 29; CCCM I:663–64, 926–27; CF 2:81.
50. Inst incl 31; CCCM I:666, 1004; CF 2:84.
51. Inst incl 31; CCCM I:672, 1224–25; CF 2:92.
52. Inst incl 31; CCCM I:667, 1043–46; CF 2:85.
53. Inst incl 31; CCCM I:668, 1091–94; CF 2:87.
54. Inst incl 31; CCCM I:671, 1187–90; CF 2:90.
55. Inst incl 31; CCCM I:672–73, 1229–37; CF 2:92.
56. Inst incl 31; CCCM I:671, 1192–93; CF 2:91. I have discussed Aelred's treatment of contemplative union with Christ in "Christ Our Mother: Aelred's Iconography for Contemplative Union," in *Goad and Nail: Studies in Medieval Cistercian History, X*, ed. E. Rozanne Elder, CS 84 (Kalamazoo, 1984), pp. 21–45.
57. Inst incl 31; CCM I:673, 1238–39; CF 2:92.
58. *S. in assumptione b. Mariae*; PL 195:306; Storey, p. 92.
59. Inst incl 31; CCCM I:668, 1076–77; CF 2:86.
60. Paschasius Radbert, *De corpore et sanguine domini*, (*passim*; see, for example, IX: 111–118); ed. Bede Paulus, O.S.B., CCCM 16:56. Macy, p. 70. Paschasius refers to this as "natural" union.
61. Inst incl 26; CCCM I:659, 769–71; CF 2:74.
62. These are the subjects of Aelred's three meditations in *On Reclusion*, though he does not suggest them as eucharistic or eschatological categories.
63. Ps 34:9.
64. Gn 2:9.
65. Sc 48:5–6; SBOp 2:70; CF 31:16–17.
66. Med 4:4, 9; PL 180:215–16; CF 3:112, 115.
67. *S. in nativitate Domini*; Talbot, p. 38.
68. SC 43:4; SBOp 2:38; CF 7:223.
69. Hum I:1; SBOp 3:17; CF 13:30. Bernard clearly does not use *viaticum* here in its usual sense. He is consciously engaging in word play throughout this passage: "Ego sum vita, id est viaticum, quo sustenteris in via."
70. Sg 5:1.
71. Dil 33; SBOp 3:146–47; CF 13:123–24.
72. Div 87; SBOp 6:331.
73. Dil 11; SBOp 3:127; CF 13:103. Si 24:21, where Wisdom speaks: "Those who eat of me will still hunger; those who drink of me will still thirst." See Jesus' words in John 4:13–14. I have discussed Aelred's use of Wisdom's self-introduction in Inst incl 14 (CCCM I:650; CF 2:63) in "Christ Our Mother," p. 25 and p. 42, n. 15.

74. Med 8:5; PL 180:231; CF 3:142.

75. Med 6:8; PL 180:224; CF 3:128–29.

76. Cant II:4. 176; SCh 82:360; CF 6:142.

77. Nat am 2:10–11; PL 184:386; CF 30:64–66.

78. Inst incl 31; CCCM I:669, 1126; CF 2:88.

79. Inst incl 31; CCCM I:668, 1090–91; CF 2:87.

80. Inst incl 31; CCCM I:668, 1065–72; CF 2:86.

81. Spec car 2; CCCM I:13. See Paschasius, *Epistola ad Fredugarum*, II. 105–109; CCCM 16:148: "Just as in the present 'we know in part' whatever we know of God, and 'in part' by the testimony of the Apostle 'we prophesy' of the future and of the kingdom of heaven, so it is in part that we pre-taste, not with the palate of our mouth, but with the palate of our heart, and by faith we believe it to be the body and blood of Christ."

82. Inst incl 32; CCCM I:676, 1339–53; CF 2:96.

83. Inst incl 33; CCCM I:681, 1523–27; CF 2:102. The phrase "and are received by his embrace" does not appear in CF 2, though Talbot indicates its absence in no MS.

84. Inst incl 33; CCCM I:681, 1499; CF 2:101.

85. Med 6:2; PL 180:222; CF 3:125–26.

INTIMACY AND IMITATION:
THE HUMANITY OF CHRIST IN
CISTERCIAN SPIRITUALITY

Marsha L. Dutton

T HE INCARNATION represents the intimacy of the human state
with God, says Gregory of Nyssa,[1] and the works of cistercian spirituality echo that understanding. In his sermons on the
Song of Songs, the great book of intimacy between the divine and
the human, Bernard of Clairvaux lays a foundation for an incarnational and sacramental spirituality of just such intimacy, explaining
the Incarnation, the Holy Spirit, and the soul's reception of God's
power and knowledge all in terms of a kiss:

> The mouth that kisses signifies the Word who assumes
> human nature; the nature assumed receives the kiss; the kiss,
> however, that takes its being both from the giver and the
> receiver, is a person that is formed by both, none other than
> "the one mediator between God and mankind, himself a
> man, Christ Jesus."[2]

> Then look at Jesus in the presence of his Apostles: "He
> breathed on them," according to St John, "and he said:
> 'Receive the Holy Spirit.'" That favor, given to the newly-
> chosen Church, was indeed a kiss. That? you say. That cor-
> poreal breathing? O no, but rather the invisible Spirit, who
> is so bestowed in that breath of the Lord that he is
> understood to proceed from him equally as from the Father,
> truly the kiss that is common both to him who kisses and to
> him who is kissed.... It is by giving the Spirit, through
> whom he reveals, that he shows us himself; he reveals in the
> gift, his gift is in the revealing. Furthermore, this revelation

which is made through the Holy Spirit not only conveys the
light of knowledge but also lights the fire of love.[3]

William of St Thierry expands this understanding, saying "The
soul in its happiness finds itself standing midway in the Embrace
and the Kiss of Father and Son.[4] And Aelred of Rievaulx defines
three spiritual significations of marriage, of which "the first was accomplished in Bethlehem, when like a bridegroom coming forth
from his chamber, emerging from the virginal womb, the Word in
our nature brought forth unity with men."[5]

THE ORIGINS OF CISTERCIAN SPIRITUALITY

The spirituality of the cistercian Fathers is profoundly incarnational, centered in the love of God made known in his intimate
union with humanity and participating in the mutual love of the
Father and the Son through the Holy Spirit. As it is always a present response to God's initiative of love both past and present, it is
in essence willed, active, and intimate.

Another way of expressing the same idea is to say that cistercian
spirituality is in essence sacramental, grounded in the meeting of
the worshipper with Christ on the altar and in Christ's revelation
of himself there through the gift of the Holy Spirit. God channels
his grace in the sacrament as in the Incarnation, through the sensible, leading humankind through creatures of bread and wine to
his son, begotten, not made, and so to himself. For cistercian spirituality, far from being rooted in a desire to escape the flesh and the
world, begins and ends in God known in the flesh in this world.
Rather than attempting to bypass the Incarnation on its way to
God, it never leaves the eucharistic feast behind in its hunger for
the heavenly banquet, nor does it turn away from the feet of Jesus
in its yearning for the eternal sight of the face of God.

The spirituality of the cistercian Fathers must then be understood through the Incarnation and its sacramental mirror, the Eucharist. There it begins and ends. Moreover, it participates in the
Eucharist and takes on its likeness, always both loving and showing
forth the humanity of Jesus. In their sermons and spiritual treatises
the Fathers insist that one becomes one with Christ by finding his
humanity in his body and blood on the altar, joining him in his

human life, and finally coming to physical and spiritual oneness with him by partaking of his body and blood once again.[6]

But the search for Christ that culminates in eucharistic spirituality also arises from the Cistercians' insistent sense that they live in exile in this world, seldom vouchsafed even a foretaste of the glory to come, in a land of unlikeness cast out from their Father's face. And in that exile they long for nothing so much as the presence of God. Recalling Paul's lamenting promise that "here we see in a glass darkly, but there face to face,"[7] Aelred titles his first known work, apparently at Bernard's bidding, *The Mirror of Charity*, so signalling its recognition that in this life love is always obscure, darkened, distorted.[8]

Repeatedly the Fathers mourn their separation from the feast of the Lord, the embrace of the Lord, the face of the Lord. Aelred speaks of Lent as representing the time between the Fall and "the last day, when we shall be finally liberated from this exile of ours," and of the fasting in Lent as a reminder "that in this life our desire for the heavenly bread can never be fully satisfied."[9] And William considers this life his hell "till I appear before your presence and behold your glory, and the eternal feast day of your face has shone upon my soul."[10]

The longing for that face in glory drives the cistercian Fathers on in unremitting yearning to see God now, to have him here, to love him in this world as in heaven. For just as the Eucharist provides a beginning and end for cistercian spirituality, the Fathers' longing for beatitude defines its necessity and its approach. As they long for God's embrace, the "feasting for ever on [his] face,"[11] they seek some temporary and partial measure of satisfaction.

As their goal is love, their route must be love, and as their goal is sensuous and intimate—dining, drinking, embracing, and looking at last on him whom they love, now at last face to face—so too must their journey be sensuous, intimate, comprised of eating and drinking, of loving and embracing, of seeking the face of God in the familiar face of a man.

Indeed, the face for which they yearn in glory is already known to them here as the face of Jesus, and Aelred insists that it is the same face. When in his meditation on the judgment he speaks of Christ the judge, who comes "in anger, his fury all ablaze and his chariot like a storm," at the left the damned drop their eyes.[12] But as the blessed stand on his right, "Jesus' face shines upon them, not terrible but lovable, not bitter but sweet, not frightening but attractive."[13] In fact within the third meditation Aelred uses the name "Jesus" only here, insistently identifying the judge as the Jesus whose loving and gentle gaze has been known on earth. For Aelred God in glory is identical to the God known here in Jesus.

So the Fathers kiss the feet of Jesus in order to come to the vision of God's face. Bernard says: "Prostrate yourself on the ground, take hold of his feet, soothe them with kisses";[14] William: "Anyone may see me lying with the sinful woman at your mercy's feet, washing them with the tears of my heart and anointing them with the perfume of heartfelt devotion!"[15] Aelred's *On Reclusion* is full of the kissing of Jesus' feet, in the manger, at the last supper, before and after the crucifixion, but Aelred often suggests a more direct link between them and the vision than do the others: "Surely you would not advise Mary to leave those feet which she is kissing so sweetly, or to turn her eyes away from that most beautiful face which she is contemplating, or to stop listening to the sweet words with which he regales her."[16]

This historical, physical approach to God through Jesus is combined with a metaphorical and at the same time eucharistic one as the Fathers speak of entering to God through Jesus, "the way, the truth, and the life."[17] William also speaks of Jesus as the door and as a bridge, even a ramp, saying:

> He who enters by you, O Door, walks on the smooth ground and comes to the Father, to whom no one may come, except by you. . . . For what better preparation, what happier arrangement could have been made for the man who wanted to ascend to his God . . . than that, instead of going up by steps to the altar, he should walk calmly and smoothly over the level of his own likeness, to a Man like himself, who tells him on the very threshold: "I and the Father are one." And he is forthwith gathered up to God in love through the Holy Spirit and receives God coming to him and making his abode with him, not spiritually only but corporeally too, in the mystery of the holy and life-giving body and blood of our Lord Jesus Christ. This, Lord, is your face towards us and our face towards you, full of good hope.[18]

The desire of the Fathers is not only to be assisted in their loneliness and separation in this world, but to come to God in the next. Eucharistic theology is always essentially concerned with salvation, of course, not contemplative union; the cistercian Fathers in seeking to see God through the Eucharist hope primarily through the Eucharist to reach salvation. Their longing to see God here is not a desire for quick thrills, temporal and temporary pleasure, but a means of enabling them to continue in the love of God.

For in the exile of this life, it is not a simple thing to keep one's eyes—and heart—set on the goal. The great difficulty, for the Fathers as for all Christians, is that voiced by William: "Who can love what he does not see? How can that be lovable that is not in some way visible?"[19] And Aelred's Mary Magdelene voices the inevitable cistercian anxiety to the risen Jesus: "Are you become less tender because more glorious?"[20] If they will come in love to God finally, they must find a way to remain in love with him now; but the difficulty seems insurmountable.

If cistercian spirituality develops through the yearning that combines loneliness, anxiety, unwillingness to accept absolute exile in this life, and the desire to dwell in eternity within God's love, "to pass through the things temporal so as not to lose things eternal,"[21] that yearning is far from despair. In consists of love not hopeless but hopeful, and that love is the means to love. William says:

> He . . . who desires loves always to desire, and he who loves desires to love always. And for him who desires and loves, O Lord, you make what he desires so to abound that the desirer is vexed by no anxiety, nor does he who has plenty ever have too much. . . . To travel always thus is to arrive.[22]

As no true lover can peacefully acquiesce to separation from the beloved, cistercian love is not peaceful, passive, experienced as merely a wait for God's longed for but unsought visits. Rather, it is on the road, active, urgent, importunate.

Bernard and Aelred both cite Peter as the prototype for such importunity, and Aelred explicitly defines him as the great lover of Jesus among the disciples, applauding his unwillingness to wait for the sight of him whom he loves. A man of violent, impetuous love, who fully clothed races the boat through the Sea of Galilee to greet his risen lord cooking breakfast on the shore, Peter is compelled to hasten by his hunger to see, to touch, to eat and drink with his Lord:

> O admirable ardor!... Only Peter, like a hart burning with thirst, devoured by internal fire, fears neither the stares nor the waves, thinks only of him whom he sees afar on the beach.... Our Spirit asks which of our fathers surpasses the others in the love of God. Now we know—our lord said it himself—that Peter loved him more than the other apostles.[23]

The importunity of cistercian spirituality, the refusal to give up the flesh of Christ, prompts some anxiety among the Fathers. Both Bernard and Aelred speak of the love of Jesus' flesh that binds the hearts of the disciples, and especially of Peter. Both declare that love to be immature, characterizing beginners in faith. But while Aelred praises it, Bernard blames it. He reminds his listeners that "the love of the heart ... is sweet indeed, but liable to be led astray if it lacks the love of the soul," then cites the example of Peter:

> When [Jesus] was speaking in the same way about his approaching death, Peter who loved him so dearly tried to stand in the way. When, as you remember, [Jesus] rebuked him, what was it but his imprudence that he was correcting? Finally, what did he mean in saying, "You do not mind the things of God" except you do not love wisely, you are following your human feeling in opposition to the divine plan.... Taught to love with his whole soul, Peter was still weak. He was well instructed but not well prepared, aware of the mystery but afraid of being witness to it.[24]

Bernard insists throughout his works that such love of the flesh is carnal, restricted, potentially dangerous, and in fact no longer possible since the Ascension.

Although Aelred applauds Peter's impetuosity, he agrees with Bernard that to love Christ only in the humanity is to be a spiritual infant, that the mature Christian must advance to knowledge and love of his divinity:

One may note, however, that the love of Peter exercises itself with more tenderness toward the humanity of the Savior while Paul is more eager to contemplate the mystery of the divinity.... Both [Peter and Paul] knew and loved perfectly the strength of his divinity and the mystery of the Incarnation, especially after the glorification of Jesus and the reception of the fullness of the Holy Spirit. However, one may say that in the affection of Peter is the milk of doctrine offered to infants, and in the love of Paul, the solid nourishment of contemplation.[25]

William agrees:

When the faithful soul has been taught by such things, however, she should begin not to need them and pass from physical to spiritual things and from spiritual things to the Maker of the spiritual and physical. Truly, then, she shall leave her baggage behind! For having left the body and all bodily cares and hindrances, she forgets everything except God.[26]

But despite their fears, despite their general sense that the mature lover of God may and must move beyond the flesh, Bernard, William and Aelred recognize that carnal man, animal souls, novices, unschooled anchoresses, all the spiritual babes to whom they preach and for whom they write, continue to need God made man as fully after the glorification of Jesus and the reception of the fullness of the Holy Spirit as before. Bernard muses:

I think this is the principal reason that the invisible God willed to be seen in the flesh and to converse with men as a man. He wanted to recapture the affections of carnal men who were unable to love in any other way, by first drawing them to the salutary love of his own humanity, and then gradually to raise them to a spiritual love.... So it was only by his physical presence that their hearts were detached from carnal loves.[27]

And William says:

It was not the least of the chief reasons for your incarnation

that your babes in the Church, who still needed your milk
rather than solid food, who are not strong enough spiritually to think of you in your own way, might find in you a
form not unfamiliar to themselves. In offering of their
prayers they might set this form before themselves, without
any hindrance to faith, while they are still unable to gaze into the brightness of the majesty of your divinity.[28]

For spiritual beginners love temporal is the only route to love
eternal; the kiss of Jesus' feet is the route to the eternal vision of
the face of God.

THE WORK OF THE EYE OF LOVE

But the difficulty in loving Jesus begins with Paul's statement,
echoed repeatedly by Bernard: "If we once knew Christ in the
flesh we know him thus no longer."[29] And William asks, How is
it possible to love him here when we cannot see him here? How
does one love what one cannot see? And where in this post-Ascen-
sion time, in this life, does one look for his sight?

Having posed the question, William gives its solution: One must
see; having seen, one will love and, what is more, possess the beloved: "For to see the good things of the Lord is to love them, and
to love them is to have them."[30] William points those who would
see toward the Eucharist, insisting that it is the Eucharist that
allows the sight of God even here:

Not that divinity may be seen by physical eyes, but that
glorification of the body by some grace manifested through
it will point out the presence of divinity. Even in this life the
religion of the physical sacraments is effective for this. Since
we understand scarcely anything besides bodies and physical
things while we are passing through as an image, we are
bound by the physical sacraments lest we draw away from
God.[31]

William even explains the mechanism of that sight:

The sight for seeing God . . . is charity. There are, however,
two eyes in this sight, always throbbing by a sort of natural

intensity to look toward the light that is God: love and
reason. . . . One of them—reason—cannot see God except
in what he is not, but love cannot bring itself to rest except
in what he is. . . . Reason . . . seems to advance through
what God is not toward what God is. Love, putting aside
what God is not, rejoices to lose itself in what he is. From
him love has come forth, and it naturally aspires to its own
beginning. Reason has the greater sobriety; love the greater
happiness.[32]

Elsewhere he explains further, now insisting on the eyes' mutual
action through grace:

One of these eyes searches the things of men, according to
knowledge; but the other searches divine things, according
to wisdom. And when they are illumined by grace, they are
of great mutual assistance, because love gives life to reason
and reason gives light to love. . . . Often when these two
eyes faithfully cooperate, they become one; in the contemplation of God, where love is chiefly operative, reason
passes into love and is transformed into a certain spiritual
and divine understanding that transcends and absorbs all
reason.[33]

So William defines the scheme of cistercian spirituality, its basis
in the Eucharist and its method: the eye of reason looks into the
bread and wine, the *sacramentum*, what God is not, and finds the
res, God in Christ, in the Eucharist; the eye of love on seeing him
there loves him, loses itself in what he is, and so possesses him.
The two eyes then work together to see God, in this life and the
next.

The work of the eye of love is parallel to that of the eye of reason. The eye of reason begins by looking into the Eucharist, finds
Christ's humanity there, and so develops a new understanding of
his humanity, of the eucharistic meal itself, and of its relationship
to beatitude and the heavenly banquet. Finally it returns to the
Eucharist with a newly integrated understanding become faith.
Bernard says of Christ, "the tree of life . . . the living bread": "His
shadow is his flesh; his shadow is faith. The flesh of her own Son
overshadowed Mary; faith in the Lord overshadows me. And yet

why should his flesh not overshadow me too, as I eat him in the sacrament?"[34] So too the eye of love begins and ends in the Eucharist, meeting and loving Christ therein.

When the eye of love looks into the Eucharist, however, it does not, like reason, ask speculative questions, probe, analyse, or discriminate, but rather works actively to seek out the beloved and to enter into intimacy with him. Its action is an imaging forth of Jesus, remembering his life, meditating on the various ways of uniting with him, and rediscovering the continuing possibility of that remembering, meditating, and uniting in this life, in the eucharistic meal itself. Love of his humanity not only begins in the Eucharist, but leads inevitably to his Passion; there his body crucified and pouring forth blood returns the beholder, the lover, the worshipper once again to the altar, to the bread that is his body, the wine that is his blood. There the two eyes become one again in unity, in charity, in the sight of God. And the fruit of that charity is the sermons and treatises of cistercian spirituality. The process is then a circle, longing for God, seeking him, loving him, becoming one with him, and leading others to begin the search again.

Although the eye of love is synthetic rather than analytic in its working, analysis may aid in understanding that synthesis. Just as charity, the sight of God, can be divided into its two parts for fuller understanding of each, so may the love of God in Christ be schematized for better understanding, for the eye of love loves Jesus in many ways, in all the ways that men are loved.[35]

THE HUMANITY OF CHRIST

The Gospel accounts furnish the ground for the Cistercians' knowledge of the humanity of Christ, and the Fathers remain close to those accounts, rarely wandering into apocrypha or blurring the distinctions between Gospel characters. Aelred, who provides the fullest life of Jesus, concentrating on the humanity[36] and not skipping from nativity to passion but detailing the principal events of Jesus' human experience, only once tells an apocryphal story, which he identifies as such, saying that it is included "in order to kindle love,"[37] and maintains the Gospel distinction between Mary of Bethany, the woman taken in adultery, and Mary Magdalene.[38]

This biblical narrative of Jesus' life lends itself naturally to Gregorian allegoresis,[39] as Aelred demonstrates in his use of historical, allegorical, and moral units in the story of Jesus at twelve. At the first level the Cistercians are concerned historically with Jesus' life as a man of Nazareth. At the allegorical level, they understand him in a series of human examples of union, as infant, lover, and mother, typologically as the bridegroom of the *Song of Songs* and as Wisdom, "the mother of fair love and of fear and of knowledge and of holy hope."[40] Finally, at the moral level, they consume him in the Eucharist and so become one with him. The stages move from the fleshly and literal to the spiritual and then back to the flesh, now known through the spirit rather than apart from it.

At the literal level Jesus is loved as an infant, child, and man, and the soul loves him as did those who loved him in his human life. It is Aelred who most commonly presents Jesus simply and clearly as a man because he is least anxious, most clear that wholly man, he is wholly God: "You adore the man in God and God in the man."[41] However, passages of devotion to Jesus in his manhood also appear throughout the works of Bernard and William.

At the historical level the soul is encouraged to involve herself intimately in the human life of Jesus, either with or in imitation of those who lived with him. All who knew Jesus—as infant, child, or adult, before, during, or after the Passion—are models for his modern-day lover. His family, disciples, friends, followers, and even strangers show the contemplative soul how to love Jesus.

Both Bernard and Aelred direct the listeners' attention to the greeting of Elizabeth and John to the unborn Jesus, Bernard saying: "[Mary hastened] to visit [Elizabeth], thus giving opportunity to the little prophet to offer the first fruits of his office to his still smaller Lord. And while the mothers ran to greet each other, affection was roused in the babes from womb to womb."[42] And he says of Joseph's love for the child Jesus: "To him it was given not only to see and to hear what many kings and prophets had longed to see and did not see, to hear and did not hear, but even to carry him, to take him by the hand, to hug and kiss him, to feed him and to keep him safe."[43]

William also directs intimacy with Jesus, leaping in one sentence from infancy to the resurrection: "You will allow [the soul], for example, to embrace the manger of the newborn babe, to venerate the sacred infancy, to caress the feet of the crucified, to hold and kiss those feet when he is risen, and to put her hand in the print of the nails and cry: 'My Lord and my God!'"[44]

Aelred's works are full of people clamoring to be with, to embrace, to love Jesus. Of those who traveled to Jerusalem with Jesus he says: "See, I beg, how he is seized upon and led away by each and every one of them. Old men kiss him; young men embrace him; boys wait upon him. And what tears do the boys shed when he is kept too long by the men? How do the holy women complain when he lingers a little longer with his father and his companions? Each of them, I think, declares in her inmost heart: 'Let him kiss me with the kiss of his mouth.'"[45]

While Bernard and William occasionally allude to incidents in the life of the adult Jesus and to the love of those who knew him between his birth and his Passion, only Aelred lingers there, directing the anchoress through scenes with strangers as well as intimates: the woman taken in adultery, the paralytic let down through the roof, the disciples, and especially Mary, Martha, and Lazarus: "But we must leave this scene and come to Bethany, where the sacred bonds of friendship are consecrated by the authority of our Lord. For Jesus loved Martha, Mary, and Lazarus. There can be no doubt that this was on account of the special friendship by which they were privileged to be more intimately attached to him."[46]

She is also directed to accompany the disciples to the Last Supper, to Mount Olivet, to the courtyard of the High Priest, to Pilate, and to the crucifixion and then to assist those who bear him to the tomb:

> But wait yet a while until that noble councilor comes to extract the nails and free his hands and feet. See how in his most happy arms he embraces that sweet body and clasps it to his breast. . . . It is for you to follow that precious treasure of heaven and earth, and either hold the feet or support the hands and arms, or at least gather up carefully the drops of the precious blood as they fall one by one, and lick the dust from his feet. See also how gently, how solicitously blessed Nicodemus handles his limbs, rubbing ointments on them, and then with holy Joseph wraps them in the shroud and lays them in the tomb.[47]

In a concern wholly appropriate for their purposes, the Fathers show the friends and followers of Jesus clinging to his flesh in love even after the Resurrection, through Mary Magdalene, Peter, and Thomas. Both Bernard and William speak of Thomas's doubt as an image of their own; hence he becomes a model for their love for Christ and for those spiritual babes for whom they write. Bernard identifies him with Joseph, whose love for the infant Christ he remarks:

> Mary's engagement is to be explained in the same way as Thomas's doubting. . . . Thus, just as Thomas, putting out his hand in doubt to touch the Lord, was to become a stout witness to the resurrection, so Joseph, in engaging himself to Mary, watched over her reputation by his protection and thus became a faithful witness to her modesty. Thomas's doubt and Mary's engagement fit beautifully together. . . . And sure enough I, weak man that I am, I find it easier to believe in the Son's resurrection when I see Thomas doubtfully touching him than when I see Cephas believing on simple hearsay.[48]

And Aelred's Mary Magdalene is an essential model for the contemplative in her yearning for the embrace of Christ, now as then:

> Do not fail subsequently to keep Magdalene company; remember to visit with her your Lord's tomb, taking with you the perfumes she has prepared. If only you might be found worthy to see in spirit what she saw with her eyes. . . . With what affection, I ask, with what desire, with what fervor of mind and devotion of heart was it that you cried "Master"?. . . She runs quickly [to tell the disciples], anxious to run quickly. She returns, but together with other women. These Jesus comes to meet with affection, restoring their spirits and banishing their sadness. And notice, the boon is now given which had previously been kept until later, for they came close and clasped his feet. Linger here as long as you can, virgin.[49]

The historical stage, however, does not allow true physical union. The women who embrace Jesus or clasp his feet remain separate from him, able to be sent away precisely as they may be welcomed back. Only a more allegorical understanding may allow imagery of physical union to represent the spiritual.[50]

At the allegorical stage Jesus is understood not as a man fixed in time and space, but metaphorically, in the ways humans love one another most intimately. This conception appears more often in the works of Bernard and William, who frequently leave Jesus the man behind as they turn to the bridegroom of the soul. For them in fact it is not always, or for long, clear that that bridegroom is Jesus, as he almost always clearly is for Aelred. In *On Loving God* Bernard moves rapidly from the Passion to the love of the bride and bridegroom and back to the Passion in one section:

> The faithful, on the contrary, know how totally they need Jesus and him crucified. . . . The Church sees King Solomon with the diadem his mother had placed on his head. She sees the Father's only Son carrying his cross, the Lord of majesty, slapped and covered with spittle; she sees the Author of life and glory pierced by nails, wounded by a lance, saturated with abuse, and finally laying down his precious life for his friends. After she beholds this, the sword of love transfixes all the more her soul, making her repeat: "Cushion me about with flowers, pile up apples around me, for I languish with love." These fruits are certainly the pomegranates the bride introduced into her Beloved's garden. Picked from the tree of life, they changed their natural taste for that of heavenly bread, their color for Christ's blood.[51]

The times in human experience when two people become most nearly one are three, closely related to one another; indeed two of the three are identical except for the perspective. They are moments of physical and spiritual union, of participation in one another, of becoming one flesh. They are the union of the unborn child with his mother, the sexual union of lover with beloved, and the union of the mother with her unborn child. The *Genesis* account of the man's joyful recognition of the partner God has given him resonates in such passages: "This at last is bone of my bones and flesh of my flesh; . . . Therefore shall a man leave his father and his mother and cleave to his wife, and they shall be one flesh."[52]

For Jesus is bone of humankind's bone, flesh of the soul's flesh as she finds union with him as mother, bride, and babe and as he reciprocally becomes her unborn child, her lover and groom, and her mother. As the soul and Jesus become one, the divine and the human become one in mutual interpenetration. The two become one in imaginative union as sacramentally and spiritually they will be one in the Eucharist.[53]

While all the fathers devote most of their allegorical attention to Christ the lover and bridegroom of the soul, they also speak of his being a child within the soul and as conceiving, bearing, or nursing the soul as a mother. Aelred says to the soul: "For just as the Lord Jesus is born and conceived in us, so he grows and is nourished in us, until we all come to perfect manhood, that maturity which is proportioned to the complete growth of Christ."[54] William sees the soul, however, as borne within him:

> Lord, where do you draw those whom you thus embrace and enfold, save to your heart? The manna of your Godhead, which you, O Jesus, keep within the golden vessel of your all-wise human soul, is your sweet heart! Blessed are they whom your embrace draws close to it. Blessed are the souls whom you have hidden in your heart, that inmost hiding-place, so that your arms overshadow them from the disquieting of men and they only hope in your covering and fostering wings. Those who are hidden in your sweet heart are overshadowed by your mighty arms; they sleep sweetly.[55]

All of the Fathers, however, present Jesus more frequently in terms describing a mother nursing rather than conceiving, carrying, or giving birth, perhaps because of greater ease in identifying the milk with the level of instruction and devotion appropriate for those whom they are teaching. So Bernard says: "Too often we must interrupt the sweet kisses [of contemplation] to feed the needy with the milk of doctrine."[56] William says: "It is your breasts, O eternal Wisdom, that nourish the holy infancy of your little ones. . . . Since that everlasting blessed union and the kiss of eternity are denied the Bride on account of her human condition and weakness, she turns to your bosom; and not attaining to that mouth of yours, she puts her mouth to your breasts instead."[57] And Aelred explicitly associates the milk of Jesus with his humanity: "Leave John to cheer himself with the wine of gladness in the knowledge of the Godhead while you run to feed on the milk that flows from Christ's humanity."[58]

Bernard and William's sermons on the *Song of Songs* consistently present Christ as the bridegroom, the lover, to the bride who is the Church or the soul. Aelred too shows Jesus as bridegroom to the contemplative bride, urging her to prepare her nuptial robe of virtues with borders of gold, "that is, of charity in all its brilliance" "a many-colored robe in which your Bridegroom will delight to see you."[59] And he describes her groom to her: "See who it is you have chosen as your Bridegroom, who it is you have made your friend. He who is the most comely of the sons of men, more resplendent even than the sun and than the stars in all their beauty.... He it is who has already chosen you as his bride."[60]

Aelred speaks of Simeon's embrace of Jesus at the Presentation in the Temple as not merely a boon of personal intimacy, but an example of the third spiritual signification of marriage, the daily union of the soul with the Word:

> [Simeon] had received the promise that he would not die before seeing the Christ, and that loving soul today embraced his Savior in his arms. Look, if you will, how the attraction wakened that love, how the desire made the ardor grow, and how, finally, it reached perfection through consent....
> He received him in his arms and his love was overwhelmed by that embrace. Ah! brothers, the tongue here can only be still, that tongue which has until this moment spoken as well as it could. But now there is only silence. These are the secrets of the nuptial couple and their intimate joys that a third person cannot share. "My secret is my own, my secret is my own." What is your secret, O bride, who alone have known the joy of this spiritual kiss in which the created spirit and the uncreated spirit merge to become two in one, that is, no longer to be more than one, justifying and justified, sanctifying and sanctified, deifying and deified.[61]

At the moral level, finally, Jesus is to be known in the Eucharist, not in memory or in imagination, in history or in allegory, but in action and in fact, once again in flesh but now veiled behind the *sacramentum* and hidden except to faith. At this stage the lover of Jesus takes him wholly into her body so that he becomes in all truth bone of her bone, flesh of her flesh.[62]

The movement from imagination to reality, the prismatic representation of a single moment of the soul, is frequently signaled by Aelred. Three times in *On Reclusion* he speaks of someone facing the judgment of Christ, the first and third times using much the same language: "Standing, sitting, and walking he so kept his face cast down and his eyes bent on the ground that he seemed to be standing in fear and trembling before God's judgment seat [*ut tremens et timens diuinis tribunalibus*]."[63] Again, "Imagine now that you are standing before Christ's judgment seat [*ante Christis tribunal*] between these two companies and have not yet been assigned to one or the other. . . . Now stand in the middle, not knowing to which company the Judge's sentence will assign you. O what a dreadful waiting. Fear and trembling [*Timor et tremens*] have come upon me and darkness has covered me. If he sends me to join those on the left I cannot complain of injustice; if he sets me among those on the right it is to be attributed to his grace, not to my merits."[64] The second such passage, though, is not hypothetical or imaginary, but fact: "I freely abandoned myself to all that is base, accumulating material for fire to burn me, for corruption to stifle me, for worms to gnaw me . . . Your anger and your indignation, God, weighed down upon me, and I did not know it. . . . How generous was his grace in following me when I fled, in allaying my fears. . . . He rescued me from the world and welcomed me with kindness."[65]

In these three passages all the facts are the same, in memory and imagination are found present realities, and he who acts as though he is before the judgment seat or imagines that he is before the judgment seat must recall that he is in fact before the judgment seat, accumulating material for fire, corruption, and worms—were it not for God's grace. So too the various ways of loving Christ, historically—in memory—and allegorically—in imagination—come finally to the same thing, uniting in the moral stage of present act and actuality.[66]

The moral stage is the stage of unity with Christ, naturally and spiritually. At the historical level his lover kissed, embraced, carried, anointed, and drank from him but remained apart. At the allegorical she progressed to the nearest human approach to oneness, but as Wisdom explains: "They that eat me shall yet hunger, and they that drink me shall yet thirst."[67] But finally in the eating of his body and blood in the Eucharist he and she are indistinguishably one. All of the fathers insist on the union there of Christ and the transfigured soul. Bernard says, recalling both traditional images of God's self-revelation and the Eucharist:

> As a drop of water seems to disappear completely in a great quantity of wine, even assuming the wine's taste and color: as red, molten iron becomes so much like fire it seems to lose its primary state; as the air on a sunny day seems transformed into sunshine instead of being lit up: so . . . all human beings melt in a mysterious way and flow into the will of God.[68]

William also refers to this uniting of the soul and Christ in the Eucharist, using much the same language as Bernard:

> In wisdom, which is the cellar of wine, are fed love and affection. The riches of the storeroom are known; the riches of the cellar of wine are tasted. In the storerooms, one must labor diligently to understand; in the cellar of wine, one has but to rejoice in experiencing fruition. . . . The cellar of wine, indeed, is a certain secret of God's wisdom; it is the state of the soul that is more fully drawn to cleave to God . . . not under the cedar beams of faith and hope, but in the fullness of charity, which is the cellar of wine. For charity . . . is the cellar of wine, and the wine of this cellar is joy in the Holy Spirit. In the cellar of wine, therefore, nothing is found but wine. Whatever enters there, whatever is brought in, either is wine or becomes wine, because the fire of the love of God wholly claims and consumes it and, in the manner of the element of fire, converts it into its own substance, since to him that loves God all things work together unto good.[69]

Not only does Aelred use recognizably eucharistic language in urging the contemplative to receive Christ's body and blood and to enter into physical union with him on the cross, he is also propositionally explicit about the unitive goal of his teaching. Echoing the language of the Mass, he says:

> Let these things serve to increase your charity. . . . From all

of them you must ascend to unity, for only one thing is necessary. That is the one thing, the unity which is found only
in the One, by the One, with the One with whom there is
no variation, no shadow of change. The man who unites
himself with him becomes one spirit with him, passing into
that unity which is always the same and whose years do not
come to an end. This union is charity, as it were the edge
and border of the spiritual vesture.[70]

This unity is for Aelred explicitly tied and indeed central to the
three stages of the humanity of Christ. He places this eucharistic
passage between an explanation of the significance of the anchoress's crucifix and a mention of her wedding garment, which introduces his consideration of charity, the portion of the treatise that
contains the three meditations provided so that "the sweet love of
Jesus [may grow] in your affections."[71]

Just as the *sacramentum* is only to humans' darkened eyes distinct
from the *res*, so the body and blood on the altar is only to mortal
eyes distinct from the swaddled babe in the manger whose crib
Christ's lovers embrace or the crucified lord whose limbs they bear
to the tomb. So too that infant, lover, and mother whose body
they kiss and hold until their lips are red with his blood[72] is only to
their darkened imagination distinct from the bread and wine they
eat and drink until their lips are red. As the Cistercians love in
memory, in imagination, and in substance, so they may see him
whom they love now and forever, the same face shining sweetly in
this world and the next.

So the route to the face of God is for the Cistercians the face of
Jesus. They love in order that they may love; they see in order that
they may see and that they may possess. The sight of Jesus in the
Eucharist leads to the eternal vision of God, and feeding upon him
there leads to the heavenly banquet, the wedding supper of the
Lord.

William explains this life's need to know God present:

When the Bride remembered the Bridegroom, or thought
of him, seeking understanding she supposed him to be absent as long as her understanding turned not into love. But
goodwill is already the beginning of love. And a passionate
will, directed as if to an absent person, is desire; drawn to

someone present, it is love; then what the lover loves is present to his understanding. For love of God itself is knowledge of him; unless he is loved, he is not known, and unless he is known, he is not loved. He is known only insofar as he is loved, and he is loved only insofar as he is known.[73]

THE FRUIT OF CHARITY: CISTERCIAN SPIRITUALITY

The newly integrated knowledge and love of Jesus culminates in the union of the two eyes in charity, as William promised. But it does not stop there. For while Aelred advises the anchoress at the feet of the risen Jesus—"Linger here as long as you can, virgin. Do not let these delights of yours be interrupted by sleep or disturbed by any tumult from without"—he immediately adds "However . . . in this wretched life nothing is stable, nothing eternal, and man never remains in the same state."[74] Indeed, a central difference between the God with whom she reaches union on the cross, at the tomb, and in the Eucharist and herself, between this world and the next, is that expressed in the words "eternity" and "temporality." In losing itself in God the eye of love has not yet attained eternal peace; the sight of God, charity, has become like God in activity and maternal love for the hungry who wait and yearn. William explains the process of participative transformation that accomplishes this likeness, saying:

Every bodily sense, in order to be a sense and to perceive at all, must be in some sort changed, by means of a certain sensible impression, into the thing perceived. . . . The sense, then, is no sense, neither can it perceive at all unless, when it has informed the reason of the thing perceived, the soul of the perceiver is changed by a certain transformation of itself into the reality perceived, or into its state. . . . That is how the soul's sense functions. For the soul's sense is love; by love it perceives whatever it perceives. . . . When the soul reaches out in love to anything, a certain change takes place in it by which it is transmuted into the object loved.[75]

So charity, produced through participation in the active, intimate love of God, through union not metaphorical but actual, becomes Godlike. It is the golden hem on the seamless garment of the soul, the nuptial robe of the bride, in which her bridegroom is surely well pleased to see her; it is the visible evidence of their oneness in flesh and spirit.

And their nuptial union at once bears fruit, offspring of an active love toward those who have not yet been fortunate enough to see, love, and possess such a lover. At the allegorical stage of the argument these are the handmaidens, the daughters of Jerusalem, who have accompanied the bride as she searched through the streets of the city for her spouse. Literally they are the monks, the new Carthusians at Mont Dieu, the perhaps unknown anchoress—all those to whom the Cistercians are drawn to give service, guidance, direction.

The fruit of charity is itself a product of and in the likeness of Jesus. It is born of the spousal union with Christ the bridegroom, signaled by the pouring of milk from the breasts of the bride or from Christ the mother:

> While the bride is conversing about the Bridegroom, he, as I have said, suddenly appears, yields to her desire by giving her a kiss. . . . The filling up of her breasts is a proof of this. For so great is the potency of that holy kiss, that no sooner has the bride received it than she conceives and her breasts grow rounded with the fruitfulness of conception, bearing witness, as it were, with this milky abundance. Men with an urge to frequent prayer will have experience of what I say. Often enough when we approach the altar to pray our hearts are dry and lukewarm. But if we persevere, there comes an unexpected infusion of grace, our breast expands as it were, and our interior is filled with overflowing love; and if somebody should press upon it then, this milk of sweet fecundity would gush forth in streaming richness.

When the bride longs to linger in the kiss the Bridegroom's companions chastise her:

> The favor you demand is rather for your own delight, but the breasts with which you may feed the offspring of your womb are preferable to, that is, they are more essential than the wine of contemplation. What gladdens the heart of one man cannot be placed on equal terms with that which glad-

dens many. Rachel may be more beautiful, but Lia is more fruitful. So beware of lingering amid the kisses of contemplation; better the breasts that flow in the preaching of God's word.[76]

The love and service produced through charity include increased love for Jesus himself, expressed in service to those whom he had defined as being equivalent to him, the poor, the hungry, the naked, the thirsty.[77] In fact, the *Exordium Parvum* includes that understanding and that service as essential to the lives of the first Cistercians, those who left Molesme: "Thus having rejected the riches of this world, the new soldiers of Christ, poor with the poor Christ, began to consult with one another as to the question of the way of life by which, and with what work or occupation, they should provide in this life for themselves as well as for guests who would come, rich and poor alike, whom according to the *Rule* they should receive as Christ."[78]

Aelred is especially clear about this responsibility. He defines beneficence—"to do good to those to whom you are able"—as a subdivision of charity, while explaining that the way in which beneficence may be practiced differs according to the life one has chosen. So while Marthas, those who follow the active life in community, are to give alms, do works of physical mercy, the anchoress, as Mary, is to exercise her beneficence in "good will." "Let this be your offering. What is more useful than prayer? Let this be your largesse. What is more humane than pity? Let this be your alms. So embrace the whole world with the arms of your love. . . . Open to all the breast of your love, shed your tears, pour out for them your prayers."[79] The language of this passage is sufficiently similar to that of the crucifixion to alert the attentive reader to the likeness between the contemplative soul and Christ in these acts of charity; she not only serves him but bears his likeness in so doing.

Aelred's youthful introduction to the linking of Jesus and the needy appears in a story from David of Scotland, at whose court he grew to manhood. David once told Aelred of an incident from his own childhood, much of which was spent at the court of Henry I of England, where his sister, Matilda, was queen. Late one night Matilda summoned her brother. Finding her washing and kissing the feet of lepers, he cried out in horror: "Surely if the king were to know of this, your lips, polluted by the feet of lepers, would never again be dignified by the kisses of his lips!'' She answered, smiling: ''Who does not know that the feet of the eternal King are to be preferred to a mortal king's lips? I indeed have called you here, dearest brother, so that you might learn from my example to perform such things.''[80]

The love to the human brother or sister who is Christ is reciprocal. Not only does it proceed from and participate in God's love for man, responding to God's initiative of love, and not only is it produced by the love between Jesus and the soul, but it is immediately mirrored by love and service from Jesus to the soul. The recluse in *On Reclusion* is to wash and dry Jesus' feet, with ''that most blessed sinner,''[81] but then to allow him to wash and dry hers: ''Give him your own feet to wash.''[82] Aelred is even more explicit in discussing the roles of Mary and Martha:

> You see, if Mary had been alone in the house, no one would have fed the Lord; if Martha had been alone, no one would have tasted his presence and his words. Martha thus represents the action, the labor accomplished for Christ, Mary the repose that frees from bodily labor, in order to taste the sweetness of the Lord in reading, prayer, or contemplation. That is why, my brothers, so long as Christ is on earth, poor, subject to hunger, to thirst, to temptation, it is necessary that these two women inhabit the same house, that in one soul the two activities occur. While we are on earth—you, me, others—for it is true that we are his members, he also will be on the earth. As long as his members endure hunger, thirst, temptation, just so long Christ also will endure hunger, thirst, will be tempted.... Do not neglect Mary for Martha, nor Martha for Mary. If you neglect Martha, who will serve Jesus? And if you neglect Mary, what will be the use of the visit of Jesus, since you will not taste his sweetness? Know, my brothers, that in this life it is necessary never to separate these two women. When the time comes that Jesus is no longer poor, no longer has hunger or thirst, is no longer tempted, then only Mary, the spiritual action, will occupy the dwelling of your soul.[83]

Mary and Martha, traditional symbols of active and contemplative love of God, both belong to cistercian spirituality as inseparable and essential elements of charity in this life.

But the preeminent fruit of the Fathers' union with Christ, the milk that spills from their union with him, is their own works of spiritual direction, their sermons and treatises, their "milk of doctrine offered to babes."[84] And as that fruit, that milk, is produced by the union with Christ through the Holy Spirit, it is identical to it. The physical, enduring manifestation of cistercian love of Jesus, the textually transmitted spirituality of the fathers, is incarnational and eucharistic; so is it willed, active, and intimate.

Cistercian spirituality is a product of will rather than emotion, insisting that action produces affection rather than the other way around, for it is produced through the grace of the Holy Spirit, always understood by the Fathers as will. In his introduction to *The Nature and the Dignity of Love*, David N. Bell says: "By love we are conformed to God; by love we are conjoined to him; by love the whole Trinity dwells within us. The basis of love, however, is will."[85] Bernard says the revelation of the Holy Spirit "lights the fire of love."[86] William explains: "When grace anticipates and cooperates, [the will] begins to cleave by its good assent to the Holy Spirit who is the Love and the Will of the Father and the Son. It begins ardently to will what God wills, and what memory and reason suggest it should will. By ardent willing it becomes love. For love is nothing other than the will ardently [fixed] on something good."[87] As Bell says, in fact, will is that which links reason and love, which allows the movement between the two eyes: "Reason 'forms' the will, directs it, endows it with the knowledge of the good and the desire for it, and reason itself finally 'mounts on high to become love [*amor*].'"[88]

Aelred reduces the theological to the practical:

> The love that comes about through feeling is pleasant but dangerous. . . . Love induced by mere feeling may well be good, but what we love in this way we love because it is pleasant and nothing more. But in the full and perfect love [that comes from the collaboration of reason, feeling, and will] we love not because it is pleasant to do so, but because it is the love of something worthy.[89]

Love based on feeling fades when the feeling fades, when one "falls out of love," but love based on feeling, reason, and wills *chosen* love, endures. That is the love of the Cistercians for Christ.

Second, cistercian love of the humanity of Christ is active rather than passive. For the Cistercians it is an error to identify contemplation with passive receptiveness, with infusion, and to distinguish it from anything resulting from activity. While the Fathers all speak of infused joy, of "the sound of the Holy Spirit's breathing"[90] or of being suddenly filled with the Holy Spirit, usually they speak of the experience as an outcome of action, seeking, longing, actively reading and praying, running and insisting. It seldom catches them off guard, rarely comes without some effort on their part. Bernard begins his sermons on the *Song of Songs* by acknowledging the soul's hunger for her bridegroom and her active request for his kiss:

> In his own person "let him kiss me with the kiss of his mouth"; let him whose presence is full of love, from whom exquisite doctrines flow in streams, let him become "a spring inside me, welling up to eternal life . " . . . For his living, active word is to me a kiss, not indeed an adhering of the lips that can sometimes belie a union of hearts, but an unreserved infusion of joys, a revealing of mysteries, a marvelous and indistinguishable mingling of the divine light with the enlightened mind, which, joined in truth to God, is one spirit with him.[91]

Later he acknowledges that the request is bold, importunate, explaining: " 'I cannot rest,' she said, 'unless he kisses me with the kiss of his mouth' . . . . There is no question of ingratitude on my part, it is simply that I am in love. The favors I have received are far above what I deserve, but they are less than what I long for. It is desire that drives me on, not reason. Please do not accuse me of presumption if I yield to this impulse of love. My shame indeed rebukes me, but love is stronger than all.' "[92] The love explains and justifies the importunity of the lover.

The activity of cistercian seeking does not diminish the role of God in the experience, nor his power to choose his time of coming. Indeed, William is especially insistent on this point, saying: "I hear the Lord say to me: 'The Spirit blows whither he will.' And knowing even in myself that he breathes not when I will, but

when he himself wills, I find everything devoid of taste and dead.
And then I know that it is to you alone, O Fount of life, that I
must lift up my eyes, that I may see light only in your light."[93]

Nonetheless, his crying out for God is constant, unremitting; he
says: "Do all you can, my soul, not so much by the exercise of reason as by the activity of love."[94] With the same explanation as
Bernard he excuses the importunity of his love through its ardor
and indicates its occasional reward:

> Yearnings, strivings, longings, thoughts and affections, and
> all that is within me, come and let us go up to the mountain
> or place where the Lord both sees and is seen!. . . But alas,
> O Lord, alas! To want to see God when one is unclean in
> heart is surely quite outrageous, rash and presumptuous,
> and altogether out of order and against the rule of the word
> of truth and of your wisdom!. . . I know I am behaving
> outrageously, but it is the love of your love that makes me
> do so, as you indeed can see for yourself, though I cannot
> see you. . . . And sometimes, when I gaze with longing, I
> do see the "back" of him who sees me; I see your son Christ
> "passing by" in the abasement of his incarnation.[95]

In fact, it may be the Fathers' very understanding that they cannot compel the Spirit to come upon them that urges them onward
in their yearning, their struggling, their crying out. For as their
longing for God is grounded in hope, they will not stop seeking.
Further, as they conceive the love between God and man to be as
ardent, as intimate, as real as that between a man and woman,
they understand that in such affairs both partners are equally eager,
equally seeking the union and reunion that defines the *Song of
Songs* and their sermons and treatises based upon it.

Aelred urges the anchoress always forward, saying: "If he still
will not let you approach his feet, be insistent, beseech him, raise
your eyes to him brimming with tears and extort from him with
deep sighs and unutterable groanings what you seek. Strive with
God as Jacob did, so that he may rejoice in being overcome."[96] In
On Jesus as a Boy of Twelve Aelred reminds Ivo of the times when
he has moaned, been on fire, sought, longed—"impatient in [his]
love"—cajoled, accused, complained, professed, presumed, tried

to conquer "by a certain spiritual wrangling." He explains the value of such behavior, saying:

> Jesus, to be sure, loving as he is, is glad to be overcome in such a contest. He is delighted by so great constancy in such a soul and says proudly to the angels who stand around: "The voice of the turtledove has been heard in our land." For it is in the land of the living that such words of a soul on fire are heard, and the sweet fragrance of such great desire charms the whole city of God.[97]

And so the lover receives his reward:

> The soul is inflamed with the fire of an unutterable longing and enters upon a certain spiritual contest with God, until the whisper of a gentle breeze makes itself felt in its inmost depths. It gently captivates the affections, imposing silence on all movements, all anxieties, all words, all thoughts; it raises the soul in contemplation up to the very gates of the heavenly Jerusalem. Then he who has been sought so long, so often implored, so ardently desired, comely beyond the sons of men, looking out of the lattice work, invites to kisses, "Rise up, hasten, my friend, and come." . . . Then there are embraces, then there are kisses, then "I have found him whom my soul loves, I have held him fast and will not let him go," then she abounds in delights and enjoys good things in Jerusalem, celebrating a feast day with joy and exultation.[98]

Here Aelred presents the essential elements of cistercian contemplative understanding: a spiritual contest rewarded by the gift of the Holy Spirit, imposing silence and bringing vision, embrace, the celestial banquet. Quiet succeeds upon struggle, but it is not a distinct state, one for which the contemplative is required merely to wait, but rather a silence after storm, a respite after rain. It is a peace, a repose that emerges from the spiritual contest itself, from the very activity of yearning, seeking, hungering.[99] In fact, only when fast in intimate relationship with Jesus is the contemplative told by Aelred to linger. At the Last Supper, after she has been told to allow Jesus to wash her feet, Aelred says, "Why are you in such a hurry to go out now? Wait a little while." Again when she observes the women clasping the feet of the risen Jesus, he says "Linger here as long as you can, virgin."[100] While peace is that sought, in cistercian spirituality the seeking itself is unremitting, urgent, active.

Finally, not only is cistercian spirituality willed and active, it is centrally intimate, constantly using the language of intimate love: the kiss, the embrace, the running to meet. It is the language of the Eucharist as well, of partaking, participating in, becoming one with, not following behind.

It is nearly universal misconception that medieval devotion to the humanity of Christ is preeminently imitative. Jaroslav Pelikan speaks in *The Growth of Medieval Theology* at length of "The Discipline of Jesus," insisting that "The summons to 'take up the cross of the Redeemer' was the core of the Christian life of self-mortification" and that "the exhortation to imitate 'the example of the Lord' pertained to all who were his 'followers.'"[101] However, for the Cistercians that is rarely so. Theirs is not primarily a spirituality of exemplarism or mortification.

There are, of course, numerous passages in which the cistercian Fathers urge imitation of Christ, most commonly in his humility, although even in imitation they tend to move rapidly to intimacy with the one they imitate. Bernard, looking at the infant Christ, says: "Let us make every effort to be like this little child. Because he is meek and humble in heart, let us learn from him, lest he who is great, even God, should have been made a little man for nothing, lest he should have died to no purpose, and have been crucified in vain. Let us learn his humility, imitate his gentleness, embrace his love, share his sufferings, be washed in his blood."[102] William's Christ says: "I shall show myself to man as a man despised and the least of all men, a man of sorrows and knowing infirmity, that he may be zealous to imitate my humility, through which he will come to the glory toward which he is hastening to rush."[103]

Aelred, like Bernard, urges imitation of the boy Jesus, saying: "Now this is the beginning of conversion, a spiritual birth as it were, that we should model ourselves upon the Child, take upon ourselves the marks of poverty, and, becoming like animals before you, Lord, enjoy the delights of your presence."[104]

While imitation of Jesus' life, suffering, and death is a less frequent theme among the twelfth-century Fathers, it also appears here and there. In a sermon on the Passion Bernard urges memory of Christ's suffering in order to take on his strength, his likeness, "that I may follow in his footsteps."[105] And in a sermon for Ascension Aelred says: "And so it is to these things that we have been called: that we may follow in the footsteps of him who, when he was reviled, did not revile, and who, when he suffered, did not threaten. Taking therefore Christ in his suffering as his model, let him who says he abides in Christ also walk even as he walked."[106]

But even in passages urging mortification, imitation of Christ's Passion, the Cistercians move quickly into sharing of his pain, joining him within it, participating in intimacy rather than separately taking his pain upon themselves. So Aelred tells his anchoress to "have a representation of our Savior hanging on the Cross; that will bring before your mind his Passion for you to imitate, his outspread arms will invite you to embrace him, his naked breasts will feed you with the milk of sweetness to console you."[107]

Imitation for the Cistercians rapidly becomes a matter of participating with Jesus, of being intimate with him in his life and through that intimacy sharing his suffering when called upon to do so. The biblical source for cistercian devotion to Christ is not Jesus' warning that "he who does not take his cross and follow me is not worthy of me,"[108] but his promise to the sons of Zebedee: "The cup that I drink you will drink; and with the baptism with which I am baptized, you will be baptized."[109] The passage in which the anchoress's actions of beneficence are described in language recalling the crucified Christ illustrate this blending of the ideas; there she might easily be understood either as imitating him and his works of mercy and thereby becoming like him or as ministering to him in the needy and so participating with him in his own works of mercy. Aelred gives no clue as to his intention, and at this point the distinction becomes insignificant.

A similarly ambiguous example appears when Aelred suggests that the recluse should share her bridegroom's poverty, exchange her state for participation in his:

> How can you dare to take pride in riches or noble birth when you seek to appear as the bride of him who became poor although he was rich and chose for himself a poor

mother, a poor family, a poor little house also and the squalor of a manger? Is it any matter for pride that you have preferred the Son of God to the sons of men, that you have despised the uncleanness of the flesh for the beauty of virginity, that you have exchanged things which will become mere dung for the eternal riches and delights of heaven?[110]

Imitation for the Cistercians then is more often a matter of becoming like Christ by dwelling with and in him than by walking in his footsteps. And that imitation is equivalent to Jesus' imitation of and intimate participation in man's condition—so the word *imitare* comes to mean for the Cistercians. For them even the idea of imitation of Christ is essentially eucharistic, a matter of acting, choosing, participating. As Christ is taken into the self, so he is known and loved, and so his lover becomes like him.

But the most important imitation for cistercian spirituality is an imitation of those who were intimate with Christ in his human life —his mother, most of all, his disciples, his friends. Mary is the great object of cistercian imitation, not Christ, for through her the worshipper may conceive the heavenly sweetness, embrace the infant and the crucified, and finally be crowned as bride and queen. Bernard says of her: "You are told that she is a virgin. You are told that she is humble. If you are not able to imitate the virginity of this humble maid, then imitate the humility of the virgin maid."[111] Aelred tells the recluse to have on her altar two figures, of Mary and of John, as signs of the excellence of virginity and "to increase your charity."[112]

More important than Bernard's explicit call for imitation of Mary, though, is his speaking of her as of the bride in the *Song of Songs*, so in the language used elsewhere by the Fathers for the church or the soul as the bride of Christ. Bernard says:

While the King was on his couch, the Virgin's nard was sending forth its fragrance, and a sweet-smelling smoke was rising up in the sight of his glory, and in this way she found grace in the Lord's eyes. . . . he was moved by so great a desire that he sped ahead of his messenger and came to the Virgin whom he loved, whom he had chosen for his own, whose beauty he ardently desired.[113]

Again, he urges Mary toward God:

> Only say the word and receive the Word: give yours and
> conceive God's. Breathe one fleeting word and embrace the
> everlasting Word. Why do you delay? Why be afraid? Be-
> lieve, give praise, and receive. Let humility take courage and
> shyness confidence. This is the moment for virginal simplicity
> to forget prudence. In this circumstance, alone, O prudent
> Virgin, do not fear presumptuousness, for if your reserve
> pleased by its silence, how much more must your goodness
> speak. Blessed Virgin, open your heart by faith, your lips to
> consent, and your womb to the Creator. Behold, the long-
> desired of all nations is standing at the door and knocking.
> Oh, what if he should pass by because of your delay and,
> sorrowing, you should again have to seek him whom your
> soul loves? Get up, run, open! Get up by faith, run by prayer,
> open by consent.[114]

Aelred echoes this language in his address to the recluse and says
to her that the Annunciation was "on your account, virgin, that
you might diligently contemplate the Virgin whom you have re-
solved to imitate and the Virgin's Son to whom you are betrothed,"
so acknowledging at once her role as mother and bride of Jesus.[115]
Cistercian spirituality outlasted the Fathers, influencing Latin
and vernacular literatures across Europe through the centuries to
come.[116] Its essence was its sacramentalism, its grounding in the
humanity of Christ, and its willed, active intimacy with Jesus. Its
story developed at three levels: historical, allegorical, and moral.
At the historical level the plot was that of the Gospels, from the
Annunciation to the Ascension, with Pentecost added to provide
the *sententia* and bring it to life. At the allegorical level, the plot
was that of the love between God and the Church, between Christ
and the soul, the story in fact of the *Song of Songs*. As William
summarizes it:

> Here we have the entire sequence of the plot of this holy love
> song from beginning to end, its entire matter and action. The
> scenes are already marked out and harmoniously arranged:
> hope hastens, desire becomes a crucifixion, wisdom sets all

in order, love speeds forward, and grace is there to meet it;
until finally, at the end of the *Song*, the grief of the soul's
desire is turned into the joy of fruition, the weariness of
delay being at last exchanged for mutual union.[117]

At the moral level there is no plot, no narrative: only action,
union with God in the flesh, becoming one with him through the
mutual, reciprocal action of God and man. The late twelfth-century
Baldwin of Ford's *Tractate on the Most Holy Sacrament of the Altar*
contains a passage striking in its faithfulness to the center of cistercian spirituality. Here is the importunity, the audacious love, the
active seeking out of God who hides to be found in the sacrament.
Here there is no passive receptivity, no waiting to be overcome by
love, no imitation. Rather, here the faithful approaches the Eucharist and finds Christ there; the lover enters the bed-chamber knowing that waiting there is the God who formerly assumed the flesh
of man.

The cistercian school of spirituality that began in the twelfth-
century Cistercians' rational inquiry into questions of eucharistic
theology has its fruition then in charity, in works of spiritual direction, and finally in a new generation of eucharistic theology:

> Christ was hidden from the beginning in the bosom of the
> Father; afterwards, he was hidden in the form of a servant
> which he assumed; and now he is hidden in the sacrament
> which he instituted. Faith finds him hidden in the bosom of
> the Father; no less does faith find him hidden in man; and it
> is faith which finds him hidden in the sacrament. The great
> power of faith possesses the great grace of intimacy with
> God. Wherever it finds him, it can approach him, and with
> a certain familiar and audacious intimacy, it rushes into his
> sanctuary and his bed-chamber. It gives no thought to being
> hindered by the guardians of the entrance or the door-keepers
> or the chamberlains; it enters carefree and unites itself confi-
> dently but reverently to the mysteries of God's intentions.[118]

The University of Michigan

NOTES

1. *De virginitate* 2; PG 46:323; tr. William Moore and Henry Astin Wilson, *Nicene and Post-Nicene Fathers*, 2d series, 5 (New York, 1893), 344.

2. SC 2:3; SBOp 1:9–10; CF 4:10.

3. SC 8:2,3,5; SBOp 1:37–38; CF 4:46, 48.

4. Ep frat 263; SCh 233:354; CF 12:96.

5. *S. in Epiphania de tribus generibus nuptiarum*, ed. C. H. Talbot, *Sermones inediti B. Aelredi abbatis rievallensis*, Series Scriptorum S. Ordinis Cisterciensis (Rome, 1952), p. 39.

6. Gary Macy, in *The Theologies of the Eucharist in the Early Scholastic Period* (Oxford, 1984), p. 47, says that Lanfranc included "contact with the humanity of Jesus as one of the principal results of the reception of the Eucharist." Macy adds: "The devotion to the Eucharist in the twelfth and thirteenth centuries was one expression of a whole movement toward a more personal love for the Human Christ. Despite the manifold forms that the devotion to the Eucharist manifested in the early scholastic period, however, the two consistent features of that devotion appear to be a strong belief in a real, nearly sensual, presence of Christ in the sacrament, and a growing interest in the Human Christ so present" (p. 95). See my "Eat, Drink, and Be Merry: The Eucharistic Spirituality of the Cistercian Fathers," above.

7. 1 Co 13:12.

8. Bernard, *Ep. ad Aelredum*; SBOp 8:486–89; see Lawrence C. Braceland, S.J., "Bernard and Aelred on Humility and Obedience," in this volume.

9. Inst incl 11; CCCM 1:647; CF 2:58.

10. Med 3:4; PL 180:212; CF 3:104. William's longing for the face of God dominates his spiritual works, especially the *Meditations*.

11. William, Med 6:2; PL 180:222; CF 3:126.

12. William too acknowledges that that face for which he longs will be terrible to the damned, saying: "In your face an enemy, by contrast, finds a fiery oven; a sinner finds the portion of his cup, fetters and flames, sulphur and stormy winds" (Med 8:6; PL 180:231; CF 3:143).

13. Inst incl 33; CCCM 1:678; CF 2:98–99.

14. SC 3:2; SBOp 1:15; CF 4:17.

15. Med 5:9; PL 180:221; CF 3:123.

16. Inst incl 31; CCCM 1:667; CF 2:86.

17. Jn 14:6; Bernard, Hum 1:1; SBOp 3:17; CF 13:30; William, Contemp 12; SCh 61:110; CF 3:60.

18. Med 10:7; PL 180:236–37; CF 3:154.

19. Contemp 3; SCh 61:67; CF 3:40.

20. Inst incl 31; CCCM 1:672; CF 2:92.

21. Proper collect 12, *Book of Common Prayer* (1979), p. 231.

22. Contemp 6; SCh 61:76–82; CF 3:46–47.

23. *S. in natale apostolorum Petri et Pauli*, ed. Talbot, pp. 132–33. Aelred even lauds Peter's cutting off the ear of Malchus, saying in the same sermon: "If the zeal of Peter was perfect when he brandished his sword, his charity had not yet attained the perfection of wisdom. . . . And however, it is necessary to praise the ardor of Peter, my brothers, and admire his devotion to the Lord. An immense love had seized his spirit and inspired him against the persecutors of Christ" (p. 135). It is not accidental, then, that Peter is one of those granted in life the loving gaze of Christ to be seen in glory. In his meditation on the life of Christ Aelred says of Jesus: "See with what a loving gaze, how mercifully, how effectually, he looks at Peter who has thrice denied him" (Inst incl 31; CCCM 1:669; CF 2:88).

24. SC 20:5; SBOp 1:117–18; CF 4:151.

25. *S. in natale*, p. 133. In "Christ Our Mother: Aelred's Iconography for Contemplative Union," in E. Rozanne Elder (ed.), *Goad and Nail: Studies in Medieval Cistercian History X*, CS 84 (1984), pp. 21–45, I have discussed Aelred's treatment of the progression from knowledge of the humanity to knowledge of the divinity, there conceived as milk and wine. But not only does Aelred not suggest that adults should in going forward to the wine of inebriation leave behind the milk of nourishment, but he insists on their mutual reception, saying: "Hasten, linger not . . . drink your wine with your milk. The blood is changed into wine to inebriate you, the water into milk to nourish you" (Inst incl 31; CCCM 1:671; CF 2:90–91). In Spec car 2:12, however, he associates wine with compunction for beginners and milk with consolation for proficients: "And when they have been torn from the milk, they will become guests at the banquet of the coming of his glory."

26. Nat am 44; PL 184:417; CF 30:107–108.

27. SC 20:67; SBOp 1:118; CF 4:152.

28. Med 10:4; PL 180:236; CF 3:152–53.

29. 1 Co 2:14; for example, Hum 8:23; SBOp 3:34; CF 13:52.

30. Ep frat 2:194; SCh 223:302; CF 12:77.

31. Nat am 44; PL 184:417; CF 30:107.

32. Nat am 21; PL 184:393; CF 30:77–78.

33. Cant 1:8.92; SCh 82:212; CF 6:74.

34. SC 48:5–6; SBOp 2:70; CF 31:16–17.

35. Aelred provides a precedent for the analytical approach here and below to unity, saying: "Now charity has two divisions, love of God and love of neighbor. Further, love of one's neighbor has two subdivisions. . . . There are two elements in the love of God, interior dispositions and the performance of works" (Inst incl 27, 28; CCCM 1:659, 662; CF 2:74, 79).

36. Aelred is so faithful to the events of Jesus' life as reported in the Gospels that he includes almost no events revealing the divinity of Christ. For example, although he reports Jesus' mourning the death of Lazarus, he does not mention his raising him. I have discussed this point in (Stuckey) *Two Middle English Translations of Aelred's* De institutione inclusarum (Diss University of Michigan, 1981), pp. 51–52.

37. Inst incl 31; CCCM 1:664; CF 2:81–82.

38. Inst incl 28, 31; CCCM 1:660–61, 665, 667, 672; CF 2:75, 79, 83, 91.

39. Gregory I, *Moralia in Job*, Ep 3; PL 75:513.

40. Si 24:24–25. See Dutton, "Mother," p. 25.

41. Inst incl 31; CCCM 1:667; CF 2:85. See Dutton, "Eat," p. 1.

42. Miss 4:6; SBOp 4:51; CF 18:51–52.

43. Miss 2:16; SBOp 4:27; CF 18:29.

44. Med 10:4, PL 180:235; CF 3:152.

45. Jesu 5; CCCM 1:253; CF 2:9.

46. Inst incl 31; CCCM 1:667; CF 2:85.

47. Inst incl 31; CCCM 1:671–72; CF 2:91.

48. Miss 2:12; SBOp 4:29; CF 18:24.

49. Inst incl 31; CCCM 1:672; CF 2:91–92.

50. It is no doubt a rational anxiety about eliciting an erotic response to Jesus that causes the Fathers generally to maintain a distinction between the literal and allegorical levels of devotion to the humanity. Bernard and William essentially avoid the historical Jesus as they use the inherently erotic texts, language, and imagery of the *Song of Songs*, concentrating on the allegorical in their treatises of love for Christ, while Aelred concentrates on the historical stage and the man Jesus while generally avoiding erotic language, even when speaking of Christ as bridegroom. Caroline Walker Bynum, *Jesus as Mother: Studies in the Spirituality of the High Middle Ages* (Berkeley and Los Angeles, 1982), p. 141, says that "*Brautmystik* (the use of nuptial and erotic imagery to describe the soul's union with God), the use of maternal names for God, and devotion to the Virgin did not oc-

cur together in medieval texts." While that statement is largely not true of the works of the cistercian Fathers, they allow significantly little blurring of the exegetical levels.

51. Dil 3:7; SBOp 3:124–25; CF 13:98–99.

52. Gen 2:23, 24.

53. This is a more difficult stage than the first because it depends on metaphors so intimate in their functioning in cistercian spirituality that twentieth-century readers resist them. Additionally, while in two of the three Jesus appears usually as male, in the third he appears as female; in this fact too the metaphors are less comfortable for modern audiences, but perhaps more accessible for the monks for whom he is so defined as an object of union in his flesh, as Bynum suggests: "For if the God with whom they wished to unite was spoken of in male language, it was hard to use the metaphor of sexual union unless they saw themselves as female. . . . But another solution was of course to see God as a female parent, with whom union could be quite physical (in the womb or at the breast)" (p. 161). She also points out that for the Cistercians "conceiving and giving birth, like suckling, are . . . images primarily of return to, union with, or dependence upon God, not images of Christ's sacrifice or of human alienation. . . . Thus the most frequent meaning of mother-Jesus to twelfth-century Cistercians is compassion, nurturing, and union" (pp. 150–51). While Bynum's attention to the maternal passages is broad and thorough, her primary concern is historical. My paper, "Christ Our Mother," *Goad and Nail*, pp. 21–45, deals extensively with the contemplative significance of such passages in Inst incl.

54. Jesu 4; CCCM 1:259; CF 2:8.

55. Med 8:4; PL 180:230; CF 3:141.

56. SC 41:5–6; SBOp 2:32; CF 7:208.

57. Cant 1:38; SCh 82:122; CF 6:130.

58. Inst incl 31; CCCM 1:668; CF 2:87.

59. Inst incl 27, 25; CCCM 1:659, 657; CF 2:74, 72.

60. Inst incl 15; CCCM 1:650; CF 2:63.

61. *S. in Ypapanti Domini*, ed. Talbot, p. 51.

62. The two predominant eucharistic theologies of the Middle Ages, the Paschasian and what Macy calls the mystical, come together here for the Cistercians in this understanding. As Macy explains the Paschasian: "The image used here is biological. Just as the food we eat becomes part of ourselves, so we, in a sort of divine reversal, become part of Christ when we receive the Eucharist. Paschasius has made this perfectly clear, 'we become part of Christ because we eat him'" (p. 70). And of the mystical, which he identifies as peculiarly Victorine and characteristic also of William, he says: "This more mystical approach to the Eucharist insisted that salvation came through a spiritual, mystical union with Christ rather than through a natural or substantial union, as the advocates of a Paschasian theology held. . . . [It] stressed the individual relationship of each believer to the risen Christ present in and through the sacrament" (pp. 103, 104).

63. Inst incl 22; CCCM 1:655; CF 2:70.

64. Inst incl 33; CCCM 1:678–79; CF 2:99–100. Aelred's shift from second to first person in this passage is characteristic of this work, as I have discussed in (Stuckey) "Translations," pp. 83–84.

65. Inst incl 32; CCCM 1:674; CF 2:94–95.

66. For William in fact the levels are sacramentally identical; meditation on the humanity of Christ is equivalent to reception of the Eucharist. See Ep frat 30: 115–17; SCh 223:237; CF 12:50–51, and Dutton, "Eat," above.

67. Si 24:29; see Jn 4:13–14; see Dutton, "Mother," p. 25 and n. 15.

68. Dil 28; SBOp 3:143; CF 13:119. The mixing of the water and wine in the chalice is often understood to represent the blending of the human and the divine in the Incarnate Christ and always to reiterate the water and blood that poured from Jesus' side.

69. Cant 10:115–16; CF 6:92–93. This passage also echoes that of the two

eyes for the sight of God, again emphasizing the distinction between reason and love, understanding and wisdom, and anticipating the banquet and the embrace.

70. Inst incl 26; CCCM 1:659; CF 2:74. In the celebration of the Eucharist according to the Roman Rite, after the consecration of the elements the priest made the sign of the cross with the Host three times over the chalice and twice between the chalice and himself, then raised the Host and chalice, saying meanwhile: "Per ipsum, et cum ipso, et in ipso, est tibi Deo Patri omnipotenti, in unitate Spiritus Sancti, omnis honor et gloria." Replacing the Host and chalice upon the altar, he said: "Per omnia saecula saeculorum" (*The Missal in Latin and English* [Westminster, 1959] p. 683). Aelred's words here are not identical—he says "in uno, apud unum, cum uno . . . in illud unum quod semper idem est"—but inescapably recall the language of the Mass.

71. Inst incl 28; CCCM 1:663; CF 2:79.
72. Inst incl 31; CCCM 1:671; CF 2:91.
73. Cant 7:76; SCh 82:188; CF 6:64.
74. Inst incl 32; CCCM 1:673; CF 2:92.
75. Med 3:7–8; PL 180:213; CF 3:105–106.
76. SC 9;7–8; SBOp 1:46–47; CF 4:58–59.
77. Mt 25:31–46.
78. *The Exordium Parvum*, trans. Bede K. Lackner, in Louis J. Lekai, *The Cistercians: Ideals and Reality* (Kent, Ohio, 1977), p. 459.
79. Inst incl 28; CCCM 1:661–62; CF 2:74, 77.
80. Gen Angl; PL 195:736.
81. Inst incl 31; CCCM 1:666; CF 2:83.
82. Inst incl 31; CCCM 1:668; CF 2:86.
83. *S. in assumptione b. Mariae*, PL 195:306; trans. Anthony Storey, "The Castle of the Soul," in *The Tablet*, 198 (1951) 93.
84. Aelred, *S. in natale*, p. 133.
85. CF 30:7.
86. SC 8:5; SBOp 1:38; CF 4:48.
87. Nat am 4; PL 184:390; CF 30:56.
88. Bell, *The Image and Likeness: The Augustinian Spirituality of William of St. Thierry*, CS 78 (Kalamazoo, 1984), p. 154.
89. Spec car 3:20; PL 195:594.
90. William, Ep frat 251; SCh 233:344; CF 12:93.
91. SC 2:2; SBOp 1:9; CF 4:9.
92. SC 9:2; SBOp 1:43; CF 4:54.
93. Contemp 12; SCh 61:116; CF 3:62.
94. Orat; SCh 61:126; CF 3:73.
95. Contemp 2–3; SCh 61:58–64; CF 3:36–38.
96. Inst incl 31; CCCM 1:666; CF 2:83–84.
97. Jesu 21; CCCM 1:265; CF 2:29.
98. Jesu 22; CCCM 1:266; CF 2:30.
99. The Fathers frequently write of repose as a mark of beatitude, a reward from the journey. But it is very often a result of the Spirit's working rather than the necessary condition for it. While Aelred three times speaks of the importance of silence, "imposing silence that her spirit may speak," "listening to Christ and speaking with him" (Inst incl 5; CCCM 1:641; CF 2:50–51), silence no more assures the coming of the Spirit than does active pursuit. God's coming is not to be compelled, his freedom to stay away or to come may not be restricted by active seeking or by passive receptivity. For further discussion of this theme, see Jean Leclercq, *Otia Monastica: Etudes sur le vocabulaire de la contemplation au Moyen Age*, Studia Anselmiana 51–52 (Rome, 1963).
100. Inst incl 31; CCCM 1:673; CF 2:86, 92.
101. Jaroslav Pelikan, *The Growth of Medieval Theology (600–1300)*, The Christian Tradition, 3 (Chicago and London, 1978), p. 126.

102. Miss 3:14; SBOp 4:45; CF 18:44.

103. Nat am 3:34; PL 184:389; CF 30:96.

104. Jesu 4; CCCM 1:252; CF 2:1.

105. *S. de Passione Domini*, SBOp 5:64.

106. *S. in Ascensione Domini de raptu Helye*, ed. Talbot, p. 103; trans. Chrysogonus Waddell, o.c.s.o., "On the Rapture of Elijah."

107. Inst incl 26; CCCM 1:659; CF 2:73.

108. Mk 10:39.

109. Mt 10:38.

110. Inst incl 24; CCCM 1:656–57; CF 2:71.

111. Miss 1:5; SBOp 4:15; CF 18:9.

112. Inst incl 26; CCCM 1:659; CF 2:73–74.

113. Miss 3:2; SBOp 4:43; CF 18:34–35; see Aelred, Inst incl 14; CCCM 1:650; CF 2:63.

114. Miss 4:8; SBOp 4:54; CF 18:54; see Aelred, Inst incl 31; CCCM 1:668; CF 2:86–87: "Let love overcome shyness, affection drive out fear." The cistercian emphasis on imitation of Mary in her intimacy with Jesus as mother and bride may explain some of the burst of Marian devotion in the twelfth century and beyond, not initially to her, but with her.

115. Inst incl 29; CCCM 1:663; CF 2:81.

116. Martin Thornton, *English Spirituality* (London, 1963), pp. 46, 48, says of this influence in England: "The Benedictine line follows into the Cistercian reform, of which the influence on England is apparent to anyone who has looked at our monastic history. This is the affective side, but English spirituality follows the Cistercianism of the more thoughtful William of St Thierry and the less austere Aelred of Rievaulx, rather than that of St Bernard. In the story of English religion, William of St Thierry plays the part of a kind of Jack-in-the-box: always popping up in unexpected places. . . . In the middle ages [England] could almost have been called the land of the Cistercians. . . . Devotion flowing from the Incarnation, necessarily coupled with the Blessed Virgin, is also Cistercian." Thornton also speaks of Bonaventure as the primary ascetic Franciscan influence on England; as Bonaventure himself was significantly influenced by Aelred, the importance of cistercian spirituality in England is then greater even than Thornton realizes. See Dutton "The Cistercian Source: Aelred, Bonaventure, and Ignatius," *Goad and Nail*, pp. 151–78.

117. Cant 146; SCh 82:310; CF 6:117.

118. PL 204:403–404.

THE SIN OF CURIOSITY
AND THE CISTERCIANS

Richard Newhauser

T HAT THE VICES, when they are not storming the castle of virtue, occasionally engage in internecine warfare, quarrels,
and debates will hardly surprise the general reader of medieval personification allegory. Works in this genre literally overflow with
the animosity of sinfulness, whether directed against the virtues or
against itself. The chief actors in this conflict are nearly always the
same: Deadly Sins, Cardinal Vices, Theological and Cardinal Virtues. Their order of appearance varies frequently; it is more unusual to find a subordinate figure advancing to take on a major role,
for this amounts, in effect, to a thorough revaluation of the psychology of evil. It is just such an act of rethinking which provides
us with the best introduction to the sin of curiosity at one of the
peaks of its medieval career. To see Dame *Curiositas* for the first
time debating on equal ground with more familiar vices is to witness
a dramatic rise in the importance of the temptation she had come to
depict. For this purpose, we must turn to Galand of Reigny's *Parabolarium*, a collection of fifty-two short fictional tales, fables, and
parables completed about a decade after the publication of Bernard
of Clairvaux's *De gradibus superbiae et humilitatis* and dedicated by
its author, a relative newcomer to the Order of Cîteaux, to Bernard himself.[1]

The importance of sinful curiosity in the Cistercian analysis of
morality can be clearly observed in Galand's parable entitled *De
colloquio vitiorum*. This colloquy presents ten sins as female figures
who, in a series of monologues, characterize themselves chiefly in
terms of their evil powers over mankind. Pride is the last to appear
and is the one to whom all the others do obeisance, recognizing

71

her as their queen. Immediately before *Superbia*, *Curiositas* holds
the stage. Her section of the parable is interesting enough to be
quoted at length:

> *Tristitia* had barely finished her speech and, behold,
> *Curiositas* was present, unforeseen. She vehemently
> and rudely asked why the vices were assembled there and
> what they were discussing among themselves. But opposed
> to this, one of the vices speaking for all of them said, "No, it
> is rather your place to speak. Since your business is
> something hidden from many, reveal the law of your
> authority in a few words!" And *Curiositas* said, "My law is
> to be idle in listening to rumors and to examine and learn
> about whatever goes on and wherever it goes on, whether
> great or small, not pertaining to me whatsoever nor having
> any use for me. I always employ all my mind to know hid-
> den and doubtful things, not only that which is on the
> earth, but also what is in the sky and sea and every abyss.
> To this study all the senses of my body have been given, the
> result being that my eyes desire to distinguish the varieties
> of colors, my ears those of sounds, my palate those of tastes,
> my hands to distinguish the smooth from the rough, and my
> nose the bad smelling from things which smell sweetly.
> Finally, it is gratifying to delve into the hidden matters of
> the human body which are horrible to sight or which it is
> not lawful for us to investigate. While I occupy the minds of
> men with such trifles I divert them from the investigation of
> what is true and useful so that, while they seek superfluities,
> they forsake necessities and expend the time given them for
> acquiring eternal life on things which are not useful for that
> task. And why do I make them investigate others' sins while
> they neglect their own? Because the more they censure
> those sins, the more they forget their own. They consider
> themselves to be saints in comparison with this or that other
> person because they do not commit the same misdeeds that
> he does—notwithstanding the fact that they commit others
> which are even worse."[2]

In Galand's image of the sin the major tendencies of previous monastic comment on *vitium curiositatis* fall together in concentrated

fashion and, as a unified phenomenon, acquire a prominence they had rarely had before the work of the Cistercians. That it is here that one finds the only *complete* depiction of *curiositas* as a personified vice produced in the literature of the Middle Ages is yet another indication of how important the concept was for Cistercian psychology.

The origins of the sin in its monastic context are much humbler than this. Its first appearance here, in the work of John Cassian, is simply as one of the many practical consequences of *accidia*. As a type of sloth, it was for Cassian an expression of the monk's *incuria* regarding his own spiritual perfection because of his *nimia cura* for hearing about the affairs of the world and especially for poking into and slandering others' imperfections. Such idle preoccupations were a further threat to the community because they kept the monk from performing his share of manual labor. Cassian's *curiositas*, and in particular its relationship to verbosity and the detraction of one's brothers, is thus more a function of mere idleness than a type of dangerous speculation.[3] The complex of behavior which the term described had already been identified as sinful in the ascetic communities of North Africa, but it was Cassian's innovation to systematize all of this under the designation of *curiositas* as a progeny of sloth and to link it to the order of cenobitic life.

The relatively restricted sense of evil curiosity seen here becomes all the more obvious when it is compared to the breadth of meaning the sin had in the works of the other major source of *curiositas*-lore from late antiquity, namely Augustine of Hippo. Augustine's ideas on *curiositas* and the central position it held in his thinking on immorality have been studied intensively in the past few years by Courcelle, Blumenberg, Oberman, Zacher, and most recently Peters.[4] Starting from a foundation laid by earlier patristic and classical sources, Augustine elevated sinful *curiositas* to a level of importance alongside pride and lust of the flesh.[5] Its position in this triad is, I think, also the key to its meaning for him. That is to say, it participated in some ways in the nature of *superbia* and in other ways in that of *voluptas carnis*. It was a danger in that it led the Christian to undervalue the teachings of the faith and substitute for them mere constructions of human thought. As a superfluous exercise, it drove human beings to collect experiences and sensations by indulging in their senses merely for the purpose of perceiving or knowing about the variety of earthly phenomena.[6] In both ways the sin remained for Augustine a basic problem of *Erkenntnis*, the act of knowing, whether conceptual or perceptual.

The disparity between these two views of the sin was clear enough to early medieval writers.[7] Yet, there was also a recognition of what they had in common. Such an acknowledgement is seen most particularly in Gregory the Great's *Moralia in Iob*. Gregory identified *vitium curiositatis* not only as the vain investigation of one's brother's life, but also as an overweening attempt to penetrate into the divine mysteries not already revealed, an undertaking which in any case went beyond human capacities.[8] But his use of the Cassianic sense of the vice with certain aspects of Augustine's analysis also reoriented evil *curiositas* to a position not on a par with pride and lust of the flesh nor as a progeny of sloth, but rather subordinate to pride. The focus of Gregory's examination was the humility of self-knowledge called for from monks; the "zeal of proud curiosity" as he termed it was a rejection of the most important virtue leading to a recognition of one's own need for correction.[9]

With these three conceptions of the vice in mind, we are in a better position to correctly place Galand's personification. There were various ways in which these variables were fit together: Bede emphasized certain aspects of Augustine's analysis; Smaragdus supported his view of *vitium curiositatis* by drawing mainly on Gregory; elsewhere Cassian's views were placed in the foreground.[10] However, with the reforming tendencies of late eleventh- and early twelfth-century monasticism one can also note a renewed emphasis on sinful curiosity's place in moral theology and on taking account of the full spectrum of ideas which have been identified in its background. This inclusiveness is seen earliest in the anonymous *Liber de humanis moribus* which represents the thinking of Anselm of Canterbury and was published shortly after his death. *Curiositas* is presented here as part of the Augustinian triad of sins, but a clear distinction is made between its perceptual and conceptual appearances, and among the forty-four types of evil curiosity delineated in the treatise one can find an idle interest in rumors as well as the impossible attempt to look into the future by sacrificing to demons or, rather more mundane, sniffing at spices in the marketplace to experience the odor of each one.[11] But at any rate not until the work of the Cistercians was the inclusive monastic view of the sin to be given its final statement.

For the early Cistercians, following the formative influence of Bernard of Clairvaux, saw in evil *curiositas* a fundamental danger to monastic life, one which could only be expressed in the most inclusive terms. In the system of sins which Bernard presented in *De gradibus humilitatis et superbiae* (before 1124/1125), sinful curiosity was the first and most dangerous step towards pride, and the one which received most of his attention.[12] That he aligned *curiositas* with *superbia* is a reflection of Augustinian and Gregorian thought, of course, but even more, these twelve steps of pride were arranged by Bernard specifically as opposites to the degrees of humility in Benedict's *Rule*.[13] In this way, *curiositas* was contrasted with Benedict's final degree of *humilitas* in which the monk was admonished to be humble in his outward behavior as well as in his heart so that he would feel and show the guilt of his own sins at all moments. Benedict recommended here that the monk, no matter what he is doing, whether sitting, walking, or standing, always have his head bowed and his eyes to the ground.[14] Bernard described the monk afflicted with *curiositas* as one who, in the same three physical postures used by Benedict, had roaming eyes, head erect, ears strained to hear whatever he could.[15]

But Bernard adopted this Benedictine degree of humility in a way which shows that the key to his thought on the sin, and its position at the head of the steps of pride, was the spiritual value of introspection. When the soul grew tired of inspecting itself, he noted, then its *incuria* for itself made it *curiosa* about others.[16] The monk's care and desire to know should be turned inward in the first instance, for it was here that the initial step towards truth was taken: the attempt to know oneself in humility.[17] The *curiosus*, on the other hand, was in retreat from himself, and the end of his flight was a thorough separation from God. The monk could legitimately concern himself with the affairs of his brothers only when this was called for by reason of mercy.[18]

The arguments Bernard received from previous writers on sinful *curiositas* were also used here to the advantage of his central concern with spiritual introspection. In Lucifer's sin against God, Bernard saw an attempt to gain more knowledge and power than the devil could master. The origins of his attempted disruption of order in heaven were traced back to his lack of knowledge about himself. Speaking directly to Satan, Bernard warned him, and through him the reader: "Keep in yourself, lest you fall from yourself if you go wandering about in the great and miraculous things above you."[19] Again, in Eve's sin Bernard identified a superfluous *curiositas* which sought a knowledge of evil as well as good. Such a knowledge did not make her wiser at all, but rather more foolish. And he further noted that if Eve's mind had not shown such a lack of care for itself, her sinful *curiositas* would not have had the leisure to investigate evil.[20]

The major portion of Bernard's section on *curiositas* in *De gradibus humilitatis et superbiae* is taken up with three figures who embody the sin in different ways. Satan's *curiositas* is proud and usurping, Eve's greedy and foolish, and in Dinah one has evidence of an idle and negligent appearance of the sin. All three of these figures are to some degree character types; together they help define the limits of *vitium curiositatis* for Bernard and show his attempt to gather and harmonize previous treatments of the sin. In Satan, Bernard found the most dangerous sort of *curiositas*, one that attempted to usurp for itself more than it could control and became the source of all sins. Even though the devil was "full of wisdom and perfect in adornment," he still sought what was too great and too high for him.[21] But the Seraphim gave proof of the order in the universe when they set the limits to his excessive curiosity and overthrew his rebellion.[22] Lucifer's knowledge could not reach into the secrets of heaven or the mysteries of the Church, but only the hearts of the proud (that is, the hearts of all sinners). Trapped there, he remains forever isolated, neither something of this world nor part of the divine. Bernard stressed the Augustinian *concupiscentia oculorum* in his examination of the method of Satan's delectation and desire. The devil "fell from truth through *curiositas* because he first looked curiously at what he desired to have illicitly and yearned to get presumptuously."[23]

Satan played a part in Eve's sin as well. Her foolishness began in innocence but was perverted by the devil into sin. She first saw the forbidden fruit with her wandering eyes; this was, noted Bernard, not in itself a sin, but it was the occasion for one.[24] She did not eat the fruit until the devil had seduced her heart into desiring consent and her reason and fear into giving consent. Here, Bernard shows plainly the systematic movement which evil *curiositas* initiates and which ends in the death of the soul. This development may begin innocently enough in perception, but continues on to the desire for and agreement to commit sin. It is, furthermore, an insatiable process, for the devil, as Bernard said to Eve, "increases your care as he excited your *gula* [to eat the fruit], he sharpens your *curiositas* as he stirs up your greed [to have knowledge of evil]."[25]

In both of these figures, Bernard found sinful curiosity reprehensible for the effects it had on others as well as on the sinner. Satan's crime led to all the other sins of mankind, and Eve's to original sin. This point is made most clearly, however, in the figure of Dinah. Verbally, at least, Bernard reflected here the earlier monastic tradition, for he found in Dinah a *curiosa otiositas vel otiosa curiositas* that brought destruction on itself and others around it, friend and foe alike.[26] Furthermore, while Dinah went out to see the women of Shechem through her idle curiosity, she was looked at with an even greater degree of useless curiosity. The misery of her sin was both her own and those who were urged by her behavior into the same sin.

Bernard's interpretation of Dinah was something new in the history of the sin, for it asserted the evil both of making a spectacle of oneself, and thus arousing the excessive curiosity of others, and of one's own engagement in a sinful *curiositas* which drove the mind away from itself and beyond its legitimate boundaries and interests. The earliest writer I know of to use this figure from the Bible in an argument against evil *curiositas* was Jonas, bishop of Orléans, in his *De institutione laicali.*[27] Jonas' work was not written for the monastery, but it reflects monastic concerns nonetheless. In supporting his use of Dinah, at any rate, Jonas referred specifically to her appearance in Gregory the Great's *Cura pastoralis.*[28] Here, Gregory employed the biblical episode allegorically to warn against being overly confident in the work of mercy. Just as Shechem comforted Dinah after raping her, so does the devil give the sinner a false hope of forgiveness after seducing him into sin.

Gregory's words served as the background for Jonas' interpretation, but it was really the latter who drew Dinah into the theme of *curiositas*. For Jonas, she was an image of the mind which had neglected its own interests and had become thoroughly absorbed by the actions of others. Haymo of Auxerre, again reflecting the monastic analysis of sinful *curiositas*, repeated the same idea.[29] When Dinah went out from her father's home, she "receded from herself," and when her virginity was violated, Haymo told the reader, this showed the *curiosus* falling into the very vices for which he had reproached others more harshly than was fitting. Bernard was the first to see her *curiositas* as both a sin and the cause of a sin.[30] He drew attention in this way not only to the *curiosi* themselves, but to the harm they did others. This particular idea was to have further implications for later analyses of the sin.

It would be difficult to overestimate the importance of Bernard's treatise on pride and humility in the history of *vitium curiositatis*. Not only did it directly influence a number of Cistercian works, but it found a place in nearly every type of religious treatise produced in the centuries following its publication, from the vast *summae* of theology down to the more limited works of pastoral interest.[31] Merely as a schematization of immoral behavior it provided one of the most satisfying methods of placing *curiositas* in a context of vices well into the modern age.[32] Part of the advantage it had was that, insofar as it was an examination of pride, it could be fit into the scheme of the Seven Deadly Sins as an expanded analysis of that list's leading member.[33]

Bernard's work on sinful *curiositas*, in *De gradibus* and elsewhere, was more than a summation of previous monastic thought and its inheritance of Augustinian ideas. This line of examination was actually intensified by Bernard. He argued, in effect, that the sin could lead to the destruction of rationality itself. The abduction by evil curiosity, he noted in *De diligendo Deo*, was one of the ways in which "a creature distinguished with the gift of reason, by not knowing itself, begins to mingle with the herd of irrational beasts. . . ."[34] This gift, provided it was exercised in the correct modes of knowing which he enumerated in his thirty-sixth sermon on the *Song of Songs*, could eventually bring mankind to *scientia veritatis*. Through *turpis curiositas*, however, it was perverted and mankind was brought "to desire to know merely for the sake of knowing."[35] The rational faculty was to be used, in the first and foremost instance at least, both to know oneself and to know that what one is does not come from one's own power. Only with this

self-knowledge could the humility be achieved which was called
for in Benedict's *Rule* and was reiterated by Bernard in *De gradibus*. This was the moral stance necessary for a monk's eventual
perfection and knowledge of truth. Without this *virtus, qua homo
verissima sui cognitione sibi ipse vilescit* the way towards pride was
opened up with unconscionable ease.[36]

Furthermore, in Bernard's analysis one can follow the systematic
development of sinful curiosity. The first step in the direction of
the vice was already taken when the monk turned his attention in
the initial stage of seeking truth from himself to something external
to him. This movement beyond the sphere of one's real concerns
was accomplished through the senses, particularly the eyes. It was
through the "windows" of all the senses that death entered the
soul, and when the monk diverted his attention from internal affairs to them he could become enmeshed in the *curiositas* of perception.[37] Even when this perceptive experience was not equated with
the sin, as in the case of Eve, it provided the occasion for sin. But it
is in any case important that all three figures in *De gradibus* were
represented as proceeding in their sin by looking at what did not
pertain to them.

Finally, when the monk was care-less of himself, and his senses
were engaged in the aimless perception of external matters, his
mind was led to seek, idly, foolishly, or proudly, a knowledge of
these matters. From perception he moved to an internal disorder
of self-disinterestedness which led to a separation from God. Bernard did not schematically distinguish the *curiositas* of perception
from that of conception; rather, the immediacy of the danger posed
by sinful curiosity, as he examined it, can be observed in its inexor-
able movement from one stage to the next.

One must hasten to add, however, that a misdirected desire for
knowledge was only the final stage of evil curiosity. In practice,
Bernard did not always make the distinction he had drawn when
examining Eve's sin, and he often associated the vice with any sen-
sory perception which distracted a monk from the tasks stipulated
in the Benedictine *Rule*. In its broadest terms, whatever perceptive
experience led to the monk's *incuria* for his monastic duties could
be conceived of as an appearance of *turpis curiositas*.[38]

This in itself was an extension of the monastic reception of Augustine's *concupiscentia oculorum* and was understood as such by the

Cistercians themselves. More immediately, Bernard's thinking on this point reflects the general desire for austerity and a return to the spiritual values of the earliest period of monastic development which showed itself in late eleventh- and early twelfth-century monasticism.[39] But by extending the concept from a testing of the senses and an interest in the grotesque to what was only unusual, elaborate, or even pleasant to perceive, Bernard added a new note of urgency to this type of *curiositas* and laid the groundwork for the later medieval, "popular" understanding of the sin.

Central to Bernard's concern here was the primacy of the Benedictine *Rule* and a spiritual life which conformed closely to the ideals of the earliest monastic communities.[40] If the monk's task was to make himself perfect for God through work, prayer, and reading, then whatever distracted him from achieving this goal was not a legitimate part of a basic monastic life and had no place in the monastery. It was this line of thinking which had brought Bernard to the Cistercian Order to begin with. However, elsewhere he saw a monasticism which he considered steeped in worldliness and wealth, an older Order where luxury, complacency and laxity had obscured an adherence to the ideals set out by Benedict. The activities of such monks were not aimed at a strict fulfillment of their monastic duties; rather, they were superfluous to this purpose. It is this very notion of superfluity which provides a key both to Bernard's view of them as sinful *curiositas* and to the reception of his ideas by later non-monastic writers.[41]

The excesses of some of the Black Monks had, in the view of many of their contemporaries, reached major proportions by the early twelfth century. It is as a response to these excesses, particularly as they were embodied in the tradition of Cluny, that one must see Bernard's charges of *curiositas*.[42] Bernard reproached the habits of the monks there and charged that the grand prior encouraged laxity: "idleness he names contemplation; gluttony, loquaciousness, *curiositas*, finally all intemperance he calls discretion."[43] Towards the end of his life, it seems, Bernard was willing to admit that there had been some change for the better in that Order, and in fact under the abbacy of another reforming monk who had once been his adversary, Peter the Venerable. After Peter had been made abbot, Bernard noted, Cluny improved "in the observance of fasts, of silence, and *indumentorum pretiosorum et curiosorum.*"[44]

In the *Apologia*, begun in 1124 or 1125 at the request of William of St Thierry, one can see the major statement of Bernard's thinking on this type of sinful *curiositas*.[45] Here, after urging his fellow Cistercians to be more moderate themselves, he turned to excesses which had become commonplace at Cluny and criticized the Black Monks for their *vanitates ac superfluitates*.[46] Their intemperance he found particularly noxious in matters of food, drink, clothing, the travelling retinues of their abbots, and the ornamentation of their churches. It was only the last of these which Bernard connected specifically with the sin of curiosity, but later a superfluity in all such areas was to be included in the common argument against the vice. For Bernard, at any rate, evidence of evil *curiositas* was observable not only in the grotesque images, the *curiosae depictiones* found painted on the cloister walls and which distracted the monks from their prayers, but also in the more "pleasant" displays of wealth in the churches.[47] Wheels gleaming with lamps and gems, enormous tree-like candleholders shining with precious stones— such things were a delight for the *curiosi* but not sustenance for humble monks.[48] For Bernard, the ideals of the monastic life demanded a relinquishing of *omnia pulchre lucentia, canore mulcentia, suave olentia, dulce sapientia, tactu placentia....*[49]

The response of the Cluniacs to the charges made by Bernard and others, and the controversy which ensued, are well known. Peter the Venerable came to see that there was more than a grain of truth to them, and his reforming decrees, which seem at least partially to have been a direct response to Bernard's criticism, are collected together in the *Statuta congregationis Cluniacensis*. It is interesting to note, however, that evil *curiositas* does not appear in the *Statuta* in connection with church ornaments, perhaps because Peter himself had been so closely associated with rebuilding the church at Cluny.[50] But he did mention the sin in two other areas of superfluity included in Bernard's reproaches. The gaily-colored material monks dressed themselves in, he noted, and their penchant for wearing catskins made them seem more secular than religious, and Peter identified the cause of this evil as a *damnata curiositas*. Likewise, the huge retinues some priors travelled with had to be reduced lest the priors be censured for their arrogance and their evil *curiositas*.[51]

Bernard's work gives evidence of an attempt to include all the major tendencies of previous thought on the sin in a discussion which is, nevertheless, more than merely a sum of its parts. His central concern remained at all times the spiritual values of the monastic life. As was seen in the examination of *De gradibus*, the Cassianic view of *curiositas* as a function of idleness took its place in Bernard's analysis next to the broader interests of the Gregorian line of thought and the ideas of Augustine. But all these were subordinated to the way in which the sin obstructed the monk's attempt to achieve spiritual perfection. He saw the culmination of this hindrance as a thorough disorder of the inner life and a misdirected orientation of the self, and so most of his attention was focused on the internal aspects of the sin. In this way, he identified an evil curiosity about others as an interior disturbance battling against virtuous piety in the human heart, and he marked out carefully the "psychological" development of the sin from perception to internal affectation.[52] When Bernard turned to the external aspects of the sin, his spiritual interests again remained in the foreground. In his analysis, a *curiositas* of perception led, of course, to the final stage of the sin, but it also evinced an intolerable worldliness at the very heart of monasticism which was antithetical to the spiritual goals of the monk.

This same attempt to be inclusive of previous material when examining the sin is characteristic of a number of later medieval works. Such a tendency can be observed particularly among certain Scholastic authors, but it is no less noticeable in treatises by the followers of Bernard. Not all of these later works, however, show the refinement of his thought and in the *Liber de modo bene vivendi*, a treatise which passed in the Middle Ages under the name of Bernard, one can see a comprehensiveness which was achieved merely by accretion.[53] In particular, the influence of Defensor's *Liber scintillarum* stands out here.[54] Completed near the end of the seventh century and transmitted frequently thereafter, this *florilegium* provided the authorities and phrasing for pseudo-Bernard's work on *curiositas*. Most of the material the *Liber scintillarum* assembled on this topic in accessible form, with the notable exception of its single quotation falsely attributed in Defensor's text to Augustine, was taken over directly in the later work. The chapter here which deals with the sin is nothing more than a tissue of quotations lifted from the *florilegium* and pieced together with admonitions to follow the advice they contain addressed to the "dearest sister" for whom the work had been undertaken.[55]

The comprehensiveness of Bernard's view of the sin, and the new prominence he gave it in monastic morality and psychology, also served as the foundation for other Cistercian texts. Galand, Aelred of Rievaulx, and others all reflect Bernard's initial influence.[56] But Galand and Aelred, in particular, also show that Cistercian thinking on the sin developed beyond Bernard. Galand made use of a literary form and drew on topics which Bernard had not covered, and Aelred's systematic analysis also extended the notion of superfluity to cover more hindrances to the monk's striving for perfection.

In Galand's image of the sin the concerns of the "Cassianic" tradition are well represented: *Curiositas* seeks only to be idle, and she drives her victims into detraction and the unnecessary reproach of their fellow sinners.[57] These ideas are found here side by side with the wider interests seen in Bernard's analysis. The superfluous, hidden, and doubtful matters of nature which *Curiositas* attempts to know are both conceptual and perceptive. For her victims they are a diversion from the knowledge needed to achieve salvation, and in particular a recognition of their own state of sinfulness. The words of Galand's personification are a valuable digest of earlier thought on the sin, though the newer areas into which Bernard had moved the concept are missing here. The senses, for example, are mentioned only in the older context of testing. Galand's *Curiositas* remains, in this way, a summation of traditional material, but it also provides further evidence of the type of comprehensiveness the Cistercians aimed for.

Less than a decade after Galand had finished his *Parabolarium*, Aelred of Rievaulx included a discussion of *vitium curiositatis* in a work he undertook expressly on the orders of Bernard. In Book II of the *Speculum caritatis* (even the title was suggested by the abbot of Clairvaux), Aelred gave a thorough and comprehensive account of the sin.[58] Unlike Galand's personification, the English Cistercian's analysis made full use of the complete range of Bernardian thought on the subject. It went, in fact, one step further, for Aelred systematized the material in a way which is not unlike one of the tendencies which can be seen in Scholastic treatments of the vice, and he moved the concept of excessive curiosity into newer areas of daily temptation which might pose a threat to the monk's task of introspection.

The distinction implied in Bernard's analysis between a *curiositas* of conception and one of perception was made explicit in Aelred's chapter on the vice. After having noted that the triad of sins mentioned in 1 Jn 2:16 (and interpreted according to Augustine) was the cause of all mankind's toiling in this world, Aelred remarked here further that sinful curiosity, in its designation as *concupiscentia oculorum*, "pertains not only to the exterior but also to the interior man."[59] The external aspects, to which he turned his attention first, amounted to the same type of worldliness which Bernard had complained of in reference to the Cluniacs twenty years earlier. Aelred, too, noted that the desire of some monks for a superfluous beauty in clothes, shoes, vessels, painting, sculpture, pet animals, architectural styling, and "the gleam of metal radiating from various objects" gave evidence of the love these men had for the world.[60] Such things only fed the eyes of the *curiosi* and did nothing to contribute to their self-knowledge. Only the monk who felt the "yoke of divine love placed on his interior neck," who knew the glory of his inner life, could know how paltry these exterior glories were.[61]

Of internal *curiositas* Aelred distinguished three general types: first, a desire for dangerous or vain knowledge; second, an examination of another's life for malicious reasons or simply to know whether it was good or evil; third, the desire to know worldly affairs. To these he added a fourth variety, limited to the most virtuous men, for they were at times driven by *curiositas* to examine their own sanctity and to tempt God through an exhibition of miracles. Particularly the first three types of the sin, noted Aelred, led to an immoderate toil in the world. Because of them, the mind became intemperate and busied itself with unnecessary matter. His concept of superfluity here was somewhat wider than Bernard's; Aelred identified the sin specifically with those who gave their souls to vain philosophy and "for whom it is a habit to contemplate the *Bucolics* with the Gospel, to read Horace with the prophets, and Cicero with Paul" and who then turned to the writing of vain literature themselves.[62] Here again the great evil posed by such types of sinful curiosity was seen by Aelred primarily as a diversion from self-knowledge. When the monk concentrated on rumors and other vanities he departed from himself, and when he returned to himself at last he brought with him not a knowledge of his inner life, but only the images of those vanities.

In Aelred's work the tendency of the Cistercians towards an all-inclusive view of the sin reached its most schematic form. The structure here which binds together previous ideas on *vitium curiositatis* was already implied in the analyses of authors from Augustine to Bernard. It distinguished the action of the sin by its area of operation, either externally on the senses or internally on the mind.[63] In both cases Aelred saw the evil posed by the vice in specifically Cistercian terms. The *curiositas* of perception was not only a hindrance to the individual monk's achievement of perfection, it was a denial of the monastic austerity sought by the Cistercians. The collections of animals kept in some cloisters angered Aelred because they were mere amusements and not the means which Anthony and Macarius had recommended for monks, nor did they in the least pertain to monastic poverty.[64] Likewise, the *curiositas* of conception was evil for Aelred because it distracted the monk from that introspective self-knowledge valued so highly by the Cistercians.

The allegorical and analytical presentations of evil *curiositas* referred to so far demonstrate clearly how central the concept was to the monastic psychology of Bernard and his followers. The inclusiveness of their definition of the sin was characteristic of their Order, and this becomes all the more obvious when the Cistercian texts are compared with other contemporary treatments of the vice. At the school of St. Victor, for example, Hugh also examined *vitium curiositatis* in detail. It held an important place in his moral analysis as a subordinate sin of pride, though evil curiosity was also related to envy. In any case, he noted, the movement initiated by the sin continued step by step until all joy was extinguished in the heart.[65] At first glance, Hugh's definition of the evil seems limited to the narrower monastic line of thought. *Mala . . . et pestilens curiositas, quae secretum alienum improbe scrutari contendit. . . .*[66] Yet elsewhere he made it plain that *alienum* implied far more than Cassian had intended. For Hugh, its real position in terms of evil *curiositas* is to be found in his epistemology. God had made the worldly knowledge of pre-Christian cultures mere foolishness; true wisdom only appeared to be foolish. After Jesus, moreover, it should have been apparent that truth could only be sought in humility. But mankind rejected this cure for its ignorance and persisted in investigating the works of creation instead of admiring them. They, in fact, amount to *aliena*, the mere external phenomena which humanity mistakenly examines in its vain curiosity (... *vana curiositate aliena investigaret*).[67] But as important as Hugh of St. Victor is for the history of *vitium curiositatis*, his ideas on the sin remain within the borders of the medieval reception of Augustine. In Hugh's works, as well, the vice describes a problem of knowledge exclusively. Nor can the full range of meaning covered by evil *curiositas* be found in the works of other monastic reformers contemporary with the Cistercians. Bruno the Carthusian, for example, only used the concept in a direct reflection of Cassian's understanding of the matter. For Bruno, however, it was not simply the deeds of the world in general outside the monastic community which posed a threat to ascetic perfection, but rather he found the hallmark of the *curiosi* in their "searching for rumors through the city."[68] But though he updated its background, Bruno's interpretation of 1 Th 4:11—which Cassian had also drawn on when examining the sin—could still assert that his Carthusian brother do his own work, "lest you look into another's affairs, hating your own tasks. And in these words Paul forbids the sin of curiosity."[69]

The treatment of sinful curiosity by Bernard and his followers can be seen as the acme of monastic development on this topic. The Cistercian view of introspection was in direct contrast to the *curiosi*'s search for a disinterested knowledge; the desire to reassert the ascetic principles of Anthony and Macarius was negated by the worldly superfluities to which the *curiosi* gave their attention. From its humble origins in Cassian's analysis, the concept of evil curiosity developed ever broader implications within the monastery. The nucleus of monastic definitions remained the Cassianic idea of an idle interest in worldly affairs or rumors and a malicious nosiness about one's brethren. Others added to it, however, by taking into account Augustine's thinking on the matter as a dangerous speculation about what did not pertain to the individual, and reoriented it to bring it into line with the conception of humility as the central monastic virtue. Finally, the spiritualizing tendencies of twelfth-century monasticism pushed back the limits covered by *vitium curiositatis* even further by identifying it also with a superfluous worldliness that interfered with the spiritual concerns of the cenobitic community. From here, it came to acquire new meanings in the criticism of the schools and in popular moral theology, but nowhere did it depict so fundamental and basic a threat as it did in the work of the Cistercians.

It should, then, come as no surprise to see that the Cistercians also seem to have acquired something of a lasting reputation for being best equipped to deal with the sin. Jacques de Vitry, in any case, relates a story which may be used to illustrate this point. It deals with a certain Master Sella who was visited once in Paris by the ghost of one of his former students. The student was dressed in a cloak covered with writing, and, when Sella asked what the writing was, he was told: "These letters are the sophisms and curiosities I spent my days on." To show his former teacher what torturous heat he now had to suffer because of them, the student let a drop of sweat fall on Sella's extended hand. It pierced his flesh as if it were the sharpest arrow. Jacques brings his *exemplum* to a close by remarking pointedly that soon afterwards the teacher quit the schools of logic and entered the Order of Cistercians.[70]

Universität Tübingen

NOTES

1. Brief information on the author's life can be found in Maur Standaert, "Galland de Reigny," in DSp 6 (1967), 74–75. See also the two articles on Galand by Sr. Colette Friedlander in *Coll.* 39 (1977) and 41 (1979) and Ferruccio Gastaldelli, "Precisazioni sul *Dictionnaire des auteurs cisterciens* a proposito di Goffredo d'Auxerre e di Galland di Rigny," *Salesianum* 39 (1977), 105. See also Jean Leclercq, "Les Paraboles de Galland de Rigny," in his *Analecta monastica*, 1ᵉ série, Studia Anselmiana, 20 (Roma, 1948), esp. pp. 167–68 where it is noted that the full *Parabolarium* was completed sometime after 1134, though it was begun as early as 1123.

2. Ed. Richard Newhauser in "The Text of Galand of Reigny's 'De Colloquio Vitiorum' from his 'Parabolarium,'" *Mittellateinisches Jahrbuch* 17 (1982), 119: "Vix illa [tristitia] sermonem conpleuerat, et ecce Curiositas adest inprouisa, uehementer et inportune perquirens cur ibi conuenissent aut quid inter se tractarent. Contra una ex illis pro omnibus respondens, "Immo," ait, "tu ipsa, quia cuius officii sis multos latet, potestatis tue ius paucis edicito." At illa, "Meum," inquit, "est rumoribus audiendis uacare et quicquid ubicumque fit, magnum uel modicum, etiam nihil ad me pertinens, nichil commodi habens, perscrutari ac discere. Omne ingenium meum in occultis et dubiis cognoscendis semper exerceo, non solum eorum que sunt in terra, sed etiam que in caelo et in mari et in omnibus abyssis. Huic studio etiam omnes sensus corporis mei dediti sunt, ut oculi discernere cupiant uarietates colorum, aures sonorum, gustus saporum, manus

lenium ab asperis, nares fetentium a bene olentibus. Denique ipsa etiam humani corporis abdita et uisu horribilia, uel que nosse fas non est, penetrare iuuat. Talibus nugis dum mentes hominum occupo, a uera et utili inquisitione auerto, ut, cum superflua querunt, necessaria relinquant et tempus eterne uite adquirende datum in non profuturis expendant. Quid quod aliorum peccata propriis negglectis eos discutere facio? Que quo magis insequntur, eo plus suorum obliuiscuntur, seseque in conparatione aliorum sanctos arbitrantur, dum non faciunt forte quod illi uel illi, cum ipsi quedam alia forsitan peiora committant."

3. See *Instituta*, 10.7 (ed. M. Petschenig, CSEL 17; Wien, 1888, p. 179): "Et ut uestra negotia agatis, non curiositate uestra actus mundi uelitis inquirere ac diuersorum conuersationes explorantes operam uestram non erga correctionem uestram seu uirtutum studia, sed ad detractiones fratrum uelitis inpendere." This is a direct response to 1 Th 4:11. On the importance of manual labor for Cassian's view of sloth, see Siegfried Wenzel, *The Sin of Sloth* (Chapel Hill, 1967), pp. 21-22.

4. Pierre Courcelle, *Les confessions de Saint Augustin dans la tradition littéraire* (Paris, 1963), pp. 101-109; Hans Blumenberg, "Augustins Anteil an der Geschichte des Begriffs der theoretischen Neugierde," *Revue des Etudes Augustiniennes* 7 (1961), 35-70; idem, "Curiositas und veritas: Zur Ideengeschichte von Augustin, Confessiones X 35," *Studia Patristica* 6, Texte und Untersuchungen 81 (1962), 294-302; idem, *Der Prozess der theoretischen Neugierde*, Suhrkamp Taschenbuch Wissenschaft 24 (Frankfurt/Main, 1973), pp. 103-121; Heiko A. Oberman, *Contra vanam curiositatem*, Theologische Studien, 113 (Zürich, 1974), pp. 19-22; Christian K. Zacher, *Curiosity and Pilgrimage* (Baltimore, 1976), pp. 22-23; Edward Peters, "*Aenigma Salomonis*: Manichaean Anti-Genesis Polemic and the *Vitium curiositatis* in *Confessiones* III.6," forthcoming in *Augustiniana*. Edward Peters and I are currently at work on a longer study of *curiositas* and its implications from antiquity into the modern era.

5. Compare *De Genesi contra Manichaeos*, 1.23.40, 2.18.27, 2.26.40 (PL 34:192, 210, 217); *De vera religione*, 38.70 (ed. Klaus-Detlef Daur, CCL 32; Turnhout, 1962, p. 233).

6. Compare Augustine's treatment of the sin in *Confessiones*, 2.6.13 and 13.21.30 (ed. P. Knöll, CSEL 33; Wien, 1895, pp. 39, 368), where the conceptual aspect of evil *curiositas* is drawn on, with the appearance of the sin in *Conf.*, 10.35.55 (p. 268), where perceptual *curiositas* is accented.

7. Isidore, for example, refers to both traditions in the same work but in widely separated chapters. See Richard Newhauser, "Towards a History of Human Curiosity: A Prolegomenon to its Medieval Phase," *Deutsche Vierteljahrsschrift* 56 (1982), 562.

8. Compare *Homiliarum in Evangelia libri duo*, 2.36.4 (PL 76:1268) with *Moralia in Iob*, 26.17.27 (PL 76:363-64). Claude Dagens, "Gregoire le Grand et la culture: de la 'sapientia huius mundi' à la 'docta ignorantia,'" *Revue des Etudes Augustiniennes* 14 (1968), 17-26, provides a good introduction to Gregory's systematic consideration of the culture of Antiquity and his emphasis on avoiding *studia exteriora*.

9. Gregory refers to *superbae curiositatis studium* in *Moralia in Iob*, 26.17.27 (PL 76:363). *Superbia* stands outside the sin heptad which Gregory developed in *Moralia in Iob*, 31.45 and is considered the root of all seven. The position occupied by *superbia* is also seen in *Moralia in Iob*, 33.2.4 (PL 76:671): "omne vitium de superbia generatur" and 34.23.47 (PL 76:744). For the primacy of this sin, Gregory had a number of authorities to which he could have referred. The most important of these was Si 10:15 ("initium peccati omnis superbia"), a text referred to frequently by Augustine (as in *De civitate Dei*, 12.6; CCL 48, p. 359) and alluded to in Cassian's "Itaque exemplis ac testimoniis scripturarum manifestissime conprobatur superbiae labem . . . omniumque peccatorum et criminum esse principium" (*Inst.*, 12.6; CSEL 17, p. 209). For the position of *superbia* in

Gregory's work, see also Leonhard Weber, *Hauptfragen der Moraltheologie Gregors des Grossen*, Paradosis, 1 (Freiburg/Schweiz, 1947), pp. 241ff.

10. See for example Bede, *In Lucae Evangelium expositio*, 1.4.13 (ed. D. Hurst, CCCL 120; Turnhout, 1960, p. 98); *idem*, *In primam epistolam B. Ioannis*, 2 (PL 93:92–93); Smaragdus, *Diadema monachorum*, 73 (PL 102:668–69)—where Smaragdus' words, "inquietudo ergo, quae et alio nomine curiositas apellatur, grande est vitium . . ." are an echo of Gregory's "grave namque curiositatis est vitium" (*Homil. in Evan.*, 2.36.4; PL 76:1268); for the emphasis on Cassian, see the discussion of Bruno the Carthusian below.

11. *Liber de humanis moribus*, 26–36 (edd. R. W. Southern and F. S. Schmitt in *Memorials of St. Anselm*, Auctores Britannici Medii Aevi 1; London, 1969, pp. 47–50). The Augustinian triad is referred to explicitly in sect. 10 (p. 41).

12. SBOp 3:1–59. For the date, see pp. 3–4. In this edition, Bernard's discussion of *curiositas* fills eight pages of print; all the other steps of pride together take up thirteen pages. On the relative importance of this first step of pride for Bernard see Etienne Gilson, *La théologie mystique de Saint Bernard*, Études de philosophie médiévale, 20 (Paris, 1934), p. 181; and Basil Pennington, "Saint Bernard's Steps of Humility and Pride, An Introduction," *Studia Monastica* 22 (1980), 43–61, here esp. p. 53.

13. This point was recognized very early in the history of the work. In a number of the oldest manuscripts a series of *capitula* has been added to the text. The twelve "Superbiae gradus in descendendo" are taken from Bernard's work; their corresponding "Duodecim gradus humilitatis" were extrapolated from *Regula Benedicti*, 7.10–66 (ed. R. Hanslik, CSEL 75; Wien, 1960, pp. 41–51). On the *capitula* see SBOp 3:9–10. See Denis Farkasfalvy, "St. Bernard's Spirituality and the Benedictine Rule in *The Steps of Humility*," ASOC 36 (1980) 248–62.

14. "Monachus . . . ubicumque sedens, ambulans uel stans inclinato sit semper capite defixis in terram aspectibus. . . ." *Regula Benedicti*, 7.63 (CSEL 75, p. 51).

15. "Si videris monachum, de quo prius bene confidebas, ubicumque stat, ambulat, sedet, oculis incipientem vagari, caput erectum, aures portare suspensas, e motibus exterioris hominis interiorem immutatum agnoscas," Hum 10.28; SBOp 3:38.

16. The absolute value of self-knowledge for St Bernard as the foundation for all other types of knowledge is seen quite clearly in CSi 2.3.6; SBOp 3:414: "Et si sapiens sis, deest tibi ad sapientiam, si tibi non fueris. Quantum vero? Ut quidem senserim ego, totum. Noveris licet omnia mysteria, noveris lata terrae, alta caeli, profunda maris, si te nescieris, eris similis aedificanti sine fundamento, ruinam, non structuram faciens." For Bernard's words on the *incuria* of the self, see Hum 10.28; SBOp 3:38: ". . . dum a sui circumspectione torpescit [animam] incuria sui, curiosam in alios facit." Bernard's use of the Delphic command is discussed by Pierre Courcelle, *Connais-toi toi-même de Socrate à Saint Bernard*, vol. 1 (Paris, 1974), pp. 258–72.

17. For Bernard two things belonged to *scientia veritatis*: first of all, the knowledge of one's self; then, the knowledge of God. As he wrote in SC 37, 1.1; SBOp 2:9 "Noveris proinde te, ut Deum timeas; noveris ipsum, ut aeque ipsum diligas. In altero initiaris ad sapientiam, in altero et consummaris. . . ." See Heinrich G. J. Storm, *Die Begründung der Erkenntnis nach Bernhard von Clairvaux*, Europäische Hochschulschriften 20, 33 (Frankfurt/Main, 1977), p. 88.

18. The avoidance of sinful curiosity did not, of course, run counter to the concept of *caritas*. Bernard noted in Hum 10.29 (SBOp 3:39) that the monk could raise his eyes towards his brother "fratris necessitate," an action which mercy commended. On what was seen in the monastery as the necessity of achieving one's own salvation (and avoiding evil *curiositas*) see Etienne Gilson, *La théologie mystique*, p. 181

19. Hum 10.31; SBOp 3:40: "Sta in te, ne cadas a te, si ambulas in magnis et in mirabilibus super te."

20. Hum 10.30; SBOp 3:39: "Nisi enim mens minus se curiose servaret, tua curiositas tempus vacuum non haberet." The word-play involved in the use of *curiose* and *curiositas* is typical of Bernard's style. It is also another indication of the term's ambiguity that the stage was set for Eve's sinful curiosity when she was not curious enough about herself.

21. Hum 10.31; SBOp 3:40: "Plenus ergo sapientia et perfectus decore. . . ." For the background of Bernard's connection between Satan and *curiositas*, see Augustine's words on the serpent and *curiositas* in *De Gen. contra Man.*, 1.23.40 and 2.18.27 (PL 34:192 and 210).

22. In Hum 10.35 (SBOp 3:43), Bernard says to the devil: ". . . per Seraphim tuae curiositati modus imponatur."

23. Hum 10.38; SBOp 3:45: ". . . per curiositatem a veritate ceciderit [reprobus angelus], quia prius spectavit curiose, quod affectavit illicite, speravit praesumptuose."

24. Eve argued that she was not forbidden to see the fruit, but only to eat it. Bernard responded by saying (Hum 10.30; SBOp 3:39–40): "Etsi culpa non est, culpae tamen occasio est. . . ." For the background of Eve's connection with sinful curiosity, see Augustine, *De trinitate*, 12.12.17 (CCL 50, p. 371) and *De Genesi ad litteram*, 11.30–31 (PL 34:445–46); Bede, *In primam epistolam B. Joannis*, 2 (PL 93:92–93). See also Donald R. Howard, *The Three Temptations*, Medieval Man in Search of the World (Princeton, 1966), p. 48.

25. Hum 10.30; SBOp 3:40: "Auget curam, dum incitat gulam; acuit curiositatem, dum suggerit cupiditatem."

26. Hum 10.29; SBOp 3:39.

27. Lib. 2, cap. 28 (PL 106:229–31) is concerned with *vitium curiositatis*. Jonas may have been an innovator in dealing with Dinah, but for the source of most of his other material on the sin, see below, n. 54.

28. *De inst. laicali*, 2.28 (PL 106:229): "Dina quippe, ut beatus Gregorius in libro Pastorali scribit. . . ." Gregory's words are to be found in *Cura pastoralis*, 3.29 (adm. 30) (PL 77:108).

29. *Homilia 112* (PL 118:603–604): "Quando enim mens infirmantium actiones curiose perscrutatur, quasi Dina filia Jacob mulieres regionis videre desiderans, a paterna domo egreditur, id est a semetipsa recedit. . . ."

30. The more traditional idea of seeing in Dinah a *vitium curiositatis* which drew the mind away from itself and into worldly cares and terrestrial pleasures which were a threat to the sinner alone is well represented in sermons by Hildebertus Cenomanensis. See *In adventu Domini sermo sextus* (PL171:368), *In coena Domini sermo secundus* (PL 171:512–13) *Sermo 112 de diversis* (PL 171:858–59).

31. For the vast late medieval importance of Bernard in general, see Giles Constable, "The Popularity of Twelfth-Century Spiritual Writers in the Late Middle Ages," in *Renaissance Studies in Honor of Hans Baron*, edd. Anthony Molho and John A. Tedeschi, Biblioteca storica Sansoni, N.S. 49 (Florence, 1970), pp. 13–19 (cited by Zacher, p. 164 n. 38). As an indication of the popularity of Bernard's Hum (and, thus, his view of *curiositas* in particular, see the following: Peraldus quoted Bernard's work in the *Summa virtutum et vitiorum*, 2.6.3.35 (Basel, 1497), fols. 105r–06r. Galienus' *Speculum iuniorum*, a mid-thirteenth-century pastoral *summa* written to educate the English clergy, probably derived its material on the sins from Peraldus (Oxford, Bodl. MS. Laud misc. 166, fol. 14r—where Bernard's twelve steps of pride are to be found). On this text, see L. Boyle, "Three English Pastoral Summae and a 'Magister Galienus,'" *Studia Gratiana* 11 (1967). 134–44. Bonaventure referred to Bernard's steps of pride in a treatise of biblical exegesis, *In Hexaemeron collatio 14*, 4 (*Opera Omnia*, vol. 5; Quaracchi, 1891, p. 420), and quoted from Bernard's text in a typical scholastic exercise, his *Comment. in libros Sententiarum*, for the *Sentences*, 2.5.1.1 (*Opera Omnia*, vol. 2; Quaracchi, 1885, p. 146). Bernard's work was taken over completely in the fourteenth-century encyclopedia, *Speculum morale* (see below, n. 33). In

the fifteenth century, Bernard's treatment of pride was used by Antoninus of Florence in his *Summa theologica*, 2.3.4 (Venice, 1477), sig. $O_2^r-O_5^r$, one of the last medieval examples of this genre. The influence of Hum probably extended to the writing of history as well. See the words of Arnoldus, abbot of the cloister of St John in Lübeck, in his *Chronica Slavorum*, 3.10 (written c. 1204– 09) (ed. J. M. Lappenberg, MGH Script. 21; Hannover, 1869, p. 154): "O monache, qui vanum servas nomen religionis et vias sectaris superstitionis, regulam profiteris, sed qua conscientia illam discutiendo legis, cum omnia in contrarium facis? Illa ascendit per gradus humilitatis, sed tu descendis per gradus elationis. Illa te vult utiliter occupari aut opere manuum, aut oratione, aut in lectione divina, tu vero otium sectaris, ad curiositatem convertis."

32. Howard Schultz, *Milton and Forbidden Knowledge* (New York, 1955, repr. 1970), pp. 7ff., documents the frequent use of Bernard as an authority by the English divines of the seventeenth century. In later editions of Cesare Ripa's *Iconologia*, Bernard's description of the curious monk (Hum 10.28—see above, p. 75) is often the only authority used to explain the emblem of *curiositas*, and it is probably this description which accounts for the ears and frogs (with large eyes) that decorate *Curiositas'* dress. See the German translation (Frankfurt, 1669–70), vol. 2, pp. 75–76, and the French translation (Amsterdam, 1698), vol. 1, pp. 57–58. On editions of Ripa's work see Mario Praz, *Studies in Seventeenth-Century Imagery*, Part 1, 2nd ed., Sussidi Eruditi, 16 (Rome, 1964), pp. 472–75.

33. This is, for example, precisely how it was used in *Speculum morale*, 3.3.2 (Douai, 1624, repr. Graz, 1964, cols. 997–1003), wrongly attributed to Vincent of Beauvais. Ps.- Vincent used Bernard's twelve steps of pride, but also added material from Thomas Aquinas and a host of other authorities.

34. Dil 2.4; SBOp 3:122: "Fit igitur ut sese non agnoscendo egregia rationis munere creatura, irrationabilium gregibus incipiat aggregari, dum ignara propriae gloriae, quae ab intus est, conformanda foris rebus sensibilibus, sua ipsius curiositate abducitur, efficiturque una de ceteris, quod se prae ceteris nihil accepisse intelligat."

35. Bernard considered that there were three modes of knowing: in what order, with what eagerness, and to what end one should know something. Correctness in the first *modus* meant that one knew first what was more fitting for salvation, in the second *modus* that one knew more ardently what was more powerful for love, in the last mode that one knew only what pertained to one's own edification or that of one's neighbor. In these terms, sinful curiosity was an incorrectness in the last category and was seen in those "qui scire volunt, eo fine tantum, ut sciant." See SC 36, 3.3; SBOp 2:5

36. Hum 1.2; SBOp 3:17. See also Storm, pp. 190–92.

37. Hum 10.28; SBOp 3:38: "Haedos quippe, qui peccatum significant, recte oculos auresque appellaverim, quoniam sicut mors per peccatum in orbem, sic per has fenestras intrat in mentem." That the eyes and ears were understood as signifying all the senses is proven by the *capitulum* cited in the following note.

38. Though the *capitula* to Hum are probably not the work of Bernard, they reflect his thought accurately enough. Here, the title given the first step toward pride is *Curiositas, cum oculis ceterisque sensibus vagatur in ea quae ad se non attinent* (SBOp 3:14).

39. The original Cistercian community, as David Knowles has pointed out in *Cistercians and Cluniacs: The Controversy between St. Bernard and Peter the Venerable*, Friends of Dr. Williams's Library, Ninth Lecture (London, 1955), p. 12, was a movement "towards simplicity and austerity." This desire to return to the spiritual ideal of apostolic Christianity can be observed in all the eremitic and ascetic movements which developed in this period. See Norman F. Cantor, "The Crisis of Western Monasticism, 1050–1130," *The American Historical Review* 66 (1960), 62–63.

40. The new ascetic movements not only interpreted the *Rule* in a stricter fash-

ion, but they appealed for inspiration and authority to a pre-Benedictine monastic tradition. Note, for instance, the mention of Anthony, Macarius, and Basil by Bernard in Apo 9.19 and 9.23; SBOp 3:96 and 100). For Aelred of Rievaulx's continuation of this tradition see below, p. 85. On the Cistercian idea of the purity of the *Rule*, see Jean Leclercq, "Les intentions des fondateurs de l'Ordre cistercien, *Collectanea Cisterciensia* 30 (1968), 247–49. As Bede K. Lackner, "Friends and Critics of Early Cîteaux," *Analecta Cisterciensia* 34 (1978), 19, has pointed out, the Cistercians were praised in particular for following the *Rule* and especially for maintaining a simple life.

41. Nearly half the Apo is taken up with an examination of these excesses under the title "Contra superfluitates."

42. See the works by Cantor and Knowles cited in note 39. For a view of Peter the Venerable's influence on Bernard see the article by A. H. Bredero in *Petrus Venerabilis 1156–1956*, ed. G. Constable and J. Kritzeck, Studia Anselmiana, 40 (Rome, 1956), pp. 53–71.

43. Ep 1.4; SBOp 7:4: ". . . otiositatem contemplationem nuncupat, edacitatem, loquacitatem, curiositatem, cunctam denique intemperantiam nominat discretionem." The letter was written in 1125, probably in the spring; see Damien van den Eynde, "Les premiers écrits de Saint Bernard," in Jean Leclercq, *Recueil d'études sur Saint Bernard et ses écrits*, Storia e Letteratura, 114, vol. 3 (Rome, 1969), pp. 395ff.

44. Ep 277; SBOp 8:190. This letter has been dated by Leclercq and Rochais 1151–1152. The words quoted here were written, as it seems in response to reforming *statuta* which Peter the Venerable had issued earlier. Epp 277 and 1 have been quoted by numerous scholars who have documented Bernard's controversy with Peter the Venerable, yet none of them has taken note of the part *curiositas* played in this argument. On the relatively late date of Peter and Bernard's friendship, see A. H. Bredero, "Une controverse sur Cluny au XIIᵉ siècle," RHE 76 (1981), 48–72. The Cistercians' emphasis on simplicity in dress remained an enduring part of their reputation. See Odo of Cheriton's parable concerning the nobleman who rejected worldly pomp and put on the habit of a White Monk, saying, "Melius in uilibus pannis salutem lucrari arbitror quam perdi in siricis" (ed. Léopold Hervieux in *Les fabulistes latins*, vol. 4; Paris, 1896; repr., Hildesheim, New York, 1970, p. 268, no. 7). See also *Catalogue of Romances in the Department of Manuscripts in the British Museum*, vol. 3, ed. J. A. Herbert (London, 1910). p. 59, no. 6; p. 397, no. 436; p. 459, no. 32; p. 564, no. 70; and Frederic C. Tubach, *Index Exemplorum*, FF Communications 204 (Helsinki, 1969), p. 320, no. 4183c.

45. See the introduction to the edition by Leclercq and Rochais, SBOp 3:63ff., for the date and circumstances of this work's composition.

46. Apo 8.16; SBOp 3:95. Of course, by the twelfth century other houses had become complacent as well, but Bernard's remarks here were levelled primarily at the Cluniacs. See his Ep 84ᵇⁱˢ in the introduction to the Apo (SBOp 3:64) and SBOp 7:219.

47. The *praeteritio* involved in Bernard's rhetorically polished accusation here has frequently been commented on. In Apo 12.28 (SBOp 3:104), he noted: "Omitto oratoriorum immensas altitudines, immoderatas longitudines, supervacuas latitudines, sumptuosas depolitiones, curiosas depictiones, quae dum in se orantium retorquent aspectum, impediunt et affectum. . . ." See also his words in Apo 12.29.

48. Apo 12.28 (SBOp 3:106): "Inveniunt curiosi quo delectentur, et non inveniunt miseri quo sustententur." The enormous wheel mentioned by Bernard has generally been taken as a reference to the large *corona* in the cathedral at Cluny. See below, n. 50. On the type of art to which the Cistercians were opposed, one which was "nourri par la superbe et la vanité, visant par amour de la gloire, à la grandeur, à l'opulence, à la virtuosité, haut en couleurs pour caresser la sensualité,

multipliant les décorations originales afin d'exciter la curiosité," see Edgar de Bruyne, *Etudes d'esthétique médiévale*, vol. 2 (Brugge, 1946), pp. 139–43.

49. Apo 12.28 (SBOp 3:105). It is interesting to note that the *Dialogus inter Cluniacensem monachum et Cisterciensem*, written after the deaths of Peter the Venerable and Bernard, continued the essence of Bernard's reproach of Cluniac intemperance by accusing that Order of sinning with all five senses. Here, however, one finds the sinful curiosity of the eyes as an argument against Cluny but that of the ears. What the writer of this dialogue objected to in terms of evil *curiositas* was the desire to hear different tones which could only be produced, so he says, by excessively heavy bells: "Multas diversi soni, & tam diversi ponderis campanas, ut aliquam earum propter nimium pondus ejus vix duo monachi pulsare possint, non requirit usus necessarius, sed aurium curiositas." See the edition by Martène and Durand in *Thesaurus novus Anecdotorum*, vol. 5 (Paris, 1717), col. 1586. On the *Dialogus* see Knowles, *Cistercians and Cluniacs*, pp. 30–32. For a detailed documenation of the continuing Cistercian attention to architectural simplicity, see Caroline A. Bruzelius, "Cistercian High Gothic: The Abbey Church of Longpont and the Architecture of the Cistercians in the Early Thirteenth Century," ASOC 35 (1979), 3–204.

50. The various *statuta* were circulated during Peter the Venerable's abbacy at Cluny. They were collected and published in this form in 1146 and are to be found in PL 189:1023–48. The exact dates of the various decrees are not known and so their relationship to Bernard's Apo must remain a matter of conjecture. Even the verbal parallels between Bernard's work and some of the decrees may only be due to commonplaces of the Cluniac controversy. Still, the areas of superfluity covered in the *statuta* often agree so closely in wording and spirit with those in the Apo that the direct influence of Bernard seems quite possible. On the *statuta* see Knowles, *Cistercians and Cluniacs*, pp. 26–29, and especially Knowles' article, "The Reforming Decrees of Peter the Venerable," in *Petrus Venerabilis 1156–1956*, pp. 1–20. For Peter's work on the building at Cluny, see Kenneth Conant, "Cluniac Building During the Abbacy of Peter the Venerable," *Petrus Venerabilis 1156–1956*, pp. 121–127. It should be noted that Peter was still led to speak of the superfluity of expenses in lighting up too often the great *corona* in Cluny's church, an ornament Bernard had found excessive in Apo 12.28. See *statutum* 52 (PL 189:1039).

51. Decrees against the evil or *damnata curiositas* of clothing are *statuta* 16–18 (PL 189:1030–31). *Statutum* 40 (PL 189:1037) is concerned with the retinues of priors.

52. Div 14.2 (SBOp 6/1:135): "Ceterum, ut gravior sit conflictus, squama squamae iungitur, et comitantia sunt in humano corde negligentia sui, et curiositas ceterorum . . . . Evidenter proinde curiositati Pietas adversatur . . . ."

53. PL 184:1199–1306; esp. *cap.* 59.130–31 (on sinful curiosity), cols. 1279–80. It has been suggested that the treatise was written by Thomas of Beverly (de Frigido Monte), a Cistercian who flourished in the 1170s. See Morton Bloomfield, *et al.*, *Incipits of Latin Works on the Virtues and Vices*, The Mediaeval Academy of America Publication No. 88 (Cambridge, Massachusetts, 1979), nos. 1712, 1759, 1762.

54. CC 117. Chapter 70 of this work is entitled "De curiositate" and is found on pp. 210–12. For the date of composition and bibliography, see H. M. Rochais, "Defensor," 14 (1960), col. 160, and Rochais' introduction (CC 117, pp. vii–xii). It should be pointed out that Defensor's *florilegium* also seems to have been responsible for much of the material on *curiositas* assembled by Jonas in his *De inst. laicali*, 2.28 (PL 106, esp, col. 230).

55. The author of the *Tractatus de interiori domo* was more selective in his use of previous material, though hardly more original. His section on sinful curiosity, *cap.* 24.50 (PL 184:533–34), is taken only from Julianus Pomerius' *Vita contemplativa*. Though he added more from this source than is given in the *Liber scintil-*

larum, his use of Pomerius may be due as much to the inclusion of material from
the *Vita contemplativa* in Defensor's chapter on *curiositas* as to the author's wide
knowledge of Pomerius' treatise.

56. For other Cistercian works in which *vitium curiositatis* plays a prominent
role, see, for example, the *Dialogus inter Cluniacensem monachum et Cisterciensem*
(above, n. 49); John of Limoges, *Morale Somnium Pharaonis* (ed. J.A. Fabricius in
Codex Pseudepigraphus Veteris Testamenti; Hamburg, Leipzig, 1713, esp. pp.
468ff.); *Ommebonum*, written in the mid-fourteenth century by an English Cistercian named Jacobus (London, British Library MS. Royal 6E.VI–VII—see 6E.VI,
vol. 2, fol. 454ra ff.).

57. It is precisely this earlier monastic tradition which is emphasized in the gloss
to proverb 135 of Galand's other major work, the *Libellus Proverbiorum*. There,
one reads: "Anime celesti sponso desiderio adherentes, in scripturarum speculo
sese perspicere, et honestis moribus indui, et magis spiritalium quam exteriorum
curam gerere, et uerecunde aspicere, id est nichil turpe in corde uoluere, et im-
pudenter nunquam loqui, id est uanum uel ociosum uerbum non proferre, et ad
publicum uix exire, id est curiositatis uitium cauere debent." See *"Galandi Regni-
acensis Libellus Proverbiorum*: le recueil de proverbes glosés du Cistercien Galland
de Rigny," ed. J. Châtillon (with a French trans. by M. Dumontier), *Revue du
moyen âge latin* 9 (1953), 87.

58. I have used the edition of the *Speculum caritatis* prepared by C. H. Talbot
in A. Hoste and C. H. Talbot, edd., *Aelredi Rievallensis opera omnia*, 1, CCCM 1
(Turnhout, 1971). The work was written 1142–43. See the introduction to *The
Life of Ailred of Rievaulx by Walter Daniel*, trans. with intro. and notes by F. M.
Powicke (Repr. Oxford, 1978). Bernard's words to Aelred are found in Ep 523
(SBOp 8:486–89), also printed before the text of Aelred's work in the edition
above, pp. 3–4. The material on sinful *curiositas* is found in Spec car 2.24.70–73
(pp. 99–101) and is summarized in the *Compendium speculi caritatis*, chaps. 52–53
(ed. R. Vander Plaetse, CCM 1:231–32).

59. "Sed iam de concupiscentia oculorum pauca dicenda sunt, quam curiositatem sancti Patres uiderunt appellandam, nam eam non solum ad exteriorem, sed
etiam ad interiorem hominem aestimant pertinere." Spec car 2.24.70 (CCCM
1:99). On the triad see Spec car 2.4.7 (CCCM 1:69).

60. Spec car 2.24.70 (CCCM 1:99): ". . . in diuersis utensilibus radiantis me-
talli splendor."

61. Spec car 2.24.71 (CCCM 1:100): "Si, inquam, interiori ceruice iugo di-
uinae dilectionis supposita, ibi ibi [sic] intus Iesus ille dulcis dulciter sapuisset, mul-
tumne, queso, gloriolas has exteriores affectasset?"

62. Spec car 2.24.72 (CCCM 1:100): "Hinc est quod plerique, qui inani philosophiae dedere animum, quibus etiam moris est cum Euangeliis Bucolica medi-
tari, Horatium cum Prophetis, cum Paulo Tullium lectitare, tunc etiam metro
ludere laciniosisque carminibus amatoria texere. . . ." The echo of Jerome's dream
is unmistakable. Aelred, of course, is not rejecting Cicero and the classics whole-
sale here; he himself describes his own avid reading of Cicero in the prologue to
Spir amic. Such works provoke a dangerous curiosity when they hinder the
monk's striving for perfection.

63. This is yet another way in which, especially for the Cistercians, evil *curiositas* was antithetical to the humility defined by Benedict. The final degree of
humilitas in the *Regula Benedicti*, 7.62–66 (CSEL 75:50–51), demanded that this
virtue be shown both externally and in the heart. See above, p. 75.

64. Such things, he said, were "non quidem Antoniana et Machariana instrumenta" (Spec car 2.24.70; CCM 1:99). There was specific legislation in the Cistercian Order forbidding those collections of animals which could provoke sinful
curiosity. Aelred probably had the words of the *Exordium Cistercii*, 15, in mind
(ed. J. B. van Damme in *Documenta pro Cisterciensis Ordinis historiae ac juris studio*;
Westmalle, 1959, p. 27): "Unde licet nobis [monachis] possidere ad proprios

usus . . . animalia, preter illa que magis solent provocare curiositatem, et osten-
tare in se vanitatem, quam afferre utilitatem, sicut sunt cervi, grues, et cetera
huiusmodi." Aelred also wrote specifically of deer and cranes here.

65. *De arca Noe morali libri 6,* 3.10 (PL 176:655–56). Hugh's position in the
history of *curiositas* has been examined by Oberman, pp. 25–26.

66. *De arca,* 3.10 (PL 176:656).

67. *Libri 10 commentariorum in hierarchiam coelestem S. Dionysii Areopagitae,* 1.1
(PL 175:925). On Hugh's use of his sources, see J. Châtillon, "Hugues de Saint-
Victor critique de Jean Scot," in *Jean Scot Erigène et l'histoire de la philosophie.* Col-
logques internationaux de Centre National de la Recherche Scientifique, 561
(Paris, 1977), pp. 415–31.

68. *Expositio in Epistulam 1 ad Thessalonicenses* (PL153:408): "per urbem . . .
rumoribus inquirendis."

69. *Ibid.:* "ne, contemptis propriis, aliena negotia curetis. In his verbis vitium
curiositatis interdicit."

70. This is *exemplum* 31, in Thomas F. Crane, ed., *The Exempla or Illustrative
Stories from the Sermones Vulgares of Jacques de Vitry* (London, 1890), pp. 12–13;
see also pp. 145–47. It was an extremely popular narrative; many other versions
(not all of which deal with the Cistercians) are listed in Tubach (see above, n. 44),
p. 89, no. 1103. The *exemplum* was examined early, though mainly in terms of
the historicity of Master Sella, by B. Hauréau, "Les récits d'apparitions dans les
sermons du moyen age," *Mémoires de l'Institut national de France, Académie des inscriptions et belles-lettres* 28, 2 (Paris, 1876), pp. 242–46.

REGULA BENEDICT: 73:8:
A RULE FOR BEGINNERS

Francis Kline, OCSO

THIS PRESENTATION will be an exercise in reading the *Rule* of St Benedict,[1] so centrally important to our Cistercian Fathers, in the light of its sources.[2] Nothing exhaustive or definitive will be attempted. Some may even disagree about the importance of the particular sources with which I will work. So I ask your pardon at the outset for any hasty judgements which I may seem to have made, and for any incompleteness.[3] John Cassian is the source I will work with—not to exclude St Basil or St Augustine. It is just that in order to exegete the particular passage of the *Rule* I have in mind, Cassian provides the most striking and ready evidence. Cassian in fact permits us to do in this passage the two things which I think any of the major sources of the *Rule* should do: 1) It sheds light on the passage to be exegeted and 2) It helps us to place the *Rule* in its role as transmitter to a future age of the primitive monastic ideals. Reading the *Rule* in this way gives us a fresh insight into the way the Cistercians used it, since they, too, were so warmly motivated by the primitive monastic ideals.

John Cassian then will help us understand what St Benedict means when he commands in Chapter 73:8 to "... keep this little rule that we have written for beginners" (*Hanc minimam inchoationis regulam descriptam . . . perfice. . .*). We need not question the appeal to Cassian to understand Chapter 73, for it is almost certain that, in this last chapter of his *Rule*, St Benedict asks his monks to read and act on the *Conferences* of Cassian, and also his *Institutes*, the *Lives of the Fathers*, as well as the Rule of "our holy Father Basil." But we must start somewhere, and by taking and searching through Cassian, there emerges a quite interesting solution to a problem that has never been rightly solved. Granted that we monks all need to be exercised daily in the cardinal benedictine virtue of humility, it does not follow that seasoned veterans of the monastery should be labelled as "beginners" whose slack observance needs to be upgraded. Even if this be the case, and we should "blush with shame," as St Benedict says, for being so slothful, so unobservant, so negligent, we should still wonder if the compassionate father of monks meant to be understood as nagging them about observances which, after all, are not so absolute in themselves. For they are to be relaxed in the case of young children and the old monks. No, we should be unworthy children of so great a parent were we not to suspect that a deeper meaning lay hidden behind St Benedict's words about beginners—that he saw a vision of a life so dazzling that we would all appear as the merest neophytes in its light. And would it not make sense that here at the end of his *Rule*, St Benedict should wax enthusiastic about the everlasting life that we should all together attain, and to which nothing whatever is to be preferred (RB 72:11)?

CASSIAN

Now Cassian, to whom we turn for guidance in our reading of this passage, is notoriously difficult to control. He is a serene, sedate, and shrewd monastic pastor, always ready to blunt the sharp edge, to blur the focussed, to deflect the pointed questions of ardent young monks with the bunting of a luxuriant classic Latin.[4] Cassian says many things about beginners, and seniors and those in between. At first glance, and perhaps second or third, we may find as many differing statements relating to our troubling passage from the *Rule* of St Benedict. The solution to the problem of getting a hold on Cassian, of finding some way to control him so that he has to be consistent here with what he said there, is to find the main structure of his system which stands behind his multifarious doctrine. Now there is one source for Cassian's writings which tends to unify and clarify his teaching where other sources would only make him diffuse. That source is Evagrius. A comparison between Evagrius and Cassian has been going on since 1936—if not before—when Salvatore Marsili published his thesis: *Giovanni Cassiano ed Evagrio Pontico.*[5] For my purpose here, I would like to talk about various aspects of the doctrine of Cassian against the backdrop of Evagrius' teaching. It will then be easier to show how St Benedict is a transmitter of this strand of Eastern Christian monasticism.

One of the important elements of Cassian's spiritual system is the three-fold division of the spiritual life. According to the image of the three books in Conference 3, Chapter 6, we learn the morals and rules of a good life at the first stage. These are found in the *Book of Proverbs*, or perhaps we should say that they are *symbolized* by the biblical book. Here, we overcome the vices and acquire the virtues. The *Book of Ecclesiastes* comes next. It teaches the transitory nature of the world and begins to turn our minds towards the unchanging and altogether different end which is spiritual. Not that the world is devalued. Rather it is seen in the light of God's purpose in creating it—to be a means by which fallen creation can return to him. Because it has no final end of its own, it is seen to be "vanity" if we should stop there without pursuing the final stage. Finally, there is the immaterial science of God—which is unitive, which only love can describe—as we have it in the *Song of Songs*. This schema, of course, does not originate with Cassian. It is one of the main structural elements in Origen's teaching on the spiritual life.[6] But it is present in Cassian as an island of solidity in the sea of his monastic talk.[7]

Cassian makes good and frequent use of this three-fold division of the spiritual life. The rudiments of the monastic discipline are set forth for the most part in the *Institutes*, but not exclusively, for there is much practical wisdom for the beginner in the *Conferences* as well. But the only reason for these ascetical practices is to bring one to the second stage where the active struggle against the vices and the acquisitions of the virtues reaches its culmination in purity of heart. Having finished with the *Institutes*, and about to embark on the *Conferences*, Cassian speaks fervently of the transition from active pursuit to the possession of purity of heart right in Conference One. Here, Abbot Moses poses the question to Cassian and Germanus like a jab with his staff. But what of the goal, if I may paraphrase him, the immediate goal which is to be pursued until it is clenched? It is, of course, purity of heart—the perfect calming of all the passions in the perfection of charity (see Conf. 1, Ch. 7 and 11). This is the first goal of the monk for which he strives day and

night with all the arts that the spiritual craft can afford him (see
Conf. 1, Ch. 4). And despite the rich and lingering flow of Cassian's prose, it catches fire when the urgency of reaching this goal
takes hold of him. For Scete was the place where *omnis commora-*
batur perfectio—where all perfection dwelt. And this perfection was
worth every labor and hardship, and the application of every spiritual skill and talent. And it was tangible and visible in the old men
who dwelt there. To see them was to catch the contagion of their
perfection.

Purity of heart, however, is not the final end of the monk. It is
only the middle, or transitional stage to the ultimate goal which is
eternal life (see Conf. 1, Ch. 5). This is to know God and to rejoice in the joy of his beauty (Conf. 1, Ch. 8). It is to pass from the
multiplicity of the active life to the love of God and the contemplation of divine things in an eternal purity of heart (Conf. 1, Ch.
10). Of these things and the prayer in which they are experienced,
Cassian will speak more at length in Conferences 9 and 10.

Not only does the passage from the active to the contemplative
life signal the perfection of charity, but it also initiates one into the
knowledge of divine realities. For we know God not only in contemplating his essence but also in the hope of his promise. We also
know him in the wonders of his creation and in the help of his daily
dispensation, that is, providence (Conf. 1, Ch. 15). We see the
reaon for the great work of the Incarnation in our salvation. These
and other innumerable contemplations arise in our understanding
according to the character of our life and the purity of our heart
(Conf. 1, Ch. 15).[8] Knowledge and charity then go hand in hand
when the monk begins to pass from the active life to the contemplative life. For what occurs is a transformation of Being and not
just the advancement of the mind or the intensity of the affections.

Elsewhere, Cassian will offer another three-fold division of the
spiritual life with another image. In Conference Eleven, he presents the active life as lived by the slave in bondage of fear to
his master. For the monk obeys the monastic discipline out of fear
of hell, rather than from the true desire of the heart (Conf. 11, Ch.
6, 7, and 8). Only one step better is the mercenary who sees the
reward at the end of his labors. It is the love of the Son for his
Father that alone is worthy of God. This love characterizes the

state of purity of heart where "love casts out fear" (see Institutes 4, Ch. 3).

Whether employing the images of love or knowledge, or the figure of the mercenary and the Son, or the three books of Scripture, Cassian hovers around his theme of the three-fold division of the spiritual life. The pivotal point is the passage from the active life into the contemplative life. And when that passage has occurred, there is a corresponding urgency to apply oneself to the pure prayer or the prayer of fire (Conf 9, Ch. 15, and Conf 10, Ch. 12) which gives one the knowledge of God alone. This three-fold schema with its various aspects can come only from Evagrius.

EVAGRIUS

Now it so happens that Evagrius, though his works have been difficult to come by in languages other than Greek and Syriac, is a man who is crystal clear in his logic and admirably, but not slavishly, consistent in his terms. Once you can locate the work, read it, hopefully in the original, and break the key to his poetic and highly symbolic language, you have before you ideas that are precise, unwavering, and uncompromising, where Cassian is diffuse and lengthy.

Evagrius says in Chapter 1 of his work the *Praktikos* (the one who is in action or is striving)[9] that the spiritual life has three stages: *praktike*—the striving stage; *physike*—the stage of nature or natural philosophy, where one comes to understand the reasons for the material and spiritual worlds; and finally, *theologia*, the union with God through *gnosis*. The translation I prefer is *Enlightenment*.[10] To explain and illustrate these three stages, Evagrius wrote three important works: the *Praktikos*, mentioned above, is first; the second, not as yet in any translation but only in Syriac (with a Greek retroversion) is the *Gnostikos* which matches *physike* or natural philosophy; the third is called the *Kephalaia Gnostika*, and it, of course, has to do with *theologia*.[11] So we have three works that mirror the three stages of the spiritual life.

Now the most important over-all characteristic of Evagrius' system is this: that once having embarked on the first stage of the return to God, one cannot neglect to pursue the course to the last

and highest stage of the essential Enlightenment of God. Though
the spiritual experience becomes more refined and reaches higher
states of knowledge, though one advances to a high degree of *apatheia* and the love that prepares the soul for God, one must not
stop one's upward flight until one's knowledge of oneself is as in
God. And it is not that in passing from the first stage to the second,
one is never aware of the third, but rather that the third and higher
stage is somehow inchoatively present even in the first stage.[12] Once
one begins the course as *praktikos*, one cannot stop until as a *theo-
logos*, there is no distraction from God. This gives to Evagrius'
writings an urgency, a tension, and direct orientation toward the
goal to be attained.

Evagrius gave to Cassian the whole ascetical doctrine based on
the struggle against the eight passionate thoughts (see Chapters
15–39 in the *Praktikos* of Evagrius and the *Institutes* of Cassian).
All through the subjugation of our passions, love emerges stronger
and stronger until at the end, with all in the state of *apatheia* (which
may be translated as self-possession), love is revealed in the soul as
free and predominant (see Conf. 1, Ch. 7, in Cassian, and the *Mirror of Monks* of Evagrius, N.N. 67 and 121).[13] "Purity of heart,"
of course, is Cassian's translation of *apatheia*.[14] It is not so much a
translation as it is a cultural adaptation. It is also the smuggling of
the suspect Evagrius into the monasteries of the West. Had Cassian transliterated *apatheia* the way he did *theoria*, for example (see
Conf. 1, Ch. 8, 2), one would have heard Jerome's roar even into
Spain, and even from his grave! Had he even mentioned the name
of Evagrius, the abbot of Marseilles would have been branded a
rebel with or without the controversy over Pelagius. But Cassian
had learned to diffuse tempers and smooth over difficulties without a drop of compromise. He made Evagrius lie low and out of
sight, forged his terms, but kept his personality and ninety percent
of his doctrine.

As Cassian adapts Evagrius, we find that he puts a greater emphasis on love or charity than on the *gnosis* which was Evagrius'
preference. And there is a largesse and an ampleness to Cassian's
diction which is the exact opposite of the tight and obscure aphor-
isms of Evagrius. Nevertheless, the forward thrust and intention of
the heart is the unmistakable quality they share, or rather that

Evagrius handed on to Cassian. This attitude of the heart is best summed up in Cassian's vocabulary as the immediate goal—which is the kingdom of heaven (see Conf. 1, Ch. 4). These two elements are what Evagrius had first called *apatheia* which leads first to the *physike*—the understanding of the physical world—and then to the essential *gnosis* or Enlightenment—which is union with God.

The radical spirit of the desert is another characteristic which Evagrius handed on to Cassian. The absoluteness which is endemic in the *Praktikos*, the *Chapters on Prayer*, and the *Kephalia Gnostika* is taken up by Cassian in such statements as this:

> For this we do endure all things, for this we make light of our kinsfolk, our country, honors, riches, the delights of this world, and all kinds of pleasure, namely in order that we may retain a lasting purity of heart. And so when this object is set before us, we shall always direct our actions and thoughts straight towards the attainment of it. (Conf. 1, Ch. 5).

This radical spirit of dedication strongly implies that the goal which is sought *can* be attained and that the spiritual love which lies always beyond our grasp is, by the very nature of love, beginning to be within our reach. This is the only plausible explanation behind the severely uncompromising system of Evagrius and the constant pleading of Cassian in Conference One to employ all the spiritual arts at one's disposal. It is the kind of attitude that sets off a golden age from a silver one. It is the very extravagance of the lives of the desert fathers which makes them an inexhaustible source of spiritual refreshment.[15] And Evagrius and Cassian, though intellectuals, are an honest representation of it.

St Benedict

Turning to the *Rule* and the problem passage of Chapter 73:8, there are several converging conclusions which we may make against the background of the *Rule*'s sources which we have examined. When St Benedict asks: "Are you hastening toward your heavenly home?", we can conclude that he refers to the ultimate

end of the monk as conceived by Cassian, the heavenly kingdom
and eternal life. The monastic life is to be viewed in the eschatological light of the kingdom of God. Until we are close on to that
blessed state, we can be described as beginners. And, indeed, this is
at least part of St Benedict's meaning.

There is also the element of hastening. "Are you hastening toward your heavenly home" [*ad patriam caelestem festinas*]? The image of hastening along the road is a frequent one in the *Prologue*
(especially *Prologue* 22) of the *Rule*, and it finds its culmination
here at the final chapter. There is only one way to aspire to the
heavenly homeland—with a rushing desire. And those who do not
run there can never hope to reach it. The idea of running is St
Benedict's expression for the radical spirit of desert spirituality
which we saw to be so apparent in Evagrius and Cassian. The images of running and rushing also include the idea of achieving the
utmost in an all-out effort. It is easy to think of St Benedict's list of
the instruments of good works (RB:4) when reading what Cassian
has to say of the monk's constant vigilance and use of all the arts of
the spiritual craft (Conf. 1, Ch. 4 and 5). Clearly, the rush of desire and the comprehensive nature of the vigilance imply a belief
that the goal can be attained. That St Benedict conceived his *Rule*
in order to achieve the goal of the heavenly homeland is set forth
right in the Prologue (21, 42, and 50). And the characteristics of
the pursuit of that goal are clear: a running and hastening, and a
comprehensive obedience of all of God's commandments, the instruments of good works.

> But as we progress in this way of life and in faith, we shall
> run on the path of God's commandments, our hearts over-
> flowing with the inexpressible delight of love. (Prologue 49).

The "delight of love" is something we enjoy on the way to the
final goal. Yet, just as it was for Evagrius and Cassian, love is also
the immediate goal for St Benedict. At the end of the twelve
degrees of humility, he describes how the monk:

> . . . will quickly arrive at that *perfect love* of God which *casts
> out fear* [1 Jn 4:18]. Through this love, all that he once per-
> formed with dread, he will now begin to observe without

> effort, as though naturally, from habit . . . no longer out of
> fear of hell, but out of love for Christ, good habit and de-
> light in virtue. (RB 7:68–69. See also: *Institutes* 4:39).

St Benedict combines the elements of hastening, all-out effort, and charity in Chapter 72, the penultimate chapter of his *Rule*. In this chapter, he is not dependent on the *Rule of the Master* as he is frequently elsewhere, but he offers instead a kind of synthesis of all the doctrine he has presented so far. There is " . . . the good zeal which monks must foster with fervent [*ferventissimo*] love." In the term "zeal" (*zelus*), we have St Benedict's own idea of the "royal road" (see Conf. 2, Ch. 2) which leads to the attainment of the immediate goal which is love. This is the love that finds its perfection (fulfillment) in the evangelical service and an attitude of humility toward the brothers and the abbot in community. And it is the love that prefers nothing to Christ. This is the victory over all the vices and the acquisition of all the virtues in fraternal service. And we may see this love as peaking in the preferring of nothing to Christ. Chapter 72 then is the equivalent of the other cardinal passages on love which we have examined, namely Prologue 49, and Chapter 7:68–69. Here, however, there is more of an emphasis on the perfection of love in a cenobitic situation.

Evagrius had described charity as the gateway to *apatheia* (see Note 10 above) and to the contemplative life. And Cassian, in Conference 1, Chapter 7, equated purity of heart, *apatheia*, with the perfection of charity. If St Benedict sees charity as the fruit of the virtue of humility, and if the twelve degrees of humility, both in the *Institutes* and in the *Rule* are a paraphrase of all the instruments of the spiritual craft and the entire monastic discipline, would it not be logical to conclude that St Benedict's charity is the equivalent of Evagrius' *apatheia* and Cassian's "purity of heart"? If so, it would also follow that St Benedict's charity would be the immediate goal of the monk and the gateway to the contemplative life and the final stages of the pursuit of the ultimate end.

St Benedict, however, does not continue with his spiritual doctrine after Chapter 7 and the degrees of humility. Instead, he embarks on the regulations of the concrete observances of his monastery. He never does come around to discussing the life of contemplation. The next hint we have of it is in Chapter 73 where we are told that

> . . . for anyone hastening on to the perfection of monastic life, there are the teachings of the holy Fathers, the observance of which will lead him to the very heights of perfection. (Chapter 73:2).

The conclusion is that St Benedict's *Rule* is for those engaged in the active struggle against the vices and the acquisition of the virtues. This is the first stage, or the stage of the beginners. And because the perfection of charity is the immediate goal of the monk and the contemplation to which it leads (*physike* and *theologia*), anyone, senior or junior, would still be a beginner were he not well on the way to attaining perfect love. St Benedict does not sound paternalistic or overly harsh when he describes his *Rule* as a "little rule for beginners." He is merely inserting his *Rule* and his spiritual system into the system of the Fathers. His *Rule* describes the first stage, and if anyone would go further, let him take up the writings of those who went before and who have given us the perfection of the monastic life in its second and third stages. This is St Benedict's advice in Chapter 73.

EPILOGUE. THE CISTERCIANS.

It is well known that the Cistercians, for all their enthusiasm about the *Rule*, cite it rather rarely in their writings. I would suggest that they take it for granted, presumed that it is being perfectly observed, and pass on to those higher teachings which St Benedict had mentioned. It is interesting to see St Bernard's deft handling of the benedictine degrees of humility in his own treatise *De gradibus humilitatis*. A study of this treatise bears out what Gilson had to say about the Cistercian use of the *Rule* and St Bernard's development of a mystical theology with the *Rule* as a foundation. But a passage I would like to highlight comes from Guerric of Igny —the *First Sermon for Epiphany*, lines 135 ff.,[16] where we offer to the infant King the same gifts as the Magi offered. The myrrh is our active striving—the *dura et aspera* of the *Rule*. We are beginners in this stage. But we pass on to frankincense. *De myrrha ad thus proficitur* (line 150). We are on the way. We put on the pallium of praise. *Convertisti planctum meum in gaudium mihi* (lines 158–59). In this stage we gain prudence, the understanding of temporal affairs and everyday concerns. The parallel with the stage of *physike* in Evagrius is striking. But the third stage—the stage of gold—who can speak of it (lines 190–94)? And Guerric's sermon ends. For those who arrive there, no words are needed. Thus we see Guerric making concrete application of the classic three stages of the spiritual life, in which the *Rule* is the first stage. It is perhaps a scheme that we should always keep in mind when reading the Cistercians—and for those of us who are monks and nuns, for reading the *Rule* as well. May it encourage us to hasten on the way.

Abbey of Gethsemani

NOTES

1. The edition of the *Rule* used throughout is *RB 1980* (Collegeville, 1981).

2. I take for granted St Benedict's dependence on the *Rule of the Master* (=RM), and in this paper, I do not attempt to distinguish between their dependence on Cassian. Thus RB reads Cassian in the same way as RM.

3. In a paper of such small scope, the following problems have not been dealt with: 1) the modification of Cassian's influence on St Benedict by his (Benedict's) other main sources—Basil and Augustine; 2) the exact balance in Cassian's works between the active life and the contemplative life. In some ways, this balance can be taken as a tension between the cenobitic and eremitic lives. See A. de Vogüé, "Understanding Cassian: A Survey of the Conferences," *CSt* XIX (1984) p. 115, n. 66.

4. I am grateful to Dom de Vogüé for this insight into Cassian's personality which he shared with us at Gethsemani in September 1984.

5. Salvatore Marsili, *Giovanni Cassiano ed Evagrio Pontico: Dottrina Sulla Carità e Contemplazione*, Studia Anselmiana 5, (Rome, 1936).

6. See Origen, *Commentary on the Song of Songs*, Prol 3.

7. Throughout this section on Cassian's threefold division of the spiritual life, I am dependent on Placide Deseille, "A Propos de L'Epilogue du Chapitre VII de La Règle," *Coll.* XXI (1959) pp. 289–301.

8. See also Conference 1, Ch. 14: ". . . per exercitationem virtutum puritate cordis ac spiritali scientia."

9. Evagrius Ponticus, *Praktikos* (Traité Pratique) SCh 170, 171, edd. Antoine and Claire Guillaumont (Paris, 1971), p. 499. English translation, see J. E. Bamberger, *Praktikos and Chapters on Prayer*, CS 4 (Spencer, 1970).

10. In a soon to be published English translation of Evagrius' text, *The Mirror*

of Monks, Jeremy Driscoll, OSB has made a cultural adaptation of *gnosis* as "enlightenment". Similarly, *praktike* becomes "Striving," *apatheia* becomes "Self-possession".

11. For the text of the *Gnostikos*, see W. Frankenberg, *Evagrius Ponticus* (Berlin, 1912). Syriac version with Greek retroversion by Frankenberg. For the *Kephalaia Gnostika*, see *Les Six Centuries des "Kephalaia Gnostika" d'Evagre le Pontique*, Syriac version, trans, and ed. Antoine Guillaumont, PO, tome 28, fasc. 1, Paris, 1958.

12. See Evagrius, *The Mirror of Monks* in H. Gressman, *Nonnenspiegel und Mönchsspiegel des Evagrius Pontikos*, pp. 152–165. See especially nn. 3 and 99. Here is a translation (Jeremy Driscoll): faith: the beginning of love; the end of love: enlightenment in God (n. 3) Out of gentleness, Enlightenment is born; out of rashness, no Enlightenment (n. 99).

13. Here is n. 67 of Evagrius' text: "Toward love, self-possession [*apatheia*] is the guide: toward Enlightenment [*gnosis*], love."

14. Marsili, *Evagrio Pontico*, pp. 114, 115, 116ff.

15. See Helen Waddell, *The Desert Fathers* (Ann Arbor, 1957), p. 24.

16. Guerric d'Igny, *Sermons* SC 166 (Paris, 1970), pp. 246ff.

ST BERNARD'S INTERPRETATION
OF THE PSALMS IN HIS SERMONS
SUPER CANTICA

Denis Farkasfalvy, O.Cist.

THE CRITICAL EDITION of St Bernard's *Sermons on the Song of Songs* (SC) identifies altogether 5526 biblical quotations. A little more than half of them are taken from the Old Testament and about half these, 1210 quotations, are from the Psalms.[1] Studying the use of the Bible by St Leo the Great, A. Lauras compiled similar statistics on longer texts by St Ambrose, St Jerome, St Augustine, and, of course, St Leo the Great. In all the texts he examined, about half of the Old Testament quotations were taken from the Psalms.[2] Our first conclusion is, therefore, that Bernard's predilection for quoting the Psalms is neither typically medieval nor especially monastic. He stands in an exegetical tradition originating with the great classics of the patristic heritage which he follows in the selection of his biblical sources.

The Vulgate's text of the Psalms consists of altogether 1775 verses. From these, in the sermons on the *Song of Songs*, Bernard quotes only 577. According to my count, an additional 790 verses are quoted or alluded to in the rest of St Bernard's works,[3] but, even so, the conclusion is that Bernard quotes only about seventy-five percent of the Psalter in his works. Thus Vacandard's contention that the Bible could be reconstructed from St Bernard's works is quite exaggerated.

What is more interesting is the relatively even spread of the quotations. In the sermons *Super Cantica* only eighteen verses recur more than four times. In other words, the abundant use of the Psalms does not consist of the continued recurrence of the same favorite verses.

From this fact two conclusions emerge. First, most of the time Bernard uses quotations from the Psalms as a stylistic feature of his sermons. He presents his thoughts as if in a "biblical wrapping", most often the words taken from the Psalms have no other purpose than that of evoking a biblical and liturgical context without essentially contributing to the development of the thought content. It seems that the majority of the quotations from the Psalms in SC pertain primarily to Bernard's biblical style, rather than his biblical doctrine. Second, to those relatively few verses, quoted with frequency by Bernard, we must pay close attention. They are the most important guides to his doctrinal preoccupations, his personal predilections, his inner world of thought and feeling. Within the framework of this paper we can cover only a few of the most preferred Psalm quotations of St Bernard. We choose the following: verse 8 of Psalm 44, verse 28 of Ps 72 and verse 54 of Ps 118.

The use of Ps 44 in SC deserves special attention. One could rightly expect that Bernard would use it extensively and abundantly, since this Psalm itself is also an 'epithalamium,' a wedding song, matching the traditional classification of the *Song of Songs.*[4] And yet the frequent use of Ps 44 is restricted to a few verses. In the eighty-six sermons only verses 3, 5, and 8 are quoted more than five times. And even from these we must put aside verse 5, for it consists of four lines and so its repeated use refers to four different phrases.

For the sake of contrast, it might be interesting to add a word on Ps 44:13, which is not quoted anywhere in the eight volumes of Bernard's *Opera omnia*, although it has been used frequently in the liturgy both as a traditional marial antiphon and as a text on holy virgins: *Vultum tuum deprecabuntur omnes divites plebis.*[5] Bernard's neglect of this passage belies the presupposition that Bernard's biblical quotations are pre-programmed by liturgical texts. Also Bernard does not use verses 4, 6, 7, 17, and 18 in the SC. Thus six of the eighteen verses of Psalm 44, altogether one third of the Psalmist's wedding song found no entry into Bernard's sermons on the Canticles.

Taking these facts into account, it is interesting to see the way in which he handles his favorite verse of the same Psalm, verse 8. It recurs thirteen times in the SC, and altogether thirty-five times in Bernard's collected works. It is one of Bernard's most frequently quoted scriptural passages. The verse consists of two lines a): *Dilexisti iustitiam et odisti iniquitatem.* ('you have loved justice and hated iniquity'); b): *Propterea benedixit te, Deus, Deus tuus, oleo laetitae prae omnibus consortibus tuis* ('therefore God, your God, has anointed you with the oil of gladness above the rest of your fellows').

The first half, line a), appears as the expression of the uncompromising righteousness of a reformer, announcing judgement and expressing a polarized attitude toward a polarized world: love for the good, hatred for evil. Less than half a century before Bernard's time, Pope Gregory VII died in exile with this Psalm verse on his lips. And indeed Bernard quotes it in a similarly righteous and militant way, but **never** in the *Sermons Super Cantica.* The use of this verse is preserved for his militancy against heretics. So, for example, he opens one of his letters against Abelard:

> To the most beloved Yvo, a cardinal presbyter of the holy Roman Church, Bernard, named the abbot of Clairvaux: *to love justice and to hate wickedness.* Master Abelard is a monk without rule, a prelate without discipline, a man who neither keeps not is kept by order, a treacherous fellow, inwardly like Herod, outwardly like St John, perfect in double-talk, with no other trait of a monk except the name and the habit....[6]

In SC only the second half, line b), of the verse is used and that with frequency and predilection. In that passage—*propterea unxit te Deus, Deus tuus, oleo laetitiae prae consortibus tuis*—Bernard finds a special combination and concentration of many of his basic theological ideas. First and foremost, for him the passage is trinitarian: the *Deus tuus* in the quotation refers to the unique relation between the Father and the Son,[7] while the ointment (*unctio*) means the Holy Spirit.[8] For Bernard Ps 44:8 describes the event of the incarnation at which Christ is constituted, made what is called, *Christos* or *unctus,* 'the Anointed One,' the possessor of the fulness of the divinity, a fulness destined for distribution among us. The expression *prae consortibus tuis* means not only that his anointing exceeds any other person's spiritual graces but also that Christ's anointing is destined to be participated in by his many brothers. In Bernard's texts the phrase *prae consortibus tuis* is often replaced

by the Patristic variant *prae participibus tuis* in order to emphasize
that Christ's fulness is the source of every grace obtained.[9] The expression *oleum laetitae*—the oil of gladness—is equally important, if
not more important, for Bernard. It illustrates the reception of any
grace, charism, and, in particular, the reception of the fulness of
God in the Incarnation, as an ecstatic event of joy which then remains forever a source of joyful exaltation for all who participate
in it.

In SC 67 Bernard reveals that Ps 44:8 has had, indeed, a great
personal impact on him, and was the source of deep spiritual experiences:

> O good Jesus, how much sweetness has he [the Psalmist] in-
> fused into my nostrils and ears by his song about the oil of
> gladness with which God has anointed you above all your
> fellows (SC 67, 7: II, 193).

Clearly, Bernard is well aware of his special attachment to this
verse as a source of renewed experience of joy—a true 'biblical experience.'[10]

Bernard worked on SC for about 20 years (1135–1153) and left
his commentary unfinished. These sermons are practically the only
sequence of texts that can be lined up in chronological order with
sufficient certainty for studying the changes that occurred in his
thinking and style during the last two decades of his life. His use of
the Psalms in SC could also be researched from such a point of
view. One example will suffice.

In the SC twenty-one Psalm verses are quoted five or more
times. Of these four refer to the human heart, as the seat of feeling
and affection.[11] It can hardly be a mere coincidence that none of
these four verses is quoted beyond sermon 57; they do not recur
in the sermons which he wrote in the last six to eight years of his
life.[12] Incidentally, none of them appears in his last treatise, *De consideratione*, either. This fact must be taken as another sign that, in
the last phase of his life, both in his thought and his vocabulary the
role of the affective or the emotional tends to recede considerably.

In contrast to this we notice the consistent frequency with which
Ps 72:28 appears throughout his eight-six sermons on the *Song of
Songs*. It is used for the first time in sermon 7, and for the last time

in sermon 85, which is the last complete sermon of the collection. The passage might appear trivially short and simple: *Mihi autem adhaerere Deo bonum est.* But Bernard uses it in a rich doctrinal context, governed by the Pauline text 1 Cor 6:17 which has been, as Yves Congar has noticed, of capital importance for shaping his thought about the soul's mystical union with God. The Pauline passage says: *Qui autem adhaeret Domino, unus spiritus est.*[13] The two quotations sometimes appear side by side,[14] but, more frequently, they are fused: the *adhaeret Domino* of the Pauline passage is replaced by *adhaerere Deo* of Ps 72. This detail is of theological importance: Bernard emphasizes that what he speaks about is a spiritual union with the Godhead, not with Christ. The mystical union, by which, according to Bernard, the soul is completely pervaded and absorbed yet fully retains its individuality, is conceivable only with the divinity, and not with the sacred humanity of Jesus.[15] Thus, the use of Ps 72:28 constitutes an interesting case: on the one hand, the Psalm verse has only a supportive and secondary role, subordinate to 1 Cor 6:17, but, on the other hand, one single word from it is so crucial that it transforms the wording of the Pauline quotation to serve an important theological qualification.[16]

I should like to conclude by taking a quick look at a quotation that appears quite closely connected with Bernard's doctrine about the monastic life. Ps 118:54 appears nine times in the SC and only six times in the rest of his works. The text of the Vulgate is: *Cantabiles mihi erant iustificationes tuae in loco peregrinationes meae.*

The *iustificationes* is interpreted by Bernard in a Pauline sense, as standing for God's deeds of justice leading to man's justification, more briefly his deeds of grace. And thus in Bernard's exegesis, the verse eloquently expresses the state of mind from which prayer, song, thanksgiving, religious writing, and poetry proceed, from which works like the sermons on the *Song of Songs* themselves are born. The verse gives voice to both the situation of the monk as being on pilgrimage, on a religious voyage toward the heavenly home, and to the experience of God's grace, causing in him exultation, joyful songs, mystical poetry. By using this verse, Bernard speaks of his own religious *ars poetica*.

The unforgettably beautiful ending of his first sermon *Super Cantica* provides the best commentary to this verse. Bernard intro-

duces this passage by the phrase "if you reflect on your own experience" (*si experientiam vestram advertatis*), and thus makes it clear
that he speaks about the inner life of his monks, the addressees of
the sermons *Super Cantica*. He then enumerates all the different
spiritual experiences of a monk's inner life and asserts that from
them a ceaseless stream of songs and canticles emanate. Then he
finishes by quoting Ps 118:54:

> Whenever temptation is overcome, or a sin gets conquered,
> or an impending danger is avoided, or the trap of the lurk
> ing enemy is detected, or some passion of the soul, which
> had turned into long-standing habit, is cured once and for
> all, or a virtue, persistently desired and repeatedly sought is
> finally obtained by God's gift, does not the soul break out,
> as the Prophet says, into thanksgiving and in songs of praise?
> Is God not blessed for his benefits, for each and every one of
> his gifts? Otherwise, on the day of judgement, she [the soul]
> would be found lacking in gratitude, if she cannot say:
> "Your deeds of justice were for me a matter of singing in
> the place of my pilgrimage."[17]

We have seen how, in the works of St Bernard, the Psalms are
essential for both style and doctrine. We have seen how certain
verses are of essential importance for expressing his thought, while
others are of little consequence. I hope to have demonstrated also
that, with the ciritical edition of his works in hand, we have reached
the point at which a thorough, reliable, and systematic study of his
biblical exegesis can be carried out, a study that promises a great
deal of progress in exploring the doctrine and the person of this
great Cistercian saint.

Our Lady of Dallas Abbey

NOTES

1. I arrived at this figure from the biblical apparatus of the critical edition of Leclercq and Talbot (SBOp 1–2).

2. However, only in the case of the texts of Jerome and Ambrose did he find a one-to-one ratio between Old and New Testament quotations. In Augustine the Old Testament texts, in St Leo the New Testament quotations were much more preponderant. A. Lauras, "Saint Léon le Grand et l'Écriture Sainte,' *Studia Patristica* VI, (1962), 127–40.

3. This is based on the unpublished biblical index of St Bernard's *Opera Omnia* to which Dom Leclercq has kindly granted me access.

4. See SC 1, 8: "epithalamii carmen" and "nuptiale carmen" (1, 6, 15, 19) See also in SC 2, 2, the long monologue pronounced in the name of the saints of the Old Testament ("perfectus quisque" or "quisquis tunc spiritualis esse poterat", that is, whoever has been given by anticipation the grace of knowing Christ in advance). This passage of eighteen lines contains four quotations of Ps 44 (v. 3 twice, verse 5, and verse 8) and is, indeed, written from the point of view of the Psalmist.

5. In the Cistercian Missal this served as Introit for the feast of the Annunciation and, was also used for liturgical texts "De communi Virginum."

6. Ep 193 (8:44–45).

7. There is, however, no indication that Bernard would have interpreted the first "Deus" as a vocative, as it appears in Heb 1:9 (ho theos). Yet Bernard would picture the "anointment of Jesus" in trinitarian terms, most explicitly in Quad 3, 1: "Unxit Pater Filium" (4:335).

8. Bernard connects Is 61:1 ("Spiritus Domini super me") with our passage in order to express that "the ointment" of Christ is the fulness of the Spirit. Most clearly in SC 16, 13 (1:96) and SC 32, 3 (1:228).

9. In SC only once, in 14,4 (1:78), but frequently in other sermons: VNat 1,1 (4,235), Quad 1, 2–3 (twice: 4:355), Asspt 2,9 (5:238), Div 33, 8 (611:227).

10. See C. Bodard, "La Bible, expression d'une expérience religieuse chez saint Bernard," *S Bernard théologien*, ASOC 9, 3–4 (1953) Rome, 24–45.

11. Ps 7:10: "Scrutans corda et renes Deus (SC 3, 2; 9, 4; 17,10; 42, 8; 55, 2)
   Ps 50:19: "cor contritum et humiliatum Deus non despicies" (SC 10, 5; 10, 6; 10, 8; 12, 10; 20, 1; 28, 12; 30, 7; 56, 7)
   Ps 38:4: "concaluit cor meum et in meditatione mea exardescet ignis" (SC 10, 5; 22, 2; 31, 4; 49, 4; 57, 7)
   Ps 103:15: "vinum laetificat cor hominum" (SC 9, 8; 16, 15; 18, 5; 23, 5; 30, 3; 44, 1; 54, 12)

12. The third phase of the redaction of the SC started (sermons no. 50–83) before 1145 and must have progressed rather quickly for in SC 80, 8 we find an allusion to the Council of Reims which took place in 1148. J. Leclercq, "Recherches sur les sermons sur les Cantiques, III. Les étapes de la rédaction" in *Recueil d'études sur saint Bernard et ses écrits*, Roma (Storia e letteratura) I (1962), 232. Leclercq points out that in 1146–1147 Bernard was constantly traveling (*ibid.*, note 4).

13. Congar thought that this was the most frequently quoted scriptural passage in St Bernard's writing ("c'est, pensons-nous, de toute l'Écriture, celui qu'il cite ou évoque le plus souvent"); "L'ecclésiologie de saint Bernard" in *Saint Bernard theologien*, ASOC IX, 3–4 (1953), 148. His conjecture was quite close. The biblical apparatus of the Opera Omnia indicates that it is the third most often used biblical passage with fifty occurrences (Rom 9:5 is used —most often as a doxology concluding the sermons—seventy-six times; Mt 11:29 occurs in the apparatus fifty-eight times).

14. In SC three times: 1:227; 2: 218 and 2:221, but four more times in other works: 4:434; 64:95; 6/1:97 and 6/2:149.

15. God alone is capable of affecting the soul with pure and unrestricted immediacy: "praerogativa haec summo atque incircumscripto spiritui, qui solus, cum
docet angelum sive hominem scientiam, instrumentum non quaerit nostrae cor-
poreae auris, sicut nec sibi oris. Per se infunditur, per se innotescit, purus capitur a
puris." (SC 5, 8; 1:25).

16. This fusion of 1 Cor 6:17 with Ps 72:28 is practically everywhere in the
writings of the twelfth-century Cistercian authors: William of St Thierry, Cant I,
130: "unus cum Deo spiritus fit" (*Sources chrét.* 82, 276); Amadeus of Lausanne,
Marial Homilies I 117–8: "qui adhaeret Deo, unus spiritus est" (*SCh* 72, 60);
Baldwin of Ford, *The Sacrament of the Altar* I: "spiritualiter adhaerens Deo unus
spiritus esset" (*SCh* 93, 92).

17. SC 1, 9; 1:7.

WISDOM AND ELOQUENCE
IN ST BERNARD'S
IN DEDICATIONE ECCLESIAE
SERMO PRIMUS

Luke Anderson, O.Cist.

At the core of St Bernard's first sermon *In dedicatione ecclesiae*, we discover a very exact epistemological formula, the understanding of which illumines not only this text but much of the matter in the five remaining Bernardine sermons on Church dedications. On the occasion of Clairvaux's dedication, probably in 1138, St Bernard *sees* one thing, but *understands* something else. What he sees is the dedication ceremony, *the sign*; what he *understands*, the *signified*, is the dedication of the monk.

> It is our own feast because it is the feast of the dedication of
> our own Church. It is still more our own [*magis autem*] be-
> cause it is the feast of our own selves.

The same distinction is made when we are told that what has transpired *visibly* in the church, *in parietibus visibiliter*, the external dedication, seen by all, must be fulfilled *spiritually* in ourselves, *in nobis spiritualiter impleri necesse est.*[2]

St Bernard in this case carefully distinguishes sign-fact from signified-fact, but he also indicates their relationship. In our texts the juxtaposition of these two dedicatory episodes, the one external, the other internal, expresses the unique dynamism extant between the seen and the understood, the sign and the signified. The exposition of Christian truth in terms of signs is an honored medieval procedure and takes its inspiration from St Augustine's rhetorical theories.

In the first portions of this sermon, there are numerous expressions concerning the signified reality, the monk's dedication:

> . . . Your souls are sanctified because of the Spirit of God
> . . . your bodies are sanctified because of your souls, and
> this house is also sanctified because of your bodies.[4]

Under another aspect, the monk's dedication is antecedent to the present sign, so that the sign is validated through a past event:

> What, I ask, can be a greater miracle than the fact that one
> who before could hardly abstain for two days together from
> luxury, gluttony, rioting, drunkenness and all the other similar and dissimilar vices, is now able to pass many years, indeed, all the rest of his life, without a fall.[5]

And summing up his understanding of the signified reality, St. Bernard repeats his ultimate concern in Clairvaux's dedication, that is, the monk's dedication:

> Accordingly, today is your festival, dearest brethren, your
> very own. You have been dedicated to the Lord and He has
> elected and adopted you as his own.[6]

To facilitate the best possible analysis of our text it is essential to review here briefly our understanding of both the nature and function of *the sign* and its relation to *the signified*. Clairvaux's dedication, the sign, manifests and makes present (*repraesentat*) to a knowing faculty something other than this visible dedication, namely, the invisible dedication of the monk.[7] It is thus that we are given two reasons why the festival is our own: it is the dedication of OUR church; and even more so is it our feast because it concerns OUR VERY SELVES, *quia de nobis ipsis*. We conclude, then, that to the sign's revelatory character must be added its essential ordination to something other than itself.

Because of its manifestive and presentative roles the sign is said to be related to the signified first by way of coincidence: there is *a partial likeness*. But when we consider the sign in its character as *ordo*, ordination toward something else, then secondarily we see the relationship of *seen* to *understood* as *antithetical*: there is a distinction because the sign represents *something other than itself*, that is, the signified.[8]

The liturgical actions present in Clairvaux's dedication make use of conventional (*ad placidum*) signs rather than purely natural (*naturale*) signs. Nevertheless, St. Bernard's choice of certain elements in the ritual allows us to see that these certain elements are not exclusively conventional signs. His sermon presents us in point of fact with an admixture of sign types.[9]

Since a partial likeness is seen in both external and internal dedications and established through the use of the quasi-baptismal rites of washing, inscription and anointing—more like natural than conventional signs—the external dedication bears a certain *intrinsic* proportion to the internal dedication. And this entitive quality of *similitude within* the natural sign is its special and peculiar intelligibility and its mediating power; and this fact of similitude and proportion renders the internal dedication or the signified (1) present, (2) initially knowable and (3) ultimately known.[10] In the case of conventional signs, the entitive quality of similitude is *not intrinsic* to the sign, or *within*, and hence the relationship to the signified is not a real relationship, but is rather a relationship of reason. Thus the knowable element in the conventional sign, other than what the sign says concerning itself, does not as signifying have the *formality of being*, but the *formality of intelligibility ad placidum*.[11] Both types of signs communicate knowledge of something beyond themselves; they differ, however, in this: the natural sign has a real relation to the signified as an *in esse rei*, but the conventional sign sets up a relation of reason and is merely *in genere scibilis* taking its origin from the will of the sign maker.[12] In the text under discussion, St. Bernard's sermon has much of its rhetorical and logical vigor from his use of the natural sign.[13]

Moreover, the natural sign is a praedicamental reality *secundum esse*; it is a real accident because it is an *ESSE IN*. But it also is an *esse ad*, and it is relational.[14] Insofar as the sign looks toward the signified it has a real relationship based on its praedicamental reality. But if we ask about the sign's relation to the mind, the second relation, we speak of *transcendental* relations because it is the "essence of the sign" under this aspect to *inform* the human mind and this differs from the praedicamental relation as it looks toward the signified.[15]

The sign usage which "informs" the mind of something "other than itself" may appear, at first glance, as a merely arbitrary predication or perhaps no more than a logical inference or innovative comparison, and this more especially in the use of conventional signs. But in fact, the sign contains the signified in another mode of existence, and informs the mind of this special mode of existence.[16] For this reason we speak of the sign as a SUBSTITUTE or as a VICEGERENT.[17] Out of the partial likeness of sign and signified come the theories of sign types, relationships and of causal actions that are *formal* not *efficient*.

Less important for our present analysis is the antithetical relationship between sign and signified; this aspect of the relationship looks toward the differences. If the sign carries *within* itself (natural sign) or *along with itself* (conventional sign) something similar to itself, yet different, this difference can not be ignored. This means that under one aspect the sign is a kind of material *in qua*, while the signified is a kind of form conferring a certain determination. In our text, the chuch dedication can be said to conceal, to hide, and to veil the monk's dedication. Yet the purpose of the sign as sign is to extend the possibility of knowability and to multiply the objects of knowledge; church dedication offers us the possibility of knowing the monk's dedication; and through the consideration of its various rites in the external consecration it multiplies the knowable objects of internal dedication.[18]

To resolve the tension between partial likeness and antithetical difference we must search for a bonding element, and element enabling and forging the relationship of sign to signified. This element is called in logic the *vis significandi*, or the power of signifying. And its use in rhetoric is extensive. St. Bernard in our text clearly identifies this element in his use of the ritural acts.

> And if you wish to know what I refer to, I am speaking of
> five things: the aspersion, the inscription, the unction, the
> illumination and the benediction.[19]

What is seen, therefore, is this series of liturgical actions; what is understood is this same series of actions transposed and repeated invisibly in the mind and heart of the monk. The thesis is this: Clairvaux's dedication is *seen* in terms similar to baptismal actions;

but such similar baptismal actions are *understood* in terms of the monk's dedication. Therefore, church dedication signifies monk's dedication. Why? Because rites similar to baptismal rites are present in both forms of dedication, ecclesial and personal. And the signified is *in* the sign *in alio esse,* in another mode of existence.[20] St. Bernard makes the same comparison in his sixth sermon on dedication:

> "Doth God take care" for dead walls? Surely no. It is not walls but human beings that can say, "He hath care of us."[21]

The aspersion, benediction, and consecration are the elements that bond the dedications in this sermon, as in sermon one. In both sermons the *vis significandi* acts as a kind of middle term joining the sign to the signified; the *vis significandi* can also be considered as a kind of analogical usage since the terms both reveal and veil rites that are only *secundum quid* the same, but really *simpliciter* different. One other complication must not be overlooked: the use of baptismal rite images becomes a sign *for* the sign.

The key which unlocks the door and grants entrance into the hidden cellars of St. Bernard's meaning is to be found in an appreciation of the power of signifying.[22] St. Bernard makes explicit the sequel of the human pontiff's action:

> . . . the same things [the five ritual acts of dedication] are being accomplished invisibly in our souls by "Christ ministering as the High Priest of the good things to come."[23]

We conclude: Christ's actions are analogous to the actions of the human pontiff; the interior dedicating rites are analogous to the external dedicating rites; and the monk's soul receives a dedication analogous to the dedication received by the church.[24]

In this sermon of dedication St. Bernard follows the usual literary lines of the rhetorical process.[25] He begins by combining introduction and statement of facts:

> My Brothers, we ought to observe today's festival all the more devoutly for the reason that it is so peculiarly our own.[26]

In paragraph two of the critical edition we find a preview calculated to capture the audience's attention and to prepare them for the sermon's essential thesis and its defense:

> Perhaps you would like to have some evidence of this earthly sanctity [the monk's] of which I speak, and wish me to show you some of the miracles of these earthly saints?[27]

The passage then traces in large lines the conversion of the monk.

In the third paragraph, St. Bernard, in a kind of apostrophe, addresses the question of the monastic life's dignity and concludes with the words of the psalmist: ". . . Blessed is the people whose God is the Lord." This paragraph can also be interpreted not as intoductory and adventitious but as part of the sermon's argument, and a kind of anticipated refutation of objections. In the following paragraph the proper rhetorical argument with some of its parts, that is, *proposition, reasons,* and *proof of reasons,* makes its appearance. Except for a brief and trenchant conclusion, the remaining portion of the text is concerned with argument.[28] We have already seen the argument: For each external rite in Clairvaux's consecration there exists a corresponding action/rite in the soul of the monk. This action/rite takes its origin either exclusively from God or from God and the monk in cooperation.[29]

The argument is developed along the lines of likenesses and differences in keeping with the doctrine of partial likenesses and antithetical relations.[30] And following the lead given by the author of the *Rhetorica ad Herennium,* St. Bernard places his stronger proofs at the beginning and the end of the argumentative section, treating *aspersion* and *blessing* more fully than the other three rites.[31]

The dedication of Clairvaux's church as a sign is a *practical* sign, not a speculative one. The practical sign, like the speculative sign, properly expresses the true, but unlike the speculative sign it sees the true in its role of leading to right action.[32] Thus it presupposes the will (the Church's, and under another aspect, St. Bernard's) as the condition for its existence. This *leading* then is the known object as a directive for operation, but in the order of formal cause, not in the area of efficient cause. For the sign looks to knowing and not to actually doing; the knowing for the practical sign is directing.[33] St. Bernard sees the church dedication as a series of practical signs; and the bulk of his argument will be aimed at showing the signified reality made present in the five dedicatory rites.[34]

The ritual aspersions in the material temple are inspired by the rite of Christian initiation. These aspersions as used in the dedication denote first the purifications and the exorcisms prior to the baptism of place; later they are considered to be the actual consecration of place. As a practical sign the washing accords with the known and expressed intention of the sign's author.[35] According to St. Bernard, what is signified is the invisible cleansing action of Christ sprinkling the monk with hyssop so that the monk's soul may be whiter than snow.[36] Then by an artistic use of figures of words, in this case repetition and accumulation-climax, St. Bernard pauses over the verb, to wash, *lavare*.

> He [Christ] washes us . . . in the confession [of sin], He
> washes us with the water of contrite tears, He washes us
> with the sweat of our penitential labor.[37]

In these three washings the monk himself provides, as it were, the water: confession, contrition, and penance. Then Christ works with these human counterparts, these "waters," these conditions and moral contributions, and produces the monk's holiness.

But the text speaks of yet another washing, this time with a special water (*aqua illa pretiosissima*), a water not produced by man's good will but flowing spontaneously from the fountain of Christ's opened side.

> . . . More particularly [*magis autem*] He washes us with that
> most precious water which has issued forth from the very
> fountain of piety, from his very side (Jn 19:34).[38]

This most precious water and the consequent washing are the direct and exclusive results of Christ's saving death, the efficacy of which is manifested primarily in baptism, and by extension, to the sign's signified reality: monastic holiness.

St. Bernard extends the sign type. The very instruments of aspersion, that is, the hyssop and the salted water, are external signs of interior purification. The hyssop points to penitential activity, and the addition of salt to water suggests that wisdom and faith are saved from insipidity by the condiments of fervor and hope.[39] Thus, washing interpreted analogously relates to baptism, to ecclesial dedication, and to monastic consecration. The seen and understood differ, but there is similitude.

The second rite, the inscription, consists of the pontiff's tracing the letters of the Greek and Latin alphabets on the church floor. And this indicates the instruction in faith and piety to be disseminated in this sacred place. As a practical sign it indicates that the invisible Christ traces invisible marks of belief and devotion upon the soul of the monk: *inscribit digito Dei* (Ex 31:18). The evident reference is to Sinai and to God's writing on the two tablets of the Testimony, because the commandments were "inscribed by the finger of God." And according to St. Bernard, when Christ cast out devils by the finger of God, he did so by the power of the Holy Spirit who is in fact the finger of God. Christ now continues to inscribe his law invisibly on the fleshly tablets of our hearts and he does this by giving us a "new" spirit, thus fulfilling the promise made by Ezechiel: the stony heart will be taken away and a heart of flesh will be given (Ezk 11:19). By the use of literary antithesis, St. Bernard then describes this new heart: it will not be stubborn or Judaic, but affectionate, but meek, but docile, but devout.[40] Happy the monk so taught of God. But faith must feed piety, and proper belief must support and prompt good behavior: be mindful of God's commands, but be mindful in order to do them (Ps 102: 18, 103:18).[41]

In this practical sign, the human pontiff's inscriptions on the church's pavement signifies Christ's and the Holy Spirit's inscriptions on the stony tablet of the monk's heart. And this invisible inscription gives the monk a heart of flesh. The similitudes here are evident and the directing office of the sign clear and the inscriptions are in highly differing modes of existence. And the causality is obviously formal.[42]

The third practical sign, the anointing of the walls of the visible temple with holy chrism, suggests to St. Bernard the invisible anointing of the monk by "the unction of spiritual grace" and the "lubricating" quality of such grace. His thought moves from a consideration of generic effects to specific ones. In general, grace should "help our infirmity" (Rm 8:26). More specifically, St. Bernard employs paradox, a special figure of thought, to stress the role of grace in dealing with a specific infirmity. We cannot, as he says, avoid the cross; yet without the sweetness of grace we can not support the bitterness of the cross. What is the resolution? The anointing of spiritual grace solves the dilemma. Such grace is an unguent which soothes and heals the abrasions caused by the specific monastic crosses of monastic observances and penances. It is necessary, therefore, that the chrism of grace penetrate every ascetical experience.

> ... Our cross is truly anointed [*crux ... inuncta*] so that, through the grace of the Spirit, who helps us, our penance is agreeable and delightful [*suavis et delectabilis*], our bitterness most sweet [*amaritudo nostra dulcissima*].[43]

Thus the sign, the chrismatic oil as a confirming and consecratory vehicle for the dedication of the church's walls, is analogous to the signified, the lubricating action of the Holy Spirit sustaining the walls of monastic observances and penances which surround and protect the monk.

The illumination rite, the fourth practical sign, receives a very brief treatment. The reason for this may be seen in St. Bernard's frequent use of certain correlatives: shining and illuminating, *ardere et lucere*.[44] According to our present text, the sacred place will shine out as a light surrounded by darkness, but it should also enlighten those upon whom it shines. This rite signifies that the monk's light should so shine upon men that they are necessarily enlightened, and thus men will be led to glorify God because of the monk's shining good works. The monk is said to be Christ's candle. And Christ will not place "his" candle, *lucernam suam*, under a bushel. No, the candle must be on the candelabrum so as to enlighten. The witness role of the visible edifice is to be repeated by the visible good works of the monk, and such witnessings are analogous.[45]

The final rite and the fifth practical sign is the blessing or benediction of the church. The signified is immediately stated:

> With regard to the benediction [of the monk], that is reserved for the end when the Lord will "open his hand and fill with blessing every living creature" (Ps 144:16, 145:16).[46]

St. Bernard then distinguishes the four earlier rites from the benediction. He unites the earlier rites under the concept of *merit*:

> The four preceding operations constitute merits [*constant
> merita*].[47]

But the last ceremony, he goes on to say, is unique for it concerns
awards.

> . . . In the benediction are the rewards [*sunt praemia*].[48]

According to St. Bernard, the four external rites as signs veil the
offer of grace, which grace when well used leads to merit, and the
external rite of benediction as sign veils the reward which is the
monk's entrance into "house not made with hands, eternal heaven"
(2 Co 5:1).

This "house" is composed, says St. Bernard, of "living stones"
(1 P 2:5); and it is built on the harmony of angels and of men. But
the full construction of this "house" awaits the end-time and the
final benediction. To explain the harmony in the eternal heaven,
St. Bernard insists that even as wood and stone *disjoined* do not
constitute a "house," so *only* by the union of angels and men can a
heavenly "house" be constituted. The union and harmony are
not, however, made by human hands, that is, by human effort.
The union is the benediction, a reward. As the grace which allows
us to merit is gratuitous, so the reward.[49]

The signified thus becomes the invisible heavenly place where
angels and men dwell harmoniously, an eternal place reserved for
the sanctified monk. But the concept of harmony is insufficient.
Using a figure of local motion, St. Bernard now conceives of God
as being also drawn to this place even as God is conceived as being
drawn to dwell in a physical place, the earthly temple. The *ultimate*
benediction occurs only when God by his presence "beatifies" the
"living stones" in the "house not made by hand," and this point
introduces the new question of the harmony of God with men and
angels.[50]

If the stones and wood were endowed with sense and intelligence
would they not, asks St. Bernard, be privy to all the words and
deeds of an earthly king in his earthly palace? They would indeed!

So it is also with the living rational souls (angels and men) in the eternal palace of the heavenly king. The "living stones" are privy to the secrets of the Trinity. God has an earthly house and a heavenly house; his presence creates the blessedness. And so St. Bernard concludes with the words of the Psalm: "Blessed are they that dwell in your house, O Lord: they shall praise you for ever and ever" (Ps 83:5, 84:5).[51]

Then, turning aside from the benediction seen as objective beatitude and "the glory of God's majesty beatifying" and the objective presence of God, St. Bernard deals with the subjective side of the benediction and with the actions of the "living stones" in the presence of this God.

> For the more they see, and the more they understand, and
> the more they know, by so much the more do they love, by
> so much the more do they praise, and so much more fully
> admire.[52]

This artistic use of repetition, polysyndeton, accumulation, gradation, and rhetorical climax should not blind us to the rich and accurate theological account of the subjective activities of the blessed in the face of the beatifying object.

St. Bernard then takes up the task of explaining the root cause of the harmony that binds the "living stones" one to another.[53] He appeals to a source other than the stones themselves.

> For the more intimate is their union with essential charity
> which is God (1 Jn 4:16), the more powerful must be the
> bonds of love that unite them one with another.[54]

To expand his concepts on the mode of harmony of the "living stones," St. Bernard makes an accommodated use of Isaiah's "The solder is good" (Is 12:7). The solder is, says St. Bernard, understood in two ways: it is full knowledge and perfect love. The "living stones" *participate* in this fulness, and in this perfection. United to one another precisely because they are perfectly united to God *in the radiance of his truth*, they penetrate all things; they have *full* knowledge. Then this understanding, shared with God, destroys the suspicions which would separate the "living stones" from each other, and so it insures *perfect* love.[55] In a deeper sense, as we have already seen, the more intimately each stone is united to essential charity, God, the more powerful will be its bonding with all others.

The benediction of Clairvaux's church is, therefore, the practical sign of reward, a dwelling place for the monk in a "house not made by hands, eternal heaven," a place constituted by "living stones" held together by full knowledge and perfect love, with God as the author of this solder.

In his rhetorical conclusion to this sermon, St. Bernard employs the classical forms of *wish, desire,* and *prayer*: if we wish to reach this happy home, the place of blessedness, we must "long and faint for the courts of the Lord" (Ps 83:3, 84:4), and pray fervently, saying, "One thing I have asked of the Lord, this will I seek after: that I may dwell in the house of the Lord all the days of my life" (Ps 26:4, 27:4). And we must go beyond this to imitate the zeal of David who took no rest until "he had found a place for Yahweh, a home for the Mighty One of Jacob" (Ps 131:5, 132: 5).[56]

The monk's soul, caught up in the external rites through his body, and visited by interior grace, is Yahweh's true home and the place of Jacob's Mighty One. Clairvaux's dedicatory ritual is but the practical sign of this higher dedication. The penitential aspersions, the inscription rites which prompt belief and piety, the anointing which issues in healing grace and the illumination which forms witnesses, each and all of these cause meritorious activity and achieve the reward of benediction. These invisible realities are understood when St. Bernard sees the dedication of Clairvaux's church.

St. Mary's Monastery

NOTES

1. St. Bernard, Ded 1; SBOp 5:370, 11.12–13. See also Ded 4: SBOp 5:396, ll. 12–15.

2. Ded. 1; SBOp 5:372, ll. 19–20.

3. "For a sign is a thing which, over and above the impression it makes on the senses, causes something else to come into the mind as a consequence of itself. . . ." St. Augustine, *De doctrina christiana*, L. 11, c. 1. See also L. 11, cc. 2 and 6; L. 111, c. 25.

4. Ded 1; SBOp 5:371, ll. 2–4. In this text the *efficient* cause of monastic sanctity is ascribed to the Holy Spirit, and through the soul to the body and ultimately to *the place* or the church. But this does not contradict the nature of the causality of the sign. Because the sign's causality is in the realm of *formal* cause; the dedication ceremony is the vicegerent of the monastic dedication and thus makes present and manifests monastic dedication *in alio esse*.

5. Ded 1; SBOp 5:371, ll. 14–16.

6. Ded 1; SBOp 5:372, ll. 3–4.

7. "Nor is there any reason for giving a sign except the desire of drawing forth and conveying into another's mind what the giver of the sign has in his own mind." St. Augustine, *De doctrina christiana*, L. 11, c. 2.

8. "Primum est *ratio manifestativi* seu *repraesentativi*. Secundum *ordo ad alterum*, scil., ad rem quae repraesentatur, quae debet esse diversa a signo . . . et ad potentiam cui manifestat et repraesentat rem a se distinctam. Et quidem manifestativum ut sic constat non dicere relationem." John of St. Thomas, *Ars logica* 11, q. 21, art. 1, in *Cursus Philosophicus Thomisticus*, ed. Reiser (Turin, 1930).

9. "Now some signs are natural, others conventional. Natural signs are those which, apart from any intention or desire of using them as signs, do yet lead to the knowledge of something else. . . . Conventional signs, on the other hand, are those which living beings mutually exchange for the purpose of showing, as well as they can the feelings of their minds, or their perceptions, or their thoughts." St. Augustine, L. 1, c. 2.

10. "Quando enim domus ista *per manus pontificum* dedicata est Domino, *propter nos* sine dubio factum est . . . ." (Italics are mine) Ded 1; SBOp 5:372, ll. 15–18. "Videte ergo si non dignum sit ut festum agamus diem, quo nos assumpsit in proprios, et investivit se per ministeriales et vacarios suos. . . . " Ded 1; SBOp 5:372, ll. 12–13. There is a slight change of venue here since the human pontiff is judged to have a ministerial role in monastic dedication as well as church dedication.

11. "Ex dicitis colliges in signis ad placitum [conventional] rationem signi etiam per relationem ad signatum explicandam esse. Sed relatio ista rationis est, et non solum consistit signum in extrinseca denominatione. . . . " John of St. Thomas, *Ars*, 11, q. 21, art. 2.

12. " . . . Quod ratio cognoscibilis et objecti in ente reali et rationis potest esse univoca; aliae enim sunt divisiones entis in esse rei, aliae in genere scibilis. . . . " John of St. Thomas, *Ars*, 11 q. 21, art. 2.

13. "Relatio signi naturalis ad suum signatum, qua constituitur in esse signi, realis est, et non rationis quantum est ex se, et vi sui fundamenti et supponendo existentiam termini caeterasque conditiones relationis realis." John of St. Thomas, *Ars*, 11, q. 21, art. 2.

14. "Nam D. Thomas expresse ponit quod signum est in genere relationis fundatae in aliquo alio; sed relatio fundata in aliquo alio est relatio *secundum esse*, et de praedicamento ad aliquid si realis sit; ergo signum consistit in relatione secundum esse." John of St. Thomas, *Ars*, 11, q. 21, art. 1.

15. "Et ideo consideratur in signo et vis movens potentiam, et ordo substituentis ad id pro quo movet. Et pimum et relatio transcendentalis, secundum praedicamentalis." John of St. Thomas, *Ars*, 11, q. 21, art. 1.

16. "Cognoscit ergo signa tum *ut contentum in signo*, et ad ipsum pertinens, et, ut dicit D. Thomas, Herculem cognoscit in statuta." John of St. Thomas, *Ars*, 11, q. 21, art. 6.

17. ". . . Ratione cujus signum dicitur instrumentale, non quidem quasi instrumentum efficientis, sed quasi substitum objecti, non informans sicut species sed ab extrinseco repraesentans." John of St. Thomas, *Ars*, 11, q. 21, art. 5.

18. Ded 1; SBOp 5:372, ll. 15–18, and 19–20.

19. "Et si vultis scire, haec utique sunt: aspersio, incriptio, inunctio, illuminatio, benediction." Ded 1; SBOp 5:372, ll. 21–22.

20. "Et si instetur: Quid est illud in signato conjunctum signo, et praesens in signo praeter ipsum signum et entitatem ejus? Respondetur esse ipsummet signatum in alio esse . . ." John of St. Thomas, *Ars*, 11, q. 21, art. 6.

21. Ded 4; SBOp 5:396, ll. 16–17.

22. In various mss the titles indicate that readers of this sermon easily discerned the importance of the ritual acts in St. Bernard's teaching on interior dedication. In Codex 344 (Maioris Monasterii) we read: *De qinque sacramentis Dedicationis*. In Codex Austriaci, and in Codex Erlangensis 282 (Fontis Salutis) we read: *Quid significet aspersio e cetera quae fiunt in Dedicatione*. And in Codex Trecensis 832 (Sancti Stephani) we read: *De Sacramento Dedicationis*. Ded 1; SBOp 5:370, note on l. 8.

23. Ded 1; SBOp 5:372, ll. 21–23.

24. ". . . Quia signum semper est minus significato, et ab ipso ut a mensura dependens." John of St. Thomas, *Ars*, 11, q. 21, art. 1.

25. *Rhetorica ad Herennium*, 1, iii, 4 (Cambridge, Massachusetts, 1954).

26. Ded 1; SBOp 5:370, ll. 9–10.

27. Ded 1; SBOp 5:371, ll. 9–10.

28. *Rhetorica ad Herennium*, 111, ix, 16–17.

29. Ded 1; SBOp 5:372, ll. 21–23.

30. See Aristotle, *Topics*, ed. Richard McKeon (New York, 1941) c. 17, 108a, 6–15; c. 16, 107b, 38–40; 108a, 1–5; c. 13, 104b, 20–25.

31. *Rhetorica ad Herennium*, 111, IX, 18.

32. John of St. Thomas, *Cursus Theologicus*, IX, *De Sacramentis*, disp. 22, art. 1, dubium quintum, 99 and 100; ed. Ludovicus Vives (Paris, 1885).

33. "Ex quo fit, quod intellectus practicus, quando respicit objectum exterius, non respiciat illud ad acquirendam cognitionem, sed ad hoc ut res ad finem aliquem intentum dirigatur, aut perducatur." John of St. Thomas, *De Sacramentis*, IX, disp. 22, art. 1, dubium quintum, 99 and 100.

34. Michael Andrieu, *Les Ordines Romani du haut moyen âge* (Paris, 1931–1961), IV, 315–36, 359–94.

35. ". . . Mensura autem veritatis practicae non est res ut est in se, sed ut concordat cum fine intento et recto." John of St. Thomas, *De Sacramentis*, disp. 22, art. 1, dubium quintum, 99.

36. "Christus . . . invisibiliter quotidie operatur in nobis." Ded 1; SBOp 5:372, ll. 22–24.

37. "Lavat, inquam, nos in confessione, lavat nos lacrimarum imbre, lavat sudore paenitentiae. . . ." Ded 1; SBOp 5:372, l. 2, and 373, l. 1.

38. Ded 1; SBOp 5:373, ll. 1–2.

39. Ded 1; SBOp 5:373, ll. 2–5.

40. ". . . Id est non obstinatum, non iudaicum, sed pium, sed mansuetum, sed tractabile, sed devotum." Ded 1; SBOp 5:373, ll. 9–10.

41. Ded 1; SBOp 5:373, ll. 10–14.

42. ". . . Quia in ratione practici sufficit, quod ex fine et directione ad eum sit operativum, non autem quod ut causa efficiens ipsum respiciat, sed id erit de perfectione practici, salvaturque vere ratio practici, si quod per aliam causam efficitur, ab ipso in finem dirigitur intentum. John of St. Thomas, *De Sacramentis*, disp. 22, art. 1, dubium quintum, 114 and 115.

43. Ded 1; SBOp 5:373, ll. 15–21.
44. St. Bernard, JB; SBOp 5:178, ll. 1–2.
45. Ded 1; SBOp 5:373, ll. 21–25.
46. Ded 1; SBOp 5:374, ll. 1–2.
47. Ded 1; SBOp 5:374, ll. 2–3.
48. Ded 1; SBOp 5:374, ll. 2–3.
49. "... Di suncta ... non faciunt ... solo vera conjunctio ... facit." Ded 1; SBOp 5:374, ll. 6–8.
50. "Sic caelestium spiritum perfecta unitas, sine illa sibi divisione connexa, integram et congruam Deo reddit habitationem, quam ineffabiliter beatificat inhabitans gloria maiestatis." Ded 1; SBOp 5:374, ll. 8–9.
51. Ps 83:5, 84:5.
52. "Quando enim plus vident, plus intelligunt, plus agnoscunt, tanto plus diligunt, tanto magis laudant, tanto amplius admirantur." Ded 1; SBOp 5:374, ll. 15–17.
53. Ded 1; SBOp 5:374, ll. 18–19.
54. "Tanto siquidem maiori ad se invicem dilectione copulantur, quando ipsi caritati, quae Deus est, vicioniores assistunt." Ded 1; SBOp 5:374, ll. 21–23.
55. Ded 1; SBOp 5:374, ll. 23–24, and 375, l. 1.
56. Ded 1; SBOp 5:374, ll. 4–6.

THE PRACTICAL THEOLOGY
OF ST BERNARD AND THE DATE OF THE
DE LAUDE NOVAE MILITIAE

David Carlson

URING THE SUMMER of 1135, just after the Synod of Pisa, Bernard of Clairvaux spent several weeks in Milan, settling a local ecclesiastical controversy officially, but then also engaged in some more impressive, more important business, according to Arnold of Bonneval, the author of the second book of the *Vita prima*. While in Milan, a woman was brought to Bernard; she was "known to all, and for seven years an unclean spirit had troubled her." Bernard bid the demon be gone, and it went, and

> all who were present rejoiced, and raised their hands to the heavens, and gave thanks to God, who had visited them from on high. Word of the event went out, and its fame increased and suddenly shook the whole city; in churches, in the plazas, and on street corners, everyone gathered; everywhere everyone was speaking of the man of God.... Work and commerce ceased; the whole city stood suspended by this spectacular event.[1]

Three days later, while Bernard was at Mass, the Milanese brought "him a little girl, gnashing her teeth and wailing, whom a devil was besetting with fearsome onslaughts." Bernard wet his fingers from the chalice and moistened the girl's lips; "and without delay, as if Satan were burning, [the devil] was unable to bear the force of the infusion, and left suddenly, bursting forth in a stream of vomit most vile. Thus was this person purged...."[2]

Now, the biographer reveals, Bernard had an epidemic on his

hands. Because of Milan's ecclesiastical deviations, demons "had been infesting very many, with free rein."[3] Bernard cured another possessed Milanese, a "great aged woman . . . once an honored matron, . . . at whose breast a devil had been sitting for many years."[4] Then word of Bernard's exorcisms began to spread beyond Milan: "Word of what was being done in Milan got out, and talk of the man of God ran through all Italy."[5] Soon, people were pouring into Milan from the surrounding countryside, bringing their possessed, their ill, their crippled. Bernard healed them all.[6] Then, even after he left Milan for Pavia, a Milanese peasant with his possessed wife followed after Bernard, and caught up with him only at the outskirts of Pavia; Bernard healed her too.[7]

Arnold magnifies the power that Bernard had wielded more facelessly behind the scenes, to heal the Milanese Church, with these public, concrete expressions of it in the exorcisms. The power that Bernard had used to heal the split in the city's church, to cast out its demons of heterodoxy, finds clearer, more tangible expression in his miracles of exorcism. In the same way that he had ended the *daemonum licencia* of the city, as Arnold points out, just so Bernard solved Milan's problems with the hierarchy and returned it *in sedis apostolicae obedientiam*.[8] These instances of exorcism serve Arnold for doubling St. Bernard's *virtus*.

But at least since Dante made Bernard his final guide to his final mystical vision of the celestial rose at the end of the *Paradiso*, we have become more accustomed to another, different Bernard, Dante's Bernard, the "one who, while still in this world, through contemplation tasted of the peace" of paradise,[9] confirmed comparatively recently in the title of Gilson's widely influential *The Mystical Theology of St. Bernard*: Bernard the mystical theologian, spiritual doctor, and contemplative mystic. For contemporaries of Bernard, however, such as Arnold of Bonneval and the citizens of Milan, Bernard was also a caster out of demons, not necessarily only in the literal sense, but also in the more figurative sense which his exorcisms take on in Arnold's account of his doings in Milan: Bernard was a powerful person who worked miracles and solved problems. Arnold and the other authors of the *Vita prima* wrote not analyses of Bernard's contemplative doctrine, nor even a spiritual or psychological biography; Arnold wrote the story of this other Bernard, who was engaged in practical problems and who was practically powerful.

Bernard's *Liber ad milites Templi de laude novae militiae* shows this side of him, the Bernard who was *potens in opera*,[10] as Arnold also describes him, as clearly as any of his writings, and it also, perhaps more importantly, shows a cooperation between Bernard the contemplative and Bernard the exorcist, a collaboration of Dante's spiritual guide and Arnold's caster out of demons, that makes the Bernard of *De laude* a "philosopher of action,"[11] exercising contemplative authority in service of concrete, practical objectives.

R. W. Southern suggests in his *Making of the Middle Ages* that "the piety of Cîteaux," or more specifically the contemplative spirituality of St. Bernard, found its "secular counterpart" in Chrétien de Troyes' secular ethic of chivalry and romance;[12] but here again, Southern too is speaking only of Dante's Bernard and so cannot quite account for the Bernard of the *De laude novae militiae*. In this treatise, Bernard is not so much pursuing spiritual lines of thought that run parallel to those laid out by Chrétien in the secular realm; rather, Bernard is bringing his contemplative experience to bear on the practical religious concerns of Chrétien's world, in an attempt to solve the practical religious problems posed by knighthood. Bernard's authority for offering solutions to chivalric problems in the *De laude* comes equally from his spiritual accomplishments, as well as from a character that found itself frequently involved with mundane affairs, exercising power in pursuit of relatively mundane goals, and from a character formed in the kind of courtly, chivalric milieu addressed also in the works of Chrétien de Troyes.

The treatise gives the impression of falling apart into two halves, the first taken up apparently with the Knights Templar and the second with a series of of meditations on the spiritual import of the holy places of the Middle East. Bernard first praises the Knights Templar, in response to whose repeated requests and insistence he wrote the treatise, as a "new kind of chivalry, recently risen on the earth," and "unknown to the ages, which ceaselessly wages a twofold war: equally against flesh and blood, and against spiritual iniquity against the heavens." And he bids the Knights Templar to dress "your souls with the armor of faith, as you have your bodies with an armor of steel."[13]

Most of Bernard's praise for the Templars, however, is offered in the form of contrasts, implicit and explicit, between what the good Knights Templar do in the Holy Land and what the bad sec-

ular knights of Europe do at home: unlike secular knights, Bernard
implies, among the Knights Templar, first of all "discipline is not
wanting and obedience is never disdained"; "in food and clothing,
they are wary of all superfluity"; and they live "without wives and
free women." The Knights Templar "at no time either sit idly or
wander on adventure"; "rank is scarcely at all recognized among
them; they give pride of place to betters, not the more nobly
born"; and finally, "rarely do they bathe, preferring to go with
unkempt hair, dirty, darkened by their armor and the sun." [14] Bernard here obliquely draws attention to the faults of secular knights
by a kind of *occupatio*, denying in each instance that the Knights
Templar are prey to what are readily identifiable as notorious
shortcomings of secular knights.

The point Bernard most emphasizes for characterizing the Knights
Templar in contrast to secular knights is that for the Knights Templar "life is secure, since they can expect death fearlessly, and even
desire it with longing and seize it with devotion": the *causa pug-
nantis* is a good one in their situation. But the secular knight, whom
Bernard addresses here in the second person, *tu qui militiam mili-
tas saecularem*, is not similarly "free from that twin peril." The secular knight "must always be fearful, lest either you should kill
your adversary bodily and yourself spiritually, or lest perhaps you
should be killed by him, both bodily and spiritually." [15] The end
or fruit of this wickedness which is secular chivalry," says Bernard,
can only be that "the murderer sins mortally and the murdered
perishes eternally," [16] since the secular knight fights only for "bursts
of senseless rage, an appetite for empty glory, or lust for some trif-
ling earthly possession." [17]

In the course of this series of contrasts, it becomes clear, first,
that Bernard of Clairvaux knows a remarkable amount about contemporary chivalry for a cloistered monk or a mystical doctor. In
chastising the chivalric nobility for having allowed vain extravagance to interfere with its military function, again addressing secular knights in the second person, Bernard incidentally provides a
good deal of detailed information about the early twelfth-century
chivalric habit:

> You dress up your horses with silks and your own armor
> with flashy fabrics; you paint your lances, shields, and sad-

dles; you decorate your bridles and spurs with gold and silver and gems; and, prepared with such pomps, you hasten
in shameful insanity and a shameless stupor to your own
deaths. . . . You burden your eyesight with womanly hair
styles; you trip up your feet with your long, full coverlets;
you bury your fine, delicate hands inside sleeves cut full and
flowing. . . . Are these the insignia of chivalry, or rather
womanly ornaments? Or perhaps you imagine your adversary's sword will be turned back by your gold, that it will
spare for your gems, and not be able to pierce your silks?[18]

And Bernard speaks of the chivalric nobility's characteristic en-
tertainments—its games of chance, its hunting and hawking, its
"mimes, magicians, and romancers, and scurrilous chanteurs," as
well as its tournaments and their attendant festivities[19]—with the
self-assurance of someone who knows what he is talking about.

In the course of this series of contrasts, it also becomes clear that
for Bernard praise and advice for the Knights Templar is only as
important as, and perhaps less important than criticism of the contemporary chivalry with which he shows himself to be so familiar.
Sidney Painter has written that "the chief expounder of the duties
of knights towards the church was, of course," Bernard of Clairvaux, "but his remarks on the subject were addressesd to the Templars. As the Templars were a military monastic order, in Bernard's
own words both knights and monks, his injunctions to them cannot be taken as an expression of his views on the duties and obliga-
tions of knights in general."[20] But the way Bernard frames his
ostensible praise for the Templars—as a series of contrasts between
them and secular knights—and the advice he offers in the *De laude*—
both directly to secular knights and indirectly to them, in the form
of exhortations to the Templars, to shun the behavior typical of
secular knights—indicate instead that the treatise was meant for a
more general audience. In the *De laude*, Bernard was not just preaching to those already converted, as Painter argues, but had in fact
undertaken at least to begin ridding knighthood of the evils to
which it seemed to Bernard to have fallen prey. In the *De laude*,
Bernard is writing not just for the Knights Templar, but also, as he
specifies at one point, "for the benefit or castigation of our knighthood, which soldiers certainly not for God, but for the devil."[21]

The De laude uses praise of a new knighthood to address the problems of contemporary secular knights, those "criminals and pro-
phaners, thieves and blasphemers, murderers, perjurers and adulter-
ers," who "bring joy even to their own, when they go away." [22]

The more enigmatic second half of the *De laude* continues to
speak to the concerns of knights, and again as much to the concerns of secular knights, as to the more limited concerns of the
Knights Templar; but now the treatise does so in the abstract, contemplative mode that we associate more easily with Bernard. The
meditations address the spiritual concerns of knights in ways that
the first five chapters do not. The first five chapters detail the symptoms of spiritual error in outward knightly practice, and offer the
concrete example of the Knights Templar as a corrective; the last
seven chapters deal more directly in spiritual solutions for the spiritual problems of knighthood. More specifically, Bernard here offers knights a version of the *imitatio Christi* adapted for their particular needs and stresses the importance of recognizing the errors
of knightly ways and then of obedience for correcting them.

In the second half of the *De laude*, chapters 6–13, Bernard seems
to leave criticism and advice and to offer a list of places the Knights
Templar are likely to see in the Holy Land, in which description
of the sites is coupled with a parallel series of meditations on the
spiritual significance of the Holy Places. The meditations are ordered not geographically, however, not quite in the form of a travelogue, but begin rather in approximate order of the major events
of Christ's life. Bernard speaks first of Bethlehem, Christ's birth-
place; then of Nazareth, where Christ grew up; of the river Jordan
and Christ's baptism; of Calvary and His crucifixion; and then, in
the longest of the meditations by far, Bernard speaks of the Holy
Sepulcher and the significance of Christ's death and resurrection.

The intention of the sequence of the meditations to this point in
the treatise would seem to be first of all to enjoin knights to follow
Christ, but not only in the comparatively restricted sense that the
travelogue form suggests, that the Knights Templar, and perhaps
other crusading knights, whose intention it was to travel to the
Middle East, would be physically following in Christ's footsteps as
they journeyed to and around the Holy Land, which would render
these meditations of interest only to this circumscript group. Nor
do the initial meditations suggest only that knights should be fol-

lowing Christ in the most general and most generally relevant sense of the *imitatio Christi*, that all Christians ought to follow Christ. Rather, the meditations' emphasis on Christ's death and the significance of his death suggests that the *imitatio Christi* has been specially adapted here.

Bernard's paramount concerns with the wasted, doubly dangerous deaths of secular knights in the first five chapters of the treatise, is matched here in the meditations by the particular emphasis Bernard builds into his explication of Christ's death: that Christ, "with his single death, redeemed both of ours." our "double death, . . . the one spiritual and voluntary, and the other bodily and necessary." [23] His death has meant that knights need not die twice, first in the flesh and then again in the spirit, as they do if they abuse chivalry in service of selfish, worldly concerns. The *imitatio Christi* here, by its dwelling on this result of Christ's death, is cast in a form specially suited to answer the particular needs of secular chivalry.

The last two meditations confirm that the series is neither limited in interest only to the Knights Templar nor so general as to be of relevance to all Christians; here too, Bernard has aimed his advice, subtly but specifically, at knighthood, and especially at unreconstructed secular knights. The last two meditations are on the towns of Bethpage and Bethany, which stand respectively for confession and obedience in Bernard's presentation; again, both topics had figured prominently in the earlier part of the treatise and are given emphatic final position here in Bernard's series of meditations.

Bernard's criticisms of secular knighthood in the first section of the treatise are arranged to provoke in knights recognition of their errors. Here in his meditation on Bethpage, Bernard calls confession "a salvific contrition in the sinner's heart" over such errors, that "takes away their noxious confusion." And he warns tellingly: "nonetheless, the confession of a dead man perishes along with him, as if it had never been," [24] emphasizing again the danger to knights of untimely, ill-prepared death in secular squabbles or tournaments.

In his final meditation, on Bethany, Bernard stresses the importance of obedience: "neither good works, nor contemplation of holy things, nor tears of repentance can be found acceptable," [25] if not in obedience to God; just as earlier, in the first part of the treatise, Bernard had identified secular knighthood's error as disobedience first of all: disobedience to secular authorities and to popular interests, to the dictates of ethical and moral behavior, to knights' own self-interest in salvation, and to the paternal, benificent authority of the church.

Here in Bethany, the *domus oboedientiae*, Lazarus, a figure for the soul dead in sin, was brought back to life in obedience to Christ's command, illustrating "the power of obedience together with the fruits of repentance."[26] To Christ, here again as throughout the meditations the model proposed as proper to knights, "a book and a mirror for life and discipline" for them,[27] such obedience was so important "that He preferred to lose His own life"—as must all knights who soldier Christ-like on God's behalf—"being thus made obedient to the Father, even unto death."[28] Obedience is the first and most prominent point of contrast between the Knights Templar and secular knights; as the subject of the last meditation of the last chapter of the treatise, it is here again prominent as the final word Bernard would leave with his knightly audience.

Others in the church subsequently undertook to criticize chivalric practice from an ecclesiastical perspective, as Bernard did in the *De laude novae militiae*, most notably John of Salisbury, as well as numerous lesser figures such as Etienne de Fougières and Jacques de Vitry.[29] But Bernard was the first to do so, and his was to remain the most subtle and searching churchly critique of knighthood, probably because he was particularly well suited, by his situation and upbringing, to undertake such a criticism. Bernard was born into and throughout his life maintained links with chivalric society, and for all his apparent preference for contemplation was also given to involving himself in relatively mundane affairs.

Clairvaux is in a part of France particularly closely associated with the efflorescence of the secular culture of chivalry and courtly love during the twelfth century.[30] Clairvaux is near Troyes, where during the 1170s and 1180s the court of the Countess Marie de Champagne patronized significant courtly writing, most notably the work of Chrétien de Troyes and probably also Andreas Capellanus, as well as others.[31] The Cistercian practice of adult recruitment meant that many monks, including Bernard himself, entered the monastery at Clairvaux, as they did other Cistercian monasteries, with some first-hand experience of chivalry and courtly love and often with literary experience of it as well.[32] The monks of Clairvaux had been or known knights, and had read or heard romances and courtly lyric by the time they entered the monastery. Leclercq has shown how the language of chivalric society was useful to Bernard in such a situation, for making his intermural *Sententiae* and *Parabolae* specially appealing to such an audience, for example. And he also suggests that the practice of adult recruitment and what it meant in terms of the expectations of adult recruits were also indirectly responsible for the nature and extent of the monastic love literature that began to flourish so notably among Cistercians in the twelfth century.[33]

Bernard's experience was typical in this regard. According to the *Vita prima*, he was born "to parents high in the age's esteem." His father Tescelin "was a man of long and legitimate standing as a knight,"[34] who might reasonably have expected his sons to grow up to be knights too. The adolescent Bernard does seem to have been well suited by nature for success in the secular, courtly society to which his paternity entitled him: he was "well shaped, good looking, gracefully well mannered, sharply intelligent, and well spoken."[35] And a number of the incidents that William of St. Thierry narrates as illustrative of the character of the young Bernard reveal that he did have direct experience of the nascent courtly culture of the twelfth century. The story of the trouvère sent to entertain an ill Bernard with the latest in literary fashion[36] recalls the persistent rumor that Bernard himself wrote secular, courtly verse at some point. This rumor is corroborated in the *Vita prima* by William's account of Bernard's brothers' attempts to encourage him to pursue a career in secular letters, for which they perceived him to have a talent.[37] William's narratives of the women who courted the young Bernard's affections[38] indicate that at least some individuals around Bernard participated in the twelfth-century's new interest in the possibilities of human romance. Bernard's brothers did follow after their father's knightly footsteps, at least some part of the way. In 1111, Bernard turned his back on the *magnas res, spes maiores*[39] that the world of secular, courtly society was offering him, just as he had turned his back on the woman who came to his bed naked one night.[40] He sought out his brothers, to persuade them to join him on his journey to Cîteaux; one of them

had to recover from a wound received in the kind of foolish sport
Bernard later criticized in the *De laude* and had to be freed from his
vanquisher's dungeon before he could assume his new religious
vocation.[41]

Bernard was never quite able to put completely behind him the
courtly, knightly society in which he was raised. It followed him
into monastic life, either in the sense that Bernard retained character traits stamped on him by his knightly upbringing, such as the
irascibility noted by Otto of Freising, for example, and which Bernard himself treated as particularly characteristic of knights in the
De laude,[42] or in the sense that the chivalric society in which he
was raised continued to pursue him actively even after he had entered the cloister. The *De laude* itself, for example, was written in
response to the repeated request of Hugh of Payne, *magister* of the
Knights Templar from their founding in 1128 until his death in
1136, who may possibly also have been Bernard's cousin.[43]

The dates of the founding of the Knights Templar at the Council of Troyes in January 1128 and the death of their first *magister*,
in May 1136, have been used as *termini* for dating Bernard's treatise; he must have written it between the founding of the order
and Hugh's death.[44] The *terminus ex quo* is indubitable: Bernard
was present at the founding of the order, he does seem also to have
written an early draft of the order's *regulae*, and the *De laude* speaks
of the Knights Templar as already in existence.[45] Another consideration, however, Bernard's involvement with another matter of
religious practice and a tangential product of this second involvement, enables reducing the *terminus ad quem* of the *De laude* by
five or perhaps six years and determining that the treatise was written after 1128 certainly, but before 1131.

On the death of Pope Honorius in February 1130, a schism
arose in the Church: the Cardinal Deacon Gregory of Sant'
Angelo was elected Pope Innocent II, and an anti-pope, the
Cluniac Cardinal Priest of St. Calixtus Peter Leonis, took the
name Anacletus II. The split seems to have been largely the result
of factionalism within the Roman Curia, compounded by various
personal ambitions, and local and imperial politics. At any rate,
the split lasted from February 1130 until some months after the
death of Anacletus in January 1138, and the period was one of

profound division of the political and ecclesiastical hierarchies of Western Europe.

The period also saw Bernard of Clairvaux turn from the parochial and monastic concerns that had occupied him up to that point towards larger concerns, those of the Church as a whole and of the relations between the Church and society.[46] Bernard was an early and active supporter of Innocent: Innocent seems soon to have come to regard Bernard as a high-value, general-purpose ambassador, to be called upon to deal with the most difficult problems most efficaciously; and for the seven years of the schism, Bernard was almost constantly on the road canvassing for Innocent, with but a brief period of rest at Clairvaux.[47]

Soon after his election, Innocent had to flee Rome's "great bloodshed, great civic destruction, and terrible profanations of the sacred,"[48] "from the Lion's jaws and the hand of the beast."[49] He travelled north, into France, where, for the first several months of his office, he held a series of consultations and councils in an effort to garner support for his disputed papacy. In addition to their main business—affirming Innocent's election and anathematizing the schismatic Peter Leonis—Innocent's early councils, held in Clermont, Liège, and Reims between November 1130 and October 1131,[50] also enacted a number of disciplinary canons, including prohibitions against clerical marriage, simony, and alienation of Church properties, and affirmations of the Peace and Truce of God and of sanctuary, an apparently regular list of some ten items reaffirmed at each of Innocent's early councils, as far as can be ascertained.

Among the canons on this apparently regular list was a prohibition against participation in tournaments, on pain of denial of ecclesiastical burial:

> We utterly forbid those detestable fairs or festivals where knights customarily gather by agreement and heedlessly fight among themselves to make show of their strength and bravery, whence often result men's deaths and souls' perils. Should any knight die on such an occasion, he should not be denied penance and the last rights if he asks for them; yet let him not enjoy church burial.[51]

The ban was a clever move, from the perspective of the relations between the Church and the chivalric class, in view of the central place tournaments had in the secular culture of knighthood:[52] the Church could in effect move to eliminate multiple immoralities of chivalry, while appearing only to inveigh against its most superficial activity; and the prohibition was reaffirmed repeatedly, by four different Popes (including St. Bernard's protege Eugenius III), up until the beginning of the fourteenth century.[53] Its periodic reinstitutions are a sign at once of the failure of the ban to achieve its desired results, and also of strong, persistent feeling on the matter within the Church; this resolve first found expression during the early months of the papacy of Innocent II, at a time of particularly close association, even intimacy, between Innocent and St. Bernard.

It is impossible to say, though perhaps still interesting to speculate, whose idea the ban was to begin with: perhaps it was a matter of local initiative, subsequently taken up by the Church as a whole, as had been the Peace of God movement of some two centuries earlier.[54] In this regard it is worth noting that the ban was not enacted at Innocent's Italian councils of a slightly later date (1134–1136),[55] but only in France, where the vogue for tournaments seems to have originated.[56] The ban may have been Innocent's own idea, and it is also possible that the ban was Bernard's idea, given his upbringing and ongoing involvement with the religious implications of chivalry. In any event, Bernard must have been aware of the Church's prohibition of participation in tournaments soon after its original enactment.

The ban was first pronounced at Innocent's first council, at Clermont in November 1130, a council that Bernard does not seem to have attended. No *acta* from Innocent's second council, convoked in Liège in April 1131, have survived, but in his continuation of Sigebert's *Chronica*, Anselm of Gembloux states that the council enacted a prohibition against clerical marriage,[57] just as Innocent's other early councils had done, first at Clermont, then again at Reims, and then later at the second Lateran.[58] So it is perhaps reasonable to assume that the ban on tournaments was also enacted at Liège, along with Innocent's other disciplinary canons, and Bernard is known to have been in attendance there, where he was instrumental in persuading the German Emperor Lothair to support Innocent's cause.[59] Bernard again took a prominent role in Innocent's third council, held at Reims in October 1131; he was called upon to preach a sermon to the assembled prelates,[60] ceedings, the Pope would not suffer the Abbot to be separated from him; rather, whatever business was transacted, be it private or public, they consulted the man of God."[61] At Reims, the ban on participation in tournaments was again enacted, and so Bernard must have known about it by October 1131 at the latest.

But for all the patent disapproval of secular knighthood that Bernard expresses in the *De laude*, and for all the social, moral, and religious sanctions he brings against chivalry there, he makes no mention of the Church's ban on participation in tournaments. Had the ban been in place when he wrote the treatise, I assume he would have used it, as an argument from authority, as he does his other arguments, on military and moral grounds, at least for criticizing tournaments in chapter 2 of the *De laude*. If the *De laude* was written after the ban had been pronounced, Bernard would have mentioned it in his treatise. He does not; therefore, the treatise was written certainly before October 1131, by which date Bernard must have known of the ban, probably before November 1130, when the ban was first enacted, and even possibly before the summer of 1130, when Bernard first became active in support of the cause of Pope Innocent.

The confluence of these two areas of Bernard's practical involvement, his concern for reforming the practice of knighthood and his concern about the exercise of papal authority, enable dating the *De laude novae militiae* more closely, then, to the period 1128–1131; but it should also, more importantly, remind us of the extent of Bernard's practical involvement in general: he was not just Dante's guide to contemplative insight. In addition to his engagement in the problems of chivalric practice and papal authority, he also preached the importance of putting Christian principles to work on Crusade;[62] he argued against Peter Abelard and Gilbert de la Porée over the practical utility of reason in Christian life;[63] and he argued with Peter the Venerable about the proper practical application of the spiritual principles of the Benedictine rule, over the vocation of a single young monk.[64] Bernard was of course the great mystical doctor of the high Middle Ages, but he was also powerfully practical, *potens in opera*; he responded readily to the

146 David Carlson

call of circumstances to work out a practical theology, by which he might put his spiritual insight to work, solving mundane problems in the ecclesiastical and personal practice of Christian life.

Southern Methodist University

NOTES

1. *Vita prima* 2.2.10: "Notam omnibus, quam annis septem immundus vexarerat spiritus"; "laetantur qui aderant et levantes manus ad sidera, Deo qui de excelso eos visitavit, gratias agunt. Auditum est hoc verbum, et percrebuit fama, et repente totam percutit urbem; per ecclesias, per praetoria, et per compita omnia conveniunt undique; de Viro Dei sermo habitur undique.... Cessatum est ab officiis et artibus, tota civitas in hoc spectaculum suspensa manet" (PL 185: 274d–75b).

2. 2.2.11: "Puellam ei parvulam,... frendentem dentibus et stridentem, quam vehementi impetu vexabat diabolus"; "nec mora, quasi ureretur Sathanas, infusionis illius virtutem ferre non potuit, sed ... festinanter egrediens, vomitu sordidissimo tremebundus erupit. Sic purgata persona ..." (275b–c).

3. 2.2.12: "effrenatis decursibus plurimos infestabant" (275d).

4. 2.2.13–14: "mulier grandaeva ... et honorata quondam matrona ... in cuius pectora pluribus annis diabolus sederet" (276a–77a).

5. 2.3.15: "Audiebantur haec quae Mediolani fiebant, et per totam Italiam Viri Dei discurrebat opinio" (277a).

6. 2.3.15–20 (277b–80a).

7. 2.4.21–22 (280b–81c).

8. 2.2.12 (275d).

9. *Paradiso* 31.110–111: "colui che 'n questo mondo,/ contemplando, gustò di quella pace." *The Divine Comedy*, III.1, ed. Charles Singleton (Princeton, 1975), p. 354.

10. 2.3.15 (277b).

11. Brian Stock, "Experience, Praxis, Work, and Planning in Bernard of Clairvaux: Some Observations on the *Sermones in Cantica*," in *The Cultural Context of Medieval Learning*, edd. J. E. Murdoch and E. D. Sylla (Boston, 1975), p. 259.

12. *Making of the Middle Ages* (New Haven, 1953). p. 243.

13. *De laude novae militiae* 1.1: "Novum militiae genus ortum nuper ... in terris," "saeculis inexpertum, qua gemino pariter conflictu atque infatigabiliter decertatur, tum adversus carnem et sanguinem, tum contra spiritualia nequitiae in caelestibus;" "ut corpus ferri, sic animum fidei lorica." SBO$_p$ 3:214, ll. 2–17.

14. "Disciplina non deest, oboedientia nequaquam contemnitur;" "in victu et in vestu cavetur omne superfluum;" "absque uxoribus et absque liberis;" "nullo tempore aut otiosi sedent, aut curiosi vagantur;" "persona inter eos minime accipitur: defertur meliori, non nobiliori;" "raro loti, magis autem neglecto crine hispidi, pulvere foedi, lorica et caumate fusci" (219.22–20.24).

15. 1.2: "Vita secura [est], ubi absque formidine mors expectetur, immo exoptatur cum dulcedine, et excipitur cum devotione;" "a duplici illo periculo libera;" "timendum omnino, ne aut occidas hostem quidem in corpora, te vero in anima, aut forte tu occidaris ab illo, et in corpore simul et in anima" (215.13–15).

16. 2.3: "Finis fructusve saecularis huius, non dico, militiae, sed malitiae;" "et occisor letaliter peccat, et occisus aeternaliter perit" (216.2–3).

17. 2.3: "Aut irrationalis iracundiae motus, aut inanis gloriae appetitus, aut terrenae qualiscumque possessionis cupiditas" (216.21–23).

18. 2.3: "Operitis equos sericis, et pendulos nescio quos panniculos loricis superinduitis; depingitis hastas, clypeos et sellas; frena et calcaria auro et argento gemmisque circumornatis, et cum tanta pompa pudendo furore et impudenti stupore ad mortem properatis. . . . Oculorum gravamen ritu femineo comam nutritis, longis ac profusis camisiis propria vobis vestigia obvolutis, delicatas ac teneras manus amplis et circumfluentibus manicis sepelitis. . . . Militaria sunt haec insignia, an muliebria potius ornamenta? Numquid forte hostilis mucro reverebitur aurum, gemmis parcet, serica penetrare non poterit?" (216.7–18).

19. 4.7: "Mimos et magos et fabulatores, scurrilesque cantilenas" (220.18–22).

20. Sidney Painter, *French Chivalry* (Baltimore, 1940), p. 68.

21. 4.7: "ad imitationem seu confusionem nostrorum militium, non plane Deo, sed diabolum militantium" (219.19–20).

22. 5.10: "sceleratos et impios, raptores et sacrilegos, homicidas, periuros atque adulteros;" "suos de suo discessu laetificant" (223.5–9).

23. 11.20: "illa sua una [morte] nostram utramque damnavit;" "gemina morte . . . altera quidem spirituali et voluntaria, altera corporali et necessaria" (231. 3–6).

24. 12.30: "in corde peccatoris . . . salutiferam contritionem;" "noxiam tollit confusionem;" "alioquin a mortuo, tamquam qui non est, perit confessio" (237. 11–13, 238.16–17).

25. 13.31: "Nec studium bonae actionis, nec otium sanctae contemplationis, nec lacrimae paenitentis . . . accepta esse poterunt" (239.1–2).

26. 13.31: "virtus oboedientiae una cum fructibus paenitentiae" (238.22–25.).

27. 11.27: "vitae et disciplinae documentum ac speculum" (235.17).

28. 13.31: "ut vitam quam ipsam perdere maluerit, factus oboediens Patri usque ad mortem" (239.3–4).

29. See John of Salisbury, *Policraticus* 6, ed. Clemens Webb (Oxford, 1909); Etienne de Fougières, *Livre des manières* 537–672, ed. R. A. Lodge (Geneva, 1979); Jacques de Vitry, *Exempla* 141, ed. Thomas Crane (London, 1890).

30. As Jean Leclercq points out in *Monks and Love in Twelfth-Century France* (Oxford, 1979), pp. 109–136.

31. See John Benton, "The Court of Champagne as a Literary Center," *Speculum* 36 (1961), 551–91.

32. Again as Leclercq has pointed out, *Monks and Love*, pp. 8–26.

33. On Bernard's *Sententiae* and *Parabolae*, see Leclercq, *Monks and Love*, pp. 86–108; on the efflorescence of monastic love literature, see esp. pp. 14–15.

34. William of St. Thierry, *Vita prima* 1.1.1: "parentibus claris secudum dignitatem saeculi;" "vir antiquae et legitimae militiae fuit" (PL 185:227a).

35. 1.3.8: "eleganti corpore, grata facie preeminens, suavissimis ornatus moribus, acri ingenio praeditus, acceptabili pollens eloquio" (230b).

36. 1.2.4 (228d).

37. Berengar, in the *Liber apologeticus*, wrote c. 1140: "Audivimus a primis fere adolescentiae rudimentis cantiunculas inimicas et urbanos modulos fictitasse" (PL 178:1857a); compare William of St. Thierry, *Vita prima* 1.3.9 (231d); see Leclercq, *Monks and Love*, pp. 17–20.

38. 1.3.7 (230d–31b).

39. 1.3.8 (231b).

40. 1.3.7 (230d).

41. 1.3.10–12 (232b–34c).

42. See Otto of Freising, *Gesta Frederici* 1.47: "Erat enim praedictus abbas [Bernardus] tam ex christianae religionis fervore zelotypus quam ex habilitudinali mansuetudine quodammodo credulus, ut et magistros, qui humanis rationibus se-

BERNARD AND AELRED
ON HUMILITY AND OBEDIENCE

Lawrence C. Braceland, SJ

T HE MIRROR OF CHARITY (1141–1142) begins with a lively
literary exchange between two great abbots, Bernard of
Clairvaulx and Aelred of Rievaulx . The two letters together are a
classic illustration of humility and obedience, quite in conform-
ance with the *Rule* of St Benedict (RB 68). The first letter, to
Aelred of Rievaulx, is not from Gervais, abbot of Louth Park, as
has been supposed, but from Bernard, abbot of Clairvaux.[1] It presupposes both a visit of Aelred to Bernard and, apparently, a letter
of Aelred objecting to Bernard's command to compose the *Mirror*. Aelred, not yet novicemaster, on a voyage to Rome for his abbot William of Rievaulx, a former secretary of Bernard, probably
met Bernard *in via* and may have presented him with written objections to undertaking the composition of the *Mirror*. Apparently
disregarding Abbot William but perhaps with his concurrence,
Bernard sent Aelred this peremptory letter intended as an introduction to the work.[2]

Beginning with a summary teaching on humility and obedience,
Bernard seems to throw both the Scriptures and the Rule Book at
Aelred:

> 1. Humility is indeed the very greatest virtue of the
> saints, provided it is genuine and discreet. Humility
> must be neither founded on fraud nor protected by the
> sacrilege of disobedience.

Bernard here recalls his own solemn command to Aelred:

> I begged you as a brother, no I ordered, or better I ad-
> jured you with God as my witness, to write a brief for
> me, in which you would respond to the complaints of

149

some who are struggling from a more lax to a more
austere way of life.

Turning to Scripture, Bernard distinguishes between Aelred's offering of excuses, which might be pardoned as humility, and his
persistence in a negative response, the equivalent of disobedience.
This is reminiscent of Bernard's advice to a brother about discern-
ment; "Brother, I'll discern and you'll obey":

> I neither fault nor blame your offering excuses, but I
> do reprove you for stubbornness. If you offered ex-
> cuses through humility, was it humility to disobey? On
> the contrary, "rebellion resembles the sin of sorcery,
> and obstinacy resembles the crime of idolatry" (1 S
> 15:23).

After such a strong reproof, Bernard repeats and demolishes Aelred's objections or representations one after another:

> 2. You object that delicate shoulders should never be
> subjected to a heavy load and that one is more prudent
> in rejecting the burden imposed, than in submitting to
> a burden only to stumble beneath it.

Bernard answers by quoting the *Rule*:

> Suppose then that my command was heavy, arduous,
> impossible. That is no reason for excusing yourself. I
> stand by my opinion and repeat my command. What
> will you do? Does not he whose rule you have vowed
> to follow, say this: "Let the junior understand that this
> is what is best for him and let him . . . trust in God's
> aid and so obey" (RB 68)?[3] You did your duty, yes,
> but no more than your duty. You went to the limit.

Noting this extreme, which is contrary to moderation, *nil nimis*,
since Aelred barely kept within the limits of the *Rule*, Bernard
lumps together a number of Aelred's objections:

> You showed the reasons why the task was impossible
> for you. You said you were no schoolmaster but al-
> most illiterate,[4] because you came to the desert not
> from the schools but from the kitchen, where living a
> rough and rustic life amid cliffs and mountains, in the
> sweat of your brow with hammer and pickaxe (1 S
> 6:7), you earned your daily bread, where one learns si-
> lence rather than speech (RB 6), and where the buskin

of orators is not worn with the togs of poor fisher-
men.[5]

Bernard parries Aelred's seven thrusts point by point, with an
abundance of scriptural references and allusions similar to those,
for example, in his letter to Henry Murdac:[6]

3. Your excuses I welcome most gladly. I feel they fan
rather than put out the embers of my desire (2 S 14:7),
because

[a, *the kitchen*:] no food should be more tasty to me,
than whatever courses you serve after lessons in the
class not of any schoolmaster but of the holy Spirit,
since "you may hold a treasure" in an earthen vessel,
perhaps for this reason, "that its transcendent power
may belong to God, not to" yourself (2 Co 4:7). How
delightful, that by some vision of things to come (Gn
41:11), you were also transferred to the desert from
the kitchen;[7]

[b, *royal kitchens*:] perhaps in a king's palace the
dispensing of food for the body was entrusted to you
for a time (1 Co 9:17), that finally in the palace of our
King you might prepare food of the spirit for spiritual
persons (1 Co 2:13) and refresh the hungry with the
food of God's word (1 Co 10:3–4).[8]

[c, *mountains, cliffs and valleys*:]

4. But I am daunted neither by mountain heights, nor
rocky cliffs, nor precipitate valleys, since in our days
"mountains distill sweet wine, hills pour milk" and
honey (Jl 3:18), "valleys are filled with grain" (Ps
64:14), "honey is extracted from the rock and oil from
flintstone" (Dt 32:13), while flocks of Christ's sheep
graze on the mountains and cliffs (Ps 99:3; Ezk 34:14).

[d, *hammer and pickaxe*:] Hence I think that from these
cliffs with your hammer you will mint ore, which
despite a keen wit you would not have mined from the
shelves of schoolmasters, and at times under shady
trees in the midday heat you will reap such experience
as you would never have garnered in the schools.

[e, *focus not on your weaknesses but on your wonderful
Lord*:]

5. Give glory then not to yourself, no not to yourself, but to his name (Ps 113*:1). "The gracious and merciful Lord, mindful of his wonders" (Ps 110:4), not only rescued one in despair "from the desolate pit and the miry bog" (Ps 39:3), from the deadly den and the morass of immorality, but to exalt the hope of sinners, also gave sight to the blind (Ps 145:8), instructed the untaught (Pr 14:33) and taught the inexperienced (Ezr 7:25).

[f, *false pretence to scholarship*:] Hence since everyone who knows you, will know also that what is exacted of you is not yours, why blush, why fret, why dissemble? At a command from the voice of your Benefactor, why do you refuse to reimburse him for his gift?

[g, *fear of presumption and envy*:] Do you dread the reproach of presumption or the envy of your peers? As if anyone ever wrote anything of value without being envied! Or as if you as a monk could incur the reproach of presumption for obeying your abbot!

Bernard now solemnly repeats his command to Aelred to record his insights into the excellence, the fruits, and the place of charity among the virtues:

6. Therefore, in the name of Jesus Christ and in the Spirit of our God, I command you without delay, to the extent of your experience in lengthy meditations, to note in writing your insights into the excellence of charity, its fruit and its rank among the virtues.

Bernard lists the contents to be treated in this treatise on charity and its opposite, cupidity:

Thus in this work of yours, let us recognize as in a mirror the nature of charity, how much sweetness exists in its possession, how much oppression is felt in its opposite, cupidity, how persecution of the outer body does not decrease, as some assume, but rather increases the very sweetness of charity, and finally what kind of discretion must be observed in its expression.

To reassure Aelred, after listing the contents, Bernard assigns both the title and the introduction to this work and assumes full responsibility:

> But to spare your modesty, let my letter introduce the
> work, that in *The Mirror of Charity*—for I am giving
> the book this title—whatever may displease the reader
> may be attributed not to you who obeyed but to me
> who coerced you.

Could Bernard's letter have been a literary device, written after
the work was complete? Although it has no introductory greeting,
it has this formal conclusion: "Farewell, dear brother, in Christ."

Had you been this junior monk, how would you have reacted
to an apparent roasting by your abbot general? On the receipt of
this letter, could you have imagined yourself being called: "the
Bernard of the North,"[9] or Bernard's being called: "the Aelred of
the South"? Twice Aelred responds to Bernard: A) at the beginning of his preface and B) when the work was finished, in the final
paragraph of the third book.

THE BEGINNING OF THE PREFACE TO THE WORK OF ABBOT AELRED
ENTITLED THE MIRROR OF CHARITY[10]

Bernard had addressed Aelred in the singular as a simple monk,
with but two formal marks of respect: *fraternitatem tuam,* and the
concluding, *dilecte frater;* Aelred keeps the respectful plural of majesty throughout. Disarmingly enough, he first emphasizes his own
lack of humility. But in an impossible task, where he can not excuse himself nor avoid criticism, he will accede however unworthily, to the command of so worthy a father! The following comment of Clement of Rome would have served him well: "The wise
man should show his wisdom not by eloquence but by good works;
the humble man should not proclaim his own humility, but let
others do so; nor must the man who preserves his chastity ever
boast of it, but recognize that the ability to control his desires has
been given him by another."[11]

> 1. Yes, genuine and discreet humility is the virtue of
> the saints, but my humility and that of others like me
> is a lack of virtue. Of our humility the prophet says:
> "notice my lowliness and rescue me" (Ps 118:153).
> He did not ask to be rescued from some virtue, nor did
> he extricate himself from humility, but in desperation
> he cried for help. How pitiful is my humility! Would

that mine were not only a genuine humility but also a discreet virtue! But lest I seem to disguise my woeful lack of humility by some overwhelming lack of obedience, I accede however unworthily, since it is for my good, to the request, the order, the solemn command of so worthy a father. Consequently I am undertaking an impossible task, both inexcusable and deserving of criticism: impossible thanks to my diffidence, inexcusable thanks to your command, and deserving criticism from any observer.

Aelred repeats his objections, from the viewpoint of readers, who will resent the work of an untutored and inexperienced writer, on a subject as sublime as the one suggested by Bernard's table of contents:

2. Who would rightly tolerate an author untutored in composition, or illiterate, as Your Reverence acknowledges, or even speechless, an infant still unable to sip milk without spilling it (1 Co 3:2; Heb 5:12) who in the preface promises a book with apostolic authority on the "more excellent way" of charity (1 Co 12:31)? How can one with little or no store of charity suggest its preeminence, someone disorderly its orderliness, someone fruitless its fruitfulness, or someone tasteless and insipid its sweetness. How can one laid low by cupidity rise to confound cupidity? Finally who am I to explain how, by harrowing the flesh and by careful cultivation, charity may flourish?[12]

Because Bernard had mentioned it three times, Aelred refers back to his past in the duties of the kitchen:

Contrary to your opinion but by your leave, I repeat that by coming from the kitchen to the desert, I changed my location but not my station.

Aelred continues to address Bernard in the plural of majesty. Yet for the sake of his readers, he asserts his freedom not to excuse but to accuse himself:

3. But your Paternity will say: you should not excuse yourself. I know, my lord, I know. Though excusing oneself is not permitted, one is free to accuse oneself. Thus a less partial reader, if warned at the en-

trance, how justified he would be in taking umbrage,
might pass by and not be forced to proceed further.

Aelred expresses his gratitude for Bernard's persevering affection:

But how reassured I am for the task of writing by your
prompt offer of the most holy affection of charity for
my acceptance of a burden which rightly could have
been imposed on me! Consequently, with slight hope
of completing what you commanded in charity, I made
what bargain I could with my hammer, to which you
referred, for the construction of a mirror, only to
rediscover the unquestionable truth, that when hope
and all else disappear, charity remains forever (1 Co
13:8, 13; Jn 15:9–10). The One who did not grant the
skill, bestowed the grace. Now just as no one's face is
reflected in any mirror, unless that person stands in the
light, so no one's likeness to charity is reflected in this
mirror of charity, unless that person remains in love (Jn
15:9–10).

Aelred explains, how following Bernard's advice, he completed
the three books with jottings from his meditations, shared with
prior Hugh, his older friend, who returned the jottings with comments of his own.

4. Yes, I was directed to undertake the present work.
I selected materials partly from notes on personal meditations and partly from notes almost as personal or
even more personal, for they were dictated now and
then to an intimate friend (Ps 54:14), my very rever-
end prior, Hugh, closer to me than life itself, who as a
private correspondent was to respond to them from
time to time. Selecting material from meditation for
my present purpose and inserting material from correspondence at intervals where it seemed to fit, I divided
the whole work into three sections.

Aelred indicates how he tried to follow faithfully the divisions of
Bernard's table of contents:

Although I mentioned each topic in each section, still I
made a valiant effort in the first especially to exalt the
excellence of charity, not only by praising its worth
but also by censuring its opposite, cupidity, then in the

second to dispose of the misguided complaints of a
few, and in the third to show how charity should be
practised.

Thanking Bernard for his prayers and the Lord for his largess,
Aelred takes the blame for all faults and suggests that Bernard scan
the titles of the chapters, placed together like a table of contents, to
decide which he should read:

> 5. If then, something to match your assignment has
> resulted from my labor, it comes from your prayer and
> the grace of our Benefactor. But if something less has
> resulted, blame it on me, for I lack both skill and prac-
> tice in writing. Lest the length of this work appal you
> with your busy schedule, first scan the titles listed
> below and then decide at a glance which chapters you
> should read or omit.

HERE THE PROLOGUE ENDS

FINAL PARAGRAPH OF AELRED'S *DE SPECULO CARITATIS*, III. 113.

Aelred concludes the work by addressing Bernard and his readers.
If he has shown a true image of charity, let Bernard's title stand.
He remains diffident; he fears public disgrace and begs the reader
to ask forgiveness for him from the just and merciful judge:

> These are my meditations on charity, most loving
> Father. If the excellence of charity, its fruit, and a com-
> petent way of displaying it are presented here in a true
> likeness, let the volume itself be entitled according to
> your letter: "The Mirror of Charity." But I beg you
> not to show this mirror in public, lest perhaps it reflect
> not the splendor of charity but rather the distorted im-
> age of its author. But if, as I fear, you may display it to
> my confusion, I beseech the reader by the sweet name
> of Jesus to assume not that I approached this work
> through presumption but that I was obliged by the
> authority of a father, the charity of a brother, and by
> my own needs. In my opinion, as it is perilous to dis-
> obey a superior, so it is sweet and pleasant to converse
> in spirit with one's dearest friend in his absence, and

vagrant and profitless distractions of my own roaming spirit.[13] If, however, any reader makes progress in thought or affection from this volume, let him reward my labors by begging pardon from the just and merciful judge for my countless sins.

HERE THE THIRD BOOK ENDS

This exchange between the two great abbots, Bernard and Aelred, is then a classic illustration of humility and obedience in the *Rule* of St Benedict (RB 68).[14]

St. Paul's College

NOTES

1. With due credit to T. E. Harvey, In *Saint Aelred of Rievaulx* (1932), pp. 27, 135, and to André Wilmart, 'L'Instigateur du *Speculum Caritatis* d'Aelred abbé de Rievaulx,' RAM, 14 (1933), 369–94, and 429. F. M. Powicke, in *The Life of Ailred of Rievaulx by Walter Daniel*, again explained the substitution of Gervase, abbot of Louth Park (the Latin corrupted from *Parcoludensis* to *Parchorensis*), and concluded, pp. lvi-lvii: "Not a single known manuscript of the *Speculum Caritatis* ascribes the letter to Gervase, whereas all the four early manuscripts . . . ascribe it to St. Bernard."

2. Sent to Rome on official business, Aelred of Rievaulx with Walter of London, archdeacon of York, "must have passed through Burgundy about March 1142," where they "would be able to consult with Bernard, . . . and possibly returned by the same route to report on what had happened in Rome." Bernard's letter and Aelred's replies were edited by Wilmart, and by A. Hoste and C. H. Talbot in *Aelredi Rievallensis opera omnia* (Brepols, Turnholt, 1971), pp. 3–6 and 161; Bernard's *Letter* also appears in SBOp 8:486–89. With an introductory note, this letter was presented in English by Bruno Scott James, in *The Letters of St. Bernard of Clairvaux* (London, 1953), pp. 245–47; David Knowles in *The Monastic Order in England*, I, 244, note 5, concludes that Bernard's, "style *clamat dominum*."

3. Bruno Scott James, p. 246, n. 3, suggests that for the understanding of this passage the entire number should be read: "If it should happen that burdensome or impossible tasks are imposed on one of the brethren he should indeed accept the command of the one who so orders with complete calm and obedience, but if he sees that the weight of the burden quite exceeds the limits of his strength, he should quietly and at a suitable moment explain to his superior the reasons why he cannot do it, not in a proud way nor with the spirit of resistance, or contradiction. But if after his explanations the one in authority remains firm in requiring

what he has ordered, the junior must understand that this is what is best for him, and let him lovingly (a word omitted by Bernard in this letter) trust in God's aid and so obey.' David Parry, O.S.B., *Households of God*, CS 39, p. 187; see also St Bernard, *On Precept and Dispensation*, XI, 26; CF 1, pp. 125–26.

4. *Almost illiterate*, see *illiterate*, an hyperbole in Aelred's Preface, parag. 2; also "Non sum sapiens, non sum legisperitus, sed homo fere sine litteris, piscatori quam oratori similior"; *Serm. Ined.*, Talbot, p. 156. Again: "Neque enim meritis id ascribendum meis, cum peccator sim; nec scholasticis quidem disciplinis, cum pene, ut scitis, illiteratus sim"; *Oner Dē Oneribus, Serm. 1 (2)*; PL 195:365C. Aelred had attended grammar schools at Hexham and Durham, where he admits that his favorite text was Cicero's *Laelius, On Friendship*; though not a scholastic from a school on the continent, in attending the Cistercian *schola Christi* he acquired a knowledge of the Church Fathers.

5. Buskin, *cothurnus*, the high-soled boot of ancient tragedy; Charles Dumont cites Augustine: "Qui autem cothurno tamquam doctrinae sublimioris elati, non audiunt dicentem: Discite a me quoniam mitis sum . . . dicentes se esse sapientes, stulti facti sunt"; Conf. Vii, ix, 3; also *De mor. Eccl.*, I, xxx, 68; PL 32:1339; and Ambrose, *De Abraham*, II, x, 70; PL 14:515A.

6. See Bernard's Letter to Henry Murdac, no. 107, in Bruno Scott James; also cited in Knowles, p. 221.

7. Bernard refers to the kitchen three times: "qui de coquinis . . . ad heremum veneris; quod . . . de coquina sis translatus ad heremum; cui forte ad horam in regia domo carnalium ciborum fuit credita dispensatio"; see Wilmart, p. 372, note 4.

8. "Fortunately Walter [Daniel] adds descriptive phrases about Ailred's high position at court; he was 'economus domus regalis, mensae regalis dapifer summus,' and dispensed (*dispensare*) the royal substance (*divitias*); and still more fortunately, a contemporary, an older friend of his boyhood at Durham, the monk Laurence, described him explicitly as 'dispensator domus regis,'" Powicke, p. xl.

9. The "Bernard of the North." "One of the most attractive figures in English monasticism. Not only a true Cistercian and a true disciple of St. Bernard, but also an able administrator"; Bruno Scott James, p. 245, n. 2.

10. *Praefatio*, a title probably suggested by *in fronte operis* in Bernard's letter, parag. 6, and by *prima fronte* in Aelred's, parag. 2; in various MSS it is called *prologus, proemium*, and even *excusatio*.

11. St Clement of Rome, *Letter to the Corinthians*, Cap. 36, 1–2, 37–38; Funk I, 145–49.

12. When Bernard asked Aelred to comment on cupidity as the opposite of charity, he was reflecting the moral theology of Augustine; Wilmart p. 373, n. 5. And Aelred's second book, "is an anatomy of cupidity in its monastic form considered under St John's three headings of lust of the flesh, lust of the eyes, and the pride of life"; Aelred Squire, *Aelred of Rievaulx: A Study*, CS 50 (Kalamazoo, 1981), p. 31. See also the appreciation of Aelred by his friend, Gilbert of Hoyland, when the latter learned of his death: "How great a honeycomb, how vast and how rich, has been transferred in these days to the heavenly banquet! I mean the Lord Abbot of Rievaulx, whose passing was announced to us while we were treating of this verse (Sg 5:1) . . . . No similar honeycomb is left in our apiary . . . . *Who was purer in life or more prudent in teaching than he?* Who was more sickly in the flesh or more hearty in the spirit than he? His speech like a honeycomb poured out honeyed knowledge"; (emphasis added) CF 26, Gilbert of Hoyland, *Sermons on the Song of Songs*, III, p. 495.

13. Obedience to his Father Bernard, affection for the prior Hugh, and his own need: "Aelred naturally places obedience first, and it is perhaps true that he would never have attempted so systematically to clarify his thoughts in writing if St Bernard had not given him the occasion to do so. But already his affection for his absent prior Hugh had led to an exchange of reflections on topics of mutual

interest and, above all, there was his urgent personal need, long expressed in minor literary efforts, to give articulate form to his problems and reconcile himself to theology and to life"; Squire, p. 27.

14. I wish to thank St Paul's College and The Social Sciences and Humanities Research Council of Canada for assistance in presenting this paper at the Twenty-first International Congress on Medieval Studies, 1986.

IMAGES OF VISITATION:
THE VOCABULARY OF CONTEMPLATION
IN AELRED OF RIEVAULX'
MIRROR OF LOVE, BOOK II

John R. Sommerfeldt

I N PURSUING AELRED's vocabulary of contemplation during the
past few years, I have been impressed with the variety of imagery which Aelred employs in an attempt to convey to us his totally
enraptured experience of the transcendent, yet immanent, Reality
which he calls God. This contemplative experience shares with all
other experiences an intrinsic ineffability, an ineffability which
Aelred himself explicitly affirms: "Neither mind nor tongue can
convey its utter delight."[1] This ineffability demands that the contemplative have recourse to poetic language when attempting to
convey to us something of his experience.

In his treatise *On Jesus at Twelve Years Old*, Aelred uses the word
"contemplation" to describe his experience of God, and tries to
explain what contemplation is by use of the imagery of the senses:
sight, hearing, and touch (particularly kisses and embraces).[2] Aelred also uses tactile imagery as a means of expressing his contemplative experience in his *On Spiritual Friendship*.[3] Books I and III
of *Mirror of Love* (*De speculo caritatis*) employ a central image of
Sabbath rest to express contemplation.[4] But Book II, while employing all of the imagery of these treatises mentioned, has as its
Leitmotiv the image of visitation.

The senses most commonly referred to in Book II are sight and
hearing. Aelred uses *visio, videre,* and *oculus* (and their various forms
and transmutations) some forty-six times, but the context in each
case indicates an intent consistently prosaic. Seeing is often the

simple act of sight and this occurs some fifteen times.[5] A mental or intellectual sight is often indicated (twenty times) in a way that can be translated by terms indicating mental examination, perception, watching, taking heed, recognition, and imagination.[6] In one case (the last of the twenty) it is the conscience which "sees."[7] A still more prosaic (though not literal) usage occurs some ten times, and is best translated by the English word "seem," as in "it seems that."[8] Similarly, the eighteen references to auditory sensation allow no more figurative interpretation than mental hearings—of the words of God or of Scripture, for example.[9] The four references to feeling (*sentio* and *sentire*) are all figurative but none helpful.[10] In one case Aelred can "feel sufferings,"[11] and twice he states he feels in the common sense of thinking or believing.[12] And smell and ordinary touch are not referred to at all!

When we turn to the special ways of touching involved in kissing and embracing, we have better luck however. Among Aelred's seven references to these sorts of touching[13] are three in which tactile imagery—one kiss and two embraces—point beyond either the literal or usual figurative meanings.[14] All three of these attempts to convey the experience of contemplation occur within the larger context of a visitation image. The same is true of Aelred's saporous imagery. All but three[15] of Aelred's twenty-two references to taste are figurative;[16] one of these points toward a foretaste of the Beatific Vision,[17] and another toward a wisdom acquired in a visitation.[18] One might expect Aelred to use the verb *experior* or the noun *experientia* to describe his experience of God. In some eleven uses[19] of these words, one stands out as clearly pointing toward the experience of contemplation.[20] That experience occurs as a result of a visitation.

The experience is also linked with one of Aelred's infrequent uses of the word "contemplation" in Book II of the *Mirror*. It is in the sweetness of divine contemplation that "you will experience in everything that the yoke of the Lord is easy and his burden light."[21] Of Aelred's three other uses of "contemplation," two indicate the activity of meditation,[22] but one points beyond the intellectual to the experiential and occurs in conjunction with the foretaste to which I have referred.[23] This contemplative foretaste occurs, one is no longer surprised to learn, in an experience described by the image of visitation.

Let us turn then to the Leitmotiv of Book II of Aelred's *De Speculo caritatis*. In this Book, Aelred describes not one, but three visitations. In Chapter 8, Aelred identifies these three visitations by their purpose:

> . . . The cause of . . . visitation is threefold. It is occasionally given as an awakener, sometimes as a consolation, and frequently also as a reward. That is, it is given to waken those sleeping, to console those laboring, and to reward those sighing for the things of heaven.[24]

These visitations are matched to three states of spiritual growth:

> The first kind awakens those who are sluggish, the second refreshes those who are laboring, and the third supports those who are making progress upward.[25]

The recipient of the third visitation is still in process; the visitation occurs in this life and not the next. The language seems sexual; though Aelred does not quote or cite the *Song of Songs*, he surely evokes its imagery:

> The first [visitation] puts terror into him who is scornful or coaxes him who is fearful; the second assists him who is striving and helps him advance; the third embraces [*amplectitur*] him who is coming. The first is like a goad correcting the devious; the second like a staff sustaining the weak; the third a bed supporting the quiet.[26]

Each visitation is a gift, of course—a gift unmerited, in its first two forms, by the holiness of the recipient.[27] But Aelred seems to suggest that the third visitation is the reward of the virtuous:

> Accustomed to frequent compunction of the second sort, nourished by frequent sips of divine sweetness, he is raised to that more sublime and excellent level which no longer strengthens and comforts the weak, but rewards the near perfect victor with more abundant grace.[28]

There is a Pelagian ring to this statement which accords badly

with Aelred's description of contemplation accomplished...
"through the Spirit of God by the infusion of grace."[29] Aelred
rather self-consciously corrects any possible confusion:

> Therefore just as in that [first] state mercy operates without
> preceding merit, so in this [third] state justice functions with
> mercy crowning his gifts—gifts which he has willed to be
> our merits.[30]

Orthodoxy is restored, and with it the possibility that Aelred's
third visitation is a contemplative union.

Aelred's description of this third visitation employs rich saporous and visual imagery and includes the word "contemplation,"
used in the sense which is the object of our search:

> In this state the soul, accustomed to countless incentives of
> heavenly affections, is raised by degrees to that most sub-
> lime visitation experienced by few. There she begins to
> foretaste her future rewards. Passing into the awe-inspiring
> tabernacle right up to the dwelling-place of God, soul melt-
> ing within, she is inebriated with the nectar of celestial
> secrets. Contemplating with purified eyes the place of her
> future quiet, she exclaims with the prophet: "This is my
> resting place forever; here I will dwell, for I have desired
> it."[31]

The contemplation described is, I believe, not the mental activity which Aelred usually means when employing that word.[32]
This contemplation occurs within "a sublime visitation experienced by few." The sublimity of the visitation indicates an ecstatic
experience.

It might be argued that Aelred's use of "experience" does not
justify this conclusion, since he most often indicates by the word
an experience of divine consolation, of "sweetness," which is not,
after all, a direct experience of the transcendent God himself.[33]
Here, I think, we can determine Aelred's meaning by an appeal to
the context, and this brings us back to the saporous and visual imagery employed. Aelred contemplates with "purified eyes"; he is
"inebriated with the nectar of celestial secrets."

And the object of Aelred's experience is the "dwelling place of

God" within which his soul melts. Could this be a description of the Beatific Vision? Surely not, for it is a "foretaste of future rewards."

Aelred continues to speak of the three visitations, employing a wild variety of images describing the third. Alternating between the first two visitations, the soul ". . . no longer grows rich with love, but eager for the hotly desired embraces of him who is the fairest of all the sons of men, she begins to desire to depart and be with Christ. . . ."[34] "When souls so blessed shall be weaned from the milk of consolation, they shall enter into his glory and feast."[35] Souls not so blessed ". . . do not rise to that sublime kind of visitation."[36] Aelred is ". . . astonished at the impudence and irreverence with which those less favored—because less virtuous . . . think that their souls defiled by earthly affections should receive caresses in the most pure embraces of Jesus."[37]

At the end of Chapter 15 of Book II, Aelred combines in one (Latin) sentence a variety of images and a riotous vocabulary describing the experience of contemplation:

> And so, consolations from God and labors due to concupiscence follow one-another; after countless struggles you will ascend to that ineffable visitation to receive your reward. Aflame with the pure ardor of love from entering the glory of God, you will be happily satiated as if by the fruit of the promised land. As the fire of divine love destroys the yoke of concupiscence, you will rest in the glow of gold, in the splendor of wisdom, in the sweetness of divine contemplation. And you will experience that the yoke of the Lord is sweet and his burden light.[38]

Words and phrases such as "ineffable visitation," "pure ardor of love from entering the glory of God," "happily satiated," "fire of divine love," "splendor of wisdom," and "sweetness of divine contemplation" do not by themselves indicate an ecstatic experience of the transcendent God. But these words and phrases reinforce one another providing a context within which we can surely affirm Aelred is here speaking of what I have called contemplation. And the context of the entire sentence makes it sure that Aelred is not speaking of the Beatific Vision, but an experience of God in this life.[39]

In Chapter 19, Aelred returns to the third visitation:

> Admitted by the grace of divine loving-kindness to that
> most sublime kind of consolation which is, as it were, the
> reward of the just, you will say with the prophet: "How
> great is the abundance of your sweetness, O Lord, which
> you have hidden for those who fear you."[40]

This brief reference reminds us that Aelred's language of contemplation—like all his language—is biblical in character, even when
Aelred is not quoting Scripture, even when not employing sense
imagery.

Book II of the *Mirror of Love* contains twenty-six chapters, and
the last explicit reference to contemplation occurs at the end of
Chapter 19 where Aelred boldly claims: ". . . I am confident that
one day I shall reach that kind of visitation which is sublime and
ineffable."[41] This not a boast, I think; Aelred writes to encourage
those who have not experienced the full gift of contemplation. In
the very last sentence of Book II,[42] Aelred reverts to a contemplative image frequent in Book I[43] and fundamental to Book III: the
image of Sabbath. To this image I hope to return next year.[44]

The University of Dallas

NOTES

1. *Sermones inediti* (ed. C. H. Talbot; Series S. Ordinis Cisterciensis, I; Rome,
1952), p. 140. See "The Vocabulary of Contemplation in Aelred of Rievaulx' *On
Jesus at the Age of Twelve, A Rule of Life for a Recluse,* and *On Spiritual Friendship,*"
in E. Rozanne Elder (ed.), *Heaven on Earth: Studies in Medieval Cistercian History,
IX,* CS 68 (Kalamazoo, 1983), pp. 72–89, and "The Vocabulary of Contemplation in Aelred of Rievaulx' *Mirror of Love,* Book I," in E. Rozanne Elder (ed.),
Goad and Nail: Studies in Medieval Cistercian History, X, CS 84 (Kalamazoo, 1985),
pp. 241–50.
2. *Heaven on Earth,* pp. 79–80.
3. *Heaven on Earth,* pp. 83–85.
4. *Goad and Nail,* pp. 245–47.
5. All references to the Spec car are to the critical edition edited by A. Hoste
and C. H. Talbot: *Opera omnia* (CC, *Continuatio medievalis,* I; Tvrnholti, 1971).
Spec car II, i, 2 (p. 66, 1. 25); ii, 5 (p. 68, 1. 87); iii, 6 (p. 68, 1. 100); iv, 7 (p.

69, 1. 130); xvii, 50 (p. 90, 1. 935); xxii, 66 (p. 97, 1. 1211); xxiii, 67 (p. 98, 1. 1236); xxiii, 67 (p. 98, 1. 1241); xxiv, 70 (p. 99, 1. 1283); xxiv, 70 (p. 99, 1. 1288); xxiv, 70 (p. 99, 1. 1292); xxiv, 70 (p. 99, 1. 1298); xxiv, 70 (p. 99, 1. 1299); xxiv, 71 (p. 100, ll. 1313–15; three times).

6. Spec car II, i, 3 (p. 67, l. 50); iii, 6 (p. 68, l. 104); v, 8 (p. 70, l. 168); vi, 12 (p. 71, l. 222); vi, 12 (p. 71, l. 223); vi, 12 (p. 72, l. 225); ix, 22 (p. 76, ll. 386–87); ix, 22 (p. 76, l. 390); xiv.33 (p. 81, l. 593); xiv, 33 (p. 82, l. 606); xvii, 43 (p. 87, l. 812); xvii, 45 (p. 88, l. 849); xix, 59 (p. 94, l. 1081); xx, 61 (p. 95, l. 1116); xx, 62 (p. 95, ll. 1139–40; twice); xx, 62 (p. 95, l. 1139); xxiv , 70 (p. 99, l. 1284); xxiv, 72 (p. 101, l. 1350); xxvi, 75 (p. 102, l. 1400.

7. Spec car II, xxvi, 75 (p. 102, l. 1400).

8. Spec car II, i, 2 (p. 66, l. 20); i, 2 (p. 66, l. 24); i, 3 (p. 67, ll. 43–44); vi, 12 (p. 72, l. 228); vi, 14 (p. 72, l. 257); vii, 18 (p. 75, l. 341); xiv, 35 (p. 83, l. 661); xvii, 41 (p. 86, l. 761); xxiv, 72 (p. 100, l. 1342); xxvi, 76 (p. 103, l. 1431).

9. Spec car II, vi, 12 (p. 72, l. 226); vii, 19 (p. 75, l. 349); vii, 19 (p. 75, l. 352); ix, 22 (p. 76, l. 390); xi, 27 (p. 78, l. 463); xi, 28 (p. 78, l. 470); xvii, 43 (p. 87, l. 821); xvii, 43 (p. 87, l. 823); xvii, 52 (p. 91, l. 963); xix, 58 (p. 93, l. 1067); xx, 62 (p. 95, l. 1140; twice); xx, 62 (p. 95, l. 1141); xx, 63 (p. 96, l. 1162); xxii, 66 (p. 97, l. 1211); xxiii, 69 (p. 98, l. 1264); xxiii, 69 (p. 99, l. 1270); xxiv, 721 (p. 100, l. 1345).

10. Spec car II, ii, 4 (p. 67, l. 76); v, 9 (p. 70, l. 181); v, 9 (p. 71, l. 187); xxii, 66 (p. 97, l. 1214).

11. Spec car II, ii, 4 (p. 67, l. 76).

12. Spec car II, v, 9 (p. 70, l. 181); v, 9 (p. 71, l. 187).

13. Spec car II, vi, 12 (p. 72, l. 230); vii, 18 (p. 75, ll. 340–41; twice); viii, 20 (p. 75, l. 366); xi, 27 (p. 78, l. 468); xii, 29 (p. 79, l. 521); xvii, 50 (p. 90, ll. 945–46).

14. Spec car II, vii, 18 (p. 75, ll. 340–41; twice); xii, 29 (p. 79, l. 521).

15. Spec car II, iv, 7 (p. 69, l. 142); xix, 57 (p. 93, l. 1053); xix, 57 (p. 93, ll. 1055–56).

16. Spec car II, v, 9 (p. 70, l. 174); vi, 12 (p. 72, l. 229); xi, 27 (p. 78, ll. 462–63); xi, 28 (p. 78, l. 485); xii, 29 (p. 79, l. 503); xii, 29 (p. 79, l. 504); xii, 29 (p. 79, l. 513); xii, 29 (p. 79, l. 516); xiv, 35 (p. 83, l. 656); xv, 39 (p. 85, l. 729); xv, 39 (p. 85, l. 738); xviii, 56 (p. 92, ll. 1029–30; twice); xviii, 56 (p. 92, l. 1035); xviii, 56 (p. 93, l. 1040); xix, 57 (p. 93, l. 1050); xix, 57 (p. 93, l. 1062); xix, 58 (p. 93, l. 1070); xxiv, 71 (p. 100, l. 1322).

17. Spec car II, xi, 28 (p. 78, l. 485).

18. Spec car II, xii, 29 (p. 79, l. 504).

19. Spec car II, iii, 6 (p. 69, l. 121); v, 10 (p. 71, l. 195); xv, 39 (p. 85, l. 739); xvii, 42 (p. 86, l. 771); xvii, 45 (p. 88, l. 854); xvii, 47 (p. 89, l. 895); xviii, 55 (p. 92, l. 1012); xviii, 56 (p. 92, l. 1037); xix, 57 (p. 93, l. 1045); xix, 58 (p. 93, l. 1074); xx, 62 (p. 95, l. 1134).

20. Spec car II, xv, 39 (p. 85, l. 739).

21. Spec car II, xv, 39 (p. 85, ll. 738–40).

22. Spec car II, xiv, 35 (p. 83, l. 642); xxiv, 71 (p. 100, l. 1313).

23. Spec car II, 28 (p. 78, l. 488).

24. Spec car II, viii, 20 (p. 75).

25. *Ibid.*

26. *Ibid.*

27. Spec car II, x, 25 (p. 77).

28. *Ibid.*

29. Spir amic, II, 24 (p. 307).

30. Spec car II, xi, 28 (p. 79, ll. 491–94).

31. Spec car II, xi, 28 (p. 78, ll. 481–90).

32. See *Heaven on Earth,* pp. 77 and 82; *Goad and Nail,* pp. 242–43.

33. See, for example, Spec car II, xi, 27 (p. 78, ll. 462–63).

34. Spec car II, xii, 30 (p. 79, ll. 517–21).
35. Spec car II, xii, 30 (p. 79, ll. 525–26).
36. Spec car II, xiii, 31 (p. 80, ll. 553–54).
37. Spec car II, xiii, 32 (p. 81, ll. 570–73).
38. Spec car II, xv, 39 (p. 85, ll. 731–40).
39. See Spec car II, xvi, 40 (p. 85).
40. Spec car II, xix, 59 (p. 94, ll. 1100–104).
41. Spec car II, xix, 60 (p. 94, l. 1110–11).
42. Spec car II, xxvi, 78 (p. 104, ll. 1465–67).
43. See *Goad and Nail*, pp. 245–46.
44. Though not bearing directly on the argument of this article, I should like to point out that in Book II, Aelred uses the adjective "mystical" and the adverb "mystically" four times: vi, 16 (p. 74, l. 302); xv, 37 (p. 84, 1, 703); xxiii, 68 (p. 98, l. 1253); xxiii, 68 (p. 98, l. 1253). In each case the meaning is "hidden" or "secret." See *Heaven on Earth*, p. 78.

In Spec car II, ix, 22 (p. 76, l. 380) occurs the only instance in Aelred's writings which I have discovered of the word *charismata*. But it surely means "charismatic gifts," not the special charism of contemplation.

THE RAPE OF THE SOUL:
THE VOCABULARY OF CONTEMPLATION
IN AELRED OF RIEVAULX'
MIRROR OF LOVE, BOOK III

John R. Sommerfeldt

A ELRED OF RIEVAULX was a contemplative. Near the end of
Book Three of his *Mirror of Love* (in Chapter XXXVII, p.
102 to be exact), Aelred describes the contemplative experience of
Paul in a way that convinces us that it is also the experience of
Aelred.

> Lastly, those words he [Paul] said: "I should willingly be
> separated from Christ for the sake of my brothers" [Rm
> 9:3] can also be appropriately understood to mean that from
> the secrecy of his prayer where he reposed with delight in
> the embraces [*amplexus*] of Jesus, from that ineffable height
> of contemplation [*ineffabili contemplationis eminentia*] where
> with totally pure eyes he viewed [*purissimis oculis perlustra-
> bat*] the secrets of heavenly mysteries, from that sweetness
> of most agreeable compunction which bathed with the sooth-
> ing dew of spiritual affection his soul—a soul thirsting for
> the things of heaven—he would have preferred to be drawn
> away to the din of the world for the salvation of his brothers.
> Anyone who, according to his measure, remains free and
> tastes how sweet the Lord is [Ps 34:8] and how blessed is
> every man who hopes in him [see Ps 40:5], does not doubt
> that to be called away in that manner should be termed
> separation from Christ.[1]

An experience is by its nature ineffable, and the contemplative experience of God so transcends man's ability to communicate it

that Aelred must resort to poetic language to convey any meaning at all.

The passage quoted contains many important features of Aelred's contemplative vocabulary. His language is clearly biblical, even when he is not quoting Scripture: the phrase "how blessed is every man who hopes in him" surely evokes Psalm 40:5—whether Aelred was conscious of the reference or not. Aelred's sense imagery is certainly self-conscious: the contemplative experience is communicated by images of touch (a most intimate touch, that of embrace), of sight and taste. And in this passage Aelred uses the word "contemplation" which is described as an "ineffable height."

Of course Aelred does not always indicate a rapturous experience of God when referring to the senses. For example, of the some thirteen uses of "hear," "hearing," and "ears" in Book Three,[2] twelve are clearly references to the literal sense of these words, to auditory sensation or perception. The sole exception[3] goes beyond the literal only to an intellectual sense in which "heard" means "learned." Again, Aelred refers to the olfactory sense on occasion, once using the word *odoramentorum*;[4] but the meaning here does not point beyond the obvious "of fragrances."

Aelred's use of other sensation words is more rewarding in our quest. We have already seen that Aelred uses saporous imagery to describe the contemplative experience,[5] but the vast majority of his twenty-five references to taste indicate the tasting, savoring, relishing of the things of this world or of persons or psychological states.[6] *Sapientia* and *sapiens* are derivative words Aelred uses some twelve times, but always in the usual sense of "wisdom" or "wise man."[7]

However, in Chapter Thirty-eight, Aelred uses the verb *sapiat* in a passage which may very well indicate contemplative experience. The savor given is a gift from Christ. Aelred writes:

> There remains a place higher than all others. Jesus, the one who has built and restored the spiritual ark, sits there alone in his beauty, without a companion. By his gentleness he keeps all the creatures below in order. May he give savor [*sapiat*] to all of them, fill all with his fragrance [*fraget*], enlighten [*luciat*] all, shed his splendor upon all, and bring the whole broad compass in a straight line to the measure of his love.[8]

But if this taste and this smell are gifts from Jesus, it is not all clear that the gift given is Christ himself. The state described through this saporous and olfactory imagery seems exalted indeed, but I am not sure that it is a contemplative state. Here is additional evidence —if needed—that words must be understood in their context, even when—or perhaps, especially when—they refer to an ineffable experience.

My last example of Aelred's use of saporous imagery comes at the very beginning of Book III of the *Mirror of Love* and is there associated with the image of Sabbath which Aelred used so powerfully in Book I.[9] Here in Book III, Aelred writes:

> . . . Every good work is founded on faith in the one God, is advanced by the seven-fold gift of the Holy Spirit, and reaches him who is truly one, where all that we are is made one with him. And because there is no division in unity, let there be there no rushing out of the mind in various directions, but let it be one in the One, with the One, through the One, around the One, sensing the One, and savoring the One—and since always One, always resting, and thus always observing a perpetual sabbath.[10]

The sensual imagery is surely here: the soul is "sensing the One"[11] and "savoring the one." But just as I was cautious in understanding "sabbath" as an image of contemplation in Book I of the *Speculum caritatis*,[12] so too am I cautious here.

Aelred's three sabbaths—the sabbaths of days, the sabbath of years, and the sabbath of sabbaths[13]—represent three loves. Aelred writes: "Let love of self, then, be man's first sabbath, love of neighbor the second, and love of God the sabbath of sabbaths."[14] Now love of God can be experienced in many ways not so rapturous as contemplation. Even the sabbath of sabbaths, I conclude, may be experienced *in* contemplation, but *is* not necessarily that contemplation.

Indeed, Aelred seems to say just this in Chapter II, 5:

> What is more, it happens in a wondrous and inexpressible way that, although all of these three loves are possessed at the same time (for it cannot be otherwise), still all three are not experienced equally at all times. At one moment rest

and joy are experienced in the purity of one's own conscience, at another they are derived from the sweetness of
brotherly love, at still another they are more fully attained
in contemplation of God.[15]

Here again, Aelred uses words which can refer to a rapturous experience of God: Aelred uses *sentiatur, sentatur* in a way which indicates experience; more importantly, perhaps, he uses the word
contemplatione.

The difficulty with the latter usage is that Aelred sometimes uses
contemplatio to indicate an intellectual activity[16] far removed from
the passive receptivity which characterizes the contemplative experience of God. In this case *contemplatio* is a synonym for *consideratio*[17] or *meditatio*.[18] Is the "contemplation" of Chapter II, 5, an
intellectual activity or an experience of man in all his faculties? I
am not sure, but I lean toward the former explanation. The quotation continues:

> Just as a king who possesses various perfume cellars enters
> now this, now that, and is steeped in the fragrant scent now
> of this perfume, now of that, so the soul preserves within
> the enclosure of her consciousness several cellars filled with
> spiritual treasures. Entering now this, now that, the measure
> of her joy varies as does the variety of her treasures.[19]

This image at once attracts me and cautions me against assigning
too exalted a meaning to Aelred's use here of *contemplatio*. For entrance into cellars—even those filled with spiritual treasures—is an
activity of the soul.

There remains a description of contemplation in Book II which
I think clearly indicates rapturous experience of God in this life. It
occurs in Chapter VI, and is again associated with the sabbath of
sabbaths which is the love of God. Aelred writes:

> The greater her [the soul's] devotion, the more securely
> does the soul purified by the twin loves [of self and neigh-
> bor] pass to the blissful embraces [*amplexus*] of the Lord's
> divinity, so that—inflamed with utmost desire—she goes
> beyond the veil of the flesh and, entering into that sanctuary
> where Christ Jesus is spirit before her face, she is thoroughly

absorbed by that ineffable light [*ineffabili lumine*] and unaccustomed sweetness. All that is corporeal, all that is sensible, all that is mutable is reduced to silence. The soul fixes her clearsighted gaze on that which *is*, which always *is*, which *is* in itself, which is *one*. Being free, she sees [*videns*] that the Lord is God [see Ps 46:10], and, in the tender embraces [*amplexus* again] of Love himself, she keeps a sabbath, without doubt the sabbath of sabbaths.[20]

Sabbath is the central image of rest, rest within the embrace of the Lord.

But Aelred also uses the word "contemplation" to describe this sabbatical embrace. He continues:

The seventh day is as the foundation of love, the seventh year love's increase, and the fiftieth year, after seven times seven, is love's fullness. In each of these there is rest, in each there is freedom, in each some keeping of spiritual sabbath. First there is rest in purity of conscience, then in most sweet conjunction of souls, finally in the contemplation of God himself. . . . In the first the soul is recollected, in the second she is extended without, in the third she is caught up [*rapitur*] above herself.[21]

Contemplation is then a holy rape, in which the Lover takes to himself his beloved—the initiative, the power is his; the delight, the joy is shared by them both.

The University of Dallas

NOTES

1. Spec car, III, xxvii, 102, p. 156, ll. 1978–92. The page and line numbers are references to the critical edition by A. Hoste and C. H. Talbot: *Opera omnia* (CC, *Continuatio medievalis*, I; Tvrnholti, 1971).
2. Spec car, III, ii, 3, p. 106, l. 41; v, 15, p. 112, l. 293; xii, 33, p. 120, l. 593; xii, 33, p. 120, l. 598; xii, 33, p. 120, l. 600; xii, 33, p. 120, l. 605; xix, 45, p.

126, l. 844; xix, 45, p. 126, l. 846; xix, 45, p. 127, l. 855; xix, 45, p. 127, l. 857; xix, 56, p. 132, l. 1049; xxxii, 77, p. 142, l. 1446; xxxvii, 99, p. 153, l. 1898.

3. Spec car, III, xii, 33, p. 120, l. 593

4. Spec car, III, xxxiv, 81, p. 145, l. 1554.

5. Spec car, III, xxxvii, 102, p. 156, l. 1988.

6. There are ten such uses: Spec car, III, iii, 8, p. 109, ll. 162–63; iv, 12, p. 111, l. 246; xix, 44, p. 126, l. 831; xix, 46, p. 127, l. 870; xx, 48, p. 128, l. 900; xxi, 51, p. 129, l. 945; xxv, 59, p. 133, l. 1086; xxvi, 62, p. 135, l. 1161; xxxv, 82, p. 145, l. 1581; xxxviii, 104, p. 157, l. 2018.

7. Spec car, III, vii, 20, p. 114, l. 378; xv, 38, p. 123, l. 701; xxix, 70, p. 138, l. 1305; xxxi, 74, p. 140, l. 1380; xxxvi, 97, p. 152, l. 1853; xl, 111, p. 160, l. 2141; xl, 111, p. 160, l. 2142; xl, 111, p. 160, l. 2143 (twice); xl, 111, p. 160, ll. 2147–48; xl, 111, p. 160, l. 2151; xl, 111, p. 160, l. 2152.

8. Spec car, III, xxxviii, 106, p. 157, ll. 2041–47.

9. Spec car, I, xviii, 51–52, pp. 33–34, ll. 766–93. See my "The Vocabulary of Contemplation in Aelred of Rievaulx' *Mirror of Love*, Book I," in E. Rozanne Elder (ed.), *Goad and Nail: Studies in Medieval Cistercian History, X*, CS 84 (Kalamazoo, 1985) pp. 241–50, especially pp. 245–47.

10. Spec car, III, i, I, p. 105, ll. 13–20

11. The latin word is *sentiens*; Spec car, III, i, 1, p. 105, l. 18. Other uses of forms of this word are: Spec car, III, i, 2, p. 105, l. 25; i, 2, p. 105, l. 26; ii, 3, p. 106, l. 60; ii, 3, p. 107, l. 99; ii, 3, p. 107, l. 101; xxiii, 54, p. 131, l. 1004; xxv, 59, p. 133, l. 1083; xxvi, 63, p. 135, l. 1171; xxvii, 65, p. 136, l. 1210; xxvii, 65, p. 136, l. 1212; xxviii, 66, p. 136, l. 1229; xxx, 73, p. 140, l. 1364; xxxiii, 79, p. 144, l. 1512; xxxvi, 98, p. 153, l. 1888; xxxvii, 100, p. 154, l. 1920; xxxvii, 102, p. 156, l. 1994. The meanings range from "feel," "sense," and "experience," to "perceive" or "understand." In no case is the feeling or perceiving related to contemplation.

12. "Vocabulary," *Goad and Nail*, pp. 246–47.

13. Spec car, III, i, 2, p. 105, ll. 21–22.

14. Spec car, III, ii, 3, p. 106, ll. 55–57.

15. Spec car, III, ii, 5, p. 107, ll. 97–102.

16. Spec car, III, ix, 28, p. 118, l. 526; xxiv, 55, p. 131, ll. 1020–21.

17. Aelred uses *consideratio* in Spec car, III, i, 1, p. 105, l. 5; ii, 3, p. 106, l. 67; v, 14, p. 112, l. 279; xii, 33, p. 120, l. 589; xxii, 52, p. 130, ll. 973–74; xxiv, 55, p. 131, l. 1026; xxvi, 62, p. 135, l. 1164; xxxiii, 79, p. 143, l. 1484; xxxv, 94, p. 150, l. 1780; xxxvi, 97, p. 152, l. 1855; xxxviii, 103, p. 156, l. 2004.

18. Aelred uses *meditatio* in Spec car, III, xxxvi, 97, p. 152, ll. 1854–55; xxxvii, 102, p. 155, l. 1971; xl, 113, p. 161, l. 2176; xl, 113, p. 161, l. 2189.

19. Spec car, III, ii, 5, p. 107, ll. 102–108.

20. Spec car, III, vi, 17, p. 113, ll. 318–28. Aelred uses *amplexus, amplexor* and *osculum, osculor* in twenty-three additional cases: Spec car, III, iv, 7, p. 108, l. 147; iv, 9, p. 110, l. 200; v, 13, p. 111, l. 264; v, 13, p. 111, l. 265; v, 15, p. 112, ll. 295–296; xi, 32, p. 120, l. 580; xii, 33, p. 120, l. 599; xviii, 42, p. 125, l. 790; xix, 43, p. 126, l. 805; xxvi, 61, p. 134, l. 1131; xxvi, 64, p. 135, l. 1182; xxvii, 65, p. 136, l. 1208; xxviii, 67, p. 137, l. 1241; xxviii, 67, p. 137, l. 1242; xxviii, 68, p. 137, l. 1251; xxix, 69, p. 138, l. 1270; xxix, 69, p. 138, ll. 1280–81 (twice); xxxvii, 102, p. 156, l. 1981; xxxix, 109, p. 159, l. 2102; xxxix, 109, p. 159, l. 2108; xxxix, 109, p. 159, l. 2114; xl, 112, p. 161, l. 2175. The meaning ranges from "likes" to "cherishes" to "the embrace [of Jesus in contemplation]." Aelred uses *video* and *oculus* some forty-eight times. Of these only two refer to contemplation in the sense used here: Spec car, III, vi, 17, p. 113, p. 326, and xxxvii, 102, p. 156, l. 1983. In Spec car III, xl, 112, p. 160, l. 2166, the reference is to the sight of Jesus in the Beatific Vision.

21. Spec car, III, 19, pp. 113–41, ll. 348–54, 358–60.

AELRED THE HISTORIAN:
THE ACCOUNT OF THE
BATTLE OF THE STANDARD*

Aelred Glidden, OSB

ELRED OF RIEVAULX'S *Account of the Battle of the Standard* is one of his neglected historical works. Although as early as 1949 Dom David Knowles described Aelred as "a historian laureate,"[1] in 1960 Aelred Squire was able to state in his article, "Historical Factors in the Formation of Aelred of Rievaulx":

> The current trend of interest in Aelred of Rievaulx as a spiritual and monastic writer still needs, it would seem, the essential corrective which would come from a more soundly based knowledge of Aelred in his English milieu, and from a closer study of his much neglected histories and hagiography.[2]

In the past twenty-six years, interest in Aelred as a spiritual writer has continued to grow; yet his historical and hagiographical works remain little known, untranslated, and unstudied.

Aelred's authorship of the *Relatio de Standardo* (variously referred to as *De bello Standarii, De bello apud Standardum,* or *Aelredus Standard'*) has never been questioned even though Walter Daniel fails to include it in the listing of Aelred's works in his *Life of Aelred.* It is attributed to Aelred in the Rievaulx library catalogue, and the internal evidence, as should become clear, leaves no reason to doubt that it was written by him.[3]

One other point worth noting before an examination of the work is to point out that Aelred never bothers to explain just what the "Standard," from which the battle takes its name, was. In fact, only one of the contemporary chroniclers provides us with a description. In Richard of Hexham's *History of the Reign of Stephen* we learn that the Standard was a large pole bearing the banners of St. Peter, St. John of Beverly, and St. Wilfrid of Ripon. At the top of the pole was a silver pyx containing the Blessed Sacrament.[4] This is a description of what was known in northern Italy as a *carrocio*. This wagon normally accompanied the city militia of the northern Italian communes on the battlefield, first being mentioned at Milan in 1039. The usual alliance of the Church with the Italian cities against the German emperors gave the *carrocio* an ecclesiastical character, as did the inclusion of the Sacrament. Its appearance north of the Alps was rare, usually with armies that had a close relationship with the Church.[5] I know of no other mention of it in England; its presence in the battle near Northallerton was probably due to the importance of the Archbishop of York in assembling the English forces.

There are only two contemporary manuscripts of Aelred's *Relatio de Standardo*, one from the Rievaulx library, now at Yorkminster, and one at Corpus Christi College, Cambridge, from Sawley.[6] Although the Rievaulx manuscript lacks the last page, the two texts are substantially the same, the most notable difference being in the way each begins. The Rievaulx text begins, "While King Stephen was occupied in the south...." The Sawley text has a large capital "R" in red and green (apparently prepared for the opening word, *Rege*) but it does not use it; instead it begins: "In the year of the Lord's incarnation 1138, while King Stephen was occupied in the south...."[7] The text in Migne's *Patrologia* includes the insertion in the Sawley text. As a result, the most commonly available text conceals the striking and abrupt opening which Aelred intended but which failed to suit the scribe who prepared the Sawley text.

Aelred's opening is significant because it has been used to date his work. In Henry of Huntington's *Chronicle* we find the opening of his account of the Battle of the Standard beginning, "While the king was engaged in the south...." The approximation to Aelred's words and other parallels in the works (in particular a speech by Bishop Ralph of Durham in Henry's account, of which a longer version appears in Aelred and is attributed to Walter Espec) indicate that one author clearly made use of the other. Since Henry's work first appeared in 1129 and was subsequently revised through 1154, his priority is established, and Aelred's *Relatio* is generally dated 1155–1157.[8]

Aelred's opening is also significant because it suggests, as does his general lack of background material, that he is not writing for posterity. His assumption that the reader knows the year in which the battle occurred and the general situation at the time suggests that he anticipates a contemporary audience, which further implies that he wrote in response to what he perceived as an immediate need.

In Squire's *Aelred of Rievaulx: A Study*, he describes the *Relatio* as "a work that has several marks of having been written for a purpose which it is hard satisfactorily to recover."[9] However, by examining Henry's work and comparing it with Aelred's, we shall see, I believe, that Aelred's primary reason for writing his account was to defend the character of King David of Scotland from the charges leveled against him by Henry of Huntingdon.

Henry's history provides the background material lacking in Aelred. The date is 1138. There is civil strife in England between the supporters of the rival claimants of the English crown: King Stephen, the son of the Conqueror's daughter, and the Empress Matilda, the daughter of the Conqueror's son. In support of Matilda's claim, King David of Scotland and his son Prince Henry launch one of the innumerable Scottish border raids into northern England. King Stephen being occupied in the south, the northern barons, inspired by Archbishop Thurstan of York and led by Walter Espec, William Peperel of Nottingham, and Gilbert de Lacy, muster their forces and repel the invaders near Northallerton.

We are told in Walter Daniels *Life of Aelred* that Aelred was reared at King David's court and that he was high in the kings's favor and close to Prince Henry.[10] Aelred corroborates this information when in his *History of the English Kings* he writes of Prince Henry:

> And in the body, but never in mind or affection, in order to serve Christ I left him, in the full bloom of his prime; as also his father, now flourishing in hale old age, whom I have loved beyond all mortals.[11]

Daniel also tells us that it was on business (presumably the king's) that Aelred was sent to Archbishop Thurstan at York.[12] With the Archbishop's blessing, Aelred and a friend traveled to Helmsley to see Walter Expec and the next day visited Walter's foundation at Rievaulx where Aelred entered the community two days later.[13] Obviously, if Aelred was so well acquainted with prominent leaders of both sides of the battle, his account promises to be of interest.

The section of Henry's *Chronicle* that deals with the Battle of the Standard is one hundred thirty-seven lines in the *Rolls Series*. Bishop Ralph's speech is fifty-one lines, the description of the battle itself thirty-eight lines, leaving forty-eight lines of other narrative, including a description of the Scottish atrocities and naming the notable figures in each army. Thus over one third of the work is one speech. The speech adds nothing to our knowledge of what occurred, since the only parts of it that are more than a simple pep talk are two references to Scottish atrocities which are related earlier in the narrative. The Bishop does make a point that many of the men in the Scottish army are unarmored, but this point is made again in the narrative describing the battle. The speech seems to serve little purpose and apparently is provided because Bishop Ralph did address the army and this speech represents what it would have been appropriate for him to say.

Aelred's *Relatio* runs to four hundred fifty-five lines in the *Rolls Series*, of which two hundred sixteen lines, or almost half, are speeches. Walter Expec's speech, based on the speech of Bishop Ralph of Durham, is one hundred twenty-one lines. There are twenty lines given to King David's leading nobles as they counsel him about the plan of battle and the marshaling of the Scottish host. Finally, there are seventy-five lines attributed to Robert the Bruce in an appeal to King David. Aelred describes the opposing armies in fifty-three lines and the battle itself in one hundred two lines. One hundred six lines of other narrative complete Aelred's account.[14]

Aelred's skill as a writer can be seen in his use of speeches. The Scottish atrocities are mentioned only in the speeches. Motivations of various characters are described in the speeches, and the reason for the Scottish battle plan is revealed in the arguments of King David's nobles. Clearly Aelred makes greater use of speeches and, unlike Henry's work, the speeches in Aelred's account serve the purpose of his narrative.

In spite of Aelred's undoubted stylistic superiority, the significance of a knowledge of Henry's *Chronicle* in understanding Aelred's purpose cannot be overemphasized.

Two sections of Henry's brief narrative are of importance in examining Aelred's *Relatio*. The first is his description of Scottish atrocities:

> Now the king of the Scots, because he had given an oath to King Henry's daughter, acted through his followers execrably, as if under the veil of sanctity. For they cleft open pregnant women, and took out the unborn babe; they tossed children upon the spear-points, and beheaded priests upon the altars; they cut off the heads of crucifixes, and placed them upon the trunks of the slain; and placed again the heads of the dead upon the crucifixes. Thus wherever the Scots arrived, all was full of horror and full of savagery. There was the screaming of women, the wailing of old men, the groans of the dying, the despair of the living.[15]

What is noteworthy is that Henry makes it quite clear that the responsibility is King David's; it is he who acts execrably, through his followers. Using his oath as justification merely compounds his offense. Assuming that Aelred's purpose in composing his work is to exonerate King David, this passage is crucial.

Of course Henry is writing in the way we would expect an English propagandist to write. We would not suspect from his account that many of the southern barons sided with the Empress Matilda, nor does he mention that Matilda is King David's niece. The fact that during King Henry's reign all of the barons (including King Stephen himself) had sworn an oath to support Matilda's right to the throne (a fact perhaps too well known to be entirely omitted) is stood on its head by focusing on the atrocities and treating them as discrediting the oath and thus (implicitly) the oath itself.

The other significant part of Henry's account is the speech of Bishop Ralph of Durham. Ralph reminds the Normans of their valor in war and their numerous conquests. He mocks the rashness of the Scots for daring to invade, and we hear once more of their atrocities. He then returns to the subject of Norman prowess and notes the large number of unarmored men in the Scottish host.[16] This speech is unmistakably the basis for the much longer oration which Aelred attributes to Walter Espec in his version.[17]

Walter is a significant figure in Aelred's account, so much so that Aelred Squire refers to him as "the real hero of the piece,"[18] and says, "He is in the centre of the picture."[19] "Picture" is a telling word, for one of the notable things in Aelred's *Relatio* is his detailed description of Walter's appearance:

> He was huge in stature, with all his members of such size that they did not exceed his size but fitted such a build. His hair was black, his beard long, his forehead open and free, his eyes large and piercing, his appearance broad but in proportion, his voice like a trumpet, adding a certain majesty of soul to the eloquence which was easy to him.[20]

Of no other character in the *Relatio* do we get such a description. His piety and place as foremost patron of the Cistercians in England are noted, and he is given the longest speech in the piece. He appears early and is the focus at the end of the story, when the English nobles gather around him to give thanks to God for their victory. Walter is given far greater prominence in Aelred than in Henry (where he is simply listed [in second place] among the English leaders), but if we read Aelred's work with one eye on Henry's version and keep in mind Aelred's relationship with King David, we see that "the real hero of the piece" is not Walter, but King David.

Two peculiarities of Aelred's *Relatio* should be noted. First, Aelred never refers to King David or Prince Henry by name, in spite of the difficulties in achieving a smooth text when referring to them only by title. At first I thought that this might be a case of avoiding lèse majesté, but this theory did not seem to hold up under examination. In the *Relatio*, Aelred does not hesitate to name King Stephen and in his *Life of King David* he calls King David and Prince Henry by name. While accepting that lèse majesté is a possibility which cannot be disproved, it seems to me more likely that Aelred is attempting to distance himself from the Scottish king and the prince. If he wishes to clear King David's character, his impartiality would be more likely to be called into question if he made a point of his closeness to King David and his son. To deal with them more formally tends to make them more distant. Aelred's use of this device must remain a speculation primarily because it does not seem to work very well. As we shall see, the conduct of the king is described in such a personal and intimate fashion that the sense of distance is lost.

The attempt to appear impartial and objective is also indicated by the second peculiarity, which is that Aelred does not talk about the Scottish atrocities in this narrative. They are described only in speeches. The first time is in Walter's speech. Walter never mentions King David in connection with the Scottish atrocities. The second time is even more noteworthy since it takes place in the presence of King David and his entourage.

These scenes with King David and his immediate followers are original with Aelred and tell us a great deal.[21] The first scene involves Robert the Bruce, a nobleman holding fiefs from both the Scottish and English kings who has sided with the English. He is granted an audience with King David and says:

> Beware moreover lest thou be involved in the sins of wicked men, at whose hands are required the slaughter of children, the grief of pregnant women, the injury of priests, contempt even for the Divinity—against whom the blood not of one Abel but of unnumbered innocents cries from the earth. Thou hast seen O king, the vile abominations which these men have done. Thou hast seen, I say, thou hast seen, hast abhorred, hast wept, hast beaten thy breast, hast exclaimed that it was done against thy command, against thy will, against thy decree.[22]

The king is moved to tears by Robert's appeal and is on the verge of withdrawing his army when his nephew, William, "the chief provoker of war," intervenes. In a rage, William accuses Robert of treason and convinces the king that he has no honorable choice but to launch the attack.[23]

Aelred does not comment directly on King David's character but illustrates it by the king's actions. Not only his remorse at the conduct of his army and his love for his vassal Robert, but also his relationship with his son, Prince Henry, show us what kind of man the king really is:

> [The prince] was a youth beautiful of face and handsome in
> appearance; of such humility that he seemed lower than all,
> of such authority that he was feared by all; so gentle, so gen-
> tle, so lovable, so affacble that he was beloved of all; so
> chaste in body, in speech so sober, in all his ways so honor-
> able—so zealous in the church, so diligent in prayer; so kind
> to the poor, against ill-doers so resolute, so submissive to
> priests and monks—that he seemed as a king to simulate the
> monk, and as a monk, the king. He was moreover of such
> bravery that none in that army was like him, either in at-
> tacking the enemy or in courageously receiving his attack—
> bolder than the rest in pursuit, keener for the repulse, un-
> readier to flee.[24]

When the course of the battle turns against the Scots, it is Prince
Henry who tries to redeem the day by leading a furious cavalry
charge with his followers while the king attempts to rally the army.
Both valiant efforts end in failure; the king is forced by his retinue
to leave the field to prevent his capture by the English. Prince
Henry, finding himself in the midst of the enemy, escapes by masquerading as an English knight and later demonstrates his charity
by giving his armor to a peasant.[25] When Prince Henry retires to
Caerleon he finds his father, deserted by the army now dispersed
and fled, but refusing to retreat further without word of his son.[26]

So in the end it appears that Aelred wrote the *Relatio* not to
provide a more accurate account of the battle than Henry (though
I believe he does so) nor to emphasize the role of Walter Espec
(which he certainly does). He wrote to correct Henry's portrait of
King David, not a bloody-handed butcher responsible for sacrilege
and atrocities, but a kind man, a brave warrior, and a loving father.

I think we need to admit that Aelred does not seem to have succeeded in his purpose. Only two contemporary manuscripts survive, and it seems possible that the work was not generally understood or influential in his time. Henry's *Chronicle* with its brief but
hostile description of King David's actions seems to have been
more widely known. Whether or not Henry's contemporaries
paid as much attention to the portion on the Battle of the Standard
as Aelred apparently feared they would seems impossible now to
determine.

Walter Espec's highly visible role in Aelred's work, while what one would expect of a Cistercian writer dealing with so important a patron, diverts attention from the skillful clearing of King David from responsibility for the Scottish atrocities. The difficulty is that the overt lauding of Walter so completely eclipses the covert defense of the unnamed Scottish king that a reader unaware of Henry's blackening of King David's character is unable even to perceive the main purpose of the work.

Perhaps it is most satisfactory to say that Aelred's apparent failure in his short term purpose was in the long term irrelevant. Today those who wish to learn about King David of Scotland do not read Henry's *Chronicle* or Aelred's *Relatio*. They are most likely to look at Aelred's earlier work, the *Life of King David*. Here they come to know the saintly man whom Aelred "loved beyond all mortals."[27]

St. Gregory's Abbey

NOTES

*This paper would not have been written without the help and support of many people, at least some of whom must be mentioned. While it may seem that I take issue with Fr. Aelred Squire, I feel obliged to point out that my work was only possible because of the groundwork laid by Fr. Aelred who replied most graciously when I contacted him about my plans to work on Aelred's *Relatio*. Fr. Jude Bell of my own monastery deserves all the credit for trying to get my thoughts into understandable English. Sr. Jane Patricia Freeland responded to a trans-Atlantic query about assistance in translating the *Relatio* by sending a complete translation, a photocopy of the text in the *Rolls Series*, and a photocopy of the Rievaulx manuscript. Finally, I must express my appreciation to Dr. Marsha Dutton who encouraged me to write this paper and was a constant help not only morally but in supplying texts to one prevented by vows of stability from doing library research firsthand. To these and others I am deeply indebted. This paper would never have been possible without them, obviously. Of course responsibility for all conclusions and any errors is entirely my own.

1. David Knowles o.s.b., *The Monastic Order in England* (Cambridge, 1949), p. 264.

2. Aelred Squire o.p., "Historical Factors in the Formation of Aelred of Rievaulx," Coll. 22 (1960) 262.

3. Walter Daniel, *The Life of Aelred of Rievaulx*, trans. and ed. Sir Maurice Powicke (Clarendon Press, 1978) p. xcv.

4. Aelred Squire o.p. *Aelred of Rievaulx: A Study* (S.P.C.K., 1969; Kalamazoo, 1981), p. 78.

5. Hans Delbrück, *History of the Art of War; Within the Framework of Political History*, III: *The Middle Ages*, trans. Walter J. Renfroe, Jr. (Greenwood Press, 1982), p. 352.

6. *Bibliotheca Aelrediana*, ed. Anselm Hoste (Steenbrugge, 1962) attributes the Corpus Christi manuscript to Hexham. Squire, *Aelred: A Study*, p. 74, states that it is from Sawley. Prof. David N. Bell of the memorial University of Newfoundland directed me to *Medieval Libraries of Great Britain: A List of Surviving Books*, ed. N.R. Ker (London: Offices of the Royal Historical Society, 1964), p. 338, for conclusive attribution of the manuscript to Sawley.

7. Squire, *Aelred: A Study*, p. 163, note 14. The Rievaulx manuscript begins with the phrase, *Rege igitur Stephano circa partes australes occupato . . .*, towhich is prefixed in the Sawley manuscript: *Anno dominicae incarnationis MCXXXVIII. . . .* See Aelred of Rievaulx, *De bello Standardii* in vol. III *Chronicles of the Reigns of Stephen, Henry II and Richard I*, ed. Richard Howless, *Rolls Series* (1886), p. 438.

8. Squire, *Aelred: A Study*, p. 76. Henry's opening is: *Occupato igitur rege circa partes australes. . . .* See Henry of Huntingdon, *Henrici Archdiaconi Huntendunensis Historia Anglorum*, ed. Thomas Arnold, *Rolls Series* (1879), p. 261.

9. Squire, *Aelred: A Study*, p. 76.

10. Walter Daniel, p. 10.

11. Alan O. Anderson, *Scottish Annals from English Chroniclers A.D. 500 to 1286* (London, 1908), p. 156.

12. Walter Daniel, p. 10. Concerning the Reason for Aelred's trip to Archbishop Thurstan, R.L.G. Ritchie, *The Normans in Scotland* (Edinburgh, 1954), p. 253, says: "The business was no doubt connected with the claims to the archiepiscopal jurisdiction over Glasgow which Bishop John was then rebutting with his accustomed vigour."

13. Walter Daniel, pp. 13–16.

14. Henry of Huntingdon, ed. Arnold. Aelred of Rievaulx, *De bello*, ed. Howlett.

15. Anderson, p. 179.

16. Henry of Huntingdon, ed. Arnold, p. 262.

17. Anderson, p. 197, note 3.

18. Squire, *Aelred: A Study*, p. 78.

19. Squire, *Aelred: A Study*, p. 78.

20. Sr. Jane Patricia Freeland, unpublished translation of Aelred's *Relatio*.

21. It is worth noting that Aelred was at Wark with Abbot William to arrange the surrender of Walter Espec's castle there to King David. While there is no evidence that King David and Aelred discussed the recent battle, it is certainly possible. See Alberic Stacpoole, "The Public Face of Aelred." *The Downside Review*, 85/280 (1967) 323.

22. Anderson, p. 194.

23. Anderson, p. 195.

24. Anderson, p. 199.

25. Anderson, pp. 203–204 and 206–207.

26. Anderson, p. 207.

27. Anderson, p. 156.

JUST HOW COGENTLY CAN ONE ARGUE FOR THE INFLUENCE OF JOHN SCOTUS ERIUGENA ON WILLIAM OF SAINT-THIERRY?

Thomas Michael Tomasic

A RESPECTRUL introductory disclaimer is in order in virtue of the fact that nowhere in this paper is the reference made to the astute and thoroughly excellent studies of David Bell, John Anderson, and Rozanne Elder about either the influence (or lack thereof) of Eriugena, or of certain Greek Patristic sources, on William. This seemingly strange absence signals neither ignorance of, nor disrespect for, those painstakingly careful and insightful studies. The necessity of reexamining the entire question "from scratch" was determined by access to a problem-solving methodology not available to Bell, Anderson, and Elder, namely, the aid of a mindless, and hence thoroughly objective, bright Burroughs B6800 mainframe. From its inception, therefore, this project has enjoyed a certain privileged independence and autonomy circumstantially not afforded other scholars.

In a paper read here last year on the influence of St. Gregory of Nyssa, as some present will recall, the computer was able to establish that fifty-one per cent of William's *Physica animae* was reproduced either verbatim or by extraordinarily close paraphrasing from Gregory's *De hominis opificio*, and that significant iterations from Gregory appeared in other works, but only those William wrote after his *De natura corporis et animae*. By comparison with the present search for Eriugenian influence on William, fixing the exact range of Gregory's influence on William was a veritable "piece of cake." William's *De natura corporis et animae* is a textbook compilation (intended undoubtedly for the education of

educable monks) of various authorities on the physics of the body
(drawn from philosophical authors) and on the physics of the soul
(drawn exclusively from theological authors). In fact, in the transition from the *Physica corporis* to the *Physica animae*, William states
these are not his words but the words of others:

> Sed iam, ut dictum est, ad animam transeamus; nec quid de
> ea philosophi vel physici saeculi sentiant vel opinentur, sed
> quid catholici Patres a Deo didicerint et homines docuerint,
> breviter perstringamus.

If the oriental Father, Gregory, might normally have been thought
an unlikely authority for a western twelfth-century monk to cite,
especially verbatim, Eriugena—given his unsavory theological
reputation in the twelfth century—is excruciatingly far less likely to
be cited verbatim or even paraphrased too closely. The difficulty
of finding any reflection at all of Eriugena in William has been
solidly confirmed by previous scholarship on this question; nevertheless, the conclusion to be drawn from this fact is far too weak
to cogently eliminate either one of two possible alternatives: (1)
either William absolutely did not incorporate Eriugena in his
works or (2) William did organically incorporate Eriugena but
camouflaged the incorporation masterfully.

We wanted to devise some way of telling which alternative is
more probably true. Let us allow, therefore, for the sake of argument, that William may have used one or more Eriugenian texts
but that he masterfully camouflaged Eriugenian concepts in his
own words, thus avoiding any noticeable and clearly identifiable
technical Eriugenian terms. Such a possible scenario, which we
may call "the best possible case argument," is imaginary and arbitrary at this point; we could just as well have chosen a "worst
possible case argument." We must, however, assume one or the
other as a starting point in order to devise a strategy which will, by
comparison and contrast, test for true and false. Just how we
might assess the probable truth or falsity of "the best possible case
argument," that is, the influence of author E on author W in the
case author W does not employ linguistic expressions indigenous
to author E, can be illustrated by providing an analogous example.

Let us imagine that student W, who is not a plagiarist, has submitted an original term paper in any field of study. Among the many authors he has consulted, as we find in his bibliography, is author E. You, patient and long-suffering hearers, are hereby help-lessly corralled into playing the role of the teacher, reading and evaluating student W's paper. As you read, you are struck by un-canny reminiscences of author E, with whose works you are thor-oughly conversant. When, however, you search the text of author E you cannot precisely locate the comparable passage for lack of recognizable strings of identical words. Competent teacher that you are, you nevertheless quite readily recognize identical con-ceptual patterns, that is, you catch genuine qualitative influence but not literal quantitative influence; significant influence is con-ceptually but not visually apparent. It is axiomatic among Platon-ists and Neoplatonists alike that the senses, in this case the unaided eye, are notoriously inaccurate and unreliable; one must rather look to conceptual patterns, paradigms, models, or isomorphisms. It is simply the case that the self-same concept can be embodied essentially in very unlike words of the same or different language-type just as genera and species can be enfleshed in very unlike in-dividuals.

Resolving the question of Eriugena's influence on William can logically be modelled on the same method one would use to locate or excavate the site of conceptual isomorphisms found in student W's paper in the text of author E. To do so with plausibility, it was necessary to devise a computer program which could override the restriction of comparing merely literal strings of words and would locate, compare, and map similar logical and conceptual structures. Such a program had to be open to generating an in-numerable amount of false comparisons. We then ran the compar-ison program on two separate groups of texts, which we shall name ALPHA and BETA. ALPHA is comprised of the five books of Eriugena's *Periphyseon*, his translations of the works of the Pseudo-Dionysius (*On the Divine Names, The Mystical Theology, The Ce-lestial Hierarchy, The Ecclesiastical Hierarchy*, and the *Ten Letters*), his translation of the *Ambigua* of Maximus the Confessor, and the translation by Thomas Gallus of the *Epistola ad Thomam*, which is reasonably closely modeled on Eriugena's now missing translation. We lacked, at the time of running, an acceptable text of the *Epis-tola ad Thalassium* of Eriugena. The ALPHA group amounts to approximately 40,000 lines. Group BETA is comprised of William's works and amounts to approximately 27,000 lines. Combined, files ALPHA and BETA contain approximately 630,000 words which were listed alphabetically and indexed or cross-referenced in less than one half hour. The amount of process time required to complete the textual comparison of ALPHA and BETA was twenty-seven hours continuous and produced a printout of 219,000 lines. As already mentioned, an output of such magnitude generated by an extraordinarily open program was bound to produce an overwhelmingly large humber of false comparisons, the elimination of which fell on the weary shoulders of the researcher.

What has the computer led us to find? First, and to eliminate a massive body of potentially influential literature, the probability that William did not incorporate a single idea directly from the Pseudo-Dionysius and Maximus the Confessor is incredibly high —so high, in fact, as to render the belief of Dionysian influence unjustified at this stage. However, since negative proofs are *never* conclusive and absolutely exhaustive, an *admonitum* must be delivered. It is always possible that a better logistical machine approach may be devised in the future which can ferret out what we did not; it is also important to note that establishing beyond reasonable doubt absence of significant or incorporated influence is not logically equivalent to the assertion William did not read the Pseudo-Dionysius or Maximus the Confessor. Anyone who reads the examination and term papers of contemporary college students cannot be ignorant of the complete lack of influence of texts that in fact were read.

Having swiftly dispensed with the Pseudo-Dionysius and Maximus, which, in effect, narrows down the question of influence to the *Periphyseon*, do we have significant probable grounds to believe Eriugena had any influence on William's thought? The computer pulled together the following comparisons:

Deus ergo, hoc nomen, quod quasi proprie proprium est summae illius naturae, a Graeco sumptum esse nemo est qui ambigat. Est autem sive a verbo	N. Huius itaque nominis etymologia a Graecis assumpta est: aut enim a verbo quod est THEORO, hoc est video, dirivatur; aut ex verbo THEO, hoc

quod est THEORO; sive ab eo quod est THEO; seu magis ab utroque: THEORO quippe, video interpretatur; THEO curro. Quid enim velocius currit stabili illo motu, qui stabilis in seipso manens, movet omnia; quid tam velociter cuncta percurrit, quam qui dixit, et facta sunt omnia? Facile etiam omnia et simul videt, in quo sunt omnia, et in semetipso videt omnia.

153. Divina ergo natura in Sponso per capream designatur, tum propter velocitatem cursus, tum propter acumen visus. Per hinnulum quoque cervorum, apte satis humana natura in Sponso exprimitur. Apparuit nempe in mundo homo Christus, quasi hinnulus cervorum, hoc est filius Iudaeorum. Ipse Ipse quippe filius dilectus "Unicornium".... (Cant, ed. Déchanet, p. 322)

est curro; aut (quod probabilius est quia unus idemque intellectus inest) ab utroque dirivari recte accipitur. Nam cum a verbo THEORO deducitur THEOS videns interpretatur; ipse enim omnia quae sunt in se ipso videt dum nihil extra se ipsum aspiciat quia nihil extra se ipsum est: cum vero a verbo THEO THEOS deducitur currens recte intelligitur; ipse enim in omnia currit et nullo modo stat sed omnia currendo implet, sicut scriptum est: "Velociter currit sermo eius." Attamen nullo modo movetur. De Deo siquidem verissime dicitur motus stabilis et status mobilis. Stat enim in se ipso incommutabiliter numquam naturalem suam stabilitatem deserens, movet autem se ipsum per omnia ut sint ea quae a se essentialiter subsistunt. Motu enim ipsius omnia fiunt. Ac per hoc unus idemque intellectus est in duabus interpretationibus eiusdem nominis quod est Deus. Non enim alius est Deo currere per omnia quam videre omnia, sed sicut videndo ita et currendo fiunt omnia. (PL 122: 452B–52D)

Igitur HYPERTHEOS, id est plus quam Deus. THEOS enim videns interpretatur. Sed si ad aliam originem huius nominis recurras, ita ut non a verbo THEORO, id est video, sed a verbo THEO, id est curro, THEOS, id est Deum, dirivari intelligas, adest tibi similiter eadem ratio. Nam currenti non currens opponitur sicut tarditas celeritati. Erit igitur HYPER-THEOS, id est plus quam currens, sicut scriptum est: "Velociter currit sermo eius." Nam hoc de Deo verbo, quod ineffabiliter per omnia quae sunt ut sint currit, intelligimus. (460A)

This passage on the spurious etymology of the Greek word THEOS, contextually nestled in bed with the *Sponsus* and *sponsa* in William's *Expositio super Cantica canticorum*, favorably compares with Eriugena, *Periphyseon* I, 452C ff. Earlier comparison of these two texts by other authors has been the focus of some controversy. Fair enough if, indeed, argument impinged solely on this single comparison.

The computer, however, noted another point of comparison between a passage in the *Expositio super Cantica*, approximately ten lines following the THEOS etymology, and a passage in *Periphyseon* I, approximately a column before the THEOS etymology. Proximity, of course, counts; more importantly, however, attention should be directed to the *semantical* proximity—even synonomy—between the two following texts, the left from William's *Expositio super Cantica*, the right from Eriugena's *Periphyseon* I:

Ipse enim cotidie venit ad sponsam suam, fidelem animam, sicut caprea visus acuti, et velocis cursus, cum efficit et mundat in ea oculum contemplationis, et veloces perficit effectus in ministerio bonae actionis. Mirabili enim condescensione gra-

Ait [Maximus] enim theophaniam effici non aliunde nisi ex Deo, fieri vero ex condescensione divini verbi, hoc est unigeniti Filii qui est sapientia Patris, veluti deorsum versus ad humanam naturam a se conditam atque purgatam, et exalta-

tiae sapientia Dei adveniens, intellectum hominis ibi subiungit et conformat; sicque ex illuminante gratia, et illuminata intelligentia, modo quodam ineffabili, fit quasi quaedam composita sapientia, complectens omnes virtutes; ut et feratur in Deum homo Dei per illuminatum intellectum, nec tamen animus virtutum, in exteriora et inferiora sanctitatis suae, deneget effectus. Ibi ergo videt, hic currit, cum nequaquam posset impleri in uno homine uniformitas tam diversa, nisi fieret ex Verbi Dei et intelligentiae humanae, ex gratiae Dei et humanae pietatis, amica quadam et efficaci conformitate. Venit etiam ad eam quasi hinnulus cervorum, hoc est sicut Filius hominis, cum sicut aliquando sponsae Ecclesiae, veniens in mundum, sacramentum susceptae humanitatis attulit in pignus amoris, sic eiusdem gratiae fidelem memoriam fideli animae efficacius inspirat, in provocatione caritatis. Sic ergo Sponsus apud sponsam similis habetur capreae hinnuloque cervorum, cum de huiusmodi quibusdam "theoriis," sive "theophaniis," esurientem pascit, reficit afflictam; quae non nisi cum vultu eius laetitia adimpletur. Et veniens non semper salit aut tran-

tione sursum versus humanae naturae ad praedictum verbum per divinum amorem. Condescensionem hic dico non eam quae iam facta est per incarnationem sed eam quae fit per theosin, id est per deificationem, creaturae. Ex ipsa igitur sapientiae Dei condescensione ad humanam naturam per gratiam et exaltatione eiusdem naturae ad ipsam sapientiam per dilectionem fit theophania. (448D–49B)

Similiter de iustitia caeterisque virtutibus exponit non aliter fieri nisi ex divinae sapientiae nostraeque intelligentiae quadam mirabili atque ineffabili conformatione. In quantum enim, ut ait Maximus, humanus intellectus ascendit per caritatem, in tantum divina sapientia descendit per misericordiam, et haec est causa omnium virtutum et substantia. Igitur omnis theophania, id est omnis virtus, et in hac vita in qua adhuc incipit in his qui digni sunt formari et in futura vita perfectionem divinae beatitudinis accepturi non extra se sed in se et ex Deo et ex se ipsis efficitur. (449C–D)

silit; sed aliquando etiam appro-
pinquat et stat, cum plusculo
quodam gaudio semetipsum ei
indulgens, taedium desideran-
tis, et lassitudinem tendentis, et
amantis pietatem abundantiore
gratia consolatur. Unde et sub-
ditur: "En ipse stat post par-
ietem nostram." (Déchanet,
pp. 324–26)

William's text marvelously reiterates Eriugena's, employing the
same conceptual structure, albeit in his own accustomed language
and inserted in his own context.

A rather fascinating comparison of notions in agreement on four
substantive issues was discovered between *Periphyseon* I (PL 122:
456A–58D) and a rather large, approximately 700-line, section of
William's *Aenigma fidei* (PL 180: 421B–34D). William sand-
wiches extensive doctrinal exfoliation in between four points of
significant agreement with Eriugena. (1) Both substantially agree
on the absence of any mode or manner of signifying the Divine
Unity or Trinity by any mode of speech because neither Unity
nor Trinity is of such a kind that it can be *conceived* by the human
intellect. As a codicil to this first point, both Eriugena and William
do focus on nonconceptual, noncategorical ways of knowing elsewhere. (2) The Divine Unity is not an individual, nor does it consist of numerical threeness; nor can Divinity be construed as bar-
ren or unproductive internally. (3) Both authors similarly expound
on the problem generated by construing the Trinitarian Persons as
"substances." Where Eriugena uses the term "substance" William
substitutes "essence," commenting that it is better to use
"essence" than "substance." In *Periphyseon* I, Eriugena paraphrases
Gregory the Theologian's, that is, Gregory of Nyssa's, reply to the
Eunomians, stating that while the names "Father," "Son," and
"Holy Spirit" can be said to denote substances, they really denote
neither nature nor operation, but pure relations; he then denies
that Persons are conditions (*accidens* or *habitus*) or are differentiated
thereby. William, correspondingly, having substituted "essence"
for "substance," similarly proceeds to speak of each Person as an

essence, construes "essence" as "relation," denies that Person denotes a condition (*accidens* or *habitus*), rejects the notion that Persons are differentiated by operation, and then informs us quite generically that this was the sort of reply made to early (unnamed) heresies in the early Church by (unnamed) Church Fathers. (4) In discussing the relation between Father and Son, both use, in a fairly similar way, the analogous relationship of Abraham and Isaac. William, however, merely mentions the paternal-filial relation of Abraham and Isaac without explanation, assuming, it would seem, that the analogy would be obvious to his readers. Eriugena develops the notion that "father " and "son" denote the distinct substances of Abraham and Isaac respectively, that is, the special and distinctive personhood of each, thus explicitly drawing out his analogical explanation of the Father-Son substantial relation in the Trinity. The proximity within the respective texts of four critical themes, which constitute a sort of subtreatise in both authors, seems sufficiently cogent probable cause to reasonably believe influence.

There appears one, isolated instance of possible influence of Eriugena in a work by William antedating the *De natura corporis et animae*. In the *De contemplando Deo* (ed. Hourlier, 8.10–13, p. 88), chronologically William's first work, he explicitly gives an eliptical or contracted version of the Pseudo-Dionysius's definition of love found in *Periphyseon* I (519B): "Amor est naturalis motus omnium rerum quae in motu sunt finis quietaque statio. . . ." Since we know beyond reasonable doubt William did not use the Pseudo-Dionysius elsewhere, the likely source is surely Eriugena. William ends with another etymological rendition of the word THEOS, meaning by it the completely uneriugenian *timor Dei*. It is almost as if William were putting his readers on notice that he is terminating his use of Eriugena at that location.

In brief, there are, in all, no less than six and not more than twelve reasonably probably instances of assimilated borrowings from Eriugena. All borrowings are drawn from *Periphyseon* I, drawn from an area limited to approximately ten pages in the Sheldon-Williams edition, or from columns 448C–519B in Migne's *Patrologia latina*. Nevertheless, this seems the appropriate place to once more issue an *admonitum*. The computer does participate in some species of infallibility, but only if the programmer tells it the right thing to do. It may well be that failings indigenous to fallible and indeterminate human minds caused us to err by defect in appropriate logistics. Some genuine comparisons may have escaped. It is important to appreciate the fact that negative proofs are indeed inconclusive because never exhaustive. By fitting extension, just because one sophisticated and open program uncovered comparable conceptual structures shared by Eriugena and William in one terribly small sector of Eriugena's *Periphyseon* I, does not, in itself, *absolutely* establish that some quite different program might locate favorably comparable structures in other sectors. Be that as it may, while my contribution to settling the question of Eriugena's influence on William is decidedly modest, it has the virtue of precision. The computer marked out with remarkable precision the boundary in Eriugena of probably influence. Although William did not incorporate far more interesting and eventful concepts from Eriugena, we can now with justification claim that he used, and of course knew, at least a minute portion of *Periphyseon* I, either directly or through some secondary channel.

John Carroll University

THE STYLE OF NICHOLAS
OF CLAIRVAUX'S LETTERS

Dorette Sabersky

NICHOLAS OF CLAIRVAUX or Montiéramey[1] was Bernard's favorite secretary from about 1146 to 1152,[2] that is, during
Bernard's last years. He appeared to be the ideal secretary, since he
adapted very easily to Bernard's style, displaying a linguistic sen-
sibility for Bernard's typical way of writing. Yet this ability does
not only show in Nicholas' continuous efforts to imitate his master's style, but also led to the numerous plagiarisms which mark
his texts. Thus Giles Constable has suggested rightly that the well-
known fact of Nicholas' repeated misuse of Bernard's seal and con-
fidence, resulting in the secretary's flight from Clairvaux, might
have been the consequence of his identification with Bernard's
authority.[3]

It has been said that the unfavorable evaluation which Nicholas'
writings received by scholars is influenced by our knowledge of his
lack of moral integrity.[4] This might be true in some respect, but
overall it is his literary work itself that reveals certain shortcomings
mainly connected with his character. It is the purpose of this paper
to examine this statement and to show Nicholas' attitude towards
literary production. The term "style" will be used here in a very
wide sense meaning the literary expression of the writer's personality.[5] While it would not be easy to exactly distinguish the structure of Nicholas' language from that of other contemporary monastic writers like Bernard, Peter the Venerable, and Peter of Celle,
the application of a more general conception of style strikingly
reveals the characteristic quality of Nicholas' texts.

Nicholas' literary output consists essentially of nineteen sermons
and about sixty letters, most of them written during his stay in

Clairvaux[6] and more than a third of which written in the name of another person.[7] The reason I will consider particularly his letters is that in them personal involvement is more conspicuous.

Nicholas' relationship to Bernard plays on different levels. First, we have Nicholas' own work, determined by his imitative style and containing many literal quotations; he even presents some of Bernard's sermons as his own.[8] Then, on the other hand, we find in some of Bernard's letters traces typical of Nicholas' style from which we can conclude that Nicholas composed these letters himself.[9] Finally, Nicholas revised some of Bernard's sermons for Pope Adrian IV after Bernard's death,[10] a practice Jean Leclercq has called "faire du Saint Bernard."[11]

In the letters Nicholas must have written for Bernard, the style is less pretentious and simpler than in his own letters.[12] This is more likely an indication of restraint on Bernard's part[13] than of the secretary's endeavor to imitate Bernard's spirit. This assumption is confirmed by Nicholas' own letters, where we see no basic difference between those he wrote in his own name and those written for someone else.[14]

It may be that a painstaking analysis and comparison could define more precisely the extent of Nicholas' participation in Bernard's work: the syntactical structure of his sentences is similar to Bernard's, but often clumsier, less clear, less elegant, and rhythmically less balanced. His very frequent use of word plays is at times rather superficial and, in opposition to Bernard's use, of little importance to the development of the contents. Repetitions of certain phrases and topics occur ever so often. He favors rather unusual words and likes to quote classical authors. His literary exertions are only too obvious. All these aspects evidence Nicholas' lack of Bernard's creative spontaneity and mastery of language.

Surprisingly, in the introduction to his letter-collection Nicholas himself refers to his abundant repetitions of commonplaces, admitting his lack of originality and noting that his forte lies more with his memory than with his imagination.[15] Also, in quoting Seneca, he expresses his taste for appropriating passages from other authors, especially from Bernard;[16] yet, such statements about himself can be quite deceiving.[17]

Since most of Nicholas' letters are written to friends, we naturally find themes characteristic of epistolary friendship. In Nicholas' texts these themes easily become mannerisms repeated again and again. The following examples will illustrate the formalized and unoriginal structure of his texts, causing absolute positions that contradict each other, without, however, touching on the fundamental diversity inherent in human complexity.

References to brevity, very common in letter writing, often occur in Nicholas' texts. While writers like Peter the Venerable[18] or Bernard[19] use comments on brevity mainly in regard to lengthy letters and vary their expressions according to the circumstances, Nicholas concludes his letters with almost the same phrases justifying the prolixity by his great love for the friend, his desire to communicate with him. An example is in Ep 6: "... ecce monachus factus sum in longitudine litterarum, sed stilum currentem instigavit plurimus affectus. Parcat affectui, qui novit affectum: et prolixitatem deputet caritati."[20]

Although a letter can console a far-away friend,[21] written communication cannot substitute for a face to face talk. The metaphors "dead-alive" reflect this: "Conspectus enim et conversatio habent aliquid vivae voluptatis, quam mortui apices non loquuntur."[22] The quotation "eye-contact and personal conversation create a vivid pleasure" appears in seven different letters.[23]

On the other hand, we frequently find reference to the dialectics of absence in epistolary friendship—that is to say, the presence of a spiritual bond in spite of spatial distance—and Nicholas stresses this idea quite strongly. Again he uses a quotation, supposedly by Cicero:[24] "Those are more present who see each other mentally than with their eyes, and it means more to be connected in the heart than in the body."[25] Nicholas hereby not only states that the spiritual unity of friends is not confined to bodily proximity,[26] but gives physical presence a negative taint. Thus, he adds to the quotation the words "chaste" and "purifying love": "In sacrario enim casti et castificantis amoris praesentiores sibi sunt, qui se animis quam oculis intuentur, quia plus est connecti corde quam corpore."[27] In another instance, he restricts the validity of the first quotation to worldly-minded people: "Scio ego quia conspectus et conversatio habent aliquid vivae voluptatis, sed hoc in saecularibus."[28] Such a rigorous point of view which omits the human level seems to offer an overly subtle remedy for the pain of separation. The fact that the letter ends with quite human feelings, expressing the

hope of seeing the friend again before death, manifests the
theoretical and unreal character of such speculations.

We can distinguish two opposing attitudes toward spiritual love
as characterized by the above quotations: first, the humanly natural desire to enjoy the company of the friend and, second, the spiritual love carried to such extremes that it rejects the idea of physical presence. Nicholas is well aware of the contradiction between
the two positions as shown by the corrections he makes in the one
quotation where the two occur together:

> Doleo igitur sed et dolebo, nec me consolabitur illa
> verisimilis, sed **non vera sententia:** Nemo sibi de absentia
> blandiatur: praesentiores sunt, qui se animis quam oculis in-
> tuentur: et plus corde quam corpore. Quamvis enim plenior
> cognitio sit in spiritu, conspectus tamen et conversatio hab-
> ent aliquid vivae voluptatis, quam isti **allegorice diligentes**
> exhibere non possunt.[29]
>
> Minime quidem deserit me quocumque iero dulcissima tui
> memoria, sed quanto memoria dulcior, tanto absentia mo-
> lestior est.[30] Absit autem ut me consoletur illa verisimilis,
> sed **non vera sententia:** Praesentiores inquit sunt qui se
> animis quam qui oculis intuentur, et plus est corde connecti,
> quam corpore. Quasi vero conspectus et conversatio non
> habeant aliquid vivae voluptatis, quae non potest absentibus
> provenire. Sed haec sicut arbitror, **ex ratione** non ex affec-
> tione locutus est ille Romanae eloquentiae splendor [sc.
> Cicero] . . . .[31]

As one can see in these texts, he twice denies the contents of the
quotation on excessive spiritual love, It is interesting that Nicholas
calls this love allegorical and attributes the quotation to rational
thinking.

One example will illustrate Nicholas' procedure in comparison
to some of Bernard's texts which he seems to have used as models:

> Quod si divisa sunt corpora, numquid corda dividi poterunt
> in aeternum? Si spatia locorum vel intervalla temporum cor-
> porum separant praesentiam, numquid unitatem et unan-
> imitatem recidere poterunt animorum? Absit! Neque enim
> diligimus nos sicut homines, qui se diligunt ut homines: qui

in carne et sanguine, carnis et sanguinis affectant praesentiam. Nostra dilectio tota de puritate descendit, tota spiritum redolet, nihil habens terrenitatis admistum. Spiritus est qui vivificat, caro non prodest quidquam [Jn 6:64]. Quid enim est aliud caro quam caro? Corpusculum fragile, vile mancipium, minima pars mei abest tibi. Spiritus tuus bonus semper est in spiritu meo, mecum manet, mecum perseverat, numquam recedit a me. memoriam suavitatis tuae eructabo [cf. Ps 144:7] quoad vixero.[32] In aeternum non obliviscar tui, nec poterit facere malitia temporis ut te vel ad horam de pectore meo subripiat; huiusmodi amor locorum et temporis incommoda penitus ignorat, semper enim licet diligere, etsi quem diligas videre non liceat. Caritas Christi, quamvis absentem, praesentem tamen te mihi reddit: et quanto longius recessisti a me, tanto ardentius in visceribus meis remansisti. Absit ut tua dilectio maris mihi fluctibus auferatur, cum scriptum sit: Aquae multae non potuerunt exstinguere caritatem, nec flumina obruent illam [Sg 8:7]. . . .[33]

The letter starts out with an expression of longing to see the friend. After an explanation why this hope could hardly be fulfilled follows the assurance that physical separation cannot destroy the unity of souls. It is a purely spiritual love, whereas human love in flesh and blood strives towards bodily presence.[34] This he bases on the opposition of spirit and flesh. Thus, Nicholas again equates the desire of physical presence with worldly love. From the context it is obvious that he does not really mean it.

This passage might depend on Bernard's *Letter 103* in which he tries to inspire the brother of one of his monks to join the monastic life.[35] Bernard offers him friendship originating not in blood and flesh but in the spirit of God and expects him to live up to it. The biblical terms "blood" and "flesh" implicate the search for material, ephemeral goods but by no means bodily presence. This idea is expressed even more clearly in *Letter 107* concerning an attempted conversion. Bernard describes the requested presence of the recipient by telling him that he is not looking for anything associated with blood and flesh, but for mutual spiritual profit.[36]

One might object that the context of Bernard's texts is totally different and therefore not comparable to Nicholas' letter. Yet that is just the point: Bernard does not use the subject of spirit and flesh

in an unnatural way. Bernard deals here with the circumstances of
a conversion where the opposites of spirit and flesh refer to the
alternative of monastery and world, but do not mirror an adverse
position of spiritual love against the body. What in Bernard's letters is quite adequate becomes with Nicholas a cluster of isolated
and exaggerated clichés. Nicholas' image of the monk shows a
tendency towards an artificial rhetorical extravagance. This unreal
attitude is actually confirmed by Nicholas' much more authentic
feelings in his lament on the absence from Clairvaux of Henry of
France.[37]

Subsequently, in Nicholas' *Letter 18* the idea appears that the absent body is the least part of him. This goes back to *Letter 208* by
Bernard, addressed to the king of Sicily.[38] In this letter, Bernard
states that his spirit is present in the monks sent from Clairvaux to
found a monastery in Sicily. This spiritual presence is something
real, not just an abstract formula as in Nicholas' text.[39]

Continuing with Nicholas' *Letter 18*, we find a reference to temporal and spatial obstacles.[40] Previously, a similar phrase led to the
opposition of flesh and spirit, here it introduces the following in-
tensification: "The farther you are from me the closer you are
united with me." Another impressive antithetic formula, but again
it merely remains on the literary level.

How much deeper is the psychological interpretation in *Letter
95* of Peter of Celle:[41] the separation renders the affection more
tender, and that is the necessary proof of perfect love. Presence
dulls the affection by habit, while absence inflames the desire further, as it always searches and never finds, and the same is true also
of the relationship with God.[42]

Nicholas' text clearly manifests his tendency to accumulate themes
and phrases, often taken out of different works by Bernard. In
Bernard's texts there is human richness; the spiritual development
of a subject is always based on a lively and individual situation. Besides the letters which served as stylistic models for Nicholas, there
are many more ideas in Bernard's letters dealing with the acceptance
of absence, for example, that "the will of God must be preferred
to our own feelings and needs,"[43] or that, with Jn 13:7: "It is not
for thee to know, now, what I am doing, but thou wilt understand
it afterwards,"[44] or that the love toward the absent friend
proves its unselfishness,[45] or that for charity's sake he gives up the

presence of a friend.[46] None of these arguments can be found in Nicholas' letters. Just once, in variation of a quotation of Bernard,[47] he mentions that his life for Christ compensates for the separation: "Minime quidem deserit me dulcis vestri memoria. Sed quanto memoria dulcior, tanto absentia esset molestior, nisi ille esset in causa, cui conveniunt omnia; cui nos et vivere, et mori felici necessitate proposuimus...."[48]

Nicholas repeats many phrases until they become abstract and empty clichés, so that the themes often are interchangeable. The texts tend to resemble formalized model letters.

The subject of speech and silence only accentuates the complacency of Nicholas' rhetoric. In his famous *Letter 89*, Bernard anticipating the addressee's retort that writing is a quiet occupation, demonstrates, on the contrary, that even without speaking, composing a letter cannot be called a silent process:

> ... rogo, ubi otium, ubi silentii quies? "Sed haec," inquies, "omnia facere potes in silentio." Mirum si ex sententia hoc respondeas. Quantus enim tumultus est in mente dictantium, ubi **multitudo** perstrepit dictionum, orationum **varietas** et **diversitas** sensuum concurrit, ubi saepe respuitur quod occurrit et requiritur quod excidit? Ubi quid pulchrius secundum litteram, quid consequentius iuxta sententiam, quid planius propter intelligentiam, quid utilius ad conscientiam, quid denique, cui, vel post, vel ante ponatur, intentissime attenditur, multaque alia quae a doctis in huiusmodi curiosius observantur? Et tu in hoc dices mihi esse quietem? Tu hoc, etiamsi lingua sileat, silentium nominabis?.... Siquidem vel monachi quod esse videor, vel peccatoris quod sum, officium non est **docere**, sed lugere.... **Docere** itaque nec indocto est in promptu, nec monacho in ausu, nec paenitenti in affectu.[49]

This passage Nicholas imitates as follows:

> At dicitis: haec omnia in silentio, et magis cum silentio operari potuisti. Mirum si hoc ex sententia dicitis. Quis enim magis in turba est, quam ille qui faciendis dictaminibus implicatur? Perstrepuit enim ut digne inveniri queat sensuum **veritas**, verborum **varietas**, quid melius ad consequentiam,

denique quid, quando, ubi et quomodo proferri oporteat.
Hoc ergo vos iudicabitis silentium et quietem, maxime
homini imperito, cui et sensus nullus adest, vel sermo non
est venustus et facilis ad sententias vestiendas?
Denique vel monachi, quod esse videor, vel peccatoris, quod
sum, non est officium **dictare**, sed flere. **Dictare** ergo nec
indocto est in promptu, nec monacho in ausu, nec paeni-
tenti in affectu.[50]

The changes Nicholas makes are significant for his style. Bernard's
vivid description of the turmoil caused in composing a letter becomes, with Nicholas, a dull and clumsy sentence.

The introduction of the word *veritas* in order to create a word
play with *varietas*, misses the point of Bernard's image of the agita-
tion. Bernard concludes by saying that those who understand the
problems of writing scrutinize these and other matters carefully.
Nicholas, on the other hand, refers to his inability to write, which,
as we shall see, is very typical of him.

It is important to realize that the circumstances under which
these two letters were written are completely different. When
asked by Oger, a regular canon, to give his advice on some doctrinal questions,[51] Bernard answers with Qo 3:1 and 7 that "all
things have their season: there is a time for speaking and a time for
keeping silence," and that the days of Lent are not suitable for
long, elaborate letters. Later on, he adds, with Jerome,[52] that it is
not the duty of the monk to teach but to lament. Thus, Bernard's
objection to writing refers to the silent time of Lent and to the
treatment of complicated questions, not just to a friendly note.

Ignoring such specific reasons, Nicholas takes an extreme point
of view. He only mentions that he swore to abstain from writing,
but he does not indicate why. In replacing the word *docere* by *dictare* he says that writing is not fitting for a monk; what an exagger-
ation! Nicholas uses silence as an effective literary scenery for his
Letter 24 to Peter of Celle who apparently had asked him for some
of Bernard's sermons. He starts out by telling his friend that it
should satisfy him if he, Nicholas, loves him as much as he loves
himself. Nicholas complains that now, by writing to him against
his own convictions, he proves that he loves Peter more than
himself. Nicholas' inappropriate reaction to Peter's request for

some books indicates that he uses Bernard's theme to stage a pose. While Bernard in his letter declines his friend's demand, Nicholas by writing complies with Peter's wishes and thus stresses the confrontation.

The beginning of *Letter 52* to Peter of Celle emphasizes even more the tension between writing and not writing:

> Anxietatem mihi generat et scribere et non scribere vobis: in altero laeditur **amicitia**, in altero propria **conscientia**. Illud quippe contra propositum, istud contra affectum est, monachi namque est non scribere, sed lugere, amici vero et loqui, et frequentibus epistolis interludere, ne muta caritas repraesentet speciem non amantis.[53] In has igitur rerum angustias incidit amicus vester; et sic [= *se*?] verbis indicare gestiens, et loqui aestuat, et veretur. Aestuat ut se aperiat, veretur ne praesumat. Timet, si loquitur, improbus; si taceat, alienus. Quis ergo vincet monachus, vel amicus? Amor qui nescit vinci, vincere consuevit et facile triumphabit de homine; qui de caelorum Domino triumphavit; et de illo quidem tanto facilius, quanto non solum amans sed et ipse amor est,[54] cuius altitudo adaequata est, cuius singularitas associata est, cuius plenitudo effusa est.[55] . . . Iudicabunt alii, prout volverint [= *voluerint*?]: ego malo in verbis excedere, quam vobis non satisfacere, et esse verbosus amicus, quam languidus. . . .[56]

This time, he uses as a model an introduction of a letter by Peter the Venerable:

> Volenti saepe mihi scribere vobis, et cor meum hoc saltem remedio amico communicare, occurrit quod alibi nusquam. Impatiens enim animus, et se verbis indicare gestiens, loqui aestuat, et veretur. Aestuat, ut se aperiat; veretur, ne displiceat. Timet, ne si multum taceat, alienus, si multum loquatur, videatur importunus. Ita fit, ut et loqui et tacere pariter reformidem. Sed malo quandoque in verbis excedere, quam quae dicenda sunt reticere. Hoc dixi, ut frequentibus, quas mitto, litteris, viam faciam, et ad eas saepe legendas, etiam pigritantem amicum oculum vestrum aperiam. Eligo magis verbosus amicus permanere, quam taciturnus sensim ab amore languere.[57]

Although Nicholas quotes literally from Peter's text, his purpose
is quite different. For Peter, who is afraid that the recipient might
disapprove of his excessive verbosity, the stated conflict between
talking and keeping silent serves to excuse his urge to communicate with his friend. Nicholas, however, fashions from it a moral
conflict between the affection of friendship and the conscience of a
monk. Here again, Nicholas declares that the monk is not supposed to write but to lament. "Who will come out on top," he
asks, "the monk or the friend?" The friend, of course, gains the
victory as in *Letter 24*. Following Peter the Venerable, he notes
that he prefers to be a wordy rather than a lukewarm friend. In
opposition to Peter, Nicholas pretends to satisfy his friend by writing. Yet one has to add that Peter of Celle is not eager at all to hear
a continuation of Nicholas' speculations on the unity of God,
which is what this letter is all about.[58] This shows again the artificial character of Nicholas' argumentation. The way Nicholas
picks up the theme of the friend in opposition to the monk again
at the end of the letter points in the direction of humor: The friend
has digressed too much and, by not leaving enough for the monk,
he has erred. By using the word play *relinquit-delinquit*, Nicholas
makes the sentence more impressive. However, his justification
for the love of the friend taking precedence over the silence of the
monk seems too ponderous for a mere joke. Nicholas argues that
love easily triumphs over man because it has triumphed even over
God since God is not only loving, but is love itself. Here, he uses
two literal quotations from Bernard's sermons on the *Song of
Songs*. All this is to prove the right of love against the position of
the tacit monk. What a reversal of the monastic perspective on
love!

In his response, Peter of Celle lets love itself say that silence is
more useful than are torrents of vain and superfluous talk which
only confuse his silence, and he asks Nicholas not to write any-
more.[59] His reprimand refers mainly to Nicholas' philosophical
discussion. But by associating love with silence, he also criticizes
Nicholas' superficial confrontation between the love of friendship
and the silence of the monk.[60]

The conflict of Nicholas is not real, the rhetorical aspect is only
too obvious, yet Nicholas likes to depict similar situations.[61] This
could reflect some of his ambivalent feelings about being a monk,

for Nicholas' texts are a strange mixture of self-satisfied rhetoric and genuine statements about himself.

This leads us to Nicholas' view of rhetoric. His unusually numerous references to style show us how important it was for him.[62] The fact that Nicholas likes to take absolute positions incompatible with each other is true also in regard to rhetoric. This differs, however, from the common ambivalent attitude of monastic writers towards rhetoric, depending on how it is used.

Nicholas' statements are mostly connected with either praise, criticism, or self-denigration. On the one side, there is his statement about the necessary effort to polish style:

> . . . nunc ergo poliendus est stilus, et venustiori respergendus eloquio, ne verborum nuditas accuset ingenii facultatem.[63]
> . . . ubi si stilus rutilantiori verborum lumine non lucet, scito quia facultas defuit, non voluntas.[64]

On the other side, there is his strong condemnation of eloquence altogether as not befitting the monk:

> Nec attendas hic splendidioris eloquentiae claritatem; quia haec est unum eorum, quae retro oblitus sum; quod mihi saepius insolentiam et extollentiam ministravit. Stilus enim sententiarum maiestate scintillans, et vernantis eloquii rutilans positura, philosophum decet non monachum, oratorem non exploratorem peccatorum suorum.[65]
> Nolo tibi longum facere prologum nec candidioris eloquentiae gratia paginam phalerare, quia sermo floridus et verborum ornamenta consectans, philosophum decet, non monachum.[66]
> Si minus splendida videtur epistola, nec eventilatis cumulata sermonibus, recole scriptum, prudenti viro non placere phalerata sed fortia. Non enim elegi quid subtilius ad consequentiam, sed quid utilius ad conscientiam esset.[67]

These declarations are contained in letters of monastic vocation, written to persuade friends to enter Clairvaux. Ironically, Nicholas, in *Letter 15* in which he complains about his work load, describes his occupation in Clairvaux in exactly such words:

> Nolo autem argui singularitatis, ut cum illi vacent, et vi-
> deant, quoniam [quondam MS] ipse est Deus, ego stilum et
> tabulas revolvam, ut revolem ad phaleras gloriamque ver-
> borum. Tamen a custodia matutina usque ad noctem nihil
> aliud facio: non illis imputetur qui mihi haec oneris impo-
> suerunt et posuerunt me multa scribere, et rescribere multis.
> Plorare enim et orare deberem.⁶⁸

Whereas his fellow-monks can meditate in peace, he is forced
to write and to take care of the embellishment and the glory of
words.⁶⁹

And, in one of the sermons, he praises the style of Gregory the
Great with the same words he uses in his condemnations: "Ita
enim actus eius, et vitam [sc. S. Benedicti] undantis eloquii clari-
tate depinxit, ut et stilus sententiarum maiestate scintillet, et sententiae stilo reluceant clariori."⁷⁰

Letter 10 is addressed to Burchard, the abbot of Balerne who had
congratulated Nicholas on the occasion of his transfer to the Cistercians. It is interesting to note that the beginning is inspired by
Bernard's only existing letter to Burchard.⁷¹ In the second part of
the letter, he comments on Burchard's style in great detail. Nicholas starts by not accepting Burchard's excuse for his modest way
of writing:

> De cetero itane ludere vultis cum puero isto [vestro MS]?
> Sane dignanter atque amicabiliter; sed si ita **luditis**, non **il-
> ludatis**; postulatis vos recipi a me in simplici stilo,⁷² cum ego
> totus obstupuerim in luce sagittarum vestrarum, in splen-
> dore fulgurantis cartae vestrae. Tota pagina phalerata est, et
> splendoribus rhetoricis inauratur, et fecundissimi sensus,
> sententiarum maiestate scintillant. Alteratis enim verba
> eadem in eadem pagina et difficillima, sed facillima vobis
> subtilitate: colores oratorum in manu vestra cerei sunt, il-
> lene ergo implumis est bestiola, qui floridissimas et multi-
> plices artium pennas sensibus suis induit, ut directior exeat
> sagitta verborum?⁷³

As an introduction he uses again a quotation of a letter by Bernard, this time to Peter the Venerable.⁷⁴ Bernard's word play
ludere-illudere, the response to a joke of Peter's, congeals under
Nicholas to a mere and rather superfluous formula.

In praising Burchard's artful style, Nicholas employs the same expressions as in the texts condemning rhetoric. Skillfully he returns Burchard's compliments, thus indirectly increasing his own praise. In his letter, Burchard cited several animals in order to praise Nicholas and to designate his own modesty. Picking up the list and enlarging upon it, Nicholas returns Burchard's praise and denigrates himself.[75] While stressing in other texts his disavowal of literature,[76] in this letter concerning his conversion to Clairvaux he practices rhetoric and uses every opportunity to discuss style.

From these examples the predominant role rhetoric plays for Nicholas is quite evident. By condemning it he reveals the negative side of his passion for style, fitting better his image of a monk.

The introductory letter of Nicholas' collection is a good example of the juxtaposition of conflicting attitudes in the same text. By degrading his letters, Nicholas pretends to express humility but seeks undoubtedly the rhetorical effect of *captatio benevolentiae*, saying that the letters were not worth remembering since neither were the words sublime nor the thoughts profound in any way. He explains that the letters were not written with the intention of publication, which for the epistolary genre in the Middle Ages is almost a contradiction in itself.[77] He justifies shortcomings in the letters by the overload of his work and, consequently, by the lack of time and the tedium of writing, which he blames for the many repetitions:

> . . . nec poteram ad plurima, sicut ad singula vigilare: ad illud solummodo vigilans, possem petentes vel exspectantes citius expedire, hinc est quod **multa similia ibi posita sunt**; multa tam de veteribus quam novis epistolis nunc quidem latenter impressa, nunc signanter expressa, **cum mihi melius memoria quam ingenium subveniret**. Nec hoc dico quasi, si voluissem, potuissem sententiosum opus in limatam eloquentiam complanare: cum hoc longe fecerit a me et ingenii tarditas, et exercitii raritas et diversitas propositi mei. Non sum orator [cf. Am 7:14], neque filius oratoris, sed **homo simplex** et domi habitans [Gn 25:27], **rusticanus** utique et vellicans sycomoros [cf. Am 7:14]. Illis **verborum venationes** tota voluntate relinquo, qui per locutionum silvas libenter deambulant, et rhetoricos modulos quasi florentes ramusculos decerpere gloriantur. Isti enim sunt, qui eloquia

Domini, eloquia casta [Ps 11:7] quasi tribulosa quaeque
refugiant; et ab asperitate segetum abhorrentes, spinarum
floribus inhiant, vanitate utique pleni, non veritate, si tamen
vanitate quis possit impleri.[78]

These reasons, he argues, should not count as excuses since his in-
genuity was sluggish and his exercise in writing rare. The latter
point appears to be contradictory to his work as a secretary rather
than an indication of the difference between writing with the aid
of Bernard's notes and composing on his own responsibility, and it
shows the merely rhetorical value of his reasons.

But now that Nicholas adds to the reasons of his inability to
write, a third point, namely that also his intention was different,
the argumentation shifts to the opposite side: "I am not an orator
nor the son of an orator, but a simple homebody," he declares, by
varying Amos who said about himself that he was not a prophet
nor the son of a prophet, and he continues with a version of Gn
25:27. Here follows an eloquent condemnation of orators who are
full of vanity instead of truth, hunting for words. Then, returning
to the subject of the publication of his letter-collection, he shifts
back to the first position, asking the addressees to suppress anything that is not elaborate and that of which the public would be
ashamed. This text shows very clearly that Nicholas inserts the
proud declaration of the *sermo rusticus* only as an especially suitable
topic serving the purpose of the *captatio benevolentiae*.

In the previously mentioned *Letter 52*, Nicholas reacts to Peter's
objections to his speculations:

Unde ergo incipiam? A litteris vestris quae non modicum
hospitaverunt apud me; quae floridioris eloquentiae, et pro-
fundioris scientiae dotibus rutilantes percusserunt me, et
vulneraverunt me nihil minus sperantem. In **simplicitate** siquidem cordis mei scripseram vobis, utpote **homo simplex**
et domi habitans [Gn 25:27]; vos autem tam verborum
venator, quam sensuum, et conclusum **retibus**, et percussum **venabulo** credidistis, utinam possemus dicere, frustra
iacitur rete ante oculos pennatorum [Pr 1:17]: nam reper-
cutere etiamsi valerem, non vellem. Sed fortassis aut ex-
clamatis aut cogitatis: O longa praemeditatio, o sensus ex-
quisiti, o verba vigilata quae et ingenii viribus et eloquii flor-

ibus debeant insigniri. Non ego id mihi adrogaverim, cum utrumque veraciter desit mihi, nec mihi super hoc hactenus cogitavi, testimonium mihi perhibente conscientia mea [Rm 9:1]. Negotiosus enim sum non otiosus. . . .[79]

He refers to his own simplicity with the same quotation from Genesis as in the first letter and uses again the metaphor of the hunt by calling Peter a hunter whose letter wounded and pierced him. Yet, he adds that even if he could free himself from the net he is caught in, he would not want to do it.

It is a difficult and obscure text; here Nicholas seems to combine in the image of the hunt its negative aspect, as in his first letter, with its positive aspect, as in the letter to Burchard whose rhetorical arrows he praises.[80] Peter is, of course, not a vain orator but, according to Nicholas, carefully works on his texts, embellishing his words by the power of his talent and by rhetorical figures. Nicholas, however, claims to be deficient in both and not to have thought about such things at all, being too busy for them. This statement bluntly contradicts Nicholas' rather stilted way of writing and illustrates again how he uses monastic simplicity[81] as a rhetorical pose.

Peter reproaches his friend quite frankly. He picks up Nicholas' sentence regarding the hunter and reapplies the expression to Nicholas, blaming him for returning bitter for sweet, vain for true, thereby ironically confirming Nicholas' presumption of simplicity.[82]

Nicholas does not seem to be able to integrate naturally his rhetoric into his monastic way of life. Bernard, on the other hand, knows how to use it as a powerful and artful yet spontaneous means to express linguistically his emotional involvement with Cistercian spirituality. Since for Nicholas rhetoric has basically the egocentric purpose of satisfying his literary ambitions to impress the recipient, there is no spiritual focal point, and thus the staged poses, theoretical and absolute, contradict each other. In fact, in his sermons, where this egotism is less conspicuous, Nicholas' style, although lacking originality, is more natural, lending more emphasis to spiritual values.

In the light of this exposition, one might wonder how Nicholas managed to get such high praise for his eloquence from his friends Peter of Celle[83] and Peter the Venerable. The latter writes in re-

sponse to Nicholas' *Letter 55*: "... Qui meam de te esuriem sa-
tiare nequeo, saltem hanc brevi tempore iucundo ac dulci tuo colloquio relevabo.... Nam si talis est stilus tuus, qualis est animus
tuus? Si talis littera tua, qualis lingua tua?..." Nicholas is not only
compared to Cicero whom he quoted in his own letter, but also to
Paul, referring to 2 Co 10:10f. Then follows: "Quia traxit fateor,
quia non parum traxit, immo rapuit cor meum epistola tua, illa
plane epistola, quae ex abundantia cordis locuta est, quae de multo
adipe et pinguedine amoris processit." Referring to Ps 118:103,
Peter then relates Nicholas' writing to the divine sphere: "Si adeo
dulce eloquium hominum, quanto magis divinum? Si adeo dulcis
terrena guttula, quam dulcior caelestis imber? Si adeo mentem
lenit ros humani sermonis, quanto magis delinit torrens voluptatis?
Multa similia ex his coniiciebam, et totum quod scripsisti ad divina
et aeterna transferebam."[84]

Such exuberant commendations have to be viewed as a genuine
expression of friendship, of joy on receiving a letter, which used to
have a much greater value than it has today. As we have seen,
Peter of Celle, on the other hand, did not hold back his strong
reprimand either, which acts as a certain counter-balance. Nicholas
was undoubtedly a skillful writer and a very charming person,
and, since his friends probably did not know his letter-collection,
they could easily get a more favorable view of his writing. Only
the comparison between all of Nicholas' texts, on which this paper
is based, completely reveals the abstract and formalized character
of his work.

Center for Medieval and Renaissance Studies
University of California, Los Angeles

NOTES

1. Nicholas, a benedictine monk of the community at Montiéramey near Troyes, was chaplain to Bishop Hato of Troyes for several years before he entered Clairvaux in 1146. Nicholas was in Rome in 1140–1141, probably as Bernard's messenger to Pope Innocent II regarding the persecution of Abelard after the Council of Sens in 1140. After his expulsion from Clairvaux in 1152, he went again to Rome and entered the service of Pope Adrian IV and of his chancellor, Cardinal Roland Bandinelli, the future Pope Alexander III. Around 1158, with the support of Adrian, he returned to Montiéramey and obtained the favor of Count Henry of Champagne, thanks to whom he became prior of Saint-Jean-en Châtel at Troyes, a dependance of the abbey of Montiéramey in 1160. He served him as a kind of secretary. See John F. Benton, "Nicolas de Clairvaux," in DSp 11 (1982) 255–59, and Giles Constable, *The Letters of Peter the Venerable* (Cambridge, 1967) 2:316–30.

2. For these dates see Constable, 2:320, 326.

3. Constable, 2:330.

4. See Benton, 258, and Constable, 2:329, note 59.

5. On defining "style," see Nils Erik Enkvist, *Linguistic Stylistics* (The Hague, 1973), pp. 11–26.

6. Nicholas seems to have written Epp 2–4 earlier, also Epp 7, 45, and 46, which concern his transfer to Clairvaux. Jean Leclercq (*Recueil d'études sur saint Bernard et ses écrits* [Rome, 1962–1969] 1:61f.) dates a letter written by Nicholas to the monks in Montiéramey to the time of his return from Rome to Montiéramey after his stay in Clairvaux. However, it resembles strongly the letters dealing with his transfer to Clairvaux. Most of the letters (Epp 1–53) were collected and published in 1149. Epp 54 and 55 were probably added later. See Peter Rassow, "Die Kanzlei St. Bernhards von Clairvaux," *Studien und Mitteilungen zur Geschichte des Benediktinerordens*, 34 (1913) 285. The rest of the existing letters dated from the time after his expulsion from Clairvaux. Leclercq (p. 74) also assumes that Ep 24 to Peter of Celle was written after Bernard's death. A large number of the letters is printed in PL 196:1593–654. This text is based on a manuscript now lost. For Epp 54–55 to Peter the Venerable, see Constable, 1:373 and 420f. There are two important surviving manuscripts containing part of the letter-collection: Paris, B. N. lat. 3012 with Epp 29–48 and parts of Epp 28 and 49; and Berlin, Phillips 1719 with Epp 3–42, 56–57 and three other letters. Two of these additional letters are published by John F. Benton; see "Nicolas de Clairvaux à la recherche du vin d'Auxerre, d'après une lettre inédite du XIIᵉ siècle," *Annales de Bourgogne* 34 (1962) 252–55, and "An Abusive Letter of Nicolas of Clairvaux for a Bishop of Auxerre, possibly Blessed Hugh of Mâcon," MSt 33 (1971) 365–70. Jean Leclercq published four additional letters from other manuscripts; see *Recueil*, 1:49–51, 61f., 66f., and *Études sur saint Bernard et le texte de ses écrits*, ASOC 9, 1/2 (1953) 62f.

7. There are also ten sequences commonly attributed to Nicholas; see John F. Benton, "Nicolas of Clairvaux and the Twelfth-Century Sequence," Trad. 18 (1962) 149–79.

8. See below, note 17.

9. See, for example, Bernard's Ep 545 (see note 40), Ep 546, SBOp 8:523f.; Ep 390, SBOp 8:358f. (see Rassow, 79f.); Ep 387, SBOp 8:355f.; Sp 389, SBOp 8:356f.

10. Nicholas writes to Adrian IV: "Ecce offero maiestati tuae quosdam sermones viri Dei non ex novo dictos, sed ex novo dictatos," This letter has been published from MS Vat. lat. 5055 by Jean Leclercq, *Études*, p. 62f. An examination of these sermons included in the Vatican manuscript, however, shows clearly that they are by no means simply the result of stylistic revisions of sermons

originally written by Bernard. For what purpose would Nicholas have done that anyhow? In fact, these texts do not really differ from Nicholas' own sermons which borrow constantly from Bernard's work. Nicholas here simply seems to hide behind Bernard's name.

11. See Leclercq, *Recueil*, 1:79, and *Études*, p. 47.

12. See Jean Leclercq, *L'amour des lettres et le désir de Dieu: Initiation aux auteurs monastiques du moyen âge* (Paris, 1956), p. 246.

13. See Leclercq, *Recueil*, 2:318

14. The reason that some of the letters Nicholas wrote in another person's name are shorter and less personal or less typical of Nicholas' style is explained by their character as mere business letters. Benton ("Recherche," p. 252), on the other hand, thinks that Nicholas tried to adopt the style and the personality of the people he wrote for. See also Jean Leclercq, "Recherches sur la collection des épîtres de saint Bernard," *Cahiers de civilisation médiévale*, 14 (1971) 208, and *Recueil*, 1:56.

15. Ep 1; PL 196:1593BC, quoted below, see note 78.

16. "Adhuc enim iuxta Philosophum, alienas sarcinas adoro" (letter to the Count of Champagne; Leclercq, *Recueil*, 1:50, 16f., quoting Seneca, Ep 22, 13), and in a sermon, he refers to Bernard: "libenter enim illius sarcinas adoro" (PL 144:849D).

17. In the same letter in which Nicholas admits that he likes to use the work of others, he states that, with few exceptions, he wrote the sermons and other liturgical texts presented to Count Henry. Leclercq (*Recueil*, 1:56–58), however, has identified a large part of that material as plagiarisms from Bernard and Hugh of St Victor.

18. See, for example, Ep 6, Constable, 1:13; Ep 49, Constable, 1:150; Ep 56, Constable, 1:178; Ep 193, Constable, 1:450.

19. See, for example, Ep 78, 13, SBOp 7:210; Ep 122, 2, SBOp 7:303. More often, Bernard, however, apologizes for his brevity due to a lack of time; see for example, Ep 365, 1, SBOp 8:320; Ep 366, SBOp 8:323.

20. PL 196:1601B. See also, for example, Ep 4, PL 196:1598CD; Ep 29, PL 196:1620BC; Ep 33, PL 196:1625CD; Ep 50, PL 196:1650C; Ep 17, PL 196:1616AB.

21. "Intolerabiles enim essent amicorum absentiae, si non intervenirent remedia litterarum" (Ep 35, PL 196:1630C, and Ep 39, PL 196:578A).

22. Ep 47, PL 196:1648D–1649A.

23. Ep 3, PL 196:1597B; Ep 39, PL 196:1576AB; Ep 50, PL 196:1649CD; Ep 6, PL 196:1601AB ("Convictus tamen et conversatio . . ."); Ep 57, PL 196:1620CD ("conspectus habeat aliquid . . ."; see also Epp 43 and 55, referred to in notes 29 and 31. These phrases are based on Seneca, Ep 35 *ad Lucilium*. There are similar formulas beginning with "utinam mihi datum esset desuper . . ." (Ep 29, PL 196:1620CD; Ep 40, PL 196:1638D; Ep 47, PL 196: 1648D).

24. See Ep 55, referred to in note 31.

25. ". . . Praesentiores enim sunt, qui se animis, quam qui oculis intuentur: et plus est connecti corde, quam corpore." This quotation reappears in Ep 29, PL 196:1621C; Ep 42, PL 196:1640AB; see also Epp 43 and 55, referred to in notes 29 and 31.

26. See, for example Bernard in Ep 65, 2; SBOp 7:160, 13ff.

27. Ep 42; PL 196:1640CD.

28. Ep 50; PL 196:1649CD.

29. Ep 43; PL 196:1642CD.

30. For this quotation from Bernard see below note 47.

31. Ep 55 to Peter the Venerable = Ep 179, Constable, 1:421.

32. Bernard, SC 43, 1; SBOp 2:43, 1f.

33. Ep 18; PL 196:1616C.

34. The term *homines* in Nicholas' sentence evokes his idealistic description of the monks in Clairvaux: "ubi vidi homines, non homines: immo vere homines; et quod verius est, supra hominem ambulantes" (Ep 45; PL 196:1645CD, and the letter published by Leclercq, *Recueil*, 1:62.

35. "Etsi facie ignotus nobis, etsi corpore remotus a nobis, amicus tamen es, et amicitia notum iam nobis, et praesentem te facit. Hanc tibi, te nesciente, comparavit non caro et sanguis [cf. Mt 16:17], sed spiritus Dei, qui Willellmum fratrem tuum aeterna nobis societate et spirituali caritate devinxit . . ." (Ep 103, 1; SBOp 7:259).

36. "Desideramus praesentiam tuam, quaerimus optatam, immo promissam exigimus. Cur tanto? Nil in ea sane expetimus de carme et sanguine. Aut proficere ex te cupimus, aut prodesse tibi. Generositas sanguinis, proceritas corporis, forma elegans, iuvenilis decor, praedia, palatia, immensa supellex, infulaeque dignitatum, adde et mundi sapientiam: de mundo sunt haec, et mundus quod suum est diligit" (Ep 107, 2 to Thomas, provost of Beverley; SBOp 7:268, 8-12).

37. See Ep 39; PL 196:1575D-8C.

38. "Accurro, et qui quaerebar, ecce adsum [Is 52:6]: non in praesentia corporis infirma [2 Co 10:10], in qua despexit Dominum Herodes [Lk 23:11]: attamen in visceribus meis. Nam quis me separabit ab [Rm 8:35] his? Sequar eos quocumque ierint [cf. Rv 14:4] et, si habitaverint in extremis maris [Ps 138:9], non erunt absque me. Habes, Rex, lumen oculorum meorum [Tb 10:4], habes cor meum et animam meam. Quid si modicum nostri abest? Corpusculum loquor, vile istud mancipium, quod etsi voluntas exponeret, sed retineret necessitas. Non valet sequi volantem animum, quoniam infirmum est, et solum paene illi superest sepulcrum [Jb 17:1]. Sed quae cura? Anima mea in bonis demorabitur, cum semen meum hereditabit terram [Ps 24:13]. Semen meum, semen bonum [Mt 13:24]. Germinabit, si tamen in terram bonam ceciderit . . ." (Ep 208; SBOp 8:67f.).

39. A letter, written by Bernard to his monks during a long absence from Clairvaux, shows quite realistically what he means by being united to each other in God: Ep 143, 2; SBOp 7:342f. On this letter, see Leclercq, "Recherches," p. 206.

40. This phrase occurs also in Ep 50; PL 196:1649D, and in Bernard's Ep 545; SBOp 8:512, 8f., obviously written by Nicholas (see Leclercq, *Recueil*, 2:317). The preceding quotation of Ps 144:7, quite common in Nicholas' letters, is taken from Bernard's *Forty-Third Sermon on the Canticle*, see above, note 32.

41. "Nescio si fortius, scio tamen quia tenerius absentia me vobis, immo vos mihi inviscerat, quam fecerit praesentia. Hoc probabile et necessarium argumentum est perfectae dilectionis, quando eo amplius incendit affectus, quo remotius separat locus. Praesentia siquidem suo visu solatiatur, et satiatur usu; famelica vero absentia, prae inopia etiam amaris iuniperi corticibus sustentatur, et ad solitam visionis dulcedinem vivacius inflammatur, et nutritur tenacius. Duris agitatur stimulius desiderium, quod semper quaerit et numquam invenit. Unde Psalmista: Quaerite Dominum, quaerite faciem eius semper [Ps 104:4]. Et in Canticis, anima liquefacta surgit, et quaerit per plateas et vicos civitatis quem diligit' (Sg 3;2; Ep 95, PL 202:545D-46AB).

42. Peter the Venerable, however, stresses the opposite aspect: "Agnosco in me, si tamen et apud alios ita est, amicitiae consuetuninem, ut quanto magis me amicus frequentat, tanto magis in corde meo fervor ipsius amicitiae crescat. Est et quoddam vestigium amoris aeterni, ut qui plus eo accensus fuerit, plus satietur, et qui magis satiatus fuerit, multo amplius accendatur. Firmus ergo amoris nexus et indissolubilis catena nos longe ab invicem remotos uniat . . ." (Ep 55; Constable, 1:176).

43. Ep 72, 5; SBOp 7:178.

44. Ep 362, 1; SBOp 8:310.

45. Ep 201, 1; SBOp 8:59.

46. Ep 73, 1; SBOp 7:179.
47. Ep 144, 1; SBOp 7:344, 8–10.
48. Ep 32; PL 196:1623A.
49. Ep 89, 1f. to Oger, a regular canon; SBOp 7:235f.
50. Ep 24 to Peter of Celle = Ep 50; PL 202:475AB.
51. See Damien van den Eynde, in Leclercq, *Recueil*, 3:350.
52. *Contra Vigilantium*, 15; PL 23:351.
53. Ennodius, Ep 1:23; CSEL 6:34, 23.
54. Bernard, SC 83, 4; SBOp 2:300, 12.
55. Bernard, SC 64, 10; SBOp 2:171, 20f.
56. Ep 52 to Peter of Celle = Ep 65; PL 202:498B.
57. Ep 60 to Henry of Winchester; Constable, 1:190.
58. On these speculations, see M.-D. Chenu, "Platon à Cîteaux," AHDL 21 (1954) 99–106.
59. "Sed monachum illum, qui cum amico in epistolae tuae principio contendebat et reticens, has iam prae taedio emittere audio voces. Utilius, inquit amor, claustra oris continuissemus, quam rescribendo tot exundantium impetus torrentum incurrissemus. Redundant enim torrentes vanitatis, et distillant ab ore amici nostri sermones superfluae garrulitatis, totus profluit et pereffluit. Silentia nostra confundit; consuetudinis nostrae morem et ordinem conturbat et concutit; ad pomposa et superflua quaeque improbitate sua, si acquieverimus, provocat et attrahit. Deinceps itaque noli scribere" (Ep 66; PL 202:513AB = Ep 53 in Nicholas' collection).
60. For Bernard, in Ep 88 to Oger, it is, on the contrary, charity that prevents him from complying with Oger's request for long letters.
61. In his Ep 49 to Peter of Celle, Nicholas, during a period of blood-letting, prefers to use the leisure to write to his friend while his fellow-monks meditate: "Reliquis reliqui subtiles et utiles illas meditationes, qui me durioris et vitae purioris exercitiis attriti et astricti in plateis supernae Sion saepius, evolantes, imaginum caelestium hauriunt theorias. Igitur a tumultu et vario rerum turbine liberatus confabulabar mecum et dicebam: Ecce iam venit plenitudo temporis, ut scribam illi quem diligit anima mea . . .' (PL 202:491D). For Peter of Celle, on the other hand, there is no conflict between epistolary friendship and meditation, both belong together (see Ep 97, PL 202:547CD). Nicholas' words about his monastic vows that prevent him from seeing his friend are quite strong: "Sed promissa stabilitas et discretioris legis praeiurata professio submovent auditorium, et viventi constituunt sepulturam" (Ep 5; PL 196:1599D).
62. His remarks about style mostly appear in the letters he wrote in his own name, with the exception of Ep 29; see above note 14.
63. Ep 3; PL 196:1596CD.
64. Ep 49 = Ep 63; PL 202:494C.
65. Ep 16; PL 196:1611BC.
66. Ep 17; PL 196:1613D.
67. Ep 38; PL 196:1636BC. The second sentence seems to depend on Bernard's Ep 89, 1, referred to above in note 49.
68. Ep 15; PL 196:1609BC.
69. However, according to his statement in *Letter 49*, he does not seem to be very anxious to meditate, see above note 61.
70. *Sermo 9*; PL 144:518CD.
71. "Vidi litteras vestras, immo vos in litteris vestris et de camino fornacis ardentissimae scintillas evolantes incurri, nec adustus sum ex eis, sed accensus et in medullas cordis, verba flammantia descenderunt et incenderunt eas" (Ep 10; PL 196:1606A). Bernard, Ep 146; SBOp 7:348, 6: "Legi illud, et concaluit cor meum intra me [Ps 38:4]: benedixi illi fornaci, de qua huiusmodi scintillae evolassent. Nonne cor tuum ardens erat in te [Lk 24:32], cum ista dictabas?" Nicholas goes on with a rhetorical catalogue in which eloquence is integrated into the

whole of human faculties. There is a similar passage in Ep 4; PL 196:1597CD and 1598B.

72. Burchard wrote to Nicholas (= Ep 9; Pl 196:1605B): "Hac vice prima in simplici stilo recipe me et sine modo, ut quadam compositione graduum liceat ascendere ad animal primum pennatum implumi bestiolae."

73. Ep 10; PL 196:1607AB.

74. Ep 228; SBOp 8:98, 6f.

75. Ep 10; PL 196:1607B. One gets the impression that Burchard's letter must have been heavily edited by Nicholas to suit his own purpose.

76. See the letter published by Leclercq, *Recueil*, 1:61f., and Ep 35; PL 196:1627CD.

77. See Giles Constable, *Letters and Letter-Collections*, Typologie des sources du moyen âge occidental 17 (Turnhout, 1976), p. 11.

78. Ep 1; PL 196:1593B.

79. Ep 52 = Ep 65; PL 202:498CD.

80. Referred to above in note 73.

81. On simplicity, see Jean Leclercq, "Sancta simplicitas," Coll. 22 (1960) 138-48.

82. Ep 66; PL 202:507AB (= Ep 53 in Nicholas' collection): ". . . Aliam vidi visionem. Rubus ardens in interiora deserti apparuit. Suspensus intenta cogitatione: Num, inquam, sicut Moysi rubus ardebat et non consumebatur, sic meus iste reddit splendorem lucentem, non calorem urentem? Amici enim increpatio, grata potius correptio est, quam molesta exustio. Est autem. Vos venator tam verborum quam sensuum, et conclusum retibus et percussum venabulo credidistis. Hic enim rubus ruborem ingerens, sed perfectae et solidae caritatis robur nescienti. Oculus pupilli pungeretur, vel etiam compungeretur, si spina huiusmodi configeretur. Non vero contingat hoc oculo caritatis, cuius solius est colligere, immo producere rosam de spinis. Sic Iesus de spina passionis rosam protulit redemptionis. Annon eius imitatione et tu reddis bona pro malis, qui mollia duris, dulcia amaris, vera retribuis vanis? Revera tu simplex et domi habitans, ut dicis, in simplicitate cordis tui."

83. See Ep 61; PL 202:489.

84. Ep 182; Constable, 1:425f.

BALDWIN OF FORD AND THE
SACRAMENT OF THE ALTAR

David N. Bell

T HE TREATISE *De sacramento altaris* of Baldwin of Ford is by far
the longest of any Cistercian treatise on the same theme. It is
five times the length of William of St. Thierry's important op-
uscule[1] and eighteen times the length of Isaac of Stella's brief
letter.[2] Indeed, it is one of the longest of all eucharistic treatises;
yet it is rarely discussed in any detail in studies of the eucharistic
controversies, and sometimes, as in Darwell Stone's compendious
History of the Doctrine of the Holy Eucharist,[3] it is conspicuous by its
absence. The reason for this is not far to seek. Baldwin's work is
not an examination or defence of what one might call the mechan-
ics of the eucharist, but an investigation of its meaning in the christian life. Nor is it polemical—the nearest Baldwin comes to dis-
putation is in his defence of the western practice of using unleavened
rather than leavened bread[4]—and Baldwin is not overly concerned
with taking individual heretics to task. This is not to say that he was
not aware of the controversies. He leaves us in no doubt that a real,
substantial change has occurred in the bread and the wine and uses
(and defends) the up-to-date term *transubstantio* to describe it;[5] he
states clearly that the entirety of Christ's body is present in each
particle of the host after the fraction, and "it is not greater in a
greater [part] and smaller in a smaller; for in the greater part or in
the smaller, it is equally and entirely contained, neither more nor
less";[6] and he is well aware of the great dangers of loose language
and careless terminology.[7] But nowhere does he mention Berengar
by name,[8] and nowhere do we find him using the subtleties of
human reason to investigate what, in Baldwin's irrevocable opinion, is entirely a matter of faith.

The philosophers, he says, have sweated over such questions as *forma* and *materia*, *species* and *substantia*, striving to discover their origins, properties, and powers, "and what may seem to them in accordance with the conjecture of human reason they will hold as definite and certain."[9] In their investigations of the ordinary course of nature, they have said much which is wondrous and in accordance with the faith (*tam mirabiliter quam fideliter*), but much else is mere supposition, "as far from the truth as it is foreign to the piety of faith [*pietas fidei*]."[10] He goes on to accuse them of being ignorant of the heavenly sacraments, ignorant of the wisdom of God,[11] and elsewhere reproaches them for their proud and curious questioning.[12] God's wisdom is not investigated by human subtlety, nor by taking long voyages and going to remote places. It is not to be found in Plato or the schools of the Academics or Stoics and does not lie in obscure writings and sayings.[13] It is not to be found by the eager use of human curiosity,[14] and compared with the simplicity of faith, the doctrines of the philosophers and the traditions of men are wholly contemptible.[15]

It is not, however, that Baldwin sees no place at all for human reason; it is simply that he insists upon its limits. In common with many other pre-scholastics he is well aware that reason may, and indeed should, complement authority, and the observations of Charles Sheedy on the matter are as true for Baldwin as they are for so many of his colleagues:

> It is incorrect . . . to set up authority and reason as two conflicting sources of knowledge, as if a man in following authority was compelled to abdicate his reason and in following reason must reject the argument of authority. The object of faith, though not derived from reason, requires the use of reason to express the truths of faith and their relations to each other, and to draw out the conclusions implicitly contained in the revealed principles.[16]

With this Baldwin would have no objection. Indeed, the whole of his *De sacramento altaris*, with its detailed and comprehensive biblical exegesis, is an example of reason being utilised in this way, and it is precisely this use of reason which is indicated by the phrase *ratio fidei*.[17] But—and it is a most important but—the faith comes first. "We cannot give a reason [*ratio*] for everything which has been handed down to us by the ancients, but in the things which are not handed down as being beyond reason [*praeter ratio-nem*], the authority of the ancients itself should be sufficient reason for us. Our faith . . . is based more on authority than human reason, and when Peter says that we should give a reason for the faith and hope that are in us to all who demand it [1 P 3:15], one can render no better reason for the faith than the authority of scripture and the authority of the ancients."[18]

One may question, for example, why the synoptic gospels present slightly different accounts of the Last Supper ("*pietas fidei* is not imperilled by such *dubitationes*"), provided we believe without any doubt (*indubitanter*) the events and words set down.[19] For this reason, says Baldwin, we may truly speak of devout knowledge and devout ignorance (*pia conscientia et pia ignorantia*): with the former we accept what God has enjoined us to believe, and with the latter we do not question what should not be investigated.[20] Reason, in other words, may elaborate revealed truth (indeed, it *should* do so, if at all possible[21]), but if, for some cause, this rational elaboration—this *ratio fidei*—is beyond us, or if we cannot understand it when it is presented to us, then let us venerate humbly "with the fervor of pious devotion" what we are unable to understand.[22] This is what "the simple" do, those who "believe simply and live innocently" (Baldwin here has been inspired by Augustine),[23] for it is not necessary for all the faithful to be versed in allegorical language or to be able to penetrate the depths of signs and sacraments. Such things are more necessary for the more perfect, those who are charged with teaching and governing, for as Christ himself said, "To you it has been given to know the mysteries of the kingdom of God; but for others, they are in parables" (Lk 8:10).[24] As Hugh of St. Victor points out, the simple are saved by their simplicity.[25]

Baldwin's faith is founded on divine authority,[26] on God, who is the Supreme Truth and Supreme Reason,[27] and on what God has revealed, directly and immutably, in Holy Scripture. Scripture is the word of God, revealed by the inspiration of the Holy Spirit, and if the Scripture is true, then the witnesses are true—and the witnesses, we are told, are the just here on earth, the angels in heaven, and God the Trinity itself—the testimonies are true, and the faith itself is true.[28] The fortifications of our faith, therefore, reduce to the authority of Holy Scripture,[29] and we shall have cause to return to this important idea later in our study. There are two sorts of knowledge, says Baldwin: a true knowledge of things which can be comprehended and a truer knowledge of things which cannot. It is this latter *cognitio* which is *scientia fidei*, and the knowledge which comes through faith is the knowledge which brings salvation (*scientia salutis*).[30] It is faith which illuminates the invisible,[31] and "if you do not believe, you will not understand."[32] Faith, as we are told by William of St. Thierry, is not based on *ratio* or *intellectus*, but on authority—the authority of God himself[33]—and if we believe worthily about God and the things which pertain to God, which he himself has seen fit to reveal in the Holy Scriptures, then our faith should be a faith in the words of God.[34] Furthermore, we must not think that this authoritative faith is no more than mere opinion. When Baldwin says that faith is knowledge (*scientia*), he means knowledge, and, as I have tried to show elsewhere, he lays more stress on this point than almost any of his contemporaries.[35] There is a place for reason, of that there is no doubt, but reason is the elaboration of faith, and faith is not the product of reason. "It is salutary to believe the mystery of faith," says Peter Lombard (who thinks he is quoting Augustine but is actually quoting Lanfranc); "it is not salutary to investigate it."[36] Or, as Guitmund of Aversa put it, "Christ did not command you to understand, but to believe!"[37]

Thus we arrive at the eucharist, for that central celebration of the christian life is also the greatest test of faith. "Faced with the power of this sacrament," says Baldwin, "the mind is dulled, the eye of reason is darkened, and every sense of the body is blunted."[38] It is the arena in which faith and reason fight together:

> This they do that one might gouge out the other's eye, and there is no end to the combat until one of them is blinded. Human reason has its eye and so does faith, but the eye of reason is dim-sighted and often cannot see things which are visible and placed near to it. The eye of faith, however, is keen and with it the invisible things of God are clearly seen.[39]

Why is it that the body and blood of Christ remain concealed by the appearances[40] of bread and wine? Not only because of "horror of the blood" (*horror cruoris*), the old Ambrosian idea,[41] but most importantly to exercise our faith. As Sheedy points out, all the opponents of Berengar were agreed on this:

> In the view of the opponents of Berengar, the Eucharist has been given by God to mankind in such a mysterious form precisely in order that we may have the opportunity to exercise our faith, and thus more surely attain to the reward of faith. The test of faith is to hold strongly to the revealed truth, even though it be contrary to the evidence of sense, even though it be beyond the capacity of the intelligence to grasp; this acceptance is indeed an agony for our minds, but the grace of God makes it possible. For what merit would there be for us if everything in the Eucharist were visible?— visible miracles are not for the faithful, but for infidels.[42]

In this tradition Baldwin stands unswervingly, and we can find no better witness for his position than the entirety of his brief tractate on the most holy sacrament of the eucharist.[43]

> Christ was hidden from the beginning in the bosom of the Father; afterwards, he was hidden in the form of a servant which he assumed; and now he is hidden in the sacrament which he instituted. Faith finds him hidden in the bosom of the Father; no less does faith find him hidden in man; and it is faith which finds him hidden in the sacrament.[44]

The teaching here is in no way different from that in the full-length treatise, but the compendious *ratio fidei* has been omitted, and what remains, therefore, has been concentrated. There is not the least doubt, in fact, that the treatise on the sacrament of the altar, the short tractate on the same subject, and the important *De commendatione fidei* all echo the same principle. They are all expositions of the same theme, and Baldwin's discourse on the eucharist could easily and accurately be entitled "Faith in Theory and Practice."

The *stupor* and *admiratio*, the *théologie admirative*,[45] which characterize Baldwin's approach to the eucharistic mystery are not restricted to that sacrament alone. They characterize his approach

David N. Bell

to the faith as a whole and apply to the eucharist only insofar as it is the greatest test of that faith. In the *De commendatione fidei*, for example, Baldwin points out how the incomprehensible mysteries of the faith always produce *admiratio*:[46] the stupefaction of the mind leads inexorably to astonishment, astonishment to faith, and faith to salvation in Christ.[47] And why, in the end, are some saved and others not? That, too, is *admiratio*![48]

Faith, then, is the heart of the eucharist, and just as the eucharist is a test of faith, so the mysteries and concealments of the eucharist are revealed to the eye of faith; and, what is even more important, it is through faith that the eucharist achieves what it is meant to achieve. The sacrament does not sanctify us automatically but requires faith, for the lack of faith is an *impedimentum* which blocks the flow of grace. Both the righteous and the wicked may eat and drink the bread and wine, but whereas the former eat it *ad salutem*, the latter eat it *ad judicium*.[49] On the other hand, since salvation comes ultimately by grace and faith alone, those who believe in Christ already possess him within themselves,[50] and as Augustine pointed out in a well-known passage from the *Tractates on John*, when Jesus was asked what was necessary to achieve eternal life, he replied: "This is the work of God: that you should believe in him who sent me. This, then, is to eat the food which does not perish, but which remains unto eternal life. So why are you preparing your teeth and your stomach? Believe, and you have eaten!"[51] Baldwin, and a great number of his contemporaries, found this idea of the utmost significance, and many of them distinguished clearly between the sacramental eating of the eucharist, which may be shared by both the good and the wicked, and the spiritual eating, which pertains only to those who have faith, and which alone, of course, was possible for those who were on earth before the Incarnation.[52] A passage from the school of Anselm of Laon distinguishes clearly between them:

> It should be noted that there are two ways of eating: one sacramental, the other spiritual. The sacramental is that such as both good and wicked receive: it profits the good, but is a judgment for the wicked. The spiritual way of eating is that in which, by faith working through love, we believe that we are united to God in a union which has now

begun and will, at the end, be complete [*plena*]. It is this way
of eating, too, which, when once received, gives everlasting
life.[53]

Baldwin himself also makes the distinction, and it was, as we
have said, a common concept. Some theologians traced it back to
Augustine[54] and some to Jerome,[55] but all were agreed on its importance. Indeed, as Alger of Liège pointed out, since the spiritual
reception is always productive of grace and the sacramental reception is not so, the former can be seen to be more important than
the latter;[56] and there is no doubt that Baldwin, whose concern for
faith was, as we have seen, paramount, might well have agreed.
He spends, in fact, a considerable amount of time dealing with the
spiritual reception, pointing out that he is not speaking of the dead
faith of sinners, but that by which the righteous live, and stating
how we are justified by faith, how it makes us participants in the
friendship of God (*amicitia Dei*), how Christ dwells in our hearts
through faith, and so on, and then goes on to divide it, in a fashion
fairly typical of Baldwin, into three modes: faith in unity (that is,
of Father and Son in the unity of the Trinity), faith in union (that
is, of the godhead and the manhood in the one person of the incarnate Christ), and faith in communion (that is, of all the faithful at
the eucharist, when the life-giving and sanctifying flesh of Christ is
communicated to us for the remission of sins).[57]
    Now there is obviously a danger here: if indeed we eat Christ by
believing in him, or, as William of St. Thierry says so dramatically,
by loving him ("hunc autem cibum plus manducat qui plus
amat"),[58] then is there any real need for actual participation in the
eucharist itself? The writers of the post-Berengarian era were well
aware of this peril, and some of them—Lanfranc, for example, and
Alger, and also William of St. Thierry[59]—demonstrate clearly and
unequivocally that both forms of reception are necessary. Baldwin
is less specific. He certainly assumes that reception will occur in
both ways—what else, after all, would one expect from a monk-
priest?—but he does not dwell upon it at length. Perhaps it was
just too obvious. His consideration of sacramental reception is
therefore brief, and reads as follows:

There is another way [of reception], when Christ is received

or, having been received, possessed in our heart not just by
faith and the power [*virtus*] of holy communion, but is
taken into us by the eating, use, and reception of his very
body and blood. He is then in us not only by the presence
of the divinity by which we were created, but also by the
presence of the body by which we were redeemed, as he
himself promised, saying: "Behold, I am with you always,
even to the end of the world" (Mt 28:20). He therefore
said: "Whoever eats my flesh and drinks my blood remains
in me and I in him" (Jn 6:56).[60]

Baldwin's major concern, then, is with the spiritual reception,
when Christ dwells within us by faith, but when Baldwin speaks
of faith he does not mean a purely individual relationship between
oneself and God, nor a purely psycho-spiritual experience which
has no practical corollaries. On the contrary, faith demands both
community and activity, for as St. Paul and almost everyone else
tells us, faith works through charity: "fides quae per charitatem
operatur" (Ga 5:6),[61] and charity, by definition, includes both
God and one's neighbour. "Great is faith," says Augustine, "but
profits nothing if it does not have charity,"[62] and "without love,
faith is useless."[63] Few were more aware of this than Baldwin, and
one need look no further than his third tractate, *On the Love of
God*,[64] or his fifteenth, *On the Common Life*,[65] to witness his recognition of the principle and its rich ramifications. The eucharist is
centrally a *communal* act, and we cannot be surprised to find Baldwin, that master-theologian of the common life,[66] leaving us in no
doubt whatsoever on this important point.

Why did Christ institute the eucharist? Not to unite himself
more closely to the individual, but to unite himself more closely to
the church.[67] Where is Christ to be found? *In unitate catholicae ecclesiae!*[68] We assemble in church *causa unitatis*,[69] for there is but one
faith, one law of righteousness (which is the law of charity), one
forma of believing and loving, and one hope of eternal life common to all the righteous.[70] There is but one christian family, says
Arnold of Bonneval, one house of the church.[71] The grace which
the eucharist communicates effects among us a spiritual unity
(*unitas spiritualis*): by the love of our neighbour we are one bread,
and by the love of God one body. "One bread for God, who rejoices in the brotherly love with which we love each other and is,

as it were, nourished [*reficitur*] by us. And we ourselves are also
one bread for each other, for our mutual love is our mutual comfort and our mutual nourishment [*refectio*]. . . . We are one body
through charity, by which Christ is loved as the Spouse, who also
loves the Church as his own body.''[72] And although it is true that
the love of God (which is the body) unites us more closely to God
than the love of our neighbour (which is the bread), yet, just as
bread is necessary for the nourishment of the body, so the love of
our neighbour is necessary for nourishing and increasing the love
of God.[73] The two loves, as I have demonstrated elsewhere,[74] cannot be separated. The communion of the eucharist, therefore, is a
communion of friendship (*communio amicitiae*)[75] and a sacrament
of fraternal charity in which each suffers with each and each rejoices with each.[76]

There is, of course, nothing new in this. The writers of the post-
Berengarian era all, without exception, lay emphasis on the importance of the unity of the faithful. Christ has three bodies—his
physical body, his sacramental body, and his mystical body (the
idea is an old one and has a long history[77])—and the sacrament of
the altar, or, more precisely, the concept of *sacramentum-et-res*,
unites all three.[78] Indeed, as Sheedy rightly indicates, ''the sacrament is only productive if it results in a union of charity and love
among the members of the Mystical Body of Christ.''[79] Baldwin
stands firmly in this tradition, and in one section of the *De sacramento altaris* explains it in a manner which is very much his own
and which reflects ideas which he expresses more fully and in more
detail in his superb tractate on the common life:

> By this authority of the apostle (namely, 1 Co 10:16) this
> drink can take the name ''communion'' [*communio*] so as to
> be called ''holy communion'' [*sacra communio*]. For it can be
> understood as a communication [*communicatio*] since it is
> given and received in common, and as a communion since it
> is possessed in common. It can also be called communion
> for another reason: for this blood works in us the charity
> through which all things become common, and the things
> which are proper to each are common to all.[80]

This is precisely the thought of the fifteenth tractate:

> By its judgment, charity knows how to convert individual
> ownership into common ownership, and it does so not by
> doing away with individual ownership, but by making indi-
> vidual ownership serve a common end. . . . Individual gifts
> are led by [charity] to [serve] the common good, and a gift
> which one person has received as his own personal posses-
> sion becomes of benefit to another because its usefulness is
> shared with him. . . . Different gifts are made common in
> two ways: [first] when the gifts given to individuals individ-
> ually are possessed in common by the sharing of love, and
> [second] when they are loved in common by the love of
> sharing.[81]

Charity lies at the heart of both communion and community,
and the grace which flows from the eucharist (and the term itself,
says Baldwin, following Isidore, means *bona gratia*[82]) is shared
among all of us by the communion of charity.[83] Furthermore,
when the community of the church offers up the oblation of the
sacramental body, it also offers up itself, whether it likes it or
not.[84] The sacrifice of Christ is also the sacrifice of the mystical
body of Christ—of the church and its members—and for Baldwin
of Ford the sacrifice of the altar is not something that happens just
once every day,[85] but a continual sacrifice, for "the sacrifice we are
now discussing is not only a sacrament which sanctifies us, but it
contains within itself an example which we should imitate. It is a
sacrament through the mystery of faith and an example of the way
we should live. As a sacrament [it brings about] the humbling of
our will, and the sacrament benefits those who imitate the example. Those who do not imitate the example, the sacrament does
not benefit."[86]

What, then, did Christ do? The answer is simple: he died. And
as he was obedient to death, so should we be obedient to death.
What is *oboedientia usque ad mortem*? It is the cup of salvation, the
cup of the passion of Christ, the perfection of the old law, the new
wine which Christ will drink in his Father's kingdom.[87] "What,
then, is it to drink this new wine if not to suffer through love of
obedience?"[88] And how is this obedience best exemplified? Undoubtedly, as everyone at the time would have agreed, by the era-
dication of self-will (*propria voluntas*). This is how Baldwin explains it:

Obedience to death should not be understood only of bodily
death, but in a certain way of every perfect mortification
and chastisement of the body, and most especially of every
perfect renunciation of self-will. Anyone who strangles self-
will puts himself to death. Whoever detaches himself from
unlawful desires for the sake of God hates his own soul for
the sake of God, and he loses it in this world; but by hating
it and losing it, he preserves it unto eternal life. Whoever
sets aside self-will in joy of soul [*mens*] and sweetness of
charity and, by a judicious choice [*discretio*], prefers his
brother's will, gives his soul for his brother. Obedience to
death is in every kind of martyr, whether we be killed by
the sword of the persecutor or by the sword of the Spirit,
which is the word of God. This is perfect obedience, which
was not in the Law, for the Law led no-one to perfection.
This is the new wine which Jesus Christ drinks with his disciples. All who rejoice in this obedience are fellow-drinkers
with Jesus, and from his cup they drink spiced wine and the
sweet juice of the pomegranate [Sg 8:2].[89]

Again, in a later section of the *De sacramento altaris* he tells us
that the chalice of Christ (*calix Christi*) can be understood in three
ways:

. . . either the very blood of Christ which was shed for us
and which we drink at the altar; or the passion of Christ,
which we are obliged to suffer with him; or the imitation
[*imitatio*] of the passion of Christ by which, in our small
measure, we make a return and a thanksgiving to him who
suffered for us by suffering with him. The spiritual drink [of
1 Co 10:4], therefore, is drunk not only by those who drink
the Lord's blood when they drink it at the reception of the
sacrament itself, but by all the righteous who, from the days
of old, have had faith in the passion of Christ and have lived
spiritually in that faith, mortifying their flesh with its vices
and desires (Ga 5:24) and displaying a likeness [*similitudo*] of
the passion of Christ by the patient endurance [*patientia*] of
their tribulations. For whoever does not suffer is not
righteous.[90]

Christ, then, is our model of obedience,[91] the *forma* and *norma* of righteousness,[92] and we can neither love him without obeying him,[93] nor have faith in him without doing what he would have us do. Baldwin is insistent on this point—more insistent, I think, than any others writing at the time. Faith is not just a matter of belief, but of service: you cannot profess to know God if you deny him in your deeds.[94] As we observed above, faith demands community and activity, and *credere* and *servare* are two sides of the same coin.[95] For Baldwin, says Gary Macy, "to receive the Eucharist without living a good life would be to cut oneself off from the society of the just, the Body of Christ."[96]

None of this is new material. Augustine, ever Baldwin's master, tells us clearly that at the eucharist, only he who imitates is filled,[97] and he sees the eucharist as the way of martyrdom.[98] He, too, says specifically that a good life (*bona vita*) is inseparable from faith, which works through love.[99] For Gregory the Great, "we ought to imitate what we receive and proclaim to others what we revere."[100] For Bernard of Clairvaux, to eat and drink Christ is to share in his sufferings,[101] and when Isaac of Stella tells us that we should die for Christ as Christ died for us, what he means is the death of abstinence and fasting (*abstinentia et inedia*).[102] What is clear is that for all these writers the eucharist is not just a daily or Sunday celebration, but a continual demand. According to Baldwin we should receive it like a starving man, and there and then, without hesitation or delay (*sine mora et cunctatione*), begin to live like Christ.[103] It is for this reason that he spends so much time in the last section of his treatise in considering the *bona vita* and the disposition of soul which is necessary for it. This material is not in any way just an appendix to his main discussion, but an integral part of it. The one grows out of the other, for faith and good works are, as we have seen, inseparable. Participation in the eucharist is the imitation of Christ, and the imitation of Christ is the christian life. We should live sacramentally and eucharistically, showing in our visible actions the invisible grace within, and living our life not as individuals swollen with self-will,[104] but as members of the *sacra communio* which is the mystical body of Christ. A high demand, no doubt, but who wants an easy life?

Self-will, says Baldwin, echoing almost everyone from Plotinus onwards, has separated us from God; by love of obedience we turn again to him.[105] The image of God which we are has been deformed through pride of reason and must therefore be reformed (*reformari*) "through the humbling of reason in this sacrament of our redemption."[106] Christ's blood redeems us, he says, that we might be reformed (*reformetur*) in the image of God,[107] and in so saying he again follows an old tradition. We find it clearly expressed, for example, in Florus of Lyons,[108] in Anselm of Canterbury,[109] in the *Summa sententiarum* (which speaks of our being "re-built" by the eucharist),[110] and very clearly in Arnold of Bonneval.[111] The reason is obvious: the restoration of the lost likeness is achieved by living a life of selfless—or self-will-less—obedience; the model for the life of selfless obedience is Christ, who was obedient *usque ad mortem*; and the *mors Christi* is celebrated every day in the sacrament and sacrifice of the altar. Thus we see, once again, the centrality of the eucharist in the christian life, for not only does it present us with an example we should imitate, but also communicates to us the grace which is so necessary for the fulfilment of that imitation.

It is this idea which stands behind the concept of the eucharist as the *viaticum*: not in the sense of communion given to a person on the point of death, but as one's "rations" or "provisions" for the whole pilgrimage through this world to heaven. Guerric of Igny calls it our food for the journey to the heavenly Galilee,[112] and according to Arnold of Bonneval, a christian finds no access to eternal life unless he is conducted there by this *viaticum*.[113] For Baldwin, too, the eucharist sustains us in our journey to the next world and guarantees our safe arrival. It is our life, our salvation, and our hope of glory;[114] it is the sacrament which bestows spiritual and eternal life,[115] and a foretaste (*praelibatio*) which prepares us for the full meal in paradise.[116] In this sacrament is hidden everlasting life and true salvation,[117] and it symbolizes the transformation of our mortality into immortality.[118] Christ, says Baldwin, has become the bread which strengthens the heart of man:

> Bread in the word of teaching, bread in the example of life, bread in every gift of spiritual grace, bread in every consolation of our misery, bread which sustains our life and comforts us in [our] labours on the road [*in labore viae*] so that, in his strength, we may arrive at Horeb, the mountain of God.[119]

By the power (*virtus*) of the eucharist we live soberly, righteously, and piously (Tt 2:12) until our death; by its power we piously fall asleep in death; and by its power we are delivered from death and raised again to life. "For such is the order of grace: a good life, a worthy death, the blessed life. *Vita bona, mors pretiosa, vita beata.*"[120]

Ordo gratiae: the order of grace; and it is, of course, grace which is, as it were, the *modus operandi* of the eucharist. After all, says the author of the *Summa sententiarum*, we have in the eucharist not just *bona gratia*,[121] but him from whom all grace comes,[122] and Baldwin tells us that from the chalice flow all graces[123] and speaks of the eucharist as the *communio generalis gratiae*.[124] Furthermore, this grace does not flow from the sacrament only at the time of its celebration, but continually. "Although the sacrament itself is transitory," says Deusdedit, "and is therefore repeated every day, the divine power [*virtus*] that is eaten in it is eternal."[125] To use a more homely example: we can drive a car a very long way after only one stop at the gas station. It is this grace, continually given and continually received in the eucharist, which enables us to live eucharistically and sacramentally, to imitate the death of Christ, to persevere in loving and obeying him,[126] to restore the lost likeness, to die a holy death, and be raised in glory in the world to come. In short, as Hugh of St. Victor says, "from the eucharist is all sanctification."[127]

Baldwin's *De sacramento altaris*, therefore, is not just a treatise on a single sacrament, but a manual of christian living. Moreover, it is a manual of *communal* christian living, whether the community be that of the monastery or of the whole mystical body of Christ. Jean Leclercq expresses the matter precisely and accurately:

> The holy communion is not primarily an individual encounter between the soul and Jesus, the occasion for an affective colloquy or of sensed and experienced relations of a psychological order; it is a real participation in the life and work of the Incarnate Word.[128]

Nowhere in his treatise—and rarely in any other treatise—does Baldwin dwell on ecstatic raptures or the *excessus* of contemplation.[129] He certainly distinguishes the *vita activa* from the *vita contemplativa*, but his description of the latter is brief, and he makes it clear that, in his view, it belongs more to heaven than to earth:

> Two ways are here [namely, in Ex 16:28–30] suggested to us: the active way, in which we should now labour, and the contemplative, for which we should labour and in which we shall be occupied in the contemplation of God alone. But although the contemplative life is most especially [a matter] for the time to come, it is represented in this [present] time by the holy repose which is symbolized by the sabbath. Of this rest [*vacatio*] Moses adds, "Let each person stay with himself and let none go forth from his place on the seventh day" [Ex 17:29], as if to say, "Let each rest in his own house and not go forth to any work on the sabbath day." By this we are taught to remain with ourselves [*apud nos*] at the time of contemplation and not to go forth through unlawful desires, but to concentrate [*colligere*] [our] whole attention [*intentio*] in purity of heart so as to love and think of God alone.[130]

And that is all we are told. Baldwin was writing just before the great surge of eucharistic devotion which characterized the early years of the thirteenth century and was not in the least interested in the sort of extravagant psychic experiences which we find occurring a little later among (for example) the *mulieres religiosae*.[131] For him, our encounter with Christ in the sacrament of the altar is not an egocentric, ecstatic rapture, but something much less individualistic and much more important:

> The effect of this sacrament *on* us is that Christ lives in us and we in him. Its effect *in* us is that, just as Christ died for us, so too we die for Christ.[132]

Alger of Liège had already attacked Rupert of Deutz for his notion of "personal union and 'deification' by means of the sacrament," maintaining, as John van Engen tells us, that this was "an assault upon Christ's uniqueness (*singularitas*) and an unwarranted (*superextendere*) exaltation of our poor humanity. Then he argued at length for Augustine's teaching that the end (*res* or *virtus*) of the sacrament is to bind believers in love to Christ and one another by grace."[133] This, too, is where Baldwin stands. He never uses the term "deification," either for our conformation to God in this life or in the life to come,[134] and neither he nor any other Cistercian envisaged the monastic life as a manic quest for ecstatic experiences: a series of rapturous oases in a vast desert of *taedium vitae religiosae*. They saw it rather as an imitation of the passion of Christ, and although it was more than possible that God, through a super-abundance of grace, might on occasion reveal himself more fully to the loving soul, that was, as it were, a bonus, and could not, in any case, be commanded. Guerric of Igny puts the matter in perspective; Christ, he says, is given to us in three ways:

> Once he was given to the world in the form of flesh; and at specific [*certis*] days and times he is given to the faithful under the appearance of bread, that is, in the eating of his sacrament; and very often [*saepius*] at unspecified [*incertis*] times he is given to those devoted [to him] in the taste [*gustus*] of his Spirit. The first [gift] was for our redemption, the second for sanctification, and the third for consolation. The first requires a right faith, the second a pure conscience, the third ready devotion [*devotio prompta*]. This [last] raises up the soul [*mens*] so that it comes in contact with grace, opens up the heart so that it can receive it, and enlarges affection [*affectus*] so that it can contain as much of it as possible.[135]

We see, then, that our redemption and our sanctification come from the incarnation and the eucharist respectively. The "visitations" are only comforts or consolations. Wonderful, no doubt, but no more than comforts, and the concern of so many modern scholars with examining and analysing "the spiritual experience" of Bernard of Clairvaux, William of St. Thierry, X, Y, or Z may mislead us into thinking that this was what the Cistercian life was all about. It was not, and Abbot Baldwin, who knew perfectly well what he was talking about, makes it clear that it was not. Three things are necessary for salvation, says Hugh of St. Victor, "faith, sacraments, and good works [*opera bona*],"[136] and not four, "faith, sacraments, good works, and ecstatic experiences." With this Baldwin is in total agreement and, as we have seen, is not only convinced that faith, sacraments, and good works are essential, but that they are intimately connected, and that one follows from the other as naturally and as necessarily as the night the day. "The sacrament, in effect, is the efficacious sign of the sanctification of man, and the spiritual life is only the 'interiorisation' or 'realisation' of what was signified and contained, as though in seed, in the sacrament."[137]

What we have, then, in this lengthy discourse is not only a detailed, conservative exegesis—a *ratio fidei* in Baldwin's sense—of the biblical text, but also a treatise on the mystical body of Christ and the life of its many members. It is true that much of what Baldwin says can be paralleled in other writers, yet the way in which he combines the materials is very much his own,[138] and his whole approach to the question of the eucharist is, I think, deliberate and significant. Baldwin was, of course, well aware of the earlier eucharistic controversies, and there can be no doubt that he was equally aware of the important role played in these controversies by the listing of patristic authorities and the reconciliation of their differences.[139] Baldwin makes no attempt to enter this field. He does indeed quote the fathers—he refers by name to Augustine, Hilary, Jerome, Ambrose, Origen, and pseudo-Dionysius[140]—but Jaroslav Pelikan is perfectly correct when he says that "among the defenders of the doctrine of the real presence in the twelfth century, Baldwin of Canterbury was outstanding for his recognition that the doctrine of the unique inspiration and supreme authority of Scripture was crucial to the orthodox doctrine of the Eucharist."[141] As we saw above, if the Scripture is true (and it is), then the witnesses are true, the testimonies are true, and the faith itself is true.[142] Baldwin's treatise, therefore, is not an exegesis of Augustine or Ambrose, but an exegesis of the scriptural text. An exegesis, it is true, in harmony with the ideas of the "orthodox fathers" (especially Augustine), but an exegesis which tries to look beyond the incredibly tangled web of patristic conflict and consensus to the relative clarity of God's own word and the purity of the faith. And if we consider for a moment when the treatise was written and to whom it was dedicated, we will find there further indications of Baldwin's purposes and intentions.

The *De sacramento altaris* was composed sometime between 1169/1170 and 1180 when Baldwin was *Fordensis monasterii servus*;[143] it was dedicated to his close friend Bartholomew of Exeter. But the year 1170 was one of great significance in the ecclesiastical

history of England, for on December 29 in that year the quarrel of
Henry II and Thomas Becket reached its apogee, and the archbishop was assassinated in Canterbury Cathedral. It is difficult to
believe that Baldwin's decision to enter the monastic life just at
this time was mere coincidence. Baldwin was a strong supporter of
Becket—indeed, he praises him directly, though anonymously, in
the *De sacramento altaris*[144] and refers to "most blessed Thomas"
by name in his second tractate[145]—and Bartholomew of Exeter,
though his conduct was at times equivocal, was regarded as a
friend of Archbishop Thomas.[146] Baldwin, furthermore, was unquestionably devout, a man well known for his piety and his
religion. He was no hypocrite, and, though sometimes a poor
judge of character, his tractates and other works reveal someone
with a real and deep spirituality.[147] Bartholomew, in many ways,
was very similar. "The bishop's personal life," says Adrian Morey,
"was one of austerity and genuine piety,"[148] and, like Baldwin, he
combined with this piety an extremely thorough knowledge of
canon law and very sound theology. His *De libero arbitrio* and *Dialogus contra Judaeos* (both dedicated to Baldwin) reveal the work of
a thoroughly competent theologian,[149] and many of his sermons,
lucid, simple, and sincere, are a pleasure to read.[150]

It is not difficult to envisage the deep distress which these devout
friends must have felt when faced with the England of the 1170s:
an England which had murdered its chief prelate, and an English
church which was caught up in conflicts and stained by scandals.[151]
The situation in the country did not even begin to approach nor-
mality until about 1175. It seems to me, therefore, that Baldwin's
treatise on the eucharist may be seen, in part, as a call for spiritual
reform, for a return to the gospel text, and, as I suggested earlier, is
not to be associated with such technical treatises as those of Guitmund of Aversa or Alger of Liège, but with Baldwin's own tractates
and his *De commendatione fidei*. That is to say, a call for a return to
the theory and practice of faith at a time in history when faith and
charity were conspicuously absent. It is a work which looks beyond the conflicts of the fathers to the text of the scripture, and
which looks beyond the complexities of ecclesiastical and secular
politics to the words of Christ. The church is, or should be, the
mystical body of Christ; the eucharist is the sacrament of his mystical body; the eucharist, therefore, is the very heart of the *via*

christiana. It is this sacrament which is the greatest test of faith, and as Baldwin has shown, we cannot have faith without love, nor love without obedience. It follows, then, that the christian life is figured in and follows from the eucharist, and it would be difficult, therefore, to spend too long in its discussion or to be too detailed in its examination. If Baldwin's own life did not always reflect these ideals, that is simply a consequence of human frailty, and if he was disillusioned by the conduct of the armies in the Holy Land, that, too, is hardly surprising. The order of grace was symbolised for him in the central sacrament of his faith: *vita bona, mors pretiosa, vita beata*, and if we may have doubts as to his attainment of the first two, we may hope that in the third, the abbot and archbishop found all that he may have desired and expected.

Memorial University of Newfoundland

NOTES

1. William of St. Thierry, *De sacramento altaris*; PL 180: 341–66.
2. Isaac of Stella, *Epistola ad Joannem Episcopum Pictaviensem de officio missae*; PL 194: 1889–96. The contributions of two other Cistercians should also be mentioned: Arnold of Bonneval and Ogier of Locedio. For the former, see his *Liber de cardinalibus operibus Christi* VI; PL 189: 1641D–50A; and J. Leclercq, "Les méditations eucharistiques d'Arnauld de Bonneval," RTAM 13 (1946) 40–56; for the latter, see his fifteen sermons *De verbis Domini in coena* in PL 184: 879–950. C. H. Talbot, in "A List of Cistercian Manuscripts in Great Britain" (Trad. 8 [1952] 407), also attributes to Arnold a *De sacramento altaris* which appears in Cambridge, Gonville and Caius College, MS 105 ff. 307–315, and Oxford, Bodleian Library, MS Bodley 569 ff. 92ᵛ–104. This is incorrect, and the work in question in actually the *De sacramento altaris/De sacramento eucharistiae* of the Benedictine Arnulf of Beauvais, bishop of Rochester from 1115 to his death in 1124.
3. D. Stone, *A History of the Doctrine of the Holy Eucharist* (London 1909), two volumes. See especially vol. I, chapter V–VI.
4. Baldwin of Ford, *De sacramento altaris* (=Sa); PL 204: 651C–52D (ed. J. Morson, trans. E. de Solms, *Baudouin de Ford, Le sacrament de l'autel*, SCh 53–54 [continuous pagination] [Paris, 1963], pp. 110–14. See Anselm of Canterbury, *De azymo et fermentato*; PL 158:541–48; Alger of Liège, *De Sacramento* II, x; PL 180:827B–30D. See D. N. Bell, "Baldwin of Ford and Twelfth-Century Theology," in E. R. Elder (ed.), *Noble Piety and Reformed Monasticism: Studies in Medieval Cistercian History VII*, CS 65 (Kalamazoo, 1981), pp. 137–38.
5. See Sa 662B (148), 678A (204). See also, *Tractatus diversae* (=Td) I; PL 204:403B (ed. and trans. R. Thomas, *Baudouin de Ford, Traités*, Pain de Cîteaux

236 *David N. Bell*

35–40 [Chimay, 1973–1975], vol. 35, p. 28). See Bell, "Baldwin," p. 138.

6. Sa 656C (126). Berengar, attributing to his opponents an ultra-realist view, had maintained that if what they said was true, then little bits of Christ would be scattered through all the churches in the land. See further C. E. Sheedy, *The Eucharistic Controversy of the Eleventh Century Against the Background of Pre-Scholastic Theology* (Washington, 1947), pp. 71–72 (Berengar's views), pp. 88–92 (the views of his opponents).

7. See Sa 641C–642A (72). It is easy to make a slip of the tongue, he says, and let a light word pop out, "but it is almost impossible to keep a careful and cautious watch on all one's expressions and weigh all one's words in the balance of judgment, so that nothing unconsidered and nothing suspect escapes. In a matter so holy, a single word brought forth incautiously or not clearly understood, though not itself erroneous, may sometimes give rise to suspicion of error."

8. The PL text of Sa ends with an appendix (769C–74C) in which the name of Berengar does appear (771C), but this appendix is not from the pen of Baldwin and did not form part of his treatise. See Bell, "Baldwin," p. 146, n. 48.

9. Sa 678D (206).

10. Sa 678D –79A (206).

11. Sa 679A (208).

12. Sa 679D (210).

13. See *De commendatione fidei* (= Cf); PL 204:590D–91A, and Bell, "Baldwin," p. 142.

14. Cf 591D.

15. Cf 609A. Again, in Cf 615A, he speaks disparagingly of *sapientia carnalis;* in Cf 625D–26A of *humani sensus interpretatio* and *humanae voluntatis adinventio sive traditio;* in Cf 634C shows how the wise of the world are confounded by the simple; and in Sa 681D (216) tells us that all worldly wisdom is hateful to God.

16. Sheedy, p. 14.

17. See Bell, "Baldwin," p. 140.

18. Sa 653B–C (116). Cp. Sa 661C (144), referring to the authority (*auctoritas*) of the Church and the orthodox fathers, and Td I 414B (35/78), referring to "the authority of God himself and of the holy fathers.' See further Bell, p. 147, n. 67.

19. Sa 669A–70A (172–74).

20. Sa 679D (210). Compare Td I 410A (35/56): "Not to see great things in oneself and to be devoutly ignorant [*pie ignorare*] of things we are not permitted to know is a good blindness. In [the realm of] heavenly mysteries and divine sacraments, every impious doubt [*omnis impia dubitatio*] should be banished far from our heart, and all inquisitive questionings [*omnis curiosa inquisitio*] should be restrained so that faith, which possesses the conviction of truth [*veritatis conscientia*], should also possess a devout ignorance [*pia ignorantia*]." See also Cf 574A.

21. See the discussion in Sa 666D–67B (164–66).

22. Sa 736D–37A (440).

23. Sa 747C (484) based on Augustine, *Enarratio in Ps.* 77, 17; PL 36:995 "There are good people in the church, weak and, as it were, carnal, who cannot apprehend and understand the profound mysteries of the faith and the customs [*instituta*] of the more perfect life, but being content with a little faith and elementary precepts, they believe simply and live innocently." Compare Sa 758A–B (524).

24. See the lengthy account in Sa 712C–13B (346–48), ending "Non igitur oportet omnes, qui fidem habent, mystici eloquii prudentes esse, vel signorum aut sacramentorum profunda penetrare. Sed mysteriorum intelligentia illis magis est necessaria, quibus docendi et regendi dispensatio est credita." Compare Cf 573D– 74A (simplicity of *conscientia* is the *comes et custos fidei*). Leclercq (Sa 50) suggests that in his distinction of the "simple" and the "perfect" (and other equivalent terms: see especially Sa 716D [362]) Baldwin may have been influenced by

Origen. This is certainly possible, but we must also remember, as Leclercq indicates elsewhere, that it was a fairly common idea (see J. Leclercq, *The Love of Learning and the Desire for God* [New York, 1962], 217–18).

25. Hugh of St. Victor, *De sacramentis* I, x, iii; PL 176:331D–32A. Compare William of St. Thierry, *De sacramento altaris, prol.*; PL 180:345A.

26. Sa 679B (208): "Our faith, therefore, which is founded immoveably on the words of God himself, is not tossed about, wavering and vacillating, by the uncertainty of human opinions. Founded on truth and grounded on the strong rock of divine authority, it stands unchanged and unshaken."

27. See Td I 407C–408A (35/46–48).

28. Cf 621A.

29. Cf 621A: "Unde constare debet quod munimenta fidei nostrae ad auctoritatem sacrae Scripturae reducuntur." See also Bell, "Baldwin," p. 140.

30. See the important discussion in Cf 583D–84C.

31. Sa 662A (146). Compare Sa 655D (124): there are things which are hidden from the eyes of human reason, but which are "wonderfully visible to the eyes of faith alone."

32. Sa 703B (300): "Nisi credideritis, non intelligetis." This is the Old Latin version of Is 7:9, which Baldwin probably found in Augustine (for example, *De Trinitate* XV, ii, 2; PL 42:1058; *Sermo 272*; PL 38:1246). See also Td VI 452C (37/26, but Fr. Thomas's identification—Is 9:9—is incorrect).

33. William of St. Thierry, *De sacramento altaris, prol.*; PL 180:345A.

34. Cf 575C.

35. See Bell, "Baldwin," pp. 138–39. The key text is Cf 583C–84D "De fidei certitudine."

36. Peter Lombard, *Sententiae* IV, xi, 3; PL 192:862: "Mysterium fidei credi salubriter potest, investigari salubriter non potest." This is traced by Lombard to the *Liber sententiarum ex Augustino collectae* of Prosper of Aquitaine, but Lombard is dependent for the text and its source on Alger, *De sacramento* I, ix; PL 180:767A:"... respondet tibi Augustinus in libro Sententiarum Prosperi: 'Si quaeris modum quo id possit fieri, breviter ad praesens respondeo: Mysterium fidei est, credi salubriter potest, investigari utiliter non potest.'" Alger, in turn, is incorrect: the sentence is actually from Lanfranc, *De corpore et sanguine Domini* x; PL 150:421D: "Si quaeris modum quo id fieri possit, breviter ad praesens respondeo: Mysterium fidei credi salubriter potest, vestigari utiliter non potest."

37. Guitmund of Aversa, *De corporis et sanguinis Christi veritate* I; PL 149:1441C: "Non enim praecepit tibi Christus: Intellige, sed crede!" See generally Sheedy, 41–43.

38. Td I 407C (35/44).

39. Td I 407B–C (35/44).

40. That is, *species*, as in Sa 678A (204) and a number of other places. Baldwin does not use the term "accidents" (*accidentia*), although Guitmund had made the term part of the standard vocabulary a century earlier (see A. J. MacDonald, *Berengar and the Reform of Sacramental Doctrine* [London, 1930], 344–46).

41. See Ambrose, *De sacramentis* IV, 20; PL 16:443A. The phrase is common from Ambrose onwards.

42. Sheedy, p. 42.

43. Td I 403–414 (35/26–81).

44. Td I 403B–404A (35/28).

45. See Sa 47–51.

46. See Cf 606C–607A.

47. Cf 587D–88A.

48. Cf 613C–D.

49. A common idea, based on 1 Co 11:27–29, which appears continually from the patristic period onwards. See J. Pelikan, *The Christian Tradition, III: The Growth of Medieval Theology* (Chicago, London, 1978), 196–97.

50. Sa 692A (258): "Christ is the bread of life for those that believe in him. To believe in Christ is to eat the bread of life; that is, to possess Christ within oneself [*Christum in se habere*]; that is, to possess eternal life." And see further the rest of this discussion to 693A (262).

51. Augustine, *In Joannis Evangelium, Tractatus 25*, 12; PL 35:1602, quoted by Baldwin in Sa 695C (272).

52. See the discussion in Sa 709D–710D (336–40).

53. O. Lottin, *Psychologie et morale aux XIIe et XIIIe siècles* (Gembloux, 1959) V, 131, #193: "Notandum quia due sunt manducationes: una sacramentalis, altera spiritualis. Sacramentalis illa est talis quam boni et mali accipiunt; bonis quidem prodest, malis vero iudicium est. Spiritualis autem manducatio est illa qua, per fidem que ex dilectione operatur, credimus nos uniri Deo, que unio iam incepit, in fine vero plena erit. Hec est illa manducatio que etiam semel accepta dat vitam eternam."

54. Peter Lombard, for example, in *Sententiae* IV, ix, 1; PL 192:858, traces it to Augustine. See the notes in E. F. Rogers, *Peter Lombard and the Sacramental System* [New York, 1917; rpt. New York, 1976], pp. 124–25.

55. William of St. Thierry, *De sacramento altaris* vi; PL 180:353B–C traces it to Jerome, *In epistolam ad Ephesios* I, i (in v. 7); PL 26:451A: "The flesh of Christ is understood in two ways: either that spiritual and divine [flesh] of which he says, 'My flesh is truly food' [Jn 6:55], or that flesh which was crucified and buried" (William's version). In the *Summa Sententiarum* VI, iii; PL 176:140C–D, it is traced to both Jerome and Augustine.

56. See Alger, *De sacramento* I, xi; PL 180:773D–74A.

57. See Sa 694C–95D (268–72). "This," he says, "is the summary of our faith: to know Christ in the Father, Christ in the flesh, Christ in the sharing at the altar [*in altaris participatione*]." Compare Td I 403B–404A (35/28) translated at n. 44 above for exactly the same idea. For a further example of the eucharist as a *communio amicitiae*, see Sa 714B–D (352–54). Compare also Cf 573B–C. Baldwin's ideas on friendship have almost certainly been influenced by Aelred of Rievaulx.

58. William of St. Thierry, *De sacramento altaris* v; PL 180:353A. The entirety of this marvellous fifth *caput* (351–53A) is wholly typical of William.

59. Lanfranc is insistent on this: see his *De corpore et sanguine Domini* xv; PL 150:425B–26A, especially 425D: "Each eating is necessary, and each is fruitful. The one requires the other . . . ." In Alger, see the whole of *De sacramento* I, xi; PL 180:771C–75A. For William of St. Thierry, see the useful discussion in G. Macy, *The Theologies of the Eucharist in the Early Scholastic Period* (Oxford, 1984), pp. 96–97. Rupert of Deutz also leaves us in no doubt on the matter: see J. H. van Engen, *Rupert of Deutz* (Berkeley, 1983), p. 155.

60. Sa 695C–D (272).

61. Baldwin quotes the verse in, for example, Sa 689A (246), Sa 763B (544), Cf 576D, Cf 587C, and elsewhere.

62. Augustine, *In Joannis Evangelium, Tractatus 6*, 21; PL 35:1435.

63. *Ibid.*, *Tractatus 10*, 2; PL 35:2055.

64. Td III 417D–30B (35/112–71).

65. Td XV 545C–62D (40/15–92).

66. See D. N. Bell, "Heaven on Earth: Celestial and Cenobitic Unity in the Thought of Baldwin of Ford," in E. R. Elder (ed.), *Heaven on Earth: Studies in Medieval Cistercian History IX*, CS 68 (Kalamazoo, 1983), 1–21.

67. Sa 661C (144): "Christus enim super petram fidei Ecclesiam aedificavit; Christus Ecclesiae coelestium sacramentorum mysteria revelavit; ut Ecclesiam sibi arctius uniret, hoc sacramentum instituit."

68. Sa 758D (528).

69. Sa 727C (402).

70. Sa 751B (498).

71. See Leclerq, "Les méditations eucharistiques . . ." (see n. 2) 52, lines 109–113. See further Macy, pp. 124–25, where Arnold's approach to the eucharist is classed as "ecclesiastical." It should be noted, however, that the difference between Macy's "mystical" approach (in which he includes Baldwin: see pp. 98–99) and "ecclesiastical" approach is, in many cases, only one of emphasis.

72. Sa 717A–B (364), and see generally Sa 716D–18D (362–68), which is a clear and impressive exegesis of 1 Co 10:17, "For we, being many, are one bread, one body."

73. See Sa 717C (364–66).

74. See D. N. Bell, "The Ascetic Spirituality of Baldwin of Ford," Cîteaux 31 (1980), 242–44.

75. See n. 57 above.

76. Sa 717B (364): "We ourselves are also one bread to each other, for our mutual love is a mutual comfort to us and mutual nourishment. Whence also we are every one members one of another (Rm 12:5), because we suffer with each other and rejoice with each other, counting as common, through the affection [affectus] of fraternal charity, the bad and good things which seem to be proper to each." See further n. 80 below.

77. For a detailed survey of the matter, see H. de Lubac, *Corpus Mysticum: L'eucharistie et l'église au moyen âge* (2nd ed., Paris, 1949), pp. 295–339.

78. See Sheedy, p. 118.

79. Sheedy, p. 123.

80. Sa 715D (358). Compare also the passage translated at n. 76 above.

81. Td XV 558C (40/71); 559B (40/75); 561A–B (40/85). See further Bell, "Heaven on Earth," pp. 8–9.

82. Sa 716B (360): "Unde et Eucharistia dicitur, id est bona gratia," following Isidore, *Etymologiae* VI, xix, 38; PL 82:255C: ". . . cujus panis et calicis sacramentum Graeci Eucharistiam dicunt, quod Latine *bona gratia* interpretatur." Everyone was aware of this etymology.

83. See Sa 760D–61A (536).

84. This is the especial contribution of Augustine to the theology of the eucharistic sacrifice, and there is surely no clearer statement of it than appears in *De civitate Dei* X, 6; PL 41:283–84. See also *ibid.*, XIX, 23, 5; PL 41:655.

85. The Cistercian *Consuetudines* make it clear that monk-priests could, if they so wished, celebrate private masses every day. Monks who were not priests normally received the eucharist every Sunday, and lay brothers just seven times a year, unless the abbot decided otherwise. See P. Guignard, *Monuments primitifs de la règle Cistercienne* (Dijon, 1878), pp. 156–57 (*Consuetudines*, lviiii); pp. 160–61 (*ibid.*, lxvi); p. 281 (*Usus conversorum*, v).

86. Td I 410C–D (35/60).

87. See Sa 676B–C (196–98).

88. Sa 676C (198). For Baldwin's teaching on the nature and importance of obedience, see Bell, "Ascetic Spirituality," pp. 234–38.

89. Sa 676C–77A (198–200). On the importance of *discretio*, see Bell, "Ascetic Spirituality," p. 232, n. 49.

90. Sa 711D–12A (342–44). The expression *imitatio passionis Christi* occurs again at Sa 733B (428).

91. Sa 646A (86): "Christus forma est oboedientiae."

92. Sa 758C (526).

93. See especially Td III 426A–26C (35/152–54), and further discussion in Bell, "Ascetic Spirituality," pp. 238–39, 244–45.

94. See Cf 575D–76D, based on Titus 1:16.

95. See Cf 575D–76A.

96. Macy, p. 99.

97. Augustine, *Enarratio in Ps.* 21, ii, 27; PL 36:178: "Coenam suam dedit, passionem suam dedit: ille saturatur, qui imitatur." Compare also *ibid.*, 48, i, 3;

David N. Bell

PL 36:545: "It says in another psalm 'The poor shall eat and shall be filled' [Ps. 21:27].... What do they eat? That which the faithful know. How shall they be filled? By imitating the passion of their Lord and, not without cause, by receiving their reward."

98. See J. Burnaby, *Amor Dei: A Study of the Religion of St. Augustine* (London, 1938), pp. 125–26.

99. Augustine, *De fide et operibus* xxiii, 42; PL 40:224.

100. Gregory, *Moralia in librum Job* XIII, xxiii, 26; PL 75:1029B: "Ut ergo in nobis sacramentum dominicae passionis non sit otiosum, debemus imitari quod sumimus, et praedicare caeteris quod veneramur."

101. Bernard, *In Psalmum xc 'Qui habitat', sermo 3*, 3; PL 183:192A; (SBOp 4:394): "What is it to eat his flesh and to drink his blood if not to share [*communicare*] his sufferings and imitate the way of life he displayed in the flesh?"

102. See Isaac of Stella, *De officio missae*; PL 194:1893B–C.

103. Sa 739D (452).

104. Baldwin speaks of *tumor propriae voluntatis* in Sa 674D (192).

105. See Sa 693B (262–64) and generally in Bell, "Ascetic Spirituality."

106. Td I 410A–B (35/58). See also the passage translated in n. 86 above.

107. Sa 647D (94): "Through the only-begotten Son of God the image of God was formed in you, and it is he and no other who will be your price, by whose blood you should be redeemed, so that through this same Son who is the image of the invisible God, the image of God might be reformed in you."

108. Florus of Lyons, *De expositione missae* 59; PL 119:51D–52A: "So that the hearts of the faithful may become heavenly and, as they have borne the image of the earthly, may also bear the image of him who is of heaven . . . they should be cleansed not with the blood of brute beasts, but with the spiritual blood of Christ [*rationabili sanguinis Christi cruore*] who, as the same apostle says, offered himself unstained to God through the Holy Spirit [Heb 9:14]. It is this which is daily renewed for us in the sacrament of the body and blood of the Son of God."

109. See Anselm, *Epistola* 107; PL 159:255A–B.

110. *Summa sententiarum* VI, ii; PL 176:139A.

111. See Leclercq, "Les méditations eucharistiques," pp. 53–54 §II, and 54 §III, lines 1–15.

112. Guerric of Igny, *De resurrectione Domini, sermo I*, 6; PL 175:144B, (SCh 202:226; CF 32:85).

113. See Leclercq, "Les méditations eucharistiques," p. 55, lines 57–59. Compare also *Summa sententiarum* VI, ii; PL 176:139B for a clear account.

114. Td I 414D (35/80).

115. See Sa 693D (264).

116. Sa 754D (512).

117. Td I 406D (35/40).

118. Sa 680D (214): "The substantial changing [*mutatio*] of true bread into the true body of Christ effects [*operatur*], in a certain way, and signifies the changing of our mortal life into immortal life...." It is these ideas which lead George Tavard, "The Church as Eucharistic Communion in Medieval Theology," in F. F. Church and T. George (edd.), *Continuity and Discontinuity in Church History*, Studies in the History of Christian Thought 19 (Leiden, 1979), p. 96, to speak of "the heart of Baldwin's sacramental theology" as "radically eschatological."

119. Sa 657A (128).

120. Sa 660C (140–42). See further Leclercq's discussion in Sa 15–18.

121. See n. 82 above.

122. *Summa sententiarum* VI, ii; PL 176:139B.

123. Sa 687A (236).

124. Sa 667D (166).

125. See Pelikan, p. 206.

126. See the long discussion in Sa 696D–98B (276–82). See especially 698B

(280–82): "This food, therefore, when it is eaten with perfect faith and worthy veneration, gives righteousness and perseverance and eternal life." *Perseverantia*, it should be remembered, is essentially an Augustinian technical term: see, for example, Augustine's *De dono perseverantiae*; PL 45:993–1034.

127. Hugh of St. Victor, *De sacramentis* II, viii, 1; PL 176–461D: "The sacrament of the body and blood of Christ is one of those on which salvation principally depends, and it is unique among all of them, since from it is all sanctification [*omnis sanctificatio*]."

128. Sa 40–41. This becomes even clearer among those whose approach to the eucharist is described by Macy as "ecclesiastical." Witness his comments on Arnold of Bonneval (p. 124): "The union achieved in the Eucharist consists in the identity of Christ and the Church, not that of Christ and the individual believer. Salvation takes place when Christ unites us to the society of eternal life, the Church."

129. For a discussion, see Bell, "Ascetic Spirituality," pp. 246–48.

130. Sa 757C–D (522).

131. Compare Hadewijch's vision of Christ in the eucharist: "Then he gave himself to me in the shape of the Sacrament, in its outward form, as the custom is; and then he gave me to drink from the chalice, in form and taste, as the custom is. After that he came himself to me, took me entirely in his arms, and pressed me to him; and all my members felt his in full felicity, in accordance with the desire of my heart and my humanity. So I was outwardly satisfied and fully transported" (*Hadewijch: The Complete Works*, trans. Mother C. Hart, Classics of Western Spirituality [New York, 1980], p. 281. [Vision 7, 64]). Caroline Bynum says, "To the nuns of Helfta, the eucharist was the equivalent of and the occasion for ecstasy" (*Jesus as Mother: Studies in the Spirituality of the High Middle Ages* [Berkeley, 1984], p. 257).

132. Td I 414B–C (35/78).

133. Van Engen, p. 170, referring to Alger, *De sacramento* I, iii; PL 180:751A-B.

134. But other Cistercians do: for example, Isaac of Stella, *De officio missae*; PL 194:1895A: there are three oblations: "the first separates [us] from the world, the second conjoins [us] to Christ, the third unites [us] to God. The first mortifies, the second vivifies, the third deifies [*deificat*]." Arnold of Bonneval, in Leclercq, "Les méditations eucharistiques," uses *deificans* on p. 52, line 101, *deifici* on p. 55, line 47, and *deiformes* on p. 56, line 89.

135. Guerric of Igny, *De nativitate Domini, sermon II*, 3; PL 185:34D (SCh 166:184). The version in CF 8:46 is a paraphrase rather than a translation. We might add that although Baldwin would have agreed with the principle enunciated here, he might not have agreed with the *saepius*. According to him, the experience occurred "seldom and superficially" (*raro et tenuiter*): see Bell, "Ascetic Spirituality," p. 247, n. 161.

136. Hugh of St. Victor, *De sacramentis* I, ix, 8; PL 176:328A-B.

137. Sa 418–419, n. 1.

138. See my comments in "Heaven on Earth," pp. 10–11.

139. See generally Pelikan, pp. 216–29, "The Problem of Patristic Consensus."

140. See Bell, "Baldwin," pp. 141–42. Aelred, Bernard, and the *Rule of St. Benedict* are also important influences, though not mentioned by name. See also M. Pellegrino, "Reminiscenze bibliche, liturgiche e agostiniane nel *De sacramento altaris* di Baldovino di Ford," *Revue des études augustiniennes* 10 (1964) 39–44; and J. C. Didier, "Le *De sacramento altaris* de Baudouin de Ford," *Cahiers de civilisation médiévale* 8 (1965) 59–60, n. 4. Tracing Baldwin's sources is by no means easy: he assimilates and digests his material and, unlike others, does not simply regurgitate it in lumps.

141. Pelikan, p. 221.

142. See n. 28 above.

143. Sa 70. For the date of Baldwin's entry into Ford, see A. Morey, *Bartholo-*

mew of Exeter, Bishop and Canonist (Cambridge, 1937), p. 121. Leclercq's statement (Sa 10) that the work was composed between 1161 and 1180 needs revision.

144. See Sa 682B–C (218–20), and see further B. Smalley, *The Becket Conflict and the Schools: A Study of Intellectuals in Politics* (Totowa, N.J., 1973), pp. 218–19.

145. Td II 416C (35/94), and see further Smalley, pp. 219–20.

146. See Morey, Chapter II, "Bartholomew and Becket," and D. Knowles, *The Episcopal Colleagues of Archbishop Thomas Becket* (Cambridge, 1951), pp. 102–104.

147. For some remarks on Baldwin's character, see my "Ascetic Spirituality," pp. 227–28.

148. Morey, p. 102.

149. See Morey, pp. 108–109, for a brief description of these two works, and pp. 163–64 for the manuscripts (three of the *De libero arbitrio* and one of the *Dialogus*).

150. See Morey, pp. 109–112, and J. B. Schneyer, *Repertorium der Lateinischen Sermones des Mittelalters* (Münster i.W., 1969) I: 424–35. To my mind there is not the least doubt that all three works deserve publication.

151. Both Bartholomew and Baldwin acted as papal judge-delegates; both were eminent authorities in canon law; and Baldwin, either directly or indirectly, was responsible for one of the most important collections of decretals to be made in England in the twelfth century (see Morey, Chapter IV, and C. Duggan, *Twelfth-Century Decretal Collections and Their Importance in English History* [London, 1963], pp. 110–17). Both, therefore, were well aware of the problems within the church.

AN UNEDITED CORRESPONDENCE
BETWEEN HELINAND OF FROIDMONT
AND PHILIP, ABBOT OF VAL
STE MARIE, ON *GENESIS* 27:1
AND THE AGES OF THE WORLD*

Edmé R. Smits

The *CHRONICON* of the Cistercian Helinand of Froidmont is the source of many points which elucidate items of twelfth-century history. Malgorzata Malewicz has published an unknown tract on astrology by Odo of Champagne which was preserved only through Helinand's *Chronicon*. Häring used this work for his edition of the Hexaemeron-commentary by Thierry of Chartres, and the great importance of the *Chronicon* as a source for the *Speculum maius* by Vincent of Beauvais was outlined by Monique Paulmier.[1] Further studies shed light on this work as an important witness for the early reception of Seneca's tragedies, as a landmark in the history of the Guntramlegend, and as a possible witness to the discussion concerning the authorship of the famous Vergil-commentary which is commonly attributed to Bernard Silvestris.[2]

In this article attention is drawn to a letter of Helinand which is an answer to a letter by Philip, abbot of the Cistercian abbey of Val Ste Marie, situated north of Paris. The subject of the correspondence is the interpretation of Genesis 27:1. As works by Philip are, as far as I am aware, unknown, and since the scope of Helinand's answer is broader than just the explanation of the beginning of the Genesis chapter, the correspondence, preserved in Helinand's own *Chronicon*, deserves to be edited.

The text printed below identifies Philip as *Philippus abbas de Valle*. Monique Paulmier pointed to Philip, abbot of Val Ste

Marie as the author.[3] This Philip, who lived until 1196, is indeed most likely to have been Helinand's correspondent. He fits into Helinand's biography nicely; Helinand lived from about 1160 until after 1229 and is known to have been at the abbey of Froidmont in this very period.[4]

Helinand, famous for his French *Vers de la Mort*, is known, beside this major poetic achievement, mostly for his sermons. His *Chronicon* of which only books 45–49 are edited, covering the period 634–1204, is rather neglected. Of the unpublished forty-four books only the first eighteen are preserved in manuscript. The rest seems to be lost. The first eighteen books, however, which treat the history of creation until the death of Alexander the Great, contain many interesting issues and form a document of great interest for twelfth-century Cistercian intellectual history.[5]

The first part of the *Chronicon* has come down to us in two manuscripts. The more important is MS Vat. Reg. lat. 535, a very large codex, dating from the first quarter of the thirteenth century. It was once in Beaupré, a Cistercian abbey situated near Beauvais and also near Froidmont. The other manuscript dates from the fifteenth century: MS London, BL Cotton Claudius B IX. This MS may have come from Canterbury.[6]

In the first books of the *Chronicon* Helinand treats the creation of the world, the angels, and man; here the historical line is provided, in the tradition of Eusebius-Hieronymus, by the Bible. Pagan history is treated simultaneously.[7] Commenting line-by-line on the Biblical text, Helinand reaches in chapter 64 of book VI the beginning of Genesis 27. The line *Senuit Ysaac et caligauerunt oculi eius* incites him to quote the interpretation of this line by the third-century martyr Hippolytus. The latter explains that the old age of Isaac points to the consummation of the world; the darkening eyes signify that faith has disappeared from the world and they point to neglect of the light of religion. Having quoted some more of Hippolytus's comments, which have their ultimate source in a letter of Jerome,[8] Helinand remarks that he has written, as he recalls, a letter to Philip who was once abbot of Val, commenting on the exposition of Hippolytus. He inserts the letter, with the one to which it responds, at this point in his *Chronicon*.[9]

Chapter 65 contains Philip's letter to Helinand. Philip quotes Genesis 27:1, and in a stylistically rather obscure letter he complains about the disadvantages of old age. He opposes the ambition of the people in the world who do not care about spiritual salvation, to the situation of Helinand. He, Philip says, has time to devote himself to study and is thus able to obtain the Lord's favor. Philip further stresses the extraordinary grace that has befallen Helinand. The situation in Froidmont, far away from the noise of this world, contributes to ample opportunity for study. Philip concludes on a light tone by promising Helinand his anger if the bearer of the reply carries home nothing but a letter.

Helinand's response is in chapter 66. His point of departure is Genesis 27:1 and Hippolytus's explanation. Helinand criticizes the lack of coherence in Hippolytus's interpretation. If Isaac, Helinand says, signifies God, how can Isaac's old age signify the consummation of the world? Would it not be better to regard Isaac as the personification of the world rather than of God? A possibility, however, is that Hippolytus applied the different ages of the world to God. God then would be as old as the world in the different ages that the world had in the course of its history. So there would be a correlation between the attitude of people in the different ages of the world regarding faith and worship, and the ages of God (11. 3–21).

The first period, *infantia*, is marked by a lack of praise of the Lord. The world was not able to speak up, *infans*.[10] Helinand adduces some evidence. Abel, though a just man, did not praise the Lord. Only his blood, the Bible says, cried out to the Lord. In addition, the Innocents praised God not by words, but by their death. Enos, the son of Seth, and Enoch, are also treated, but they too, can not be found shown to be evidently praising God (11. 22–52).

Helinand continues by describing God's *infantia*. God can be compared to an infant child. He did not give permission to speak, that is, to praise Him. A quotation from Statius's *Thebaid* fits this situation well. Isiphile cries out in pain over the death of her infant son Archemorus. The different traits of the son, his beautiful face, his stammering words, his smiling and his little cries only understood by the mother, are explained as pointing to the physical beauty of early mankind which faded away in the course of history. This gradual disappearance was due to the increasing wickedness of the world, to the ignorance of its early inhabitants who were not as yet aware of the Trinity, and, lastly, to the fact that only God knew what eternal joy was about. By a wordplay *obliuio/ diluuium* (*obliuio* removes remembrance of the *infantia*)[11] Helinand reaches the flood which brings to an end the first period of the history of the world (11.53–101).

The *puericia mundi* Helinand argues, rightly started with Noah. Three verses of Horace's *Ars Poetica* illustrate this point. The little boy renders words, can walk deliberately, longs to have playmates, is quickly angered, but this emotion is of short duration and his emotions change incessantly. These lines of Horace are applied to Noah and his behavior toward God. Noah did everything God urged him to do, and this is explained by Helinand as rendering words to God. Noah also walked deliberately, since the Bible tells us that he walked with God. The remaining qualifications of the boy in Horace's poetry refer to the wicked of the second age. They longed to have playmates who built together the tower of pride and who started to adore idols. In anger they thought that a brick tower could sustain God's wrath and their emotions changed every few minutes when, by the confusion of the languages, they were spread over different countries. The aftermath of the building of the tower of Babel marks the end of the second period, *puericia* (11. 101–168).

After the first two ages mankind reached the age of discretion which Helinand illustrates by the symbol of the letter Y.[12] Two ways are open for man and there is a possibility to make a choice. This period is the world's *adolescentia* and starts with Abraham. There are different reasons to assume that the *adolescentia mundi* starts here. From now on man is subjected to chastity and, as a sign to stick to this virtue, to circumcision. Also Matthew begins his genealogies of the Lord with Abraham. Augustine stresses the procreative force that belongs to the *adolescens*. The Church Father also makes Abraham a starting-point for the third age of the world in his various historical schemes. Although Augustine and Isidore distinguish six ages of the world, Gregory the Great counts only five. He uses for his own scheme the metaphor of the hours of the day, but, again, Abraham is at the beginning of the third period. Helinand discusses various different solutions to divide the world's history at some length. (11. 169–239).

The fourth age of the world, *iuuentus*, starts with David and lasts until the Babylonian exile. The history of Israel expanding its power during David's reign corresponds rather well to what is to be expected of *iuuenes*. Horace's unfavorable description of *iuuenis* on the other hand, fits this period too, especially when Israel was disobedient to God's law and devoted itself to idolatry (11. 240–71).

The fifth age of the world, *grauitas* or *uirilitas* or *uirilis aetas*, saw the vices of Israel come to an end. The period is marked by temperance. Moreover, interest changed for the better and virtue, friendship of the prophets, and divine honor were much sought after. This fifth period ended with the coming of Christ. Then the world had grown old and had lost its power to defend itself. Therefore, the coming of Christ came at the right time. Old age also may make people weak and unable to do good works. Consequently, it was written that Isaac grew old and that his eyes darkened, which was interpreted by the martyr Hippolytus that faith became neglected and overcome by ambition (11. 272–316).

At this point, Helinand proposes a different interpretation of this verse of Genesis. He finds it hard to believe that this passage could mean anything else than praise for the Patriarch, especially since the holy scripture ascribes elsewhere wisdom and innocence to old age. Old age refers to *otium*, monastic leisure, and freedom from involvement in worldly affairs. The disappearing vision refers to two things which disappear in elderly people: love for the world and love for oneself. For this interpretation Helinand derives an argument from 3 Kings 1:1: David had grown old and did not get warm when he was covered with blankets. Here, the blankets are interpreted as affluence of worldly wealth.

This favorable view of old age differs greatly from the picture that Horace presents in his *Ars Poetica*. Old people are depicted as being a great nuisance. Cicero, however, expresses a more discreet opinion, arguing that there are, of course, foolish elderly people as there are foolish younger ones. A negative assessment of old age, Cicero says, is, however, unjust. Helinand concludes by excusing himself wittily for his limited talent (11. 317–94).

The letter can be divided into three parts: an introduction in which Hippolytus's explanation of Genesis 27:1 is quoted, criticised, and adapted, a lengthy central section that develops the adapted interpretation and which itself is subdivided into six paragraphs, and a conclusion with Helinand's own diverging interpretation.

Hippolytus's explanation quoted in chapter 64 is by no means unknown. It finds its origin in *Letter 36* of Jerome and is also used

by, for example, Isidore of Seville, Claudius of Turin, Hrabanus
Maurus, and the *Glossa Ordinaria*.[13] For his criticism of and alternative to this interpretation, Helinand uses first the motif of *mundus senescens*, widely known in the Middle Ages through Ambrose,
Jerome, and, especially, Augustine,[14] in combination with the
equally traditional periodization of history into six *aetates*.[15] The
principal theme of the introduction is the development of the strength
of faith and of the love for God. In the first period *fides* and *dilectio*
are judged by the presence or absence of *laus Dei*. The absence of
praise of God and the hesitant beginning of it are analyzed in Biblical texts,[16] but quotations from classical authors are used as well:
Statius for the *infantia*, Horace for the *pueritia*. This theme recedes
at the beginning of the *adolescentia* to make room for another one.
It is now important that man has the possibility to make a choice
between a righteous and an unjust life, a division which can be
seen again in the following *aetates* with the exception of the fifth.
This period covers the time from the Babylonian exile up to the
coming of Christ. Perhaps Helinand sees this period as a chasten-
ing of the people of Israel which is ended by Christ's birth, linking
this period typologically to his own days where the righteous in
this world of misery will be rewarded by the second coming of
Christ. Notable too is the fact that Helinand stresses that Christ
came at a time when the world had grown weak and lacked *duces,
reges, principes, prophetae*, and *sacerdotes* (11. 294–96). This echoes
yet another repartition of history: the era of the patriarchs, judges,
kings, and priests, preceding the age of Christ.[17]

At the end of the central section Helinand shows that he is not
satisfied with his proposal. He turns now to another solution,
which analyzes Isaac's *caligo oculorum* as *odium mundi* and *contemptus sui* respectively.[18] His proposal ends with the words: "Beati
quorum oculi caligine Ysaac cecutiunt et quorum seniles artus frigiditate Dauitica torpescunt." Helinand's view of history overall
does not seem to be pessimistic. He is critical of his contemporaries, but suggests that ways to reach salvation are open for those
who follow the lead of those who flee from the world (*sermo 24*
[684C]):

> Igitur tria sunt genera fugiendi mundum. Primi abrenunti-
> ant mundanis rebus, sed non desideriis; secundi desideriis,
> sed non rebus; tertii rebus et desideriis. Primi mundum fugi-

unt corporaliter, secundi mentaliter, tertii dupliciter, id est mente et corpore. Primi sunt falsi claustrales, secundi boni saeculares, tertii boni claustrales. Primi ignem fugiunt, et in sinu suo ignem abscondunt; secundi pendulo gradu stant in sublimi, quasi funambuli; tertii via recta et regia incedunt exonerati et securi.

It is the monks—and, presumably for Helinand, more in particular the Cistercians—who lead a life which will bring salvation.

Remarkable is the way in which Helinand uses quotations from classical authors. A few lines from Statius's *Thebaid*, the lamentation of Isiphile over the death of her infant son, provide him with ample opportunity for allegorizing. More important, however, is the role played by Horace's *Ars Poetica*. Helinand makes use of Horace's description of the four characters in drama which the latter describes in lines 158–74 of this famous work: *puer, iuuenis, uir*, and *senex*. These were particularly appropriate because of the weight given in the descriptions to *mores*. Helinand employs Horace's "vignettes" with a skillful sense of variation.

In the description of *puericia* Horace's *Ars* is the point of departure. *Reddere uoces* is allegorized and the actions of Noah and Adam are analyzed from this angle. In passing, contemporary practices in the Easter liturgy are explained as deriving from Adam's disobedience. The remaining elements from the three lines of Horace are commented on as though they were a piece of literature treated by a schoolmaster. For the discussion of *iuuentus* Horace's role is less important. Helinand mentions David and the successors of this period first. Unjust people, however, could be found in this age as well. To characterize them Helinand uses Horace's description of the *iuuenis*, at times merely glossing Horace's poetry. Treatment of the fifth age is short but on the whole positive. Horace's *uirilis aetas* illustrates this thesis. It is striking to see how Helinand varies his methods, because the commentary now precedes the quotation. Horace's *senex* can be found at the end of the letter. Helinand has given his own interpretation of Genesis 27:1 and Horace's *senex* is introduced as a rather superfluous added extra. Horace's very negative approach to old age in these lines consequently triggers a mitigation of this view in the words of Cicero.

It is hard to decide whether the quotations from Statius and Horace were taken from a full text or a medieval anthology. The lamentation of Isiphile is found among the famous *Carmina Canta-brigiensia*[19] and Horace's verses formed part of the well-known *Florilegium Gallicum*. In the latter anthology the titles of the four subdivisions of this part of the *Ars Poetica* point to the interpretation Helinand gave: 1. *De proprietatibus diversarum etatum*, 2. *De temeritate iuvenum*, 3. *De sapientia adultorum*, 4. *De incommodis senum*.[20]

Helinand was not the only Cistercian to write at the end of the twelfth century in France on the issue of historical periodization. Garnier de Rochefort[21] (died after 1225) in his *Sermon 19* divides history into seven periods just like, he says, the world turns around in seven days. The first period is treated rather similarly to Helinand:[22]

> Sed quoniam nec verbis nec operibus factori suo et benefactori respondit [*scil.* Adam], imo multiplicatis hominibus multiplicata sunt mala filiorum Adam, ita ut dolere cordis tactus intrinsecus, compelleretur Dominus ad dicendum: *Poenitet me fecisse hominen* (*Gen.* VI), id est faciam quod homo poenitens facere solet; delet enim quod fecit; quod et factum est. . . . Hinc est etiam, quod in vigilia Paschae lectionem primam istam nullum sequitur responsorium, quia divinis beneficiis Adam Domino non respondit.

History in the second period is treated by Garnier in a different way, but he also makes mention of the tower of Babel. Helinand's third age, which runs from Abraham to David, is divided into two by Garnier. Moses marks the end of the third and the beginning of the fourth *aetas*. The last period is known, as it is in Helinand's, for its vigor and strength. The description of the remaining periods has, however, less in common with Helinand's letter.

It appears that the system of historical periodization was well known at the time in Cistercian France. The two examples show that the Cistercians had their own reflections on the schemes that had come down through tradition. An obvious question which arises is whether the theory was put into practice by Helinand when he wrote his largest work, the *Chronicon*, which treats the history of the world from the creation up to Helinand's own days (1204 is the last year that is mentioned). The answer is negative. The *aetates* theory is present in the *Chronicon*, but plays no role in the structure and contents of the work as a whole. As an illustration, I point to the end of the first period which is briefly mentioned in book IV, chapter 41 (MS Vat. Reg. lat. 535, p. 55):

> De fine prime etatis.
> Capitulum XLI.
> Notandum quod hic desinit prima etas cuius annos ponunt LXX duo milia ducenta quadraginta quatuor, Ieronimus non plane duo milia, Methodius duo milia. Ipse tamen per ciliades disponit nec apponit annos si supersint, et ideo nichil certum de numero annorum tradidit. Hugo in Cronicis secundum Hebreos ponit annos huius etatis mille sescentos quinquaginta sex, secundum aliam translationem que usitatior est, annos duo milia sescentos quadraginta duos.

It is just a brief note, taken for its greater part from Peter Comestor's *Historia scholastica*,[23] discussing the different calculations of various learned predecessors for the number of years that had passed. The end of the second period coincides with the end of the last chapter, 89, of the fourth book (MS Vat. Reg. lat. 535, p. 63):

> Hic terminatur etas secunda et incipit tercia cuius inicium est primus annus Abrahe partriarche, ubi incipiunt Cronica Eusebii que transtulit Iheronimus; et nos hic librum quartum terminabimus, ostenso prius quanta sit diuersitas in computatione annorum huius etatis inter LXX et Hebraicam ueritatem.[24]

No mention has been made of the end of the third period,[25] but we find the beginning of the fifth at a more or less significant place, at the start of book fifteen. Although the examples from the end of book four and the beginning of book fifteen might seem interesting, there seems to be no reason to attach much significance to this point. As far as we can judge now, Helinand does in no way develop the theme in his work, and, if this were the case, it would indeed be surprising. Helinand's *Chronicon* is basically an annalistic compilation.[26] The very nature of this kind of historical work makes it difficult to mold theoretical concepts into a more concrete form.

For the establishment of a date for the correspondence edited below, some useful information is at hand. Philip died in 1196; he became abbot of Val Ste. Marie in 1194.[27] Since Helinand calls him *abbas*, the letters must have been produced between 1194 and 1196. Insertion of the correspondence into the *Chronicon* took place after Philip's death; Helinand's very words, "scripsisse epistolam quandam ad Philippum *quondam* abbatem de Valle," provide the evidence.[28]

The text edited below is based on the two manuscripts of this part of the *Chronicon* which have come down to us: MS Vat. Reg. lat. 535 (V), dating from the first quarter of the thirteenth century, and MS London, BL Cotton Claudius B IX (L), dating from the fifteenth century. Chapter 64–66 of book 6 are in V on pp. 106b–111a, and in L on ff. 72ra–74vb. V and L are independent witnesses. The spelling of V is followed throughout and the punctuation is modern. The marginal notes are for the greater part in V only. They have been edited as well since they belong clearly to the *Chronicon* as a means for making the work easily accessible.[29]

University of Groningen

NOTES

*Completion of research for this article was made possible by a grant from the Netherlands Organization for the Advancement of Pure Research (Z.W.O.). Thanks are due to the students of a seminar in Medieval Latin (1984–1985) at the University of Groningen where this correspondence was discussed. I also owe gratitude to Dr. Simon Forde who corrected the English, and to Mr. J. B. Voorbij for some helpful suggestions. At the University of Groningen research is in progress on Helinand's *Chronicon*: an edition of books 17 and 18 by Mr. J. B. Voorbij and a study of books 45–49 by Mr. M. M. Woesthuis. The present writer is engaged in editing books 1–16.

1. M. H. Malewicz, "Libellus de efficatia artis astrologice. Traité astrologique d'Eudes de Champagne (XIIe siècle)," *Mediaevalia Philosophica Polonorum* 20 (1974) 1–95; N. M. Häring (ed.), *Commentaries on Boethius by Thierry of Chartres and his School*, Studies and Texts 20 (Toronto, 1971), pp. 50–52; M. Paulmier-Foucart, "Ecrire l'histoire au XIIIe siècle. Vincent de Beauvais et Hélinand de Froidmont," *Annales de l'Est* 33 (1981) 49–70.

2. E. R. Smits, "Helinand of Froidmont and the A-text of Seneca's Tragedies," *Mnemosyne* 36 (1983) 324–58; J. B. Voorbij, "The Legend of Guntram in Helinand of Froidmont's 'Chronicon,'" in M. Gosman and J. van Os (edd.), *Non Nova, Sed Nove: Mélanges de civilisation médiévale dédiés à Willem Noo-*

men, Mediaevalia Groningana 5 (Groningen, 1984) pp. 261–77; E. R. Smits, "New evidence for the authorship of the commentary on the first six books of Virgil's 'Aeneid' commonly attributed to Bernardus Silvestris?," in *Non Nova*, pp. 239–46.

    3. M. Paulmier-Foucart, "Hélinand de Froidmont: Pour éclairer les dix-huit premiers livres inédits de sa Chronique. Edition des titres des chapitres et des notations marginales d'après le ms. du Vatican, Reg. lat. 535," *Spicae. Cahiers de l'Atelier Vincent de Beauvais* (forthcoming).

    4. For Helinand's biography, see Fr. Wulff and Em. Walberg, *Les Vers de la Mort par Hélinant, moine de Froidmont* (Paris, 1905), VII–XVII, and W. D. Paden, "Documents concernant Hélinant de Froidmont," *Romania* 105 (1984) 332–41.

    5. Smits, "Helinand," pp. 332–37.

    6. Smits, "Helinand," p. 334.

    7. Smits, "Helinand," pp. 336–37.

    8. Jerome, Ep. 36, 16 (CSEL 54, 283–84).

    9. See the text edited below pp. 25–43.

    10. For the etymological link *infantia/non fari*, see, for example, Augustine, *De civitate Dei* 16, 43 (CCSL 48, 550): "A pueritia namque homo incipit loqui post infantiam, quae hinc appellata est, quod fari non potest"; Bede, *Liber de temporibus*, cap. 16, *De mundi aetatibus*: "Secunda [aetas] a Noe usque ad Abraham generationes similiter complexa decem, annos autem ccxcii; quae in lingua inventa est, id est hebraea, a puericia namque homo incipit nosse loqui post *infantiam*, quae et nomen inde accept quod fari, id est loqui, non potest" (ed. Jones, p. 303).

    11. For the origin of this idea, see Augustine, *De Genesi contra Manich.* I, 23 (PL 34:190): "Quasi vespera hujus diei fit diluvium; quia et infantia nostra tanquam oblivionis diluvio deletur"; see also Augustine, *De civ. Dei*, 16, 43 (CCSL 48, 550).

    12. See M.-A. Dimier, "La lettre de Pythagore et les hagiographes du moyen âge," *Le Moyen Age* 60 (1954) 403–418; W. Harms, *Homo viator in bivio. Studien zur Bildlichkeit des Weges*, Medium Aevum, Philologische Studien, Band 21 (München, 1970) esp. pp. 193-94; H. Silvestre, "Nouveaux témoignages médiévaux de la 'Littera Pythagorae'", *Le Moyen Age* 79 (1973) 201–207; H. Silvestre, "Pour le dossier de l'Y pythagoricien: Nouveaux témoignages,'" *Le Moyen Age* 84 (1978) 201–209. Helinand uses the image of the Y differently in Sermo 2 (PL 212:526B); see Harms, *Homo viator*, p. 90.

    13. Isidore of Seville, *Quaestiones in Vetus Testamentum in Genesin*, cap. 23 (PL 83:256AB); Claudius of Turin, *Commentarii in Genesim*, Liber II (PL 50:987D); Hrabanus Maurus, *Commentaria in Genesin*, Liber III, 13 (PL 107:587CD); *Biblia sacra cum glossa ordinaria . . . et Postilla Nicolai Lyrani . . .* (Paris, 1690) col. 312. Different interpretations by, for example, Augustine, *Sermones de Vetere Testamento*, IV, 11 (CCSL 41, 27); Remigius of Auxerre, *Commentarius in Genesim*, cap. 27 (PL 131:103D); Bruno of Segni, *Expositio in Genesim*, cap. 27 (PL 164:205C); Guibert of Nogent, *Moralia in Genesin*, VII, 27 (PL 156:206A).

    14. G. J. M. Bartelink, "Le thème du monde vieilli," *Orpheus* N.S. 4 (1983) 342–54; M.-D. Chenu, *Nature, Man, and Society in the Twelfth Century: Essays on New Theological Perspectives in the Latin West* (Chicago, 1968), pp. 181–84.

    15. R. Schmidt, "Aetates Mundi: Die Weltalter als Gliederungsprinzip der Geschichte," *Zeitschrift für Kirchengeschichte* 67 (1955–1956) 288–317; R. Häussler, "Vom Ursprung und Wandel des Lebensaltervergleichs," *Hermes* 92 (1964) 313–41; P. Archambault, "The Ages of Man and the Ages of the World: A Study of Two Traditions," *Revue des Etudes Augustiniennes* 12 (1966) 193–228; C. Gilbert, "When did a man in the Renaissance grow old?," *Studies in the Renaissance* 14 (1967) 7–32; B. Guenée, *Histoire et culture historique dans l'occident médiéval* (Paris, 1980), pp. 148–54.

254 Edmé R. Smits

16. For example, Gn 4:10; for the exegesis of *uox sanguinis*, see G. Dahan, "L'exégèse de l'histoire de Cain et Abel du XIIe au XIVe siècle en Occident: Notes et textes," RTAM 49 (1982) 21–89, 50 (1983) 5–68, especially (1982) 63–65. Similar thoughts in Idung, *Dialogus duorum monachorum* II, 602 ff.: "CLUNIACENSIS. *Ex ore infantium et lactentium perfecisti laudem.* Ore non poterant laudare Christum, quia infantes et lactentes erant, nisi 'ore' ponatur ibi pro morte: morte enim sua laudaverunt Christum. Sed quod 'ore' possit pro morte poni numquam audivi, nusquam legi et ideo videtur michi valde absurdum CISTERCIENSIS. Sacra scriptura non multum curat proprietates verborum observare. Clamor non est nisi aut oris aut cordis. Clamor oris hominibus est audibilis, clamor cordis soli deo, quia ipse dixit ad Moysen non ore, sed corde clamantem: *Quid clamas ad me?* Sanguis Abel in terram fusus nec os nec cor habuit et tamen deus dixit ad Cain: *Ecce vox sanguinis fratris tui clamat ad me de terra.* Simplex divinus es, si nescis quod et inanimatae creaturae, sensu et vita carentes, deo locuntur et deum laudant," R.B.C. Huygens (ed.), *Le moine Idung et ses deux ouvrages: "Argumentum super quatuor questionibus" et "Dialogus duorum monachorum"* (Spoleto, 1980), pp. 138–39.

17. See Chenu, p. 180. This division in history is important for Helinand as he discusses the theme in sermo 7, taking Ga 4:4–5 as his point of departure.

18. A recently published voluminous monograph on the subject of the eye in the Middle Ages is: G. Schleusener-Eichholz, *Das Auge im Mittelalter*, 2 vols., Münstersche Mittelalter-Schriften 35 (München, 1985). A related thought in the commentary of Thomas the Cistercian on Sg 4:1: "Quam quidem simplicitatem exprimit, dicens: *Oculi tui columbarum.* Nam in columbis signatur simplicitas, et innocentia. Oculi autem sunt duo, intellectus videlicet et affectus. Isti oculi columbini sunt innocentes et simplices, cum intellectus est sine errore; et in veritate Scripturae nihil intelligit nisi veritatem, cum affectus in Deum est absque mundana concupiscentia, et in opere Dei nihil concupiscit mundanum, nihil quaerit nisi Deum" (*Commentarii in Cantica Canticorum*, II, 27; PL 206:149D).

19. No. 31; K. Strecker (ed.), *Die Cambridger Lieder*, MGH 40 (3rd ed., Berlin, 1966), p. 83.

20. R. Burton, *Classical Poets in the "Florilegium Gallicum,"* Lateinische Sprache und Literatur des Mittelalters 14 (Frankfurt a/M, 1983), pp. 288–90. For the use of Horace's *senex* in Biblical exegesis, see R. Sprandel, *Altersschicksal und Altersmoral: Die Geschichte der Einstellungen zum Altern nach der Pariser Bibelexegese des 12.–16. Jahrhunderts*, Monographien zur Geschichte des Mittelalters 22 (Stuttgart, 1981) pp. 90, 124. See, for the *puer*, Helinand's *Epistola ad Galterum* (PL 212:755D–56A): "De isto [*scil.* puero] Horatius: *Cereus in vitium flecti . . .* Periculosa enim est aetas pueri. . . ."

21. For Garnier, see J.-Ch. Didier, "Garnier de Rochefort: Sa vie et son oeuvre. Etat des questions," Coll. 17 (1955) 145–58; N. M. Häring, "The Liberal Arts in the Sermons of Garnier of Rochefort," MS 30 (1968) 47–77.

22. PL 205:696AB.

23. PL 198:1081A.

24. See PL 198:1091A.

25. It could be expected in book XIII, chapter 21 which treats the reign of David.

26. Smits, "Helinand," pp. 335–37.

27. *Gallia Christiana* (Paris, 1744), VII, 877.

28. Text edited below cap. 64, 1. 21.

29. Smits, "Helinand," pp. 334, 345–46.

Helinandi Frigidi Montis Monachi Chronicon. Liber Sextus
[106b].

Mysterium de senectute Ysaac secundum martyrem
Ypolitum.
Capitulum LXIIII.

Ieronimus et
Ypolitus
martyr

Senuit Ysaac et caligaverunt oculi eius. Senectus
Ysaac, sicut ait Ypolitus martyr, consummationem mundi
significat, oculi caligantes, fidem periisse de mundo et
religionis lumen neglectum. Quod filius maior uocatur,
acceptio legis Iudeorum. Quod escas eius et capturam
diligit pater, homines sunt ab errore saluati, quos per
10   doctrinam iustus quisque uenatur. Sermo patris,
benedictio repromissionis est et spes regni futuri, in
quo cum Christo sancti regnaturi et uerum sabbatum
celebraturi sunt. Duo hedi, duo populi utique peccatores,
teneri et boni, docibiles et innocentes anime,
15   afferri iubentur. Stola Esau, fides et scriptura
Hebreorum que illis primo date sunt, quibus populus
gentilium postea indutus est. Pelles circumdate
bra[107a]chiis Iacob, peccata sunt utriusque populi in
extensione manuum Christi in cruce affixa.

Auctor

De hac senectute Ysaac memini me scripsisse
epistolam quandam ad Philippum quondam abbatem de Valle
quam in hoc loco inserere placet cum ipsa Philippi
epistola cui illa respondet, propter quedam dubitabilia
que in expositione martyris Ypoliti continentur.

Epistola Philippi abbatis de Valle de eadem re. Capitulum
LXV.

Elinando suo Philippus salutem.
Caligant oculi Ysaac in quibusdam, et inueterata iam
5   mundi facies in plerisque calore simul et colore
marcido lumen perdidit intellectus. Cecat mortalium
mentes uana uite huius ambicio, et proiectis intimis
suis telas texunt aranee, bono intimo non utentes. In
te aliter, qui ut felicitate Moysi perfruaris, animum
10   colis, rodis inmotis dentibus panem tuum, et exercens
ingenium caliginem euitas oculorum. Beatus tu quoniam
appropinquasti pedibus dei accepturus utique de
doctrina illius. Nichil te plus habuit prior Plinius
aut secundus, nichil ceteri qui omne tempus perire
15   arbitrati sunt quod studiis non daretur. Immo tu illos

precedis in gratia qui in loco suo queris ueritatem
ideoque reperturus quod negatum est illis quorum pes in
uanitate ambulauit, et sonitus fauoris et glorie semper
in auribus eorum. Quanquam ipsius que uidebatur
20   uirtutis eorum emulacio non sit inefficax ad
beatitudinem consequendam si uitato illorum deuio
incedatur.

Vellem diu, sed occupationibus meis miserri-
mis et hore ipsius breuitate prohibeor. Tu uicem cui
25   uacat ut arbitror magna tibi indulta prerogatiua. Nam
et ipsa loci tui desolatio horas uacationis longiores
et spatia dat protractiora. Irascar si preter epistolam
nichil attulerit lator horum. Vale.

Epistola alia de eadem re et de sex etatibus mundi.
Capitulum LXVI.

Frater Elinandus Philippo suo salutem.
Legimus super illum locum Genesis *Senuit Ysaac etc.* sub
5   nomine martyris Ypoliti per Ysaac significari deum
patrem, per senectutem eius mundi consummacionem, per
caliginem oculorum eius defectum fidei et religionis
lumen in mundo neglectum. Sed priores huius
expositionis particule non satis inter se conuenire
10   uidentur. Si enim Ysaac in persona propria deum patrem
significat, quomodo senectus eius consummacionem mundi
designat? Aut si recte senectus accipitur mundi
consummacio, quomodo ipse in persona mundi non rectius
accipitur quam in persona dei? Quidenim mundo ad deum
15   uel deo ad mundum? Nisi forte gradus etatum quos in
mundano cursu solemus distinguere secundum augmenta et
decrimenta religionis et fidei, figuratiue ad deum
patrem predictus martyr uoluerit transferre, quod eum
puto intellexisse ut uidelicet deum patrem quasi talem
20   mundi etatem per diuersa mundi tempora habere
intelligeret, qualis etatis uirtutem in eius fide et
dilectione ipse mundus haberet.

Dicemus ergo deum patrem uelut quandam similitu-
dinem gessisse infantie, quandiu mundus per fidem et
Quare tempus   dilectionem aut nichil aut parum fari potuit de eius
quod fuit ante di- laude. Licet enim prothomartyr Abel iustus fuisse
luuium appelletur dicatur et respectus a domino ipse et munera eius et
infantia mundi   per fidem sacrificium deo obtulisse, non ipse tamen
quidem legitur laudasse deum, sed tantum sanguis eius
30   clamasse dicitur ad deum de terra. Quod saluis aliis

intellectibus sanis et mysticis eo eciam modo dictum
potest intelligi quo de Innocentibus dictum est, quod
scilicet non loquendo, sed moriendo diuinum preconium
sunt confessi. Enos quoque filius Seth legitur quidem

35   inuocasse dominum. Sed quia qualis fuerit eius
inuocatio non exprimitur, ideo et ipsa pro infantili
uagitu uel silentio reputatur. Quamuis non plene
dicatur inuocasse dominum, sed cepisse inuocare
uel secundum aliam translationem sperasse inuoare, ut

40   ipsa illius inuocatio magis ad futurum uideatur
pertinere quam ad preteritum, magis ad suos posteros
quam ad se ipsum. Enoch eciam septimus ab Adam legitur
quidem placuisse deo per fidem, et adeo placuisse ut
eciam raptus sit ne malitia mutaret intellectum illius,

45   aut ne fictio deciperet animam illius. Prophetasse
quoque legitur et propheciam suam iuxta testimonium
Taddei apostoli litteris mandasse. Sed quia liber eius
tum pro nimia antiquitate, tum pro quibusdam fabulis de
Gygantibus locutioni prophecie non satis competenter

50   insertis numeratur inter apocrifos, ideo et ipse non
immerito computatur inter primi temporis infantes
iustos.
    Durauit ergo infantia dei patris usque ad diluui
um, quia usque ad illud tempus ipse uelut infans mutus

55   laudem suam tacuit, cum eam hominibus fari non conces-
sit. Mundus enim usque ad illud tempus aut in laude
omnino dei mutus fuit aut eam uelut infans fandi
potestatem cupiens non capiens balbutiuit potius quam
expressit, ut ad sanctos illius temporis a futura mundi

60   malitia celeriter ereptos fortassis non incongrue
possit referri planctus ille cuiusdam mulieris de suo
infantulo sibi premature subtracto:

Stacius   Heus ubi siderei uultus? ubi uerba ligatis
            imperfecta sonis risusque et murmura soli

65   intellecta mihi?
Quomodo planc- Nam quod attinet ad sydereos uultus per quos infantis
tus Ysiphile de   Archemori pulcritudo significata est, certum est
Archemoro ad   in illa prima mundi etate formas humanorum coporum longe
sanctos primi   amplioris fuisse decoris et gracie [108a] quam modo
temporis aptari sint, quod et hystorici gentilium testantur, non quod
possit   creator longinquitate temporis a scientia plasmandi
             desciuerit, sed quia mundi malitia successiuis accessi-
             onibus enormiter increscens uasa humanorum corporum
             naturaliter in honorem formata peruersitate uite

75   deformauerit in uasa contumelie, ideoque superno illi
             artifici et iusto iudici satis indignum ducitur, ut

turpi habitatori, animo, formosi corporis paretur
hospicium. Quasi autem uerba erant sonis imperfecta
ligatis, rara tunc in mundo fides et nouicia, solam

80   adhuc in deo unitatem substantie confitens necdum in
personis mysterium trinitatis agnoscens. Quid autem
aliud erant iam prelibata a quibusdam perfectioribus
beatitudinis eterne gaudia, priuatim et secrete
inspirata paucissimis, nondum passim et publice

85   predicata uniuersis quam uelud quidam risus et infanti-
lia murmura soli intellecta deo. De quo risu est

In Genesi   illud Sare: *Risum mihi fecit deus. Quicumque audierit,
corridebit mihi.* Hoc igitur modo deus pater uelut
infans fuisse dicitur usque ad diluuium, quod ad

90   cognitionem sui uelut in infantia reliquit genus
humanum, laudem suam in infidelibus omnino reticens, in
fidelibus autem quodam uelut infantili murmure balbu-
tiens magis quam exprimens. Sicut autem infanciam delet
obliuio, sic etas illa mundi siue dei deleta est

95   diluuio. Est autem in sacra scriptura satis usitatus
iste locutionis modus, ut quemadmodum frigus pigrum
dicitur quia homines pigros facit, sic eciam metonomice
efficiens pro effecto, deus infans aut puer et cetera
huiusmodi dicatur, quia homines mystice   tales facit;

100 facit dico in bonis causaliter, in malis permissi-
ue. Hec de infantia dicta sint.

Quare puericia   Recte autem a diebus Noe post diluuium dicitur
mundi dicitur   incepisse mundi puericia, iuxta illud epiteton puero
incepisse a Noe.   rum:
Horatius

    Reddere qui uoces iam scit puer, et pede certo
    signat humum, gestit paribus colludere, et iram
    colligit, et ponit temere, et mutatur in horas.

Quomodo epi-   Vere enim Noe sciuit reddere uoces deo, de quo legi-
theta puericie   tur: *Fecit ergo Noe omnia quecumque mandauerit ei
que ponit Ho-   deus,* quod de nullo sanctorum ante illum legitur. Quod
ratius possint ap-   autem facere iussionem dei sit reddere uocem ei, innuit
tari ad puericiam   mos ille ecclesiasticus, quo in celebratione diuini
mundi   officii solet responsorium subiungi lectioni. Lectioni
quippe subiungere responsorium est uiriliter et

115 hylariter exercere in opere quod diuina precipitur
lectione. Adam nesciuit reddere uocem deo qui uocem
uxoris sue preponere non timuit iussioni diuine. Vocem
deo reddere nesciit cum se a facie illius querentis et
dicentis: *Adam, ubi es,* abscondit et ait: *Vocem tuam

120 audiui et abscondi me eo quod nudus essem* [108b]. O
uere stulta responsio quasi factori suo displiceret
nudus qui talis ab eo fuerat factus. Vocem deo nesciuit

reddere quando culpam suam refundens in alium hoc se modo conatus est excusare: *Mulier quam dedisti mihi sociam, dedit mihi et comedi.* Non culpam suam simpliciter confessus est, non ueniam precatus est, sed declinauit cor suum *in uerba malitie ad excusandas excusationes in peccatis.* Hinc est quod ad illam primam lectionem Genesis de formatione hominis que legitur in sabbato sancto Pasche nullum sequitur responsorium, nec aliquid loco responsorii quia nostri prothoparentes ad primam domini iussionem nullum obediencie dederunt responsum. Sed et illud quod sequitur in poeta de puero quod uidelicet pede certo signat humum, non incongrue Noe attribuitur. Certo siquidem pede signauit humum qui, ut de illo legitur, *cum deo ambulauit.* Quid enim aliud est cum Deo ambulare, nisi sanctitatis et iusticie semitam terere, diuine gratie ductu preambulo et subsecutiua arbitrii libertate? Est enim diuina gratia nos preueniens tanquam nutrix et baiula pueri manum tenens. Huius nutricis ductum Adam subsequi nesciuit, qui cum dei gratiam ad manum haberet, eam deseruit et temptatori ualens sed non uolens resistere, non se erexit ut uinceret, sed succubuit ut prostratus iaceret. Iacuitque resupinus imbecillus et impotens non solum tanquam infantulus in cunabulo, sed eciam tanquam paralyticus in grabatto, ut iam de cetero naturalibus adiumentis posset non resurgere, sed medicinalibus fulciri indigeret remediis. Reliqua puerorum epiteta ad reliquos illius etatis reprobos referenda sunt. Gestierunt quippe paribus colludere illi omnes qui unanimi consensu superbie turrem edificare et ydola adorare ceperunt. Nam et ydolatria ludus appellatur, ubi dicitur: *Sedit populus manducare et bibere et surrexerunt ludere.* Qui ludus significatus est per ludum Ysmaelis cum Ysaac. Quintus eciam Curcius agens de fortunatis, idest felicibus, dicit eos semper parem aleam querere, et apud Tullium de senectute loquitur Cato dicens: Vetere prouerbio pares cum paribus facillime congregantur. Iram uero temere collegerunt qui contra omnipotentis assultus terribiles et infatigabiles impetus in una turre latericia satis se presidii habere putauerunt. Quasi uero aquarum inundatio par priori diluuio si rursus inundasset, unam turrem non posset subuertere que totum iam subuerterat orbem terre. In horas eciam mutati sunt quando subita et inopinata linguarum confusione confusi per diuersas regiones diffusi sunt. Hec de puericia.

Marginal: 125, 130, 135, 140, 145, 150, In Exodo 155, Quintus Curcius, Tullius in persona Catonis, 165

His duabus etatibus transcensis, infancia scilicet
et puericia, quarum prima pre humiditatis habundantia
quodam uelut obliuionis et igno[109a]rantie absorbetur
diluuio, altera naturalium appetituum multiformi
uarietate distincta uelud quadam linguarum confusione
punitur, mundus a naturalis ignorantie uniformi stipite
iam emergens tanquam ad biuium figure Pytagorice Y
peruenit. In cuius ancipiti constitutus inicio cepit in
paucissimis dextrum et arduum uirtutis callem terere,
in plurimis autem ad sinistrum et facilem uoluptatis
anfractum uiator erroneus declinare. Quia ergo homo ab
adolescentia discretionis et precepti capax incipit
esse aut ex innocentia et obedientia laudabilis, aut ex
incontinencia et contumacia uituperabilis, iccirco
tercia mundi etas numerari cepit ab Abraham. A cuius
tempore et uirtus castitatis primo cepit hominibus
districtissime precipi et scelus libidinis acerrime
puniri. Tunc enim propter ignominiosos incestus
Sodomiticos et regio Pentapolis ad terrorem futurorum
celesti igne subuersa est, et ritus circumcisionis sub
eterne mortis interminatione in signum castitatis
obseruari preceptus est. Denique Matheus dominice
generacionis per tres tesserescedecadas contexturus
ordinem, iccirco teste Augustino ab Abraham quasi ab
adolescentia mundi sumpsit exordium, quia homo ab
adolescentia iam incipit generare. Ad confirmationem
quoque huius opinionis quod uidelicet tercia mundi
etas, idest adolescentia ab Abraham inceperit, idem
Augustinus quasi pro mystica significatione inducit
sacrificium Abrahe de animalibus trimis, idest de
uacca et capra et ariete annorum trium. Quam etatem in
libro De Ciuitate Dei extendit ab Abraham usque ad
Dauid in quo uelut articulum quendam iuuentutis populi
dei constituit. In tractatu quoque super Iohannem sex
hydrias ad sex etates mundi sic refert: Prima, inquit,
ab Adam usque ad Noe, secunda a Noe usque ad Abraham,
tercia ab Abraham usque ad Dauid, quarta a Dauid usque
ad transmigrationem Babylonis, quinta a transmigratione
Babylonis usque ad Iohannem Baptistam, sexta a Iohanne
usque ad finem mundi. Has etates eodem modo distinguit
Ysidorus in libro Ethimologiarum quinto. Gregorius
tamen in omelia uidetur uelle non sex etates mundi, sed
quinque tantum computari debere. Dicit enim primam
mundi etatemd que fuit ab Adam usque ad Noe fuisse quasi
mane unius diei, secundam uero que fuit a Noe usque ad
Abraham quasi horam diei terciam. Terciam uero etatem

170

175

Quare adole-
scentia mundi in-
cepisse dicitur ab
Abraham

185

190

195

Augustinus in
libro De Ciuitate
Dei XVIII
Idem

205

Ysidorus

Gregorius in
omilia dominica
in septuagesima

215 que incepit ab Abraham per horam diei sextam significa-
tur quam non terminat in Dauid sicut alii, sed in
Moyse. A quo dicit incepisse quartam mundi etatem,
idest horam diei nonam, quam horam uel etatem extendit
usque ad [109b] aduentum domini. Inde uero incepisse
220 dicit quintam mundi etatem uel horam diei undecimam
quam extendit usque ad finem mundi. Ad easdem quinque
distinctiones horarum idem Gregorius quinque tantum
hominis etates retulit, idest puericiam, adolescentiam,
iuuentutem, senectutem et decrepitam etatem, sed sub
225 puericia comprehendit infantiam, sicut sub mane
comprehenditur non solum hora prima, sed eciam secunda. Idem tamen Gregorius in alia omelia adolescentiam
et iuuentutem pro una computat etate propter scripturam

Ysidorus Etimo-   que dicit: *Letare iuuenis in adolescentia tua.* Ysidorus
logiarum libro   autem in libro Ethimologiarum XIo gradus etatum sex
XI   esse dicit: infantiam, puericiam, adolescentiam,
                  iuuentutem, grauitatem, senectutem. Horatius tamen
Horatius   sicut et Gregorius adolescentiam sub iuuentute compre-
                  hendit dicens:
235   Inberbis iuuenis, tandem custode remoto
                      gaudet equis canibusque et aprici gramine campi,
                      cereus in uitium flecti, monitoribus asper,
                      utilium tardus prouisor, prodigus eris,
                      sublimis cupidusque et amara relinquere pernix.
240   Verum iste due etates usitatius discernuntur in duas
                  quam coniunguntur in unam. Incepit ergo secundum
                  Augustinum quarta etas mundi, idest iuuentus, a Dauid
Quare iuuentus   et durauit usque ad transmigrationem Babylonis. Merito
mundi dicitur   autem a Dauid qui interpretatur manu fortis, fortissima
incepisse a Dauid dicitur etas incepisse. Tunc enim populus de sub iugo
                  inimicorum suorum ceruicem suam potenter excussit. Tunc
                  filii Israhel tanquam iuuenes expediti et ad bella
                  fortissimi, in toto mundo florebant quippe qui nationes
                  alienigenarum a sancta terra promissionis expulerunt et
250   per manum Dauid regis prudentissimi, iustissimi,
                  bellicosissimi, fortissimi, regni sui terminos amplis-
                  sime dilatauerant. Porro hec eadem etas secundum quod
                  multis adolescentie uitiis respergitur, non incongrue
                  ad reprobos eiusdem populi et refugas legis dei
255   coaptatur qui dixerunt: *Non est nobis pars in Dauid*
Quomodo   *neque hereditas in filio Ysai.* Illi namque qui recesse-
epitheta iuuenum runt a Roboam sub Iheroboam filio Nabath qui peccare
que ponit   fecit Israhel quasi imberbes iuuenes, idest nulla
Horatius possint grauitatis et sapientie signa preferentes, tandem
aptari ad   custode remoto, idest iugo legis excusso quam apostolus

reprobos etatis tercie

265

270

pedagogum uocat, ruperunt uincula timoris dei qui custos est anime, et non solum equis et canibus et aliis mundanis uoluptatibus illecti sunt, sed etiam ad ydolatriam et ceteros immundos et efferatos ritus gentium transierunt, cerei in uitium flecti, monitoribus, prophetis, asperi, utilium tardi uel potius nulli prouisores, prodigi eris, idest salutis proprie contemptores, nam substantia anime uiri proprie diuicie, [110a] sublimes cupidique et amara relinquere celeres tam pernices ad suam perniciem quam ad errorem precipites et effrenes ad uoluptatem.

Quare quinta mundi etas dicitur incepisse a transmigratione Babilonis

280

285

Successit postea quinta etas quam Ysidorus grauitatem, Horatius uirilitatem appellat, siue uirilem etatem que populum illius temporis captiuitate seruitutis opprimens et captiuitatis miseriam multis calamitatum oneribus accumulans iuuenilem illius temperauit audaciam, frenauit licentiam, petulentiam castigauit. Nam et impiorum euersa potentia est, et piorum mens per penitenciam est conuersa. Siquidem uexatio que dedit intellectum auditui eorum, fecit eos conuersis studiis et moribus emendatis querere opes uirtutum et amicitias prophetarum et inseruire diuino honori et cauere de cetero ne talia committerent que mutare postea laborarent, sicut ait Horatius:

Conuersis studiis etas animusque uirilis
querit opes et amicitias, inseruit honori,
commisisse cauet quod mox mutasse laboret.

Quare senectus mundi dicitur incepisse a Christo

295

300

In sua epistola prima
305

Senescente autem iam mundo et crescente animarum periculo *uenit* illa sacri *plenitudo temporis* in quo *misit deus filium suum* in terris *factum ex muliere, factum sub lege, ut eos qui sub lege erant, redimeret.* Vere enim mundus senuerat cum ad defendendas legis ceremonias nullas prorsus uires habebat. Ablatum enim erat *sceptrum de Iuda et dux de femore eius. Non erat* dux qui duceret, rex qui regeret, princeps qui defenderet, propheta qui argueret, sacerdos qui oraret. Iccirco deficientibus et iamiamque perituris illud singulare et unicum restabat subsidium ut expectatio gentium et earum desideratus adueniret. In tali mundi uespera uerus sol iusticie de centro sublimissimo equalitatis paterne ad nostre mortalitatis se inclinauit occasum. Hec *est hora nouissima* quam Iohannes apostolus iam dicit aduenisse. Nos enim sumus *in quos fines seculorum deuenerunt.* Porro senectus ista alios efficit plenos dierum et sapientie ditat consiliis, alios ad omne opus bonum reddit fluidos et enerues, et quoniam

ipsa magis ac magisuergit in senium, ideo scriptum
est de Ysaac quod non tantum *senuerit*, sed etiam quod
oculi eius caligauerint. Nam iuxta martyrem Ypolitum
lumen religionis et fidei paulatim in mundo negligitur,
et prope est ut ad illam cecitatem perueniat per quam,
sicut scriptum est de Ysaac, *uidere non possit*; adeo
inueteratos pannos et induratas maculas et condensatas
albugines oculis mortalium pestilens ambitiosuper-
duxit, illa, inquam, ambitio, de qua est illa sancti
Bernardi elegans exclamatio: O ambitio ambientium crux,
quomodo omnes torquens, omnibus places?

Salua tamen ista communi et autentica expositione
[110b] ego in senectute Ysaac et caligine oculorum eius
aliquid altius intelligendum puto. Nullo enim modo
crediderim quod spiritus sanctus qui tanti patriarche
totam reliquam uitam laudauerat, de senectute eius et
caligantibus oculis mentionem faceret, nisi hoc aliquo
modo ad eiusdem uiri spiritale preconium pertine-
ret. Grecorum siquidem prouerbialis sententia senectutem ipsam morbum esse asserit, sed scriptura uirtutem
sapientie uel innocentie per etatem senectutis intelli-
gere consueuit. Vnde est illud: *Cani sunt autem sensus
hominis, et etas senectutis uita immaculata.* Talis
autem senectus concupiscentie carnalis ardorem refrige-
rat et uitiosas uires anime frangit penitus et ener-
uat. Senectus enim que hominem reddit inactuosum et
languidum significat in Ysaac ocium ipsius et omnium
sanctorum laudabile et uacationem quietam et tranquil-
lam a negotiorum secularium implicatione, et illum
languorem sanissimum de quo sponsa dicit in Canticis: *Fulcite me floribus, stipate me malis quia amore
langueo.*

Sunt autem oculi duo qui semper in huiusmodi
senibus caligant: amor mundi et amor sui. Hi ergo senes
uidere non possunt, quia mundum et que in mundo sunt,
diligere nesciunt, et uoluntatem propriam propter
obedientie meritum relinquunt. Quod autem amor ad
oculum pertineat, habemus ex illa uulgata sententia: Vbi amor, ibi oculus. Senectus ergo Ysaac secundum
quod in bono accipitur, est perfecti cuiuslibet sancta
et fructuosa uacatio. Odium uero mundi et contemptus
sui est oculorum eius caligo. In eandem significationem
uidetur mihi scriptura mentionem fecisse de senectute
Dauid, ubi ait: *Et rex Dauid senuerat cumque operiretur
uestibus non calefiebat.* Quid enim sunt uaria operimen-
ta uestium, nisi affluentia rerum mundanarum? Vestem

**In Genesi
Iuxta Ypolitum
martirem**

**315
Sermone**

**Anagogicus
intellectus de
senectute Ysaac**

325

**In libro Sa-
pientie
330**

**335
In Canticis**

340

Prouerbium

**Misterium de
senectute Dauid**

ta uestium, nisi affluentia rerum mundanarum? Vestem
tynea comedit, fur subripit, uetustas consumit. Similiter diuitias huius mundi corrumpit superbia, corrodit

355   luxuria, subtrahit dum contrahit ipsa auaricia, qui
sunt tres uermes diuitum semper eos comedentes. *Figura*
quoque que *preterit huius mundi*, secum eas silenter
trahit in interitum et demergit in profundum. At ut
eciam perpetue essent et immortales, auaritia tamen iam

360   possessas subripit, prodigalitas uero disperdit et
Seneca   dissipat possidendas. Vnde eleganter quidam: Multas
diuicias habet ille. Si auarus est, non habet; si
prodigus, non habebit. Et certe in diuitibus mundi
nichil est medium: aut auari suntaut prodigi aut quod

365   omnia prodigia superat, et auari et prodigi, auari ut
rapiant, prodigi ut perdant. Operitur ergo uestibus,
sed non calefit, qui si diuitie affluant, cor suum non
In Psalmo LXI   apponit. Iuxta illud: *Diuitie si affluant, nolite cor
apponere.* Ac si aliis uerbis dicat: Etsi uestes

370   habetis unde operiamini, nolite tamen in uestram
perniciem operimentis talibus confoueri. Etsi in hac
uita temporales diuitie [111a] nobis affluant, illece-
brose tamen earum blandicie uos ad uoluptatum deuia non
seducant. Beati quorum oculi caligineYsaac cecutiunt

375   et quorum seniles artus frigiditate Dauitica torpescunt. Ab his enim longe sunt illa uitiose senectutis
incommoda que poeta enumerat dicens:

Horatius   Multa senem circumueniunt incommoda, uel quod
               querit, et inuentis miser abstinet, et timet uti,
380   uel quod res omnes timide gelideque ministrat,
               dilator, spe longus, iners, auidusque futuri,
               difficilis, querulus, laudator temporis acti
               se puero castigator censorque minorum.

Tullius ex uoce   Huiusmodi uitia, sicut ait Cato apud Tullium, sompnicu-
Catonis   lose senectutis sunt, non senectutis. Sicut enim
petulantia et libido magis est adolescentium quam
senum, non tamen omnium adolescentium sed non proborum,
sic ista, inquit, senilis stulticia que deliratio
appellari solet, senum leuium est, non omnium.

390   Hec de caligine oculorum Ysaac sumpta ex tuis
litteris occasione dicta sint, cum uenia tamen caligan-
tis ingenii cuius nimirum imbecillem aciem et molesta
domus nostre retundit desolatio et praue consuetudinis
rubigo iam corrosit.

Apparatus Criticus

LXIIII

  8 Iudeorum V: est *add.* L
 19 manuum L: mannuum V

LXV

  3 suo V: filio L

LXVI

  8 neglectum L: -turum V
150 etatis V: et *add.* L
239 amara V: -ata L
245 populus V: dei *add.* L
256 filio L: fili V
269 amara V: -ata L
299 earum desideratus V: expectatus L
326 scriptura V: sacra *add.* L
329 senectutis L: -ctus V

Apparatus Fontium

LXIIII
  4 Gn 27:1; Hier. *epist.* 36, 16 (CSEL 54, 283–84)

LXV

  7 Sir 10:10
  8 Is 59:5
 12 Dt 33:3
 13 cf. Plin. *epist.* 6, 16, 3
 17 cf. Jb 31:5
 18 cf. Jb 15:21

LXVI

  4 Gn 27:1
 26 Mt 23:35; Heb 11:4
 27 Gn 4:4
 29 Gn 4:10
 32 Coll. de Innoc.
 34 Gn 4:26
 36 cf. Aug. *ciu.* 15, 18 (CCSL 48, 480–81)
 42 Gn 5:18–24
 45 cf. Aug. *ciu.* 15, 23 (CCSL 48, 491) et 18, 38 (*ibid.* 633)
 63 Stat. *Theb.* 5, 613–15

 86 Gn 21:6
105 Hor. *ars* 158–60
109 Gn 7:5
119 Gn 3:9–10
124 Gn 3:12
127 Ps 140:4
136 Gn 6:9
147 cf. Mc 2:4
154 Ex 32:6 (cf. 1 Co 10:7)
155 Gn 21:9
156 Curt. 5, 5, 12
159 Cic. *Cato* 3, 7
190 Mt 1:17
192 Aug. *ciu.* 16, 43 (CCSL 48, 550)
199 Aug. *ciu.* 16, 43 (CCSL 48, 550)
202 Aug. *in euang. Ioh.* 9, 6 (CCSL 36, 93–94)
209 Isid. *orig.* 5, 39
210 Greg. M. *in euang. 40* 1, 19 (PL 76:1154C–55B)
227 Greg. M. *in Ezech.* 1, 2, 3 (CCSL 142, 19; Eccl 11, 9)
229 Isid. *orig.* 11, 2, 1
235 Hor. *ars* 161–65
255 3 Rg 12:16
261 Ga 3:24
268 cf. Pr 13:8
285 Hor. *ars* 166–68
289 Ga 4:4–5
294 Gn 49:10
298 cf. Gn 49:10
299 Agg 2:8
302 1 Io 2:18
303 1 Co 10:11
308 Gn 27:1
312 Gn 27:1
316 Bernardus Claraevall. *De Consideratione* 3, 1, 5 (ed. Leclercq 3:434)
325 cf. Ter. *Phorm.* 575; Sen. *epist.* 108, 28
328 Sap 4:8–9
337 Ct 2:5
345 Walther, *Sprichw.* 32036
350 3 Rg 1:1
352 cf. Lc 12:33
356 1 Co 7:31
361 Ps. Sen. *De Rem. Fort.* 10, 3
369 Ps 61:11
378 Hor. *ars* 169–74
384 Cic. *Cato* 11, 36

DEED AND WORD: HELINAND'S TOULOUSE SERMONS I

Beverly M. Kienzle

A MONG HÉLINAND of Froidmont's sermons, those which recently have received the most critical attention were delivered in Toulouse around 1229. We have the text of at least four sermons given there: the focal point for this study will be the two sermons associated with a 1229 council.[1] It has been suggested that one was the opening and the other the closing sermon for the council.[2] The themes of both relate to the church's authority and responsibilities of the clergy. Hélinand's preaching in Languedoc followed that of earlier Cistercians charged with the impossible task of stifling heresy by their own words and example. As far as we know, Hélinand's role in Toulouse was exclusively that of a preacher, but he was known for the conversion of his poetic talents to God's service, and consequently as one who personally affirmed spiritual values by his example and verbal talents. He thus embodied the special Cistercian province as described by Innocent III in *Etsi nostri navicula* (31 May 1204): to be strong in deed and word (*potentes in opere et sermone.*[3] In the Toulouse sermons, Hélinand confronts with characteristic verve and acerbity the controversial issues facing the times.[4] Likewise, he displays his literary talents to impress and persuade his listeners.

To examine Hélinand's preaching in Toulouse, we first briefly trace what is known of his life before 1229 and continue with a summary of early Cistercian missions in Languedoc. Next, the immediate background for the two 1229 council sermons is established. Finally, these sermons are analyzed as they relate to the council canons and Hélinand's continuation of the theme of excellence in deed and word.

From what we know of Hélinand's life, the Toulouse sermons represent the apex of literary talents perfected in the schools, then displayed frivolously, and ultimately put to the service of God and church. Hélinand studied with Ralph of Beauvais, an Englishman and pupil of Abelard,[5] whose method is particularly notable for its abundant usage of illustrative citations. Ralph was at the height of his fame in the late eleven sixties and seventies.[6] Hélinand states in his own *Chronicle* that he studied with Ralph *a puero* (PL 212: 1035D). The date 1160 suggested for Hélinand's birth[7] would place him as a boy in Ralph's school while it flourished. A young Hélinand led a wandering poet's life, always seeking someone to devour (1 P 5:8) with flattery or chiding (*quaerens quem devoraret, aut adulando, aut objurgando*; PL 212:748D). Suddenly, he experienced a conversion and entered the Cistercian monastery at Froidmont around 1182.[8] From the monastery he issued his powerful *Vers de la Mort*, dated 1193–97,[9] to decry the scandal and abuses surrounding Philip Augustus' attempts to divorce Ingeburga of Denmark. Historical records are still being searched for information about Hélinand's life between the *Vers de la Mort* and the 1229 synod in Toulouse. For Hélinand to journey to Toulouse for such a crucial assembly allows us to infer that during those thirty years his fame as a preacher had come to surpass even his reputation as a poet. He had transformed his earlier flattery of patrons into praise of spiritual values and his chiding was now directed at those whose lives betrayed Scripture's teaching.

Hélinand's presence in Languedoc was part of a larger Cistercian involvement there, an effort including preaching, negotiating, and organizing the new university at Toulouse. Bernard had made a tour of the region in 1145. His letters describe the deplorable state of popular worship and urge the continuance of efforts to eradicate heresy.[10]

Alexander III sent Cistercian legates to Languedoc, and later Innocent III commissioned Cistercians as legates charged with conducting a preaching mission to attempt to stifle heresy by word and example.[11] His bulls affirm the necessity for strength in deed and word, the special province of the Cistercians. In the 31 May 1204 bull *Etsi nostri navicula*, Innocent states: "We rejoice that there are many in your order who possess the zeal of God grounded in knowledge [and who are] strong in deed and word . . . and all the more fit for confounding fabricators of perverse dogma as there is so little in them to reprehend ."[12] In the autumn of 1203, Pierre of Castelnau and Raoul, both of Fontfroide, were designated legates.[13] Arnaud, abbot of Cîteaux and former abbot of Grand-selve, was directed in late May 1204 to join them.[14] These preachers encountered resistance not only from heretics, but also from feudal lords and corrupt resentful local clergy.[15] In January 1205, Innocent reminded the discouraged legates that the active life is useful and expressed his hopes for success in their *opus evangelistae*.[16]

Pierre of Castelnau described the discouragement felt because of the double task of reforming and preaching.[17] The preaching mission was revitalized in the summer of 1206 when in Montpellier the legates encountered Dominic and Diego, bishop of Osma. The Cistercians were encouraged to present an example of irreproachably strict poverty, travelling without escort and without the one mount they had obtained from the local archbishop.[18] Later the same year, Innocent also appealed to Raoul of Frontfroide to follow the Spaniards' method, imitating Christ's poverty, *in despecto habitu et ardenti spiritu*, and correcting the heretics with example of deed and substance of preaching (*per exemplum operis et documentum sermonis*).[19] In 1207, twelve learned abbots and other accompanying monks journeyed from Cîteaux to support the effort.[20] Nonetheless, as a contemporary poet wrote, the Cathars paid no more attention to the sermons than they would to a rotten apple.[21]

Innocent, already disappointed at the paucity of converts and urging Philip Augustus to take up arms, was outraged when the legate Pierre of Castelnau was brutally murdered in January 1208. The indignant pope suspected the excommunicated count of Toulouse (*diabolus monstruum suum*) of instigating the crime[22] and persuaded Philip that a crusade should be undertaken to punish the guilty and expel the heretics.[23] Force took the place of preaching, and nearly twenty years of war ensued.

At the termination of hostilities, Hélie, abbot of Grandselve, was involved in negotiating the Treaty of Paris between the king and the count of Toulouse. That 1229 treaty included a clause providing for the foundation of a university at Toulouse. Organizational details and in particular the choice of masters were entrusted to the same Hélie.[24] It was possibly Hélie, then, who in-

vited Hélinand to preach in Toulouse. Among the masters brought
to the new university, the most notable was John of Garland whose
epic poem, *De triumphis ecclesiae*, describes Hélie's role in the be-
ginnings of the new university.[25]

Hélinand's sermons revive the message of strength in deed and
word, bringing it to bear on the 1229 council at Toulouse. Two
sermons have been associated with the council: *Twenty-six* because
of the MS rubric *In synodo Tolosana in ecclesia S. Jacobi habitus*,
and *Twenty-eight*, *De potestate et probitate ecclesiae*, because of its
theme and direct reference to the papal legate. It has been suggested that *Twenty-eight*, defending the church's authority, was the
opening sermon for the council and that *Twenty-six* on the responsibilities of the priesthood, was the closing sermon. While the exact occasions for the sermons cannot be definitely established,[26]
their content does relate directly to the council and its canons. The
first sermon defends ecclesiastic authority, and the second advises
her representatives to be worthy of it.

The council brought together both ecclesiastic and lay leaders of
the region. According to a contemporary chronicler, the papal legate Romano, cardinal of Sant' Angelo, arrived in Toulouse shortly
after Pentecost in 1229, and then called a council sometime after
the summer (*post aestatem*).[27] There is no clear evidence that Hélinand traveled in the cardinal's retinue. A nineteenth-century historian makes that suggestion, and a recent historian revives it.[28]
Hélinand does refer to the cardinal's arrival in Toulouse (PL
212:720C), but without saying that he himself accompanied the
legate.

The council issued forty-five canons which are dated from November 1229.[29] The first eighteen deal with searching for heretics,
judging them, penalities for sheltering or hiding them, treatment
of converts, administration of an oath abjuring heresy, and required signs of faith: confession and receiving the Eucharist three
times per year. Six canons (19–24) define eccleiastic privileges:
freedom from taxation and tolls and the legal rights of clerics. Three
canons (25–27) order attendance at church on Sundays and feast
days, requiring fines for absentees. Another seventeen concern
preserving peace, punishing disturbers of the peace, dealing with
stolen goods, the responsibilities of judges, and providing legal assistance to the poor. The final canon (45) declares that all the preceding canons are to be set forth (*exponantur*) by the parish priests

four times per year. Parish priests, bishops, and the legate were involved in the implementation of the canons. Following the council, the legate himself adjudicated the inquest, carrying the records with him to Rome in an unsuccessful attempt to protect those who identified suspects.[30]

In *Sermon Twenty-eight*, Hélinand affirms the church's power and appeals for obedience. He justifies the legate's presence in the region and the purpose of the council. Traditional garden imagery laces the sermon together; the garden workers are clergy and the thorns are vices, and undoubtedly heretics. God, the great *pater familias*, sends workers into his vineyard to guard against thorny vines, nettles, and vipers (PL 212:712). Jeremiah was thus made a cultivator of the Lord's vineyard, set up over peoples and kingdoms to pluck out, destroy, spoil, build, and plant (Jr 1:10). Likewise every prelate is established by God over peoples and kingdoms (PL 212:712D), and from the beginning the Lord appointed all secular authority subject to the church. Numerous historical examples illustrate the wisdom of that subordination. As the Lord is the source of authority, so, too, he is the author of peace (PL 212:716); his delights are purity of bodies and peace of souls PL 212:716D). The prelate or preacher plants a garden of delights for God when by his word and example (*verbo et exemplo*) he plants peace and holiness in the hearts and bodies of his listeners (PL 212:716D). Hélinand explains that legates are sent from the pope to perform this planting, an *opus evangelistae* (PL 212:716D). Like Jeremiah, they are to pluck out, destroy, build, and plant. Virtues can not be planted unless vices are first extirpated (PL 212:717A). For this task, there is need of discipline and obedience. The new legate, to whom reverence and obedience are owed, has brought a new hoe of discipline and has set forth numerous rules, necessary for eradicating the many thorns. Hélinand praises the legate as a modest teacher, a lover of justice, a zealous seeker of souls, and a *contemptor* of riches. By the example of his unpretentious arrival (*non pompatice incedit*), the legate has shown that he is not moved by riches. Of the virtues praised, this disdain of wealth is extolled over others.[31] Perhaps this practical preacher intends not only to praise virtue, but to discourage attempted bribes. Finally, Hélinand urges his audience to listen humbly and devoutly to the legate's orders and to be obedient (PL 212:720).

Sermon Twenty-six expounds the theme of deed and word, offering traditional yet timely advice to a clergy charged with implementing council canons. Hélinand's Cistercian predecessors had struggled to convert by good example, and his message, presumably the final words to the council, reaffirms the value of strength in deed and word. Ps 132:9 is the sermon's theme: your priests are vesting in integrity (*justitiam*). Images of putting on clothing link the various sections of the sermon. The message is at first directed to all the faithful (PL 212:692D), a chosen people made a kingdom and a priesthood but later focuses on priests. *Sacerdos* is explained as *sacrum dans*, because the four things a priest gives are all holy: example, word, food, and judgment (PL 212:697). Holy example involves moderation in good fortune and patience in adversity; holy word includes prayer and preaching; holy food consists of giving Holy Communion and feeding the poor; holy judgment requires absolving those who are repentant and binding (*ligare*) those who are rebellious and unyielding. These responsibilities are crucial to clerical efforts in the region, for virtue distinguishes true priests from the devil's false priests and from heretics whose infernal doctrine lurks behind seeming austerity.

The clothing of integrity worn by priests has four chararteristics and purposes. Childlike, it covers nakedness like an alb (*alba*), preserving innocence or restoring lost innocence through repentance. Manly, it warms like a cloak (*penula*), protecting the needy from the cold. Kingly, it adorns and honors like the purple robe of Christ (*purpura*), suffering all things with patience and enduring them with forbearance. Soldier-like, it covers and protects like armor (*lorica*), giving to each his due, leaving none of the body uncovered (PL 212:698-99).[32]

The sermons's final image is the sword. The prophet Ezekiel calls it a sword of great slaughter. But Hélinand states that the slaughter is meagre when an evil custom is relinquished and evil action is retained. For the prophet speaks of a sword on two or three accounts (Ezk 21:19). Its blow is doubled when both evil custom and perverse action are relinquished, and tripled when even evil will is cut off at its original root. The sword of which Hélinand speaks does not level a crusader's blows at heretics; it slays the vices of his fellow clergy. With the sermon's final sentence, Hélinand boldly affirms: "Then we are truly priests of God when we strike our own body and soul with such a sword" (*Tunc vere sacer-*

dotes Dei sumus, quando tali gladio corpus nostrum et animam macta-
mus [Ezk 21]).

Hélinand thus urges his listeners to examine their own conduct
before they set out to search that of others. He does condemn heretical doctrine—the Cathars' abstinence from food and likening of
marriage to incest in their prohibitions[33]—but those denunciations
occupy less than one of nearly eight columns of text for this sermon (697D, 698ABC of 692D-700B). He is clearly warning that
adherence to a strict Christian code of priestly virtue is all the
more essential as the council canons will be difficult to implement.
A person charged with surveying and judging others must be beyond reproach.

In summary, Hélinand, with a considerable reputation as poet
and then preacher, journeyed to southern France at a tense and
crucial moment in that region's history. He followed a course
similar to that undertaken some twenty-five years earlier by fellow
Cistercians at the request of Innocent III. With their reputation
for knowledge and an irreproachable way of life, they seemed the
best agents for reform and conversion in Languedoc. Innocent's
letters praised them for strength *in opere et sermone* and requested
that they excel even further in both. The task was unsurmount-
able, but the message of excellence in deed and word, counsel to
preachers for centuries, endured to be reaffirmed. A 1229 council
in Toulouse promulgated forty-five canons with the double and
perplexing aim of searching for heretics and maintaining peace. Although the assembly included lay delegates, the preponderant responsibility for implementing these canons was ecclesiastical.
Hélinand's sermons to the assembled prelates, nobles, and city
representatives urge obedience to the church, but advise the clergy
to deserve the reverence and obedience owed them.

The two synod sermons are among at least four Hélinand delivered in Toulouse. He complains in an unedited passage that he had
to preach three times in one week (*Ter in ista hebdomada sermonem*
facere coactus sum).[34] The remainder of that sermon, as it appears in
edited versions, is filled with citations and literary devices
undoubtedly designed to impress his university audience, at the
same time admonishing them that learning without a spiritual dimension is worthless and dangerous.

While verbal displays may not appeal to modern tastes, Hélinand's style was appreciated in his day. Vincent of Beauvais, who borrowed heavily from Hélinand's *Chronicle*,[35] describes the sermons as *peroptimos*.[36] With his preaching talent and the example of his conversion to the Cistercian way of life, Hélinand's journey to Toulouse must have brought a living example of excellence in deed and word.

St. Anselm College

NOTES

Research for this paper was begun under a 1983 Faculty Summer Research Grant from St. Anselm College. I am especially grateful to Chrysogonus Waddell, O.C.S.O. for his several suggestions and reading of the paper, to Stanley Ceglar, S.D.B. for the date of Bernard's *Tolosanum iter*, to Edmé Smits for information from his reading of the sermon manuscripts, and to Eugene A. Green, C.O. for his suggestions and thoughtful reading of the paper's various versions.
1. Twenty-eight of Hélinand's sermons are edited in B. Tissier, *Bibliotheca patrum cisterciensium* (Bonnefontaine, 1669), VII, 206–306; and PL 212: 481–720. All further references from PL 212 appear in the text. Brial, in *Histoire littéraire de la France* XVIII, 87–103, identified the 1229 council in Toulouse. The four sermons are Ss XV, XXVI, and XXVIII in PL 212 and an unedited sermon for Rogation in B.N. ms. lat. 14591 f. 35vb. See J.-Th. Welter, *L'Exemplum dans la littérature religieuse et didactique du moyen âge* (Paris, 1929), p. 111. The unedited sermon is summarized by Yves Dossat, "Les premiers maîtres à l'Université de Toulouse: Jean de Garlande, Hélinand," in *Les Universités du Languedoc au XIIIe siècle*,Cahiers de Fanjeaux 5 (Toulouse, 1970), p. 200.
2. Adophe-Félix Gatien-Arnoult, "Hélinand," *Revue de Toulouse et du Midi de la France* 22 (1866) 287–302 and 345–56; and "Notes sur les commencements de l'Université de Toulouse," *Mémoires de l'Académie des sciences, inscriptions et belles-lettres de Toulouse* E.I (1857) 202–220; and "Histoire de l'Université de Toulouse," *Mémoires* G.IX (1877) 455–94.
3. PL 215:359B.
4. On Hélinand's preaching, see my article, "The Sermon as Goad and Nail: Preaching in Hélinand of Froidmont," in E. Rozanne Elder (ed.), *Goad and Nail; studies in Medieval Cistercian History, 10*, CS 84 (Kalamazoo, 1985), pp. 228–40.
5. PL 212:1035D: "Hujus etiam Petri Abaelardi discipulus fuit magister meus . . . Radulphus, natione Anglicus cognomento Grammaticus, Ecclesiae Belvacensis." See also R. W. Hunt, "Studies in Priscian in Twelfth Century II," *Medieval and Renaissance Studies 2* (London, 1950; rpt. Liechenstein, 1969), pp. 1–56.
6. See Hunt, "Studies . . . II," pp. 11–12.
7. Anselme Dimier, "Elinando di Froidmont," *Bibliotheca sanctorum* (Rome, Pontificia Università Lateranse, 1964), IV, col. 1073. The year 1170 was suggested by A. Lecoy de la Marche, *La chaire française au moyen âge*. (2nd. ed., Paris, 1886), p. 157.

8. Dimier, col. 1074.

9. See William D. Paden Jr., *De monachis rithmos facientibus,"* *Speculum* 55 (1980) 669–85.

10. The letters are in Martin Bouquet, *Recueil des historiens des Gaules et de la France* (Paris, 1869–1904), XV, 597–98, 609–610. Bernard's *Tolosanum iter* began in May and ended in late August of 1145. The beginning date is established in Georg Hüffer, *Der heilige Bernard von Clarivaux: Eine Darstellung seines Lebens und Werkens,I, Vorstudien* (Munster, 1886), pp. 27–28, n. 4; the ending date is given in *Ep. Gaufridi Archenfredo.*PL 185:412D; and the journey is discussed om Robert Lechat, "Les Fragmenta de vita et miraculis S. Bernardi, par Geoffroy d'Auxerre," *Analecta Bollandiana* L (1932) 83–122

11. Information on the preaching mission is contained in Christine Thouzellier, *Catharisme et Valdéisme en Languedoc* (Paris, 1969), pp. 183–203; Pierre Belperron, *La croisade contre les albigeios* (Paris, 1942); and Joseph R. Strayer, *The Albigensian Crusades* (New York, 1971). See also the thirteenth-century chronicles: Pierre of Vaux-de-Cernay, *Hystoria Albigensis,*ed. Pascal Guébin and Ernest Lyon, Société de l'histoire de France (Paris: 1926–1930); and Guillaume of Puy-Laurens, *Chronique,* ed. and trans. Jean Duvernoy (Paris, 1976).

12. PL 215:359B: "Gaudeamus autem . . . in Ordine vestro multi reperiunter habentes zelum Dei secundam scientiam, potentes in opere et sermone . . . qui tanto sunt ad confutandos fabricatores perversorum dogmatum aptiores, quanto minus in eis quid reprehendere valeat."

13. Thouzellier, pp. 184–85.

14. Thouzellier, p. 187.

15. Thouzellier, p. 189.

16. 26 January 1205, in PL 215:525–26. See Thouzellier, p. 189.

17. Thouzellier, p. 193.

18. Thouzellier, p. 194–95.

19. PL 215:1025B; Thouzellier, p. 196.

20. Thouzellier, p. 199.

21. Guillaume de Tudèle in *La Chanson de la croisade albigeoise,* ed. and trans. Eugene Martin-Chabot, Les Classiques de l'Histoire de France au Moyen-Age (Paris, 1960), I, 2, v. 25.

22. PL 215:1354–62; Thouzellier, pp. 204–206.

23. Thouzellier, p. 206.

24. See Cyril E. Smith, *The University of Toulouse in the Middle Ages,*(Milwaukee, 1958) 33–35.

25. *De triumphis ecclesiae libri octo,* ed. Thomas Wright (London, 1856).

26. See Gatien-Arnould, *Mémoires* (1877), G. IX, 463ff.; Dossat, pp. 197–99; and Smith, p. 38.

27. The council, its preparations, arrival of the legate, etc., are described by Guillaume de Puy-Laurens, pp. 134–39. Smith, pp. 37–38, n. 18, dates the cardinal's arrival in the autumn.

28. Gatien-Arnoult, *Mémoires* (1857) E. I., 207, and *Mémoires* (1877) G. IX. 457; Dossat, pp. 191–92.

29. Jean-Dominique Mansi, *Sacrorum conciliorum nova et amplissima collectio* (1784) XXIII, cols. 192–204.

30. See Smith, p. 49; and Guillaume de Puy-Laurens, pp. 138–41.

31. A further comment on the legate is found in MS Paris BN lat. 14591 f. 48 v. There Hélinand states that this legate is not like the others, whom Hélinand compares to the furies released from Hell: "In summa, si auderem dicere: romanus non est, id est non abiit post aurum, nec sperat in thesauris pecunie. Non est de legatis illis quos aliquandos novimus sic egressos fuisse a latere domini papae, ac si ad ecclesiam flagellandam egressus esset Sathan a facie Domini. Ita plerique versantur in ecclesiis, in provinciis debachantur ac si ad tedas in facinus excitandam egressa sit ab inferis iuxta Claudianum, Thesiphone vel Megera. . . ."

Edmé R. Smits (ed), *Peter Abelard, Letters IX–XIV* (Groningen, 1983), pp.
109–110. The remark is somewhat humorous because Hélinand says, "romanus
non est," referring to traditional Latin satire of Roman avarice. The legate's
name, however, was Romano, and he came from a noble Roman family. On Romano Frangipani, cardinal of Sant'Angelo, see Jonathan Sumpton, *The Albigensian Crusade* (London, 1978), p. 214.

32. This passage probably refers to four vestments: alb (*alba*), chasuble (*penula*),
cope (*purpura*), amice (*lorica*) and their corresponding vesting prayers. For the
alba, Hélinand uses Rv 16:5 and Ps 32:1; for the *penula*, Jb 31:19 and Pr 31:21;
for the *purpura*, an allusion to Christ's purple robe and Passion; and for the *lorica*
Ep 6:11–15. The innocence and penitence that Hélinand associates with the *alba*
are found in other prayers emphasizing the contrast between the alb's white color
and the filth of sin. Joseph A. Jungmann, *The Mass of the Roman Rite*, trans. Francis A. Brunner (New York; 1950), I, 282. For Hélinand, the chasuble's warmth is
given to the poor; in other vesting prayers the chasuble is variously represented as
a garment of love, a fortress, a piece of armor, and so on (Jungmann, p. 286). The
amice took on a warlike significance as early as the ninth century; and in a ninth-
century source, the amice and alb are combined in one prayer (Jungmann, p.
282). Hélinand seems to recall a similar prayer when he says of the *lorica*: "totum
corpus circumtegenti, et nihil intectum deserenti." Symbolic value is given to
vestments in Hugh of St. Victor's *Sermon Fourteen* (PL 177:927–29). The semon,
possibly for a synod (*In synodo, aut in festo confessorum sacerdotum, de vestibus sacris*)
has Ps 132:9 as its theme, but does not otherwise directly correspond with Hélinand *Sermon Twenty-six*.

33. On the Cathar's heretical beliefs, see Perron, pp. 68–100.

34. See Lecoy de la Marche, p. 166. Tissier gives "Cum sermonem hunc facere
coactus sum . . . . ." VII, 254.

35. Monique Paulmier-Foucart, "Ecrire l'histoire au XIIIe siècle: Vincent de
Beauvais et Hélinand de Froidmont," *Annales de l'Est* 33 (1981) 49–70.

36. *Speculum historiale* XXIX, c. 108, in PL 212:479A.

ERUDITION AT GOD'S SERVICE:
HELINAND'S TOULOUSE SERMONS II

Beverly M. Kienzle

ELINAND'S SERMON *Fifteen for the Ascension* was delivered in Toulouse at the Church of St James to an audience of students (*ad clericos scholares*) and, undoubtedly, university masters.[1] Its exact date is uncertain, but must be tied to the opening of the new University of Toulouse, established in accordance with the provisions of the 1229 Treaty of Paris. The University opened sometime in 1229.[2] One historian concludes that Hélinand delivered this Ascension sermon for the University's opening on 24 May 1229, and that it counters a letter issued by the university masters.[3] Hélinand exhibits his literary talents and the extent of his reading while at the same time admonishing his listeners that the highest knowledge is with God. The sermon illustrates its own message: a display of erudition at God's service and intended to caution against learning without a spiritual dimension. Height and ascension provide the theme, vocabulary, and images for the sermon, an exemplary model of Hélinand's style of sermon writing. After briefly recalling the background of Hélinand's presence in Toulouse, we discuss the occasion for the sermon and its theme. We then examine selected examples of its style to elucidate what features typify Hélinand's writing and make him at once a representative and a unique figure for his time.

Hélinand presumably journeyed to Toulouse sometime before the council there that issued its canons in November 1229. According to a contemporary chronicle, the papal legate, Romano, cardinal of Sant'Angelo, had arrived in Toulouse shortly after Pentecost and called the council sometime after the summer (*post aestatem*).[4] Two of Hélinand's sermons, *Twenty-six* and *Twenty-*

eight, have been associated with the council.[5] Also in 1229 a new university opened in Toulouse; a clause providing for its foundation was included in the Treaty of Paris, signed on 12 April 1229.[6] A Cistercian abbot, Hélie of Grandselve, was responsible for organizational details, including choosing the university masters.[7] Hélie possibly invited Hélinand to Toulouse. The recruiting of masters was facilitated by a quarrel in Paris, where in late March the university issued an ultimatum demanding redress of its grievances within a month after Easter, by 15 May. Unsatisfied students and masters began to leave Paris; some journeyed to Toulouse, including John of Garland who recorded the event in his *De triumphis ecclesiae.*[8] A nineteenth-century historian, Gatien-Arnoult, concludes from John of Garland's poem that the legate accompanied the masters from Paris to Toulouse and that Hélinand may have traveled with them.[9]

Gatien-Arnoult presumes that the new University's opening was marked by a solemn assembly where Hélinand preached. This would have taken place on 24 May 1229 in the Church of St. James.[10] Furthermore, Gatien-Arnoult suggests that Hélinand criticized, at least indirectly, some passages in the letter issued by the masters, and that his sermon warned the University to examine itself as the Church examined it.[11]

The letter is addressed from the Toulouse masters to schools of other regions. It announces the intention to establish a new basis for study in Toulouse: continuance of the good life (*vitae bonae perseverantiam, exitu cum beato*); and praises the new University, affirming the possibility for studying freely and living well in Toulouse. For example, Aristotle's *Libri naturales,* forbidden in Paris, could be heard in Toulouse; Bacchus reigned in the region's vineyards; and the cost of living was not high.[12] Civil law was taught, as well as medicine, and scholastic freedom was promised.[13] The masters also claimed to make Christ the foundation for their philosophical studies and proclaimed that the cedar of Catholic faith would be raised as high as the stars.[14] Yet the prospective students would be soldiers of philosophy (*philosophiae milites*), not of Christ. The reading of forbidden works, the teaching of civil law, also forbidden, and the importance accorded philosophy defy the prevailing opinions and restrictions of Paris theologians.[15]

Whether or not Hélinand intended to specifically criticize that one letter, his sermon stands in opposition to the currents of thought it espouses. Ps 24:3-4 is the sermon's theme: "Who shall climb the mountain of the Lord, or who shall stand in his holy place? One with innocent hands, and a pure heart." Hélinand explains each of the verses' elements: going up to the mountain, standing in the holy place, innocence, and purity of heart. Christ, our model of innocence and purity, lived in heaven before coming down to earth, and then ascended, returning to heaven and preparing a place for us. Before we go up to the mountain, heaven and the true knowledge that dwells there, we must first reside on earth. In order to go up and live in heaven, our earthly lives must be led in innocence and purity of heart (PL 212:596D-98A). Our efforts on earth, including the pursuit of knowledge, must be directed towards the true knowledge that dwells with God in heaven (PL 212:603C).

Yet Hélinand is going to tell his listeners that many pursue another end in their studies; greedy and vain, they devour learning in order to swell their pocketbooks with lucre or their heads with pride. Hélinand will upbraid these seekers of vain and saleable information, lamenting their folly and exhorting them to reform. He will warn seekers of false riches and of false knowledge that they endanger their souls as they labor and sweat in vain (PL 212:604A).

After delivering approximately the first half of the sermon, an impersonal treatment of the theme, Hélinand begins to intensify and personalize his message. His first target is philosophers. We can imagine that he spoke to the university masters present. Divine wisdom teaches ways of going up, yet many fall because of their ignorance of its great art and teaching (*tantam artem, et tantum magisterium*). Joining Lucifer, Alexander, and Simon the Magician in their precipitous pursuit of falsehood are the philosophers, whether followers of Pythagoras, Plato, Epicurus, the Stoics, or any others (PL 212:602B). These and other proud and rebellious men do not climb to heaven, but onto horses of pride and lust (PL 212:602C). The ambition that drives them also destroys them (PL 212:602D).

Hélinand next addresses the students present, announcing that his speech will be more simple to accomodate the simple so that they, too, may climb up with the others (PL 212:603A). Many travel great distances to study; they endure many things in order to earn money, traversing city and globe. Yet their reward is insanity, the inevitable outcome of worthless letters (*nihil salvantes litterae*) (PL 212:603B).

Nowhere is virtue sought, and nowhere life. The book of life is the book of knowledge, the wisdom of God, now in its bookcase (*armarium suum*) raised to heaven. However, Hélinand laments, "the clerics in Paris pursue liberal arts; in Orléans, authors; in Bologna, codices; in Salerno, medicine boxes; in Toledo, magic; and nowhere, virtue" (PL 212:603B). The students of Toulouse, while not listed in that frequently quoted passage, were surely its target.

During this lengthy exhortation (over fifteen columns in PL 212), Hélinand presents an extensive repertoire of sermonic techniques—some personal, some belonging to monastic homiletic tradition, and others to the newer school sermon. The combined features that distinguish his style are often forceful, entertaining, and even moving, but at times are tiresome in their accumulation. To modern tastes, Hélinand's sermon writing is most appealing when it is most personal, in occasional moments of gentleness, in frequent attacks on his contemporaries, and in his apparent delight at telling a good story. His own audience, however, and especially the audience for this Ascension day sermon, would have also been impressed by a display of erudition, and Hélinand provides just that.

In the sermon's preface, Hélinand discusses the art of speaking, apologizing for the sermon's hasty composition. In the unedited version he states that he had to speak three times in one week;[16] in the edited text he speaks only of being obliged to do the sermon and implies that time was lacking. Leaning on Horace, Quintilian, Sallust, and Statius, he warns of the risks taken when attempting to please an audience. Fortune has little regard for talent in the recognition it awards writers and orators. Not all audiences will be as moved as the one that greeted the recitation of Statius' *Thebaid* with wild enthusiasm.[17] Expounding on the fickleness of human favor provides Hélinand the context to demonstrate his own reading on oratory, and later to call his listeners to look for favor and knowledge from God. He himself is laden with a heavy burden, a weak person given a short period of time to complete a matter requiring considerable effort (PL 212:595D–96B).

Earlier we noted a shift in tone about midway through the sermon where Hélinand announces a change in style.[18] His expressed desire to reach the simple in his audience clearly shows us that he deliberately uses a cultivated style in the first part of the sermon. In the second part he seems to relax. Supportive quotations are no longer from classical authors, but from Scripture and early Christian writers. He continues to use word play, but his language is simpler and more emotive.[19] He employs techniques of the patristic sermon: numerology and explanation of the senses of scripture. The divisions and distinctions of the second part are shorter and simpler. He denounces the shortcomings of education in his day, and he calls up his talent as story-teller, recounting three lengthy *exempla* in the remainder of the sermon.

The entire sermon, but especially the first half, abounds in citations—from Scripture, early Christian writers, and classical literature. Within just over fifteen columns of text appear nearly one hundred identified citations, and doubtless more. Scriptural passages, at least fifty-one of them, appear seventy-four times; early Christian writers, especially Augustine and Jerome, are used eleven times. Classical authors are cited at least thirteen times, but are absent from the second half of the sermon in its expressedly simpler style.

The frequency of references to classical authors is unusual for a sermon composed around 1230. Alain of Lille had stated that, on occasion, statements from pagan writers could be inserted just as Paul used the opinions of philosophers.[20] The occasions were apparently rare in Hélinand's day. The 1230 university sermons, representative of the Sorbonne's position on such matters of controversy, contain only eight quotations from classical writers out of a total of 1295.[21] Hélinand apparently did not agree with the Paris theologians' proscriptions of profane reading.

An abundance of illustrative citations, including those from classical sources, was characteristic of the school of Hélinand's teacher, Ralph of Beauvais. Ralph's school is credited with reapplying the study of authors to grammar, and at least one glossator of the school seems to have made his own selections from Virgil instead of taking them from another source.[22] Hélinand apparently continued using Ralph's methods even in his sermons. Current research on Hélinand shows that some of his references to ancient authors, Seneca for example, are so extensive that he may have been familiar with complete texts of their works and did not simply consult *flori-legia*.[23]

Figures of rhetoric and wordplay occur throughout the sermon. Hélinand, like Bernard,[24] is fond of the "tricolon," a series of three more or less rhyming or rhythmic clauses, for example:

> Vae, qui vocati exemplo, non veniunt; procati verbo, non audiunt; provocati miraculo, non accurrunt (PL 212:597C). 'Woe to those who do not come when called by his example, do not heed when charged by his word, and do not hasten when called forth by the miracle [of his Ascension].

Here Hélinand plays on the prefixes (*vocati, procati, provocati*), the -o endings (*exemplo, verbo, miraculo*), and the verb endings (*veniunt, audiunt, accurrunt*) to establish a certain rhyme and rythym.

Hélinand also plays on suffixes and other word endings. An example follows:

> Quantum desiderabilis ad dexteram, tantum intolerabilis ad sinistram id est ineffabilia redditurus innocentibus praemia, nocentibus tormenta: illis ascensuris ad coeli palatia, istis in tartara ruituris (PL 212:597D).
> ... [It shall be] as desirable [for those] on his right hand as it is unbearable [for those] on the left; that is, he shall bestow unutterable remuneration on the inculpable, and punition on the culpable: the inculpable shall be raised up to the eternal palaces, and the culpable cast down into the infernal places.

He repeats -*abilis* (*desiderabilis, intolerabilis*), and -*uris* (*ascensuris, ruituris*, with *redditurus* an imperfect third). In the same sentence he plays on prefixes to underscore the contrast in meaning (*innocentibus, nocentibus*). Again, he repeats word endings (*ad dexteram, ad sinistram; ineffabilia, praemia, tormenta; palatia, tartara*).

Hélinand is also fond of rhetorical questions.[25] About divine wisdom, he asks:

> Quid hac arte subtilius, quid hac utilius scientia, quid ista facultate salubrius, quid hac sublimius potestate? (PL 212: 602A) What [could be] more subtle than this art, what

> more beneficial than this knowledge, what more healthful
> than this ability, what more noble than this authority?

The rythym of the questions is enhanced by the repetition of the suffix *-ius* (*subtilius, utilius, salubrius*), and of a second "u" sound in each word. We see that he also varies the rythym, making the word order parallel in the first and third, and second and fourth clauses.

In this sermon to an academic audience, Hélinand delights in seemingly endless lists, using word associations to move from one idea to another. Here he is typical of the early thirteenth-century sermon writer who lists, distinguishes, and divides, but lacks an imposed structure, an overall division with subdivisions.[26] The distinctions and lists (perhaps early or imperfect forms of distinctions)[27] he makes for innocence, for example, demonstrate how the sermon is expanded with this technique.[28] He distinguishes narrow and broad interpretations of innocence, supporting these with authorities. The broader understanding of innocence as justice is given two meanings, and the first of these is divided into two parts. The definition then proceeds by negation, and Hélinand elaborates what the just or innocent do not do. Evil can be done by word, deed, or consent alone. As an example, verbal evil doings are divided into many categories. Disparagement can be done three ways, one of them verbal insult. Insulting speech is divided into blasphemy against God and anger against one's neighbor. Then blasphemy and insult are both divided twice. One of the ways to insult is to tell lies, the other to keep silent. Three ways of lying are distinguished and then eight types of lies are drawn from Augustine. Truth is divided into two categories, and, finally, Hélinand ends the development of evil deeds in word. The list of types of lies represents the seventh division of doing evil verbally! The entire development of the definition of innocence by negation extends over three and one half columns of text before Hélinand finally returns to the Ascension theme, stating that these two parts of innocence are two rungs of the ladder which reaches to heaven (*sunt duo gradus scalae quibus in coelum scanditur*, PL 212:601D).

In the second half of the sermon, we see the usage of a simpler style. Lists are fewer and shorter. There is still wordplay, and Hélinand uses emotive language. He frequently employs the apostro-

phe at emotional moments in his sermons. Here he exalts humankind's fortune at having Christ as mediator:

> O singularis dignitas conditionis humanae, cujus preparator
> hospitii ascensor est coeli, cujus loci mundator est mundi fa-
> bricator! O quam nobilis creatura homo purus! cujus servus
> homo Deus ad preparandum illi hospitium praecurrit ad
> coelum... (PL 212:607B).
>
> O matchless dignity of the human condition, whose home is
> prepared by one who ascends to heaven, whose dwelling is
> cleansed by the one who made the world! O how noble a
> creature is a cleansed man whose servant, man and God,
> went before him to heaven to prepare his place...

Exalting Christ's suffering in an emotive passage, he selects the
verbs *aspicere* and *respicere*, [29] and uses them in a series of powerful
imperatives [30]:

> *Aspice in Christum tuum...; Respice in corpus ejus...;*
> *Aspice in Christum tuum...; Respice in corpus ejus...;*
> *Aspice in Christum tuum...; Respice in nos miseros...* (PL
> 212:608BCD).
> Behold your Christ...; Be mindful of his body...; Behold
> your Christ...; Be mindful of his body...; Behold your
> Christ...; Be mindful of our wretchedness....

Also in the second half of the sermon we find Hélinand using
patristic sermon techniques, distinguishing the anagogical from the
historical interpretation of scripture, and using numerology. A tale
about St. Dunstan, archbishop of Canterbury, is connected to
scripture and interpreted on literal and anagogical levels. Just prior
to death, Dunstan and his bed were raised three times to the raf-
ters and then lowered. That story is connected to Christ's healing
the paralytic and saying: Rise, pick up your bed, and go to your
home (Mt 9:6). Hélinand states that what was fulfilled historically
for the paralytic will be fulfilled anagogically for all the chosen.
Dunstan could not be taken up body, soul, and bed, to heaven,
but the bed's lifting him body and soul showed that he would first
be taken up without the body, and then later with it.
    The one example of numerology in this sermon is short and sim-

ple.[31] Hélinand explains the significance of 120, the number of those witnessing Christ's ascension. 120 consists of multiples of fifteen. Fifteen is composed of seven plus eight, the seven saints of the Old Testament and the eight of the New. Therefore, 120 represented all those true disciples of Christ who will go up to heaven with him at his second coming.

Finally, in the second part of this sermon, Hélinand recounts three *exempla*, a technique for sermon development in which he excelled and delighted. Many of his anecdotes found their way into preaching aids copied throughout the remainder of the Middle Ages. Where Hélinand found his many tales is being investigated by researchers of his *Chronicon*. There is evidence that some of the sermon *exempla* are taken from the *Chronicon*,[32] and that some of its *exempla* draw on the oral and written tradition of Clairvaux. Beaupré was a center where oral traditions were gathered and combined with written materials. A daughter-house of Clairvaux in the same diocese as Froidmont, it was located near the main route between England and Paris, Clairvaux, or Cîteaux.[33] In fact, Beaupré was about twelve miles from Froidmont.[34] Further study of *exempla* in the *Chronicon* will illuminate Hélinand's indebtedness to Clairvaux and her daughter-houses in France and England.

Hélinand's recounting of stories enlivens his preaching and sets his sermons apart from others of the early thirteenth century. One long anecdote selected for *Sermon Fifteen* heightens local interest and provides a relevant message. It concerns William, once lord of Montpellier, and then a monk at the monastery of Grandselve, not far from Toulouse. In his great fondness for William, Bernard visited him in a vision on the night he left this world for the Father. He took William by the hand and led him to a very high mountain near Jerusalem. When William asked why Bernard had to climb that mountain, Bernard replied: so that I may learn (*ut discam*). For William, Bernard was the wisest of all mortals, but Bernard assured him that he would not be wise until he had first climbed the mountain. As Bernard rapidly climbed it, the clock striking for vigils (*signum horologii*) woke William (PL 212:603D).

Two stories illustrate how and how not to make oneself ready for preparing a hospice in heaven. The tale of a nobleman of Macon demonstrates that some have a place prepared for them in hell. On some solemn occasion, the nobleman was surrounded by soldiers when a man riding a horse entered the palace. The man insisted that the nobleman follow him. Bound by an invisible power, the nobleman followed and obeyed an order to mount a horse at the palace door. Suddenly, the horse rose up and ran through the air for a very long time. Unlike Dunstan's bed, the horse did not come down. It disappeared and the nobleman was made the devil's companion. In horror, the townspeople blocked the palace door with stones.

In contrast, Dunstan prepared himself well for his heavenly home (PL 212:609CD–610AB). An assembly of cherubim and seraphim visited Dunstan as he was praying and preparing to preach on the following day, the feast of the Ascension. Dunstan declined the angelic invitation to celebrate the Ascension in heaven, insisting that he could not disappoint his people's expectations and his hopes to show them how to reach heavenly joy. Dunstan did indeed speak to his people, like an angel, then foretold his death, pointed out his preferred burial site, and collapsed into bed at the stroke of six. His wondrous preaching and the spectacle of the rising bed served to confirm his people in faith and fulfill the intention he expressed to the angels.

The visual images created by these lively *exempla* remain as Hélinand rapidly concludes the sermon, offering a brief interpretation of Dunstan's tale and then returning to Christ's Ascension. As he brings the sermon to its conclusion, he completes his display of literary devices: classical citations, rhetorical figures, and *exempla*.

In summary, Hélinand delivered his *Sermon Fifteen for the Ascension* in Toulouse to an audience of students and university masters, some of whom had left Paris to join the new University of Toulouse. According to a nineteenth-century historian, Gatien-Arnoult, Hélinand preached to an assembly marking the University's opening. Gatien-Arnoult contends that Hélinand rebuffs a letter issued by the parisian university masters. Certainly, we find his sermon opposing the ideas espoused in the letter. Hélinand attacks philosophers while the university masters proclaim themselves soldiers of philosophy. He also criticizes students who endure hardships, including long journeys, in order to earn money. Study not dedicated to God is worthless.

Hélinand's abundant use of classical citations in a sermon is a display of erudition that contrasts with his contemporaries' practice in university sermons. Hélinand delivered this Ascension sermon in 1229, only one year before the collection of university sermons edited by Davy in which classical references are sparse. The frequent use of illustrative citations is a feature of the methods Hélinand learned from his teacher, Ralph of Beauvais. Perhaps he intended to differ from parisian practices on yet another ground, by demonstrating that he could put his command of classical literature to the service of God.

Rhetorical devices are also a feature of Hélinand's style. In that respect his writing reflects the thrust of the monastic sermon, attempting to influence the emotions with various figures of rhetoric.[35] We note his taste for wordplay reminiscent of Bernard, and his use of rhetorical questions and apostrophe.

Finally, Hélinand is a story-teller. His *exempla* serve to move and to instruct his audience. In *Sermon Fifteen*, they create vivid and active visual images, which must have remained with his listeners long after the figures of rhetoric faded. We imagine Bernard climbing stairs to heaven, the knight's horse flying in the air, and Dunstan's bed being raised and lowered. Research continues on the sources of Hélinand's *exempla* and their presence in both his sermons and *Chronicon*.

We know nothing of how the sermon was received in Toulouse, but we can appreciate the energy and effort Hélinand brought to his task. He clearly intended to present a personal example of erudition at God's service in order to persuade his listeners, a university audience, that divine knowledge is supreme. Perhaps he felt obliged to convince the students that his own erudition surpassed that of their university teachers. In doing so, he left us yet another testimony to his way of molding the practices of his day to leave his own distinctive mark.

St. Anselm College

NOTES

Research for this paper was begun with a 1983 Faculty Summer Research Grant from St Anselm College. An earlier version was presented at the Sixteenth Conference on Cistercian Studies held in conjunction with the International Congress on Medieval Studies. Western Michigan University, May 1986. I am grateful to Conference participants for their suggestions, and especially to Chrysogonus Waddell, O.C.S.O. for his comments on the conference paper, and to Eugene A. Green, C.O. for his reading of the paper's preliminary versions.

1. PL 212:595D–611A: "Tolosae habitus ad clericos scholares in ecclesia B. Jacobi."
2. Cyril E. Smith, *The University of Toulouse in the Middle Ages* (Milwaukee, 1958), p. 38 and pp. 32–55 on the Treaty and the University.
3. Adolphe Félix Gatien-Arnoult, "Notes sur les commencements de l'Université de Toulouse," *Mémoires de l'Académie des sciences, inscriptions et belles-lettres de Toulouse* E.I (1857), 202–220; and "Histoire de l'Université de Toulouse," *Mémoires* G.IX (1877), 455–94.
4. Guillaume of Puy-Laurens, *Chronique*, ed and trans. Jean Duvernoy (Paris, 1976), pp. 134–39. Smith, *The University*, pp. 37–38, n. 18, prefers autumn as the time of the legate's arrival, and discusses the problems in establishing the date.
5. PL 212:692–700 and 711–20. See Beverly M. Kienzle, "Deed and Word: Hélinand's Toulouse Sermons I," forthcoming in *Studies in Medieval Cistercian History*.
6. Smith, *The University*, pp. 31–32.
7. See Smith, *The University*, p. 35; John of Garland's *De triumphis ecclesiae libri octo*, ed. Thomas Wright (London, 1856), is the source of information on the choice of masters. More on Grandselve is found in M. Moustier's "L'abbaye cistercienne de Grandselve du XIIᵉ au début du XIVᵉ siècle," Cîteaux 34 (1983) 53–76 and 221–44.
8. See Smith, *The University*, pp. 37–38.
9. *Mémoires*, 207–208, 463.
10. *Mémoires*, 463.
11. *Mémoires*, 464–65. The text of the letter, *Epistola transmissa a Magistris tholosanis ad universalia Studia alibi florentia*, is reproduced from *De triumphis ecclesia*, Book 5, and translated in *Mémoires*, 209–215. Gatien-Arnoult cites three or four passages which seem to criticize the letter in *Mémoires*, 463–64. In an 1866 lecture, Gatien-Arnoult goes as far as to claim that Hélinand's sermon is a manifesto of the Church against the letter, a manifesto of the University, "Hélinand," *Revue de Toulouse et du Midi de la France* (1866) 287–302.
12. "Libros naturales, qui fuerant Parisius prohibiti, potuerunt illic audire...;" "Bacchus regnat in vineis;" "Pro parvo vinum...," *Mémoires*, 210–11.
13. "Decretistae Justinianum extollunt, et a latere Medici praedicant Galienum;" "Quid deerit vobis igitur? Libertas scholastica? Nequaquam; quia nullius habenis dediti, propia gaudebitis libertate," *Mémoires*, 210–11.
14. "Conati sumus in Christo Tholosae studii philosophici fundamentum durabile collocare"; "cedrus fidei catholicae per vos ad sidera sublimetur," *Mémoires*, 209.
15. M. M. Davy, *Les sermons universitaires parisiens de 1230–1231* (Paris, 1931), pp. 82–90.
16. "Ter is ista hebdomada sermonem facere coactus sum," in BN MS lat. 14591, fº 1; A. Lecoy de la Marche, *La chaire francaise au moyen age* (Paris, 1886), p. 166, n. 1.
17. Tradition held that Statius was born in Toulouse. Hélinand, referring to

the *Thebaid*, states: "... cujus auctor Statius, cognomento Surculus, hujus civitatis oriundus" (PL 212:596A).

18. PL 212:603A: "Sed nunc sermone simplici pauca loquamur ad simplices, ut et ipsi nobiscum pariter ascensuri, invenire possint per Dei gratiam in sermone nostro viam et vehiculum, lucernam et viaticum." This announced division into two sections with different styles recalls Jean Leclercq's theories on Bernard's sermons with two versions, particularly the *Sermon on Conversion*. Bernard's shorter text, probably the one delivered, is followed by a longer, written text. See *Sermons on Conversion*, trans. Marie-Bernard Said, CF 25 (Kalamazoo, 1981), p. 16.

19. For a study of Hélinand's language, I am indebted to Jean Leclercq's article on Bernard, "Sur le caractere littéraire des sermons de S. Bernard," *Studi Medievali* 7 (1966) 701–744. A more detailed examination of wordplay, specifically *paronomasia* or *adnominatio* is found in Dorette Sabersky, *Studien zur Paronomasie bei Bernhard von Clairvaux* (Freiburg, 1979).

20. *The Art of Preaching*, trans. Gillian R. Evans, CF 23 (Kalamazoo, 1981) 22; PL 210:114C.

21. Davy, pp. 49–51. The texts in Davy's collection are summaries. Jean Longère, *La prédication médiévale* (Paris, 1983), p. 77, cautions that the surprising uniformity and repetition in the Davy collection probably indicate that the copyist did considerable reworking of the texts. Bernard occasionally cited classical sources, but generally opposed their study for monks. Thomas Renna, "St Bernard and the Pagan Classics: An Historical View," *The Chimaera of His Age: Studies on Bernard of Clairvaux*, edd. E. Rozanne Elder and John R. Sommerfeldt, CS 63 (Kalamazoo, 1980), pp. 122–31.

22. See R. W. Hunt, "Studies in Priscian in the Twelfth Century II," *Medieval and Renaissance Studies* 2 (London: 1950; rpt. 1969), 10–11, 23–32, 39.

23. Edmé E. Smits, "Hélinand of Froidmont and the A-Text of Seneca's Tragedies," *Mnemosyne* 36, (1983) 339.

24. On Bernard and the "tricolon," see Leclercq, p. 721.

25. On Bernard's use of rhetorical questions, see Leclercq, p. 727.

26. See Richard H. and Mary A. Rouse, *Preachers, Florilegia and Sermons: Studies on the Manipulus florus of Thomas of Ireland* (Toronto, 1979), pp. 65–72, on the sermon in transition and Hélinand.

27. Rouse and Rouse discuss the development of the distinction in the thirteenth century, stating that "early in the century, the commonest use is the dry recitation of three or so meanings of a word, or of several words, in the Bible text which serves as the theme of a sermon." They state that Hélinand uses distinctions, but only rarely (pp. 9, 71).

28. PL 212:598C: "Hujus innocentiae duae sunt partes: nec facere miserum, nec deserere miserum. Facimus autem miserum, aut verbo, aut facto, aut consensu solo. Verbo tripliciter: aut detrahendo, aut adulando, aut contumeliam inferendo. Detrahis vero tripliciter: aut ut inventor, aut ut relator, aut ut non invitus auditor."

29. Ps 84:9: "Protector noster aspice, Deus, et respice in faciem Christi tui." God, our protector, behold us, and be mindful of the face of your [son] Christ.

30. Bernard was fond of developing the stylistic possibilities of verbs, notably the imperative. See Leclercq, p. 726.

31. See Henri de Lubac, *Exégese médiévale* (Paris, 1964), II.2, pp. 14–31, for other examples of numerology in Hélinand's sermons.

32. I am grateful to Edmé Smits for identifying the sources of the three *exempla* in *Sermon Fifteen*. The story of Bernard and William of Grandselve, not found in the *Chronicon*, appears in some of the *Vitae* of Bernard, for example in PL 185: 363–64, 522. The tale of the nobleman of Macon is from Peter the Venerable's *Liber Miraculorum* II, 1 (PL 189:909ff), and is also in Hélinand's *Chronicon* (PL 212:734Dff and MS Vat. Reg. lat. 535, p. 168). Smits discusses the tale of St Dunstan in his "Vincent of Beauvais: a note on the background of the *Speculum*,

(forthcoming). The story is found in Hélinand's *Chronicon* PL 212:913B–14B) where he expresses his indebtedness to William of Malmesbury, although the tale of St Dunstan, in a more elaborate form, is actually found in Eadmer's *Life of St Dunstan*. Smits suggests that Hélinand took the St Dunstan *exemplum* from his *Chronicon*, using it as a preacher's aid.

33. Brian Patrick McGuire, "The Cistercians and the Rise of the *Exemplum* in Early Thirteenth Century France: A Reevaluation of Paris BN MS lat. 15912," *Classica et Medievalia* 34 (1985) esp. 245–52.

34. See Maur Cocheril, *Dictionnaire des monasteres cisterciens* I, La documentation cistercienne, vol. 18, no. 1 (Belgium, 1976), France, map 4, p. 77.

35. Rouse and Rouse, p. 68.

THE CISTERCIAN AUTHORS
IN THE
REGISTRUM LIBRORUM ANGLIE

David N. Bell

A CCORDING TO RICHARD and Mary Rouse (who know more about the work than anyone else), the *Registrum Librorum Anglie* is

> a location list of selected books available in the cathedrals
> and monasteries of England and southern Scotland, compiled
> by Franciscans probably at Oxford in the second half of the
> 13th century. It survives in three 15th-century manuscripts:
> MS. [Oxford, Bodleian] Tanner 165; Cambridge, Peter-
> house 169; and London, B.L. Royal 3.D.I, a copy of the lat-
> ter. Under the name of each of the some 100 authors is a list
> of his works. Following each work is one or more numbers,
> referring to a key list of 187 ecclesiastical institutions. Thus,
> for example, 1 = Christ Church, Canterbury; 15 = St. Al-
> bans; 82 = Bury St. Edmunds. The location references
> record information gathered by visitation of the houses con-
> cerned and examination of the actual volumes—or at least
> (as first documented by Richard Hunt) by consulting the
> tables of contents at the beginning of the volumes.[1]

The Oxford manuscript, as M. R. James suggested, undoubtedly represents the earlier recension of the work,[2] and it contains, so far as I can see, ninety-eight authors (of which one, Hesychius of Jerusalem, appears anonymously and must be identified with the aid of the second recension of the work in the Cambridge and London manuscripts).[3] A complete list of these authors appears in Appendix II of this present article.[4] Of the libraries recorded, forty-four are Cistercian: Aberconway, Basingwerk, Beaulieu, Biddlesden, Bordesley, Boxley, Buckfast, Buildwas, Coggeshall, Combe, Croxden, Dieulacres, Dore, Dunkeswell, Flaxley, Ford, Fountains, Furness, Garendon, Holme Cultram, Jervaulx, Kirkstead, Louth Park, Margam, Melrose, Merevale, Newbattle, Newminster, Pipewell, Quarr, Revesby, Rievaulx, Robertsbridge, Rufford, Sibton, Stanley, Stoneleigh, Stratford Langthorne, Thame, Tiltey, Valle Crucis, Warden, Waverley, and Woburn.[5] Surviving manuscripts from most of these houses are very few—in some cases, none at all—and the lists and records we can find in other sources are, again, somewhat limited.[6] For many of these monasteries, therefore, the *Registrum* provides us with our only record of the volumes they once contained.

This record, however, is only partial. The *Registrum* is list of *auctoritates*, not a series of library catalogues. "The absence from the *Registrum* of certain books which are in nearly every monastic catalogue suggests how strictly the selection has been limited. Aristotle, Juvenal, Ovid, Sallust, Statius, Terence, and Virgil are not included; while books on grammar, rhetoric, music, logic, astronomy, geometry, and civil and canon law, are not catalogued at all or are few in number."[7] Nevertheless, there is no reason to doubt that the vast majority of what does appear was to be found in the monasteries concerned, and a record of even half-a-dozen texts is half-a-dozen better than none.

Six Cistercians are listed in the *Registrum*: Aelred of Rievaulx, Baldwin of Ford, Bernard of Clairvaux, Geoffrey of Auxerre, Gilbert of Hoyland, and John of Ford. Peter Cantor also appears, but although he died as a member of the order at Longpont in 1197, he cannot meaningfully be called cistercian. Included among these six we also find William of Saint-Thierry masquerading, as usual, as Saint Bernard, and a number of other writers, not of the order of Cîteaux, who also appear pseudonymously.[8] In the following pages the reader will find the entry for each of these writers transcribed from the Oxford manuscript (variants in the London manuscript are listed in Appendix I) and notes on the identification of each work.[9] An excellent, complete, and authoritative edition of the entire text is to be published in due course by Professor Rouse, but given the speed at which publishers move, it may be a convenience to my friends and colleagues to have at least these few items more readily to hand.

NOTES

1. R. H. and M. A. Rouse, "The *Registrum Anglie*: The Franciscan 'Union Catalogue' of British Libraries," in A. C. de la Mare and B. C. Barker-Benfield, *Manuscripts at Oxford: An Exhibition in Memory of R. W. Hunt* (Oxford, 1980), p. 55. The colophon to the work (MS Tanner 165 f. 120b) reads "Explicit Registrum Anglie de Libris Doctorum et Auctorum Veterum. Ihesu Mercy." E. A. Savage, in his "Co-operative Bibliography in the 13th and 15th Centuries", in *idem. Special Librarianship in General Libraries* (London, 1939), pp. 288–92, has argued that the original text was compiled between 1250 and 1296, and this seems to be generally accepted. For further information on the history of the *Registrum*, together with further references, see R. H. Rouse, *Catalogus de Libris Autenticis et Apocrifis: A Critical Edition* (Diss Cornell University, 1963; available from University Microfilms International), pp. viii–xii.

2. See M. R. James, "The List of Libraries Prefixed to the Catalogue of John Boston and Kindred Documents," in C. L. Kingsford *et al.* (edd.), *Collectanea Franciscana* II (Manchester, 1922), p. 38. But the second part of James' argument, that "the *Tabula* [the text in the Cambridge and London manuscripts] includes a few more writers than the *Registrum* [the text in the Oxford manuscript]" (p. 38), is incorrect. See n. 4, below.

3. See Appendix II, n. 4.

4. James, "List of Libraries," p. 38, gives the number of writers in the *Registrum* as "some 70"; Savage, "Co-operative Bibliography," p. 286, as 94; Rouse, *Catalogus*, lii, as 97, which, if we exclude the anonymous Hesychius, is correct.

5. But as James points out ("List of Libraries," p. 47), there are some odd omissions: for example, Byland, Hailes, Kirkstall, Meaux, Netley, Sawley, and Whalley, all of which were houses of major importance.

6. See D. N. Bell, "Lists and Records of Books in English Cistercian Libraries," ASOC, forthcoming in 1987.

7. Savage, "Co-operative Bibliography," p. 294.

8. See Appendix III for an index of these writers.

9. For the identification of the libraries I have followed James, "List of Libraries," pp. 37–60, and the reader must be referred to his study for details and discussion.

ABBREVIATIONS

Bale-Poole	J. Bale, edd. R. L. Poole and M. Bateson, *Index Britanniae Scriptorum* (Oxford, 1902).
Bale	J. Bale, *Scriptorum Illustrium Maioris Brytanniane Catalogus* (Basle, 1557–1559; two parts).
CCCM	*Corpus Christianorum, Continuatio Mediaevalis.*
Catalogus	R. H. Rouse, *Catalogus de Libris Autenticis et Apocrifis: A Critical Edition* (Diss Cornell University, 1963; available from University Microfilms International), cited by a) page number, b) author number, and c) item number. For example, *Catalogus* 95/85/2 = *Catalogus* page 95, author 85

(= Bernard of Clairvaux), item 2 (= *De diligendo Deo*).

Glorieux	P. Glorieux, *Pour revaloriser Migne*, Mélanges de science religieuse IX (Lille, 1952).
LR	D. N. Bell, "Lists and Records of Books in English Cistercian Libraries," ASOC, (forthcoming, 1987).
Landgraf	A. M. Landgraf, *Introduction à l'histoire de la littérature théologique de la scolastique naissante* (Montréal, Paris, 1973).
PL	J. P. Migne (ed.), *Patrologiae Latinae Cursus Completus*
Pits	J. Pits, *Relationum Historicarum de Rebus Anglicis* (Paris, 1619).
RBC	J. Leland, ed. T. Hearne, *De Rebus Britannicis Collectanea*, volume 4 of the second edition (London, 1774).
Registrum	*Registrum Librorum Anglie*, cited by folio number of MS Oxford, Bod. Lib., Tanner 165.
S	F. Stegmüller, *Repertorium Biblicum Medii Aevi* (Madrid, 1940–1980).
SB	J. Leland, ed. A. Hall, *De Scriptoribus Britannicis Commentarii* (London, 1709; two volumes with continuous pagination).
SBOp	J. Leclercq *et al.* (edd.), *Sancti Bernardi Opera* (Rome, 1957–).
SCh	*Sources chrétiennes.*
Schneyer	J. B. Schneyer, *Repertorium der lateinischen Sermones des Mittelalters*, Beiträge zur Geschichte der Philosophie und Theologie des Mittelalters XLIII: 1–9 (Münster i.W., 1969–1980).
Tabula	*Tabula septem custodiarum* (the second recension of the *Registrum*), cited by folio number of MS London, B. L. Royal 3D.i.
VV	M. Bloomfield *et al.*, *Incipits of Latin Works on the Virtues and Vices, 1100–1500 A.D.* (Cambridge, Massachusetts, 1979).

AELRED OF RIEVAULX
TEXT (*Registrum* f. 116b).

Opera Elredi Abbatis

1 *De virginitate beate marie*   43 Woburn
2 *Super cantica*   43 Woburn
3 *De quattuor hominibus*   163 Newminster   120 Valle Crucis
                             125   Coventry   126 Combe
                             116   Shrewsbury
                             123   Croxden   129 Burton
4. *De 12 oneribus in adventu domini*   163 Newminster   105 Margam
5 *Sermones eiusdem*   163 Newminster   160 Jervaulx   114 Bordesley
                     105 Margam
6 *De spirituali amicicia*   43 Woburn   160 Jervaulx
7 *De inclusis*   43 Woburn   124 Merevale
8 *Super illud: Cum factus esset Iesus annorum 12*   160 Jervaulx
9 *Speculum eiusdem*   105 Margam
10 *Dialogus*   105 Margam
11 *De anima*   105 Margam
12 *Epistole*   105 Margam
13 *De vita sancti Edwardi*   43 Woburn

NOTES

See A. Hoste, *Bibliotheca Aelrediana*, Instrumenta Patristica ii (The Hague, 1962).

1. Neither here nor anywhere else are we provided with an *incipit* for this work, but the reference may very well be to the anonymous *Rhythmus de laude virginitatis B.V.M.* which appears in Douai, Bibl. Mun., 392, ff. 94–97b (from Anchin). It has been attributed to Aelred since at least the early seventeenth century, though there is no sound evidence for the ascription, and Hoste has suggested that the work may possibly be the *Rithmus* of Maurice of Rievaulx noted in the Rievaulx catalogue (see further Hoste, pp. 108–109).

2. For the commentary on Canticles attributed to Aelred, see the full discussion, with further bibliographical references, in Hoste, pp. 104–106. The work remains either untraced or unidentified.

3. This work, which also appears as *De tribus hominibus*, is attributed by Bale and his followers to Aelred of Warden, an obscure figure who was supposed to have been abbot of Warden round about 1220 (see Bale, I: 268 [lxxx]; Pits, 294–295 [#318]). But although Hoste, p. 110, accepts (cautiously) this view, I myself do not. I do not believe that Aelred of Warden ever existed, and one can make a tentative case for identifying the mysterious *De iii/iv hominibus* with the *De spiritali amicitia* (see #6 below) of Aelred of Rievaulx. For details of these arguments, however, the reader must be referred to my article, "Aelred of Warden: A Man Who Never Was," to appear in *Studia Monastica* in 1987.

4. *Sermones de oneribus*: see Hoste, pp. 55–61.

5. In the *Catalogus* (68/5/18) these sermons appear as *sermones in causis et synodis* 100; in Bale (I: 209 [xcix]) and Pits (230) as *centum sermones synodales*; and there are similar entries in other early cataloguers. No such collection of one hundred dred sermons has survived and it is impossible to identify them with precision. For another collection of Aelredian sermons which may have disappeared (though this is not certain), see LR s.v. Rievaulx, II, 11.

6. *De spiritali amicitia*: see Hoste, pp. 63–73. See also #3 above and #10 below.

7. *De institutione inclusarum*: see Hoste, pp. 75–80.

8. *De Iesu puero duodenni*: see Hoste, pp. 51–54.

9. *Speculum caritatis*: see Hoste, pp. 41–46.

10. This is a reference either to the *De spiritali amicitia* (#6 above, or to the *abbreviatio* of this work which appears as *Dialogus inter Aelredum et discipulum* (see Hoste, pp. 71–72)), or to the *Dialogus inter hominem et rationem*, recorded by Leland (SB 200) and his followers, which is the same as the *Soliloquiorum lib. i* listed elsewhere (for example, *Catalogus* 67/5/4), and now lost. It is unlikely to be the *Dialogus de anima*, since this is listed separately at Margam immediately below. The *De spiritali amicitia* appears in Walter Daniel's *Vita Aelredi* (F. M. Powicke [ed. and trans.], *Walter Daniel: The Life of Ailred of Rievaulx* [London, 1950] p. 41), early catalogues (for example, Bale-Poole, 11; *Catalogus* 67/5/3), and in certain manuscripts (for example, B.L. Royal 5B.ix, f. 137) as *De spirituali amicitia sub dialogo* or *Dialogus de spirituali amicitia*, but the compiler of the *Catalogus* obviously thought that the work here listed was the volume of *Soliloquies*, not the treatise on spiritual friendship (see *Catalogus* 67/5/4: he has omitted the *Dialogus* and shifted the library number—105 Margam—to the *Soliloquiorum liber*). He was probably correct.

11. *De anima*: see Hoste, pp. 81–82.

12. On Aelred's letters, of which only fragments remain, see Hoste, pp. 137–139. Bale, I: 209 (xcix), provides a slightly longer *incipit* than those listed by Hoste: "In quieto littore degens adhuc."

13. *Vita S. Edwardi Confessoris*: see Hoste, pp. 123–26.

Editions of ##6–9 and 11 will be found in CCCM I (1972) which was published after the appearance of Hoste's *Bibliotheca Aelrediana*.

Note Hoste, pp. 43, 59, 81, 137, records copies of the *Speculum caritatis*, *Sermones de oneribus*, *De anima*, and *Epistolae* at Cirencester. His authority for this is T. W. Williams, "Gloucestershire Mediaeval Libraries," *Transactions of the Bristol and Gloucestershire Archaeological Society* 31 (1908) 94. Williams, however, was incorrect: he misread the 105 (Margam) of the *Catalogus* (pp. 67–68) as 104 (Cirencester), and as a location for these four works, Cirencester must therefore be excluded.

BALDWIN OF FORD

TEXT (*Registrum* f. 118b).

Opera Baldewyni

1 *De commendacione fidei*   105 Margam

2 *De sacramentis*   105 Margam

3 *Sermones eiusdem*   105 Margam

NOTES

See D. N. Bell, "The *Corpus* of the Works of Baldwin of Ford," *Cîteaux* 35 (1984) 215–34.

1. *De commendatione fidei* (PL 204:571–640). I have a critical edition of this interesting treatise in preparation.
2. *De sacramento altaris* (PL 204:641–769; SCh 93–94 [1963]).
3. *Tractatus diversi* (PL 204:403–572; R. Thomas [ed.], *Baudouin de Ford: Traités*, Pain de Cîteaux 35–40 [Chimay, 1973–75]).

For further discussion of all these texts, together with lists of manuscripts both extant and lost, see my "*Corpus* of the Works of Baldwin of Ford," *passim*.

BERNARD OF CLAIRVAUX

This is one of the longer entries in the *Registrum*, being exceeded only by Augustine (3½ entire folios), Jerome (114 entries), Ambrose (82 entries), Hugh of St Victor (70 entries), Isidore of Seville (58 entries), and Bede (56 entries). But of the fifty-one Bernardine entries, only about sixty percent represent authentic works.

TEXT (*Registrum* ff. 115b–16).

Opera Bernardi Abbatis Clarevallensis

1 *Ad Senonensem archiepiscopum de tribus virtutibus*   43 Woburn   13 Waltham
2 *De cohabitacione fratrum*
3 *Quedam questiones eiusdem*
4 *Quomodo imitetur Christus*   154 Melrose
5 *Exhortaciones bernardi*   154 Melrose
6 *Ad David Nepotem suum*   154 Melrose
7 *De operibus 6 dierum*   105 Margam
8 *Ad clericos de conversione*   94 Ford
9 *De colloquio Simonis et Iesu*   94 Ford
10 *Super illud: Intravit Iesus*   63 Crowland
11 *Super illud: Cum esset desponsata*   63 Crowland
12 *Super Ysayam "Memor promissi mei"*   128 Kenilworth   15 St Albans   20 Lewes
13 *De vi verbis domini in cruce*   154 Melrose   114 Bordesley   111 Evesham   105 Margam
14 *Sentencie contemplative eius*   42 Reading   153 Kelso   139 St Mary's York   xx Witham
15 *Planctus eius super morte fratris eius*   153 Kelso

16 *Super epistolam Jacobi*   111 Evesham
17 *Omelie eius*   156 St Andrews   9 Merton   xii Buildwas
18 *Super regulam*   93 Buckfast
19 *Defloraciones eius*   93 Buckfast
20 *Ad romane ecclesie diaconum*   93 Buckfast   126 Combe   20 Lewes
21 *Super cantica canticorum lib. 1 "Vobis fratres alia quam"*   163 New-
            minster   164 Durham   9 Merton   19 Waverley or St
            Paul's 37 Oseney   15 St Alban's   1 Canterbury
            Cathedral   115 Much Wenlock   xii Buildwas
            23 Southwick   25 Quarr   20 Lewes 139 St Mary's
            York   53 Lenton   39 Eynsham   57 Rufford 49 St
            James Northampton   63 Crowland   x Holy Trinity
            Aldgate   104 Cirencester   53 Lenton   46 St Neots
            xxiiii Goldcliff   xxv Bradenstoke   xxvii Farleigh
            97 Athelney   124 Merevale   159 St Agatha's Easby
22 *Sermones eiusdem*   94 Ford   92 Dunkeswell   82 Bury St Edmunds
            9 Merton   108 Gloucester Cathedral
            13 Waltham   15 St Albans
23 *Ad fratres de monte*
24 *Epistole eius lib. 1 "Oportet ad vestrum referre"*   164 Durham
            Cathedral   127 Stoneleigh   126 Combe
            89 Bodmin   19 Waverley or St Paul's   13 Waltham
            xii Buildwas
25 *De consideracione lib. 5*   127 Stoneleigh   94 Ford   92 Dunkeswell
            19 Waverley or St Paul's   13 Waltham
            xii Buildwas   25 Quarr 39 Eynsham
            63 Crowland   46 St Neots   xx Witham
            xxv Bradenstoke   xxvi Stanley
26 *De precepto et dispensacione*   163 Newminster   94 Ford
            92 Dunkeswell   43 Woburn   9 Merton   19
            Waverley or St Paul's 15 St Albans   1 Canterbury
            Cathedral   xii Buildwas   57 Rufford   xxiiii
            Goldcliff   xx Witham   xxv Bradenstoke
27 *Super Missus est lib. 1*   163 Newminster   165 Brinkburne
            9 Merton   19 Waverley or St Paul's   15 St Albans
            1 Canterbury Cathedral   xii Buildwas
            57 Rufford   43 Woburn   46 St Neots
            xxvi Stanley   xxvii Farleigh
28 *De 12 gradibus humilitatis lib. 1 "Locaturus autem de"*
            163 Newminster   94 Ford   92 Dunkeswell
            43 Woburn   8 Battle   9 Merton   19 Waverley or St
            Paul's   13 Waltham   15 St Albans 1 Canterbury

Cathedral   xii Buildwas   57 Rufford   49 St James Northampton

29 *De gratia et libero arbitrio lib. 1 "Loquente me coram"*   94 Ford   93 Buckfast   9 Merton   19 Waverley or St Paul's 13 Waltham   xii Buildwas   25 Quarr   20 Lewes [xii, 25, 20 repeated]   53 Lenton   57 Rufford 63 Crowland   46 St Neots

30 *De diligendo deo lib. 1 "Vultis igitur a me"*   94 Ford   43 Woburn 8 Battle   9 Merton   19 Waverley or St Paul's 108 Gloucester Cathedral   115 Much Wenlock 23 Southwick   xii Buildwas   20 Lewes   53 Lenton 63 Crowland   46 St Neots   xxv Bradenstoke

31 *De amore dei*   94 Ford   89 Bodmin   42 Reading   127 Stoneleigh 80 Holy Trinity Ipswich   13 Waltham 63 Crowland   53 Lenton   xx Witham

32 *De videndo deo*   161 Gisburn

33 *Super psalmum Qui habitat*   161 Gisburn   43 Woburn   57 Rufford

34 *Ad quendam monachum de superfluitatibus*   161 Gisburn 157 Holyrood   43 Woburn   9 Merton   13 Waltham

35 *Ad Eugenium lib. 5 "Subit animum"*   163 Newminster   9 Merton 1 Canterbury Cathedral   xii Buildwas 23 Southwick   20 Lewes   53 Lenton   57 Rufford v Flaxley   xx Witham   xxv Bradenstoke xxiii Muchelney

36 *De virtutibus et viciis*   161 Gisburn   43 Woburn

37 *Vita eiusdem*   163 Newminster   118 Chester Cathedral 127 Stoneleigh   126 Combe   93 Buckfast

38 *Exposiciones ecclesiasticarum regularum*   163 Newminster (end of f. 115b)

39 (f. 116) *Super illud: Dixit Simon Petrus ad Iesum*   163 Newminster 57 Rufford   102 Bristol Cathedral

40 *Epistola ad Robertum monachum fugientem*   163 Newminster 46 St Neots

41 *Ad milites templi*   162 Tynemouth   43 Woburn   1 Canterbury Cathedral   63 Crowland

42 *Ad Willelmum abbatem*   163 Newminster

43 *Sermo in nativitate beate Marie*   163 Newminster

44 *Sermo de Jepte*   166 Hexham

45 *Epitalamium*   166 Hexham

46 *Meditaciones*   127 Stoneleigh   160 Jervaulx   154 Melrose xii Buildwas

47 *De concepcione beate Marie*   126 Combe   154 Melrose

48 *De varietate ordinis monastici*
49 *De caritate ad fratres cartusie "Illa inquam verba"*   161 Gisburn
    63 Crowland
50 *Apolegeticum eius*   94 Ford   89 Bodmin   43 Woburn
    105 Margam   8 Battle   108 Gloucester
    Cathedral   20 Lewes   46 St Neots
51 *De visitacione Infirmorum*   xii Buildwas

NOTES

1. *Epistola 42 ad Henricum archiepiscopum Senonensem/De moribus et officio epis-coporum* (PL 182:809–834; SBOp 7:100–31).

2. ps-Bernard = Hugh of Barzelle, *De cohabitatione fratrum*, ed. J. Morson, "The *De Cohabitatione Fratrum* of Hugh of Barzelle," *Studia Anselmiana* 4 (= *Analecta Monastica* IV) (1957) 119–40. No location for this work is provided in the *Registrum*, but the *Tabula* (see Appendix I, Bernard of Clairvaux, T30 = R2) and the *Catalogus* (97/85/27) record the work at 126 Combe.

3. This work appears in the *Catalogus* (97/85/35) as *Quaestionum quattuor*, but I cannot offer an identification.

4. Although there are certain sermons in which Bernard elaborates on this (for example, *Sermo 4 de duplici adventu*, PL 183:47–50; *Sermo de passione Domini*, PL 183:263–70) and also certain ps-Bernardine works in which it is considered, the title is too vague to permit precise identification. The *De imitatione Christi* of Thomas à Kempis very occasionally appears attributed to Bernard, but the *Registrum* was compiled before Thomas was born. L. Janauschek, *Bibliographia Bernardina* (= *Xenia Bernardina* IV; Vienna, 1891) x #115, reports "in MSS" a *Tractatus quomodo homo compati debeat Christo crucifixo*, but I have not seen a copy.

5. The obvious identification here is Bernard's *De consideratione* (see ##25 and 35 below) which commonly appears in the manuscripts as *Exhortationes* (see SBOp 3:382–91). The situation is confused, however, by the *Catalogus* (97/85/22) which refers to the work as *Exhortationum de passione Christi lib. i* and provides the *incipit* "Dominus noster" (which precludes our identifying it with the *De passione Domini* in PL 183: 263–70). If this *incipit* is correct, then both it and the work remain untraced.

6. So far as I know, Bernard had no *nepos* called David, and the reference is presumably an error for Robert [de Castillione]. *Ad Robertum nepotem suum* is the well-known *Epistola 1* (PL 182:67–79; SBOp 7:1–11).

7. ps-Bernard = Arnold of Bonneval, *De operibus sex dierum* (S 2251; VV 3690; PL 189:1515–70). Arnold's *De sex* (PL: *septem) verbis Domini in cruce* (S 2254; PL 189:1677–726) is also listed s.v. Bernard (see #13 below), and he himself appears twice in the *Registrum*, once as Abbot Arnulph and once as Ernaldus. As Arnulph, Arnold was sometimes confused with Arnulph of Rochester, and the *De sacramento altaris* written by the latter (see, for example, London, B.L. Royal 7C.viii, ff. 100 foll.) is sometimes attributed incorrectly to the former (as in, for example, the *Catalogus* 76/31/2, or C. H. Talbot, "A List of Cistercian Manuscripts in Great Britain," *Trad.* 8 [1952] 407). Under *Opera Arnulphi Abbatis* (*Registrum* f. 116) we find the following works:

    1 *De operibus sex dierum*   94 Ford
    2 *De vi verbis domini in cruce*   94 Ford

And under *Opera Ernald* (*Registrum* f. 119) the following:

1 *De vi verbis Christi in cruce*   43 Woburn
2 *De cardinalibus virtutibus*   43 Woburn
3 *De vi diebus*   43 Woburn

The *De cardinalibus virtutibus* is presumably the *De cardinalibus operibus Christi* (PL 189:1609–78). We might also note that a treatise *De operibus sex dierum* also appears in the *Registrum* f. 110b s.v. Isidore of Seville with a location at Bodmin, but there is no evidence to indicate that it is the same work.

8. *De conversione* (VV 0195; PL 182:833–56; SBOp 4:69–116).

9. ps-Bernard = Geoffrey of Auxerre, *Declamationes de colloquio Simonis cum Jesu* (PL 184:435–76). This work is listed again at #39 below. For some brief but important notes on the dating, nature, and Bernardine attribution of this interesting text, see J. Leclercq, *Recueil d'études sur saint Bernard et ses écrits* (Rome, 1962) 1:16–20 (this paper, "Saint Bernard et ses secrétaires," originally appeared in *Revue Bénédictine* 61 [1951] 208–229).

10. *Sermo in assumptione B.V.M.* (PL 184:1001–1010). For the attribution to Bernard rather than ps-Bernard, see J. Leclercq, "Sermon pour l'Assomption restitué à saint Bernard," RTAM 20 (1953) 5–12.

11. The sermon "Cum esset desponsata" (Mt 1:18) attributed to Bernard has not, so far as I know, been printed, but for an example see Oxford, Bod. Lib., Fairfax 17 (3897) (from Louth Park) ff. 33–38, *inc.* "Propositum nobis est."

12. The *incipit* is that of Book II of the *De consideratione* (PL 182:741C), the *Apologia super consumptionem Ierosolymitarum*, but there seems no special reason why it should be titled *Super Ysayam* (provided, of course, that the compilers of the *Registrum* read the word correctly, which they did not always do).

13. ps-Bernard = Arnold of Bonneval: see #7 above.

14. Possibly the ps-Bernardine *Liber sententiarum* printed in PL 184:1135–56, but there were certainly other similar collections of sententiae in circulation (cf. PL 183:1197–204).

15. *Planctus super morte[m] [Girardi] fratris* = *Sermo 26 in Cantica* (PL 183:903–12; SBOp 1:169–81).

16. There is no other record of any such commentary, and whatever the compilers of the *Registrum* saw, it was not by Bernard of Clairvaux.

17. The *Registrum* does not specify which sermons are included here, but there is a surviving manuscript from Buildwas which could well be that recorded by the compilers. It is Oxford, Balliol College 150, an early thirteenth-century manuscript containing 173 sermons (primarily *de tempore*, but including a number *de diversis* and a few others which do not appear in the PL collection): for details, see R.A.B. Mynors, *Catalogue of the Manuscripts of Balliol College, Oxford* (Oxford, 1963), pp. 135–36.

18. The *Super regulam* is surely the *De praecepto et dispensatione* recorded below at #26. See *De praec.* I, i, PL 182:861D: "Prima igitur quaestio circa Regulam nostram versatur...."

19. See, for example, M. Bernards, "Flores Sancti Bernardi," in J. Lortz (ed.), *Bernhard von Clairvaux: Mönch und Mystiker* (Wiesbaden, 1955), pp. 192–201. But since there were numerous such compilations in circulation (S 1731.1, though very important, is only one of many), we cannot specify which is recorded here.

20. Possibly, but not certainly, *Epistola 105 ad Romanum Romanae curiae/ecclesiae subdiaconum* (PL 182:240–41; SBOp 7:264–65).

21. *Sermones in Cantica* (S 1721; PL 183:785–1198; SBOp 1–2).

22. Sermons, otherwise unidentified. See #17 above.

23. ps-Bernard = William of St Thierry, *Epistola ad fratres de Monte-Dei* (PL 184:307–354; SCh 223 [1975]). No locations are recorded for this work in either the *Registrum* or the *Tabula*, but the *Catalogus* (96/85/17) s.v. Bernard of Clairvaux notes copies at Bury St Edmunds, Crowland, and Ramsey. In *ibid.* 276/632/2, s.v. Wilhelmus monachus et abbas S. Theodorici, no locations are given.

The pseudonymous third book of the work (PL 184:353–64) is correctly listed in the *Catalogus* (63/3/18) under Anselm of Canterbury, with copies at Norwich and Colchester St John's.

24. The *incipit* is that of *Epistola 190 contra quaedam capitula errorum Abaelardi* (PL 182:1053–72).

25. *De consideratione* (VV 5830; PL 182:727–808; SBOp 3:393–493). See also #35 below.

26. *De praecepto et dispensatione* (VV 4330; PL 182:859–94; SBOp 3: 253–94). See also #18 above.

27. *Homiliae iv super "Missus est"/In laudibus Virginis matris* (S 1726; PL 183: 55–88; SBOp 4:13–58).

28. *De gradibus humilitatis [et superbiae]* (VV 5208; PL 182:941–72; SBOp 3: 15–59).

29. *De gratia et libero arbitrio* (PL 182:1001–1030; SBOp 3:165–203).

30. *De diligendo Deo* (PL 182:973–1000; SBOp 3:119–54).

31. ps-Bernard, *De amore Dei* = William of St Thierry, *De contemplando Deo* (PL 184:365–80; SCh 61 [bis] [1968]) and *De natura et dignitate amoris* (PL 184: 379–408; the best edition at present available is R. Thomas [ed. and trans.], *Guillaume de S. Thierry: Nature et dignité de l'amour*, Pain de Cîteaux 24 [Chambarand 1965], but Fr. Stanley Ceglar has completed a superb critical edition which is to be published shortly). The *Catalogus* (95/85/3), but not the *Registrum* or the *Tabula*, provides an *incipit* and *explicit* for this work: "Venite ... benedicimus," which indicates only the *De contemplando Deo* (Venite = PL 184:367A; benedicimus = PL 184:380B), but the two treatises are most commonly found together.

32. *De videndo Deo* must surely be *Sermo 31 in Cantica, de excellentia divinae visionis*, and other similar descriptions (PL 182:940–45; SBOp 1:219–26).

33. *Super psalmum xc "Qui habitat"* (PL 183:185–254; SBOp 4:383–492).

34. *Ad quendam monachum de superfluitatibus* = *Apologia, cap.* viii (or, more rarely, vii) –xiii (PL 182:908–918; SBOp 3:95–108).

35. *De consideratione*: see #25 above. The *incipit* is PL 182:727A.

36. This title is as vague as it is common, and there are so many possibilities that speculation is of little avail.

37. Almost certainly the *Vita prima s. Bernardi* by William of St Thierry, Arnold of Bonneval, and Geoffrey of Auxerre (*Bibliotheca Hagiographica Latina* 1211 foll.).

38. I cannot identify this work.

39. ps-Bernard = Geoffrey of Auxerre, *Declamationes*, recorded at #9 above.

40. Presumably *Epistola 1 ad Robertum* (see #6 above), who "fled" from the Cistercians to the Cluniacs.

41. *De laude novae militiae* (PL 182:921–40; SBOp 3:213–39).

42. *Ad Willelmum abbatem* = the *Apologia*, recorded above at #34 and below at ##48 and 50 (PL 182:895–918; SBOp 3:81–108).

43. *Sermo in nativitate B.V.M./De aquaeductu* (PL 183:437–48; SBOp 5:275–88).

44. There is no authentic sermon of Bernard *de Jepte*, and the reference may possibly be to the *Sermo de filia Jephthae* of ps-Hugh of St Victor in PL 177:323–24 (see R. Goy, *Die Überlieferung der Werke Hugos von St. Viktor* [Stuttgart, 1976], p. 491).

45. This may possibly refer to one of the ps-Bernardine poems, but I cannot identify it with any certainty. *Epithalamium* is also one of the titles of Origen's commentary on Canticles (S 6200; tr. Rufinus), which is recorded in the *Registrum* on f. 111b, but I have never seen the work attributed to Bernard of Clairvaux.

46. The very popular *Meditationes piisimae* (VV 3126; PL 184:485–508). The *incipit*, "Multi," is provided by the *Catalogus* (97/85/21).

47. *De conceptione B.V.M.* = *Epistola 174* (PL 182:332–36; SBOp 7:388–92).

48. *De [discreta] varietate ordinis monastici* = the *Apologia*, already recorded at #42 above and again at #50 below.

49. So far as I know, this sermon, either by or attributed to Bernard, remains unpublished. For an example, see Oxford, Bod. Lib., Bodley 96 (1919) (from Peterborough) ff. 193b–196. For *illa inquam verba* in the *Registrum*, the *Tabula* (f. 107b) has (incorrectly) *illa inquam vera.*

50. The *Apologia* already noted above at ##42 and 48.

51. Presumably ps-Bernard/ps-Augustine (but most probably by Baudri de Bourgueil: see Glorieux, 30), *De visitatione infirmorum* (PL 40:1147–58). See C. de Visch, *Bibliotheca Scriptorum Sacri Ordinis Cisterciensis* (Cologne, 1656), p. 42: "In Monasterio Parcensi, Ord. Praemonstrat. iuxta Lovanium, servatur liber huius tituli: Sancti Bernardi *Tractatus de visitatione infirmi.* Teste Sandero in Bibliotheca M.S. Belgica." The same title appears again in the *Registrum* s.v. Augustine (f. 104), together with the *incipit* "Visitacionis gratia" (PL 40:1147) and a location at Jervaulx.

GEOFFREY OF AUXERRE

Geoffrey of Auxerre appears twice in the *Registrum*, once as Galfridus and once as ps-Bernard of Clairvaux.

TEXT (*Registrum* f. 118).

Opera Galfridi

1 *Super matheum*   165 Brinkburne   153 Kelso   115 Much Wenlock
2 *Super apocalipsim*   105 Margam
3 *Super cantica canticorum*   105 Margam

NOTES

See J. Leclercq, "Les écrits de Geoffroy d'Auxerre," R Ben. 62 (1952) 274–91.

1. The commentary on Matthew is not by Geoffrey of Auxerre, but as is clear from the *incipit* provided in the *Catalogus* (132/216/3), "Dominus ac . . . personam Christi," it is the well-known commentary by Geoffrey Babio (S 2604). It also appears attributed to Anselm of Laon (as in PL 162:1228–1500), Anselm of Canterbury, and Alvarus.

2. S 2436; ed. F. Gastaldelli, *Goffredo di Auxerre: Super Apocalypsim*, Temi e Testi 17 (Rome, 1970).

3. S 2414; ed. F. Gastaldelli, *Goffredo di Auxerre: Expositio in Cantica Canticorum*, Temi e Testi 19–20 (Rome, 1974).

The *Declamationes de colloquio Simonis cum Jesu* (PL 184:435–76) is recorded in the *Registrum* s.v. Bernard of Clairvaux ##9 and 39, with locations at Ford, Newminster, Rufford, and Bristol Cathedral; and the *Vita S. Bernardi*, to which Geoffrey contributed Bks. III–V, s.v. Bernard of Clairvaux #37, with locations at Newminster, Chester Cathedral, Stoneleigh, Combe, and Buckfast.

GILBERT OF HOYLAND

Of the nine works listed, only one (#9) is unquestionably an authentic work of Gilbert of Hoyland, but confusion among the various Gilberts was very common.

TEXT (*Registrum* f. 118).

Opera Gilberti

1 *Sentencie eius*   xii Buildwas
2 *Super epistolas Pauli*   163 Newminster   19 Waverley or St Paul's
3 *Super psalterium*   163 Newminster 160 Jervaulx 127 Stoneleigh
        124 Merevale   19 Waverley or St Paul's   15 St
        Albans 104 Cirencester 20 Lewes 130 Lincoln
        Cathedral 22 Chichester Cathedral
4 *Super matheum*   163 Newminster
5 *Super apocalipsim*   163 Newminster
6 *De casu diaboli*   165 Brinkburne
7 *De anima*   165 Brinkburne
8 *De disputacione christiani et gentilis*   165 Brinkburne
9 *Super cantica canticorum*   94 Ford 43 Woburn 114 Bordesley
        124 Merevale 115 Much Wenlock xii Buildwas
        20 Lewes 139 St Mary's York 39 Eynsham
        57 Rufford

NOTES

See E. Mikkers, "De Vita et Operibus Gilberti de Hoylandia," *Cîteaux* 14 (1963) 33–43, 265–79.

1. This is an interesting entry. It does not refer to the *Theologicae conciones* seen by Leland at Byland (SB 291), for despite the difference in title, these refer to the Byland copy of the sermons on Canticles reported by Leland in RBC 38 (see LR, s.v. Byland I, 4). One text comes immediately to mind: the *Sentences* of Gilbert de la Porrée, admirably edited by N. M. Häring, "Die Sententiae magistri Gisleberti episcopi Pictavensis," in AHDL 45 (1978) 83–180 and 46 (1979) 45–105 (there seem to be only two surviving manuscripts providing two different recensions of the same *lectura*). But if indeed this is what is recorded at Buildwas, it is a rare text to find in an English monastery. The *Sententiae divinitatis* of the school of Gilbert de la Porrée (See Landgraf, pp. 112–113) cannot, I think, be considered. There is no evidence that they were ever attributed directly to Gilbert, and both surviving manuscripts (Munich, Clm 16063 [whole manuscript] and Clm 18918 ff. 81–108) are anonymous.

2. ps-Gilbert of Hoyland = Gilbert de la Porrée, *Commentary on the Pauline epistles* (S 2497 = S 2515–2528). See Mikkers, p. 276; Landgraf, pp. 109–110.

3. ps-Gilbert of Hoyland = Gilbert de la Porrée, *Commentary on Psalms* (S 2495 = S 2511). See Mikkers, p. 276; Landgraf, p. 108.

4. This may possibly be the work which survives in Oxford, Bod. Lib., Bodley 87 (1872) ff. 89b–149b. The prologue is titled "Incipit prologus Gileberti abbatis super Evangelium secundum Matheum", *inc.* "Lusisti utiliter ubertimque in ista iam pridem materia," and this is followed by a series of thirty-seven sermons on Matthew which constitute the exposition. So far as I know, the first to suggest that this might be Gilbert's "lost" commentary was Thomas Tanner (see his *Bibliotheca Britannico-Hibernica*, ed. D. Wilkins [London, 1747], p. 317), and the same suggestion appears in Stegmüller (supplement) 2492.

5. On this commentary, which may possibly have been a work of Gilbert de la Porrée (see S 2498, 2529), see Mikkers, p. 276.

6–8. These three works are all by Gilbert Crispin, not Gilbert of Hoyland; see J. A. Robinson, *Gilbert Crispin, Abbot of Westminster: A Study of the Abbey Under Norman Rule* (Cambridge, 1911), Chapter 5, especially pp. 72–73 (##6, 7) and 73–76 (#8). With regard to #8, it should be noted that the text of the *Registrum* is quite clear: it is not the well-known dispute between a Christian and a Jew which is listed here, but that between a Christian and a Gentile. By the time of the *Catalogus* (131/214/1), the latter had been transformed into the former, but it is not the reading of the *Registrum*.

9. Gilbert of Hoyland's authentic *Commentary/Homilies on Canticles* (S 2493); see Mikkers, pp. 266–72.

JOHN OF FORD

TEXT (*Registrum* f. 117).

Opera Johannis

1 *Super cantica canticorum*   94 Ford
2 *Super Jeremiam*   94 Ford
3 *Omelie eius*   94 Ford

NOTES

1. John's *Commentary/Homilies on Canticles* (S 4467; Schneyer, 3:471–80), edited by E. Mikkers and H. Costello in CCCM XVII–XVIII (1970). Leland also saw this work at Ford (see RBC 150 and SB 231), and there is but one surviving manuscript of unknown provenance: Oxford, Balliol College 24, ff. 1–264.

2. This commentary on Jeremiah was also seen at Ford by Leland (RBC 150; SB 231), and has been identified with a (lost) commentary on Lamentations by a Benedictine of Norwich, John de Fordeham (S 4470; Bale-Poole, 203). But as J. C. Russell, *Dictionary of Writers of 13th Century England* (New York, 1936), p. 62, remarks: "Ford is not Fordeham, and the similarity of name hardly justified Bale in changing 'Benedictinus' to 'Cisterciensis.'" I would assume, therefore, that John wrote a commentary on Jeremiah and that it, like so much else, has not survived.

3. These *Omelie* may well be the same as the *Omelie super cantica* noted at #1 above. On the other hand, the single sermon which survives in Oxford, Bod. Lib., Bodley 705 (2564) ff. 76–80, "Sermo Johannis monachi de Forda in do-

minica in Ramis Palmarum" (ed. by H. Talbot, "Un sermon inédit de Jean de Ford," Coll. 7 [1940–45] 36–45; CCCM XVIII: 812–21) is unquestionably all that remains of what was once a collection of *sermones de tempore*, and it may well have been such a collection, now regrettably lost, which is recorded here. Bale's record of "Ioannes abbas de Forda, sermones de triplici cruce, *inc.* 'Vetus homo noster simul crucifixus est'" (Bale-Poole, 203) is most probably erroneous; these sermons are almost certainly by Baldwin of Ford, John's illustrious predecessor, and they survive as Baldwin's *Tractatus XI* (PL 204:517–30; Thomas [see Baldwin of Ford, #3 above] 39:54–111). The manuscript which contained them, however ("ex collegio corporis Christi, Oxon." [Bale-Poole, 203]), has disappeared.

APPENDIX I

Correspondences Between the Registrum and the Tabula

In the following lists, R = *Registrum* (Oxford, Bod. Lib., Tanner 165) and T = *Tabula* (London, B.L., Royal 3D.i). In neither text are the items numbered, but there is little difficulty in counting them in T, and no difficulty at all in R.

AELRED OF RIEVAULX (*Registrum* f. 116b; *Tabula* f. 111 col. 2)

R1 = T1
R2 = T2
R3 = T3　T adds 127 Stoneleigh, 124 Merevale; T omits 120 Valle
　　　　　Crucis, 126 Combe, 116 Shrewsbury, 123 Croxden
R4 = T4
R5 = T10
R6 = T5　T adds 163 Newminster
R7 = T6
R8 = T7
R9 = T8
R10 = T9
R11 = T11
R12 = T12
R13 = T13

BALDWIN OF FORD (*Registrum* f. 118b; *Tabula* f. 107 col. 2)

R1 = T1
R2 = T3
R3 = T2

BERNARD OF CLAIRVAUX (*Registrum* ff. 115b–116;
Tabula f. 107b col. 1–2)

R1 = T29
R2 = T30 T adds 126 Combe
R3 = T31 T adds 156 St Andrews
R4 = T32
R5 = T33
R6 = T23
R7 = T24
R8 = T25
R9 = T26 T adds 163 Newminster, 57 Rufford, 102 Bristol
Cathedral (these three locations are taken from R39: see
note below)
R10 = T27
R11 = T28
R12 = T12 T gives no locations for this work
R13 = T13 T adds 103 Malmesbury, 128 Kenilworth, 15 St Albans,
20 Lewes, xx Witham, xxvi Stanley; T omits
105 Margam
R14 = T14 T adds 123 Croxden
R15 = T15
R16 = T16
R17 = T17
R18 = T18
R19 = T19
R20 = T20 T omits 93 Buckfast
R21 = T1   T adds 13 Waltham, xx Witham, xxvi Stanley, 159 St
Agatha's Easby, 128 Kenilworth, 122 Dieulacres, 114
Bordesley, 154 Melrose, 153 Kelso; T omits 53 Lenton
R22 = T2 T adds 89 Bodmin, 29 Christchurch Twynham, xii
Buildwas, 25 Quarr, 139 York St Mary's, 55
Thurgarton, 63 Crowland, 53 Lenton, 46 St Neots
R23 = T46
R24 = T3 T adds 9 Merton, 8 Battle, 23 Southwick, 25 Quarr,
37 Oseney, 57 Rufford, 46 St Neots, xxiiii Goldcliff; T
omits 89 Bodmin
R25 = T4 T omits xx Witham, xxv Bradenstoke, xxvi Stanley
R26 = T5 T writes 13 Waltham for 15 St Albans; T omits xxiiii
Goldcliff
R27 = T6 T writes 3 Canterbury, St Gregory's for 1 Canterbury
Cathedral, and 49 St James Northampton for 43
Woburn; T omits xxvii Farleigh

R28 = T7   T adds 63 Crowland, 46 St Neots
R29 = T8   T writes 43 Woburn for 63 Crowland; T adds 16
           Robertsbridge
R30 = T9   T omits xii Buildwas
R31 is omitted in T
R32 = T10
R33 = T21 T omits 57 Rufford
R34 is omitted in T
R35 is omitted in T
R36 is omitted in T
R37 = T22
R38 = T34
R39 is omitted in T and the library locations combined with R9
R40 = T35
R41 = T36 T adds 46 St Neots
R42 = T37
R43 = T38 T38 appears twice
R44 = T39
R45 = T40
R46 = T41
R47 = T42   T adds 108 Gloucester Cathedral; T omits 154 Melrose
R48 = T43   T adds 126 Combe, 154 Melrose
R49 = T44
R50 = T11   T writes 99 Totnes for 89 Bodmin
R51 = T45   T adds 94 Ford, 89 Bodmin

Note:

T omits R31 *De amore Dei*, R34 *De superfluitatibus*, R35 *De considera-*
tione, R 36 *De virtutibus et vitiis*, and combines together R9 and R 39,
the *De colloquio Simonis et Iesu* of Geoffrey of Auxerre.

GEOFFREY OF AUXERRE (*Registrum* f. 118; *Tabula* f. 111 col. 2)

R1 = T1
R2 = T2
R3 = T3

GILBERT OF HOYLAND (*Registrum* f. 118; *Tabula* f. 111b col. 1)

R1 = T1
R2 = T2
R3 = T3
R4 = T4

R5 = T5
R6 = T6
R7 = T7
R8 = T8
R9 = T9   T adds x (= 10) Holy Trinity, Aldgate; T omits 124
          Merevale, 139 York St Mary's

JOHN OF FORD (*Registrum* f. 117; *Tabula* f. 233 col. 1)

R1 = T1
R2 = T2
R3 = T3

APPENDIX II

Alphabetical Index of Authors in the Registrum

In the following index, each name is followed by a number in parenthesis indicating where the author appears in the *Registrum* list (Augustine is Author #1; Richard of St Victor is #98) and the folio of Oxford, Bod. Lib., Tanner 165 on which his works are recorded.

Aelred of Rievaulx (39)   116b
Albertus Magnus (61)   118b
Albinus (26)   114 (= Alcuin)
Alcuin (38)   116b (= Albinus)
Alexander Neckham (42)   117
Ambrose of Milan (3)   106b–107b
Andrew of St Victor (43)   117
Angelomus of Luxeuil (45)   117
Anselm of Canterbury (33)   115a–b
Arnold of Bonneval (69, as Ernaldus)   119 (= Arnulf)
Arnold of Bonneval (36, as Arnulph)   116 (= Ernaldus)
Athanasius of Alexandria (17)   112b–13
Augustine of Hippo (1)   103–106b
Avicenna (88)   119b
Bachiarius (75)   119
Baldwin of Ford (64)   118b
Basil the Great (15)   112b
Bede (7)   109b–110
Berengaudus (49)   117b
Bernard of Clairvaux (34)   115b–16
Boethius (58)   118b
Bruno[1] (63)   118b
Brutus (89)   119b

Caesarius of Arles (20)   113
Cassian: see John Cassian
Cassiodorus (14)   112a–b
Cicero (= Tullius) (84)   119a–b
Claudius of Turin (68)   119
Cyprian of Carthage (21)   113a–b
Didymus of Alexandria (16)   112b
ps-Dionysius the Areopagite (5)   108
Ephraem Syrus/Ephraem Latinus (76)   119
Eusebius[2] (13)   112
Eutropius (40)   116b
Fulgentius of Ruspe (25)   114
Gennadius of Marseilles (12)   112
Geoffrey of Auxerre (55)   118
Gilbert[3] (56)   118
Gregory the Great (2)   106b
Gregory of Nazianzus (18)   113
Gregory of Nyssa (19)   113
Haymo (mainly Haymo of Auxerre) (27)   114a–b
Hegesippus (78)   119
Hesychius of Jerusalem[4] (67)   119
Hilary of Poitiers[5] (4)   107b–108
Hugh of St Victor (97)   119b–20b
Innocent III (30)   114b
Isidore of Seville (8)   110a–b
Ivo of Chartres (35)   116
Jerome (6)   108–109b
John Beleth (73)   119
John Cassian (32)   114b–15
John Chrysostom (9)   110b–11
John of Ford (44)   117
Jordanes (82)   119
Josephus (31)   114b
Julianus Pomerius[6] (65)   118b
Julian of Toledo[7] (70)   119
Lanfranc of Canterbury (51)   117b
Leo the Great (28)   114b
Macrobius (90)   119b
Martin of Braga (41, as Martin)   117
Martin of Braga (47, as Maximus[8])   117b
Maximus of Turin (48)   117b
Methodius of Olympus (77)   119

Odo[9] (50)   117b
Origen (10)   111a–b
Orosius (79)   119
Palladius[10] (93)   119b
Papias (92)   119b
Patrick of Dublin (72)   119
Paschasius Radbertus (22)   113b
Peter Alphonsus (52)   117b
Peter Babilon[11] (66)   119
Peter of Blois (46)   117
Peter Cantor (53)   118
Peter Comestor (60)   118b
Peter Damian (74)   119
Peter of Poitiers[12] (59)   118b
Pliny (the Elder and the Younger) (91)   119b
Pompeius Festus (86)   119b
Prosper of Aquitaine (23)   113b
Prudentius (29)   114b
Quintilian (85)   119b
Rabanus Maurus (11)   111b–12
Ralph of Flaix (37)   116b
Rases[13] (96)   119b
Richard of St Victor (98)   120b
Robert[14] (54)   118
Rufinus of Aquileia (24)   114
Sedulius (94)   119b
Seneca (83)   119
Smaragdus[15] (81)   119
Stephen Langton (57)   118b
Tyconius (80)   119
Vegetius (95)   119b
Vigilius of Thapsus[16] (71)   119
Vitruvius[17] (87)   119b
Zacharias Chrysopolitanus (62)   118b

NOTES

1. A combination of Bruno of Asti/Segni and ps-Bruno the Carthusian.
2. Primarily a combination of Eusebius of Caesarea and ps-Eusebius of Emesa.
3. A combination of Gilbert de la Porrée, Gilbert of Hoyland, ps-Gilbert of Hoyland, and Gilbert Crispin.
4. This author is not listed by name in the *Registrum* and the entry on f. 119 line 3 reads simply *Super leviticum*. Cambridge, Peterhouse 169 and B.L. Royal 3D.i, however, list the work under *Opera Esicii*, and this serves to identify it as the Leviticus commentary of Hesychius of Jerusalem (S 3290).
5. On my microfilm of Tanner 165 Hilary's name is illegible, but we may reconstruct it from Peterhouse 169 and Royal 3D.i.
6. A combination of Julianus Pomerius (*De vita contemplativa* [E. Dekkers, *Clavis Patrum Latinorum* (*Sacris Eruditi* III, 1961) #998], which is also listed s.v. Prosper of Aquitaine) and Julian of Toledo (*De origine mortis humane = Prognosticon futuri saeculi* [*Clavis* #1258] lib. 1, which is also listed s.v. Julian of Toledo).
7. The *Prognosticon futuri saeculi* which is also listed s.v. Julianus Pomerius: see n. 6 above.
8. With the addition of a single entry—*Sentencie eius*—the *Opera Maximi* at the top of f. 117b simply reproduces the *Opera Martini* at the top of f. 117. The next Maximus in the *Registrum*—f. 117b lines 8–9—is Maximus of Turin.
9. A combination of Odo of Canterbury, Odo of Cheriton, Odo of Cluny, Odo of Morimond, and Ado of Vienne.
10. The Palladius of the *De agricultura*, not the Palladius of the *Lausiac History*.
11. A combination of the *De missa* of the obscure writer Peter Babilon or Babio (see Pits, 406, [#462]) and the widely-distributed sermon-collection, "Dicite pusillanimes" (Is 35:4), of Geoffrey Babilon/Babion/Babio.
12. None of the three works listed is actually by this author. Two of them—commentaries on Boethius' *De Trinitate* and *De hebdomadibus*—are by Gilbert of Poitiers, and the other—the *Sic et Non*—is by Peter Abailard.
13. Rases (Muhammad ibn Zakariyā al-Rāzī) is not listed by name, but appears as one of his works: the Amasor/Almansoris/Kitāb al-Mansūrī.
14. A collection of biblical commentaries and sermons by an inextricable combination of Roberts: possibly Robert Grosseteste, Robert Pullus, Robert of Bridlington, Robert of Sorbonne, Robert of Cricklade, and Robert of Tombelaine. It is impossible to determine which was written by whom.
15. Smaragdus is not listed by name, but appears as his *Diadema monachorum* (PL 102:593–690).
16. Vigilius appears as Virgilius papa.
17. Vitruvius appears as Victrinius.

APPENDIX III

Index of Authors Appearing Pseudonymously in This Article

Aelred of Warden   See Aelred of Rievaulx, 3
Alvarus   See Geoffrey of Auxerre, 1

Memorial University of Newfoundland

KNIGHTS AND THE FOUNDATION
OF CISTERCIAN HOUSES
IN BURGUNDY

Constance B. Bouchard

WHEN KNIGHTS FIRST APPEARED in France in the late tenth century, it was as armed dependents of noble lords. During the next two centuries, however, they gradually improved their position, from being retainers to being considered members of the lower aristocracy, and finally, in the thirteenth century, to being accepted without question as members of the noble social group.[1] The rise of the knights was accomplished in several ways: through marriages with the daughters of the longer-established aristocracy, through careful accumulation of wealth, and through emulation of the more powerful nobles. This emulation included such things as wearing rich clothing and building miniature towers on the corners of their houses to make them look like tiny castles, as Georges Duby has noted.[2] But this emulation also included, as I shall discuss here, trying to become founders and patrons of monasticism, an attribute which had been identified with great secular wealth since at least the ninth century.

Knights first began to found monasteries in the twelfth century, at a time when they had reached the lower fringes of the aristocracy but were not yet considered the social equals of noble lords. The knights who first became monastic patrons at this time, it must immediately be noted, did not patronize the same houses as the more powerful nobles. Instead, they gave their attention in particular to houses of the new Cistercian order. In the tenth and eleventh centuries, the foundation of a new monastery, or the re-foundation of a long-ruined house, had generally been carried out by a duke, count, or viscount, or at any rate by someone no less

powerful than a castellan. But the Cistercian houses of the twelfth
century were generally founded by knights and petty landowners,
at any rate by someone no more powerful than a castellan. I shall
illustrate this process using examples from the duchy of Burgundy,
the heart of the Cistercian order.[3]

In the tenth and eleventh centuries in Burgundy, monasteries
were generally founded or refounded by a single very powerful individual, acting with his immediate family. The monastery of
Cluny, for example, was founded in 909 by William I, duke of
Aquitaine, and his wife Angilberga, who was sister of the emperor
Louis the Blind. Paray-le-monial, a house that later became part of
the Cluniac order, was founded around 970 by Lambert, first of
the hereditary counts of Chalon. St -Bénigne of Dijon, an old
house which had been sacked by the Vikings, was refounded in 990
by a small group of powerful relatives: Duke Henry of Burgundy,
who was Hugh Capet's brother, along with the duke's step-son,
Count Otto-William, and Otto-William's brother-in-law, Bishop
Bruno of Langres. And, at the very end of the eleventh century,
the long-deserted abbey of St -Étienne of Nevers was rebuilt and
refounded by Count William of Nevers, great-grand-son of Otto-
William.[4]

In all these cases, the dukes and counts endowed their new foundations with generous gifts, usually of arable land, often the rights
to certain pastures and tolls, and sometimes even elaborate and
costly bowls and cups for use in the liturgy, such as those Count
William of Nevers gave St -Étienne. The foundation, dedication,
and endowment of such houses was always recorded in formal
foundation charters, drawn up at the time or very shortly thereafter. Such a charter would be quite long and elaborate, detailing
how the lay donor had determind to found or refound the monastery, exactly what he gave the monks, the monastic rule or order
they should follow, some comments on how future abbots would
be chosen, and lists of the donor's relatives who agreed to the
foundation and of his neighbors who witnessed. The diocesan
bishop and heads of other monasteries might also witness.

But both the foundation and the formal record of the foundation of the twenty Cistercian houses in Burgundy in the twelfth
century were very different. Rather than being the refoundation of
an old, long-ruined monastery, these houses were either completely

new foundations or else the establishment of the Cistercian order at locations which had supported cells of hermits for several years. Rather than being founded by a single powerful lord and his family, the Cistercian houses were founded by a large number of unrelated small landowners, primarily knights, though sometimes the group was headed by a castellan. Although Cîteaux's principal founder was the viscount of Beaune, and her first daughter, La Ferté, was founded by the count of Chalon, all subsequent Cistercian houses in Burgundy were founded by much less powerful men. Pontigny was founded by small landowners of the Auxerrois, Clairvaux by a number of knights and petty aristocrats of the region, and Morimond by the lord of Aigremont and his knights.[5] The rest of the Cistercian houses in the duchy were similarly founded on land given by a large number of individuals, all petty allodists.

An illustrative example is the foundation of Auberive in 1135. There are forty-eight separate donors listed in the charter comfirming the foundation of this house. Each of these men gave a small piece of property, "whatever he owned in that area," as it was later recorded. These small pieces of property, taken together, provided enough for the establishment of the monks.[6] The property involved was generally uncultivated land or waste, often indeed, as at Cîteaux, Clairvaux, and La Ferté, rather marshy land that the monks had to drain before they could begin cultivation. Although none of the donors owned enough land, even deserted or marshy land, to have founded a monastery by himself, their small holdings, taken together, provided enough for the monks to live on.

In contrast to the pattern for houses established earlier, these foundations by many petty aristocrats were usually not recorded at the time in a formal foundation charter. Neither Cîteaux herself nor any of the Burgundian Cistercian houses founded in the first two generations of the order's existence have a foundation charter drawn up at the time—although, rather amusingly, the monks of Clairvaux, when compiling their cartulary over a century after the house's foundation, found it necessary to forge a "foundation charter" which said that the house was founded by the count of Champagne.[7] Instead, the first written record of a house's foundation was a pancarte, always drawn up by the diocesan bishop, as much as ten years later. This pancarte confirmed the house's foundation and listed in summary fashion the many small gifts that made it possible.

It is indicative of how thoroughly the Cistercians were integrated into the diocesan hierarchy that it was always the bishop, rather than the abbot of the new house or of its mother house, much less any of the lay donors, who had the charter drawn up. While houses of the Cluniac order always tried, with greater or lesser success, to free themselves from episcopal control, sometimes specifying in their foundation charters (as did Cluny herself) that no bishop should interfere in the house's internal affairs, the Cistercians deferred without question to the rights of the Burgundian bishops, both those bishops who had once been monks themselves and those from the secular clergy. Whereas the tenth- and eleventh-century foundations by great nobles had included enough transfer of wealth that both the nobles themselves and the monks would prefer to have it spelled out in writing, the Cistercians, whose houses were founded on a much smaller material base even when all the small pieces of land were put together, did not fear in the same way that the individual donors or their heirs might jeopardize their monastery's existence by reclaiming their gifts. And of course the donors themselves, unlike the great nobles of previous centuries, did not have chaplains who might have drawn up such foundation charters.

There seem to be several features involved in the very close identification of knights and petty aristocrats with the foundation of the Cistercian houses. Perhaps most importantly for Burgundy, *all* of the monasteries founded entirely anew after the first decade or so of the twelfth century were Cistercian houses, rather than being Cluniac or other Benedictine establishments. The reforms of previously existing Burgundian houses in this period all entailed the establishment of canons regular, rather than monks—though here too knights often took the initiative. At least in Burgundy, then, knights may have been involved in the foundation of Cistercian monasteries in particular because they were the only houses being founded at a time when the knights had finally accumulated enough wealth to make monastic patronage possible.

But this surely cannot be the whole answer, for in other parts of France, further from the Cistercian heartland, many non-Cistercian monasteries were established during the twelfth century. And in theory there was nothing to stop a group of knights, who among them owned some land suitable for a monastery, from inviting black monks to settle on their land. There must have been some particular attraction which the Cistercians had for the knights, as is further suggested by the fact that when making pious gifts to already-established monasteries, as opposed to founding monasteries, knights still chose overwhelmingly the Cistercian houses. The cartularies of the Cistercian houses are full of small gifts of land and pasture rights from the local petty aristocrats, but the records of such houses of black monks as Cluny, St-Seine, or St-Germain of Auxerre reveal very few gifts from this group in the twelfth century. The older houses attracted gifts almost entirely from dukes, counts, viscounts, and castellans, the same sorts of men as those who had originally founded them and had always patronized them, whereas the knights were generally associated, whether in founding houses or endowing them, with the Cistercians.

Part of the connection was surely the fact that almost all Cistercian monks themselves came from the knightly or petty landowner class. For example, Bernard of Clairvaux, certainly the best-known monk of the twelfth century, was the son of a knight, a retainer of the lord of Châtillon, who was given a small tenancy at Fontaines-lès-Dijon, though he never had a castle of his own.[8] The comrades whom Bernard brought with him to Cîteaux—described later in terms suggesting the US Cavalry riding to the rescue—were also all of knightly, rather than more powerful, families. Certainly the knights who wished to found or endow monasteries might have felt more comfortable with houses of monks whose social origins were close to their own, and who may in some cases have been the sons of their friends and neighbors. But this explanation only shifts the focus of the question: why should knights and other petty aristocrats in particular have decided, as young men, to leave the world and become Cistercian monks?

I would suggest that the attraction of the Cistercian order for men at the lower fringes of the nobility, whether they wished to found a monastery, make gifts to one, or actually enter the monastic life themselves, was that this new order represented the most radical rejection yet of the aristocratic way of life. This may seem paradoxical, because these same knights had been struggling for several generations to be able to join the aristocracy.

Yet it is quite clear that the Cistercian way of life, even more so than the life of the monks in the longer-established Benedictine houses, was opposed at every point to the life of twelfth-century nobles. The nobles, and the knights who imitated them, lived in what passed for luxury in the twelfth century, in castles (or fortified houses), wearing silk and furs and gold jewelry and eating well. Cistercian monks, in contrast, lived in deliberate poverty, in simple monastic buildings, where even the churches in which they worshipped were dark and without decoration, wearing homespun robes made from the commonest sheep's wool (hence white), and eating an austere vegetarian diet. Noble lords spent their days commanding others, and had much of their energy directed toward fighting and raising sons to succeed them, while the Cistercians lived chastely, in absolute obedience to their abbots, engaged almost entirely in manual labor or prayer.[9]

Therefore, I would argue that what the knights saw in the Cistercians was a way of life that was almost by definition holy, just because it was so diametrically opposed to their own. The knights had been struggling for a century and a half to become nobles by the time they first began joining and helping spread the Cistercian order, and they were acutely aware of what being a noble entailed, probably much more so than members of the longer-established lineages, who took their position for granted. The knights were also well enough educated, especially in a time when the church was increasingly trying to redirect warrior energies towards crusade and the protection of monks and widows, to realize that luxurious living and fighting were not going to save their souls. The knights also possessed great energy and determination, which had made it possible for them to advance as far as they had, but this energy was left without an outlet once they had at least reached the lower fringes of the aristocracy, the goal toward which they had been aiming. There may even have been a sense of frustration. In these circumstances, it is scarcely surprising that the knights threw their energies into the support of a monastic order which rejected everything that they had been seeking for a hundred and fifty years.

In spite of their limited resources, then, the knights of the twelfth century could, like more powerful lords, establish a body of monks who would pray for them. That they could do so by acting together reveals the strength of the almost invisible social structures which united the lower levels of the aristocracy. These structures are also revealed by the way that they stood as witnesses and guarantors for each other if any of them had a quarrel or was involved in a lawsuit, the fact that they often married each other's sisters, and that, when they went on Crusade, they generally went together. But this sort of social link, revealed only occasionally in other documents, is best revealed in the virtual unanimity of purpose with which they were able to act in founding Cistercian monasteries.

To conclude, the explosive growth of the Cistercian order in the twelfth century can be seen as due at least in part to its appeal to the knights and petty aristocrats, men who far outnumbered the better-established nobility, and who had acquired enough land and wealth to make gifts to monastic houses possible, at precisely the time that the order began to spread. These newly-wealthy men needed monastic houses to which to make gifts, to prove that they, like generations of lords before them, were aristocratic patrons of the saints. Preferably they required small, poor houses, where what they had to offer would not be lost in a welter of larger gifts, and where, at least if they acted in concert with the friends and neighbors to whom they were bound by social ties, they might be able to establish monks praying especially for them. And, perhaps even more importantly, the Cistercians fulfilled the knights' need to find salvation, through association with monks whose holiness was guaranteed by a way of life so directly opposite to the knights' own.

University of California, San Diego

NOTES

1. Georges Duby, *The Three Orders: Feudal Society Imagined*, trans. Arthur Goldhammer (Chicago, 1980), pp. 154–61, 293–307. Joachim Bumke, *The Concept of Knighthood in the Middle Ages*, trans. W.T.H. Jackson and Erika Jackson (New York, 1982), *passim*, esp. pp. 22–26, 46–57, 72–106.

2. Georges Duby, "The Diffusion of Cultural Patterns in Feudal Society," in *The Chivalrous Society*, ed. Cynthia Postan (Berkeley and Los Angeles, 1977), pp. 171–77.

3. I am presently completing a broad study of the relations between monasteries and the aristocracy in Burgundy in the High Middle Ages.

4. Auguste Bernard and Alexandre Bruel (edd.), *Recueil des chartes de l'abbaye de Cluny* (Paris, 1876), I 124–28, no. 112. Ulysse Chevalier (ed.), *Cartulaire du prieuré de Paray-le-monial* (Paris, 1890), pp. 2–3, no. 2. E. Bougaud and Joseph Garnier (edd.), *Chronique de l'abbaye de Saint-Bénigne de Dijon,* Analecta Divionensia, 9 (Dijon, 1875), pp. 129–31. René de Lespinasse (ed.), "Les chartes de Saint-Étienne de Nevers," *Bulletin de la Société nivernaise des lettres, sciences et arts,* ser. 3, 12, (1908) 76–78, no. 2; see also Bernard and Bruel, *Recueil des chartes de Cluny* (Paris, 1894), V 67–74, no. 3724.

5. *Exordium parvum,* ed. Jean de la Croix Bouton and Jean Baptiste Van Damme, *Les plus anciens textes de Cîteaux,* Commentarii Cistercienses, Studia et documenta, 2 (Achel, 1974), pp. 56–60. Georges Duby (ed.) *Recueil des pancartes de l'abbaye de La Ferté-sur-Grosne, 1113-1178* (Paris, 1953), pp. 41–42, no. 1. *Gesta pontificum Autissiodorensium,* ed. L.-M. Duru, *Bibliothèque historique de l'Yonne* (Auxerre, 1850), I 406; Martine Garrigues (ed.), *Le premier cartulaire de l'abbaye de Pontigny (XIIᵉ–XIIIᵉ siècles),* Collection de documents inédits sur l'histoire de France, 14 (Paris, 1981), pp. 152–54, no. 84. Louis Dubois (ed.), *Histoire de l'abbaye de Morimond* (Paris, 1851), pp. 411–12; a slightly abbreviated version of this charter is printed in *Gallia christiana,* Vol. 4, instr. col. 159, no. 36.

6. *Gallia christiana,* Vol. 4, instr. cols. 165–69, nos. 42, 45.

7. Jean Waquet, *Recueil des chartes de l'abbaye de Clairvaux, XIIᵉ siècle* [Troyes, 1950], p. vii.

8. William of St -Thierry, *Vita prima Sancti Bernardi,* 1, 1; PL 185:227. Geoffrey of Clairvaux, *Vita tertia Sancti Bernardi,* 1; PL 185:523–24.

9. Richard Roehl, "Plan and Reality in a Medieval Monastic Economy: The Cistercians," *Studies in Medieval and Renaissance History* 9 (1972) 84–86, 104. Louis J. Lekai, "Ideals and Reality in Early Cistercian Life and Legislation," in *Cistercian Ideals and Reality,* ed. John R. Sommerfeldt, CS 60 (Kalamazoo, Michigan, 1978), pp. 4–13.

NOTES ON THE 850th ANNIVERSARY
OF AMELUNGSBORN

Nicolaus C. Heutger

ABOUT THE YEAR 1129, Count Siegfried IV of Homburg founded the monastery of Amelungsborn near the newly-built
Castle Homburg in Lower Saxony. Count Siegfried was the protector of other monasteries and wished to enlarge his influence and
prestige by the foundation of this new monastery. So he made his
younger half-brother Henry the first abbot of the new foundation.

The first monks came to Amelungsborn on November 20, 1135,
from Kamp (today Kamp-Lintford) near the lower Rhine, which
itself had been founded in 1123 by Morimond, a daughter-house
of Cîteaux. Kamp was the first Cistercian monastery in German
territory.

And so, in 1985, the Lutheran abbot of Amelungsborn, the
Lutheran coventuals, and the friends of the monastery celebrated
the 850th anniversary of the abbey. A book on this event in now
in print.

In 1143, Pope Celestine II granted Amelungsborn the protection of St. Peter and himself. An earlier privilege of Honorius II
and a letter from St. Bernard, warmly addressing the new convent,
are forgeries.

In the middle of the twelfth century fifty monks prayed and
worked at Amelungsborn. At its peak some ninety *conversi* worked
for the well-being of the house. In 1272, the *conversi* rebelled, and
the abbot and monks escaped only narrowly, for the monastery
could not function without its lay brethren.

In 1145, Amelungsborn sent some of its community to found
Riddagshausen near Braunschweig, and many of the Amelungs-

born's monks went still farther eastward. One of them, Berno, became bishop of Schwerin in 1158. He succeeded in converting the pagan population of Mecklenburg to the Christian faith by preaching, destroying their idols, and building Christian churches. His successor to the see of Schwerin, Brunward, also came from Amelungsborn. About 1171, Amelungsborn founded the monastery of Doberan, near the Baltic sea, by sending out the new abbot, Conrad, with twelve monks. But these eastern foundations were not always left in peace by their pagan neighbors, and, in 1179, seventy-eight monks and *conversi* suffered martyrdom. In 1186 a new and valiant team from Amelungsborn appeared in Mecklenburg. Doberan founded the monasteries of Pelplin, south of Danzig, and Buckow in the margravate of Brandenburg. In a grange of Doberan, the monk Peter Kalff wrote his Easter play in 1464; this work is perhaps the most impressive of its genre written during the Late Middle Ages.

The bishops of Hildesheim often visited Amelungsborn and donated much land to the monks. His and other gifts to the abbey were not made unconditionally; they were generally given to secure masses for the souls of the donors and their ancestors.

In 1372, a monk of Amelungsborn, John of Braunschweig, illuminated the splended Wigalois manuscript, a work of Arthurian literature commissioned by a duke and now housed in Leyden. Another illuminated manuscript, the Amelungsborn Bible, is today found at Wolfenbüttel. The catalog of the abbey's library dates from 1412 and shows some intellectual interest by the monks; however, works on spirituality comprised the bulk of the collection. The stained glass of the abbey church dates from the fourteenth century. There were originally twelve large windows, but only one has survived in which are portrayed twelve figures representing the ancestors of Christ.

The abbey declined in the Late Middle Ages. Rather than farming their own estates, the monks were forced to lease them out, owing to the lack of *conversi*.

The year 1542 saw the introduction of the Lutheran reform. The first Lutheran abbot, Steinhower, was born in England and died at the time of the Spanish Armada. His gravestone includes a miter and two *baculi*. Steinhower's widow was married by his abbatial successor. Following the suggestion of Martin Luther, Amelungsborn founded a school in 1569. Wilhelm Raabe gave the monastery and its school a place in German literature by his work *Das Odfeld.*

About 1810, corporate life at Amelungsborn disappeared, and the cloister was destroyed. Until 1912, the abbey of Amelungsborn retained only titular status. However, in 1960 the liturgist Christhard Mahrenholz became abbot and brought new life to the old walls. Dom Sighard Kleiner, formerly Abbot General of the Order of Cîteaux, has twice visited the reborn abbey.

Today one can see a complete ring wall encircling the whole monastery. A gate house is extant. The church has a single, small tower over the crossing; the nave is Romanesque and the choir Gothic. Other edifices which remain are a large building called the Stein, the workhouse of the *conversi* (today a guest house), the old priory, and the school. The buildings are monuments of a treasured past which we thankfully commemorated on the abbey's 850th anniversary.

Hildesheim

Bibliography

Nicolaus Heutger, *Das Kloster Amelungsborn im Spiegel der zisterzienischen Ordersgeschichte.* Hildesheim: August Lax, 1968.

Nicolaus Heutger, *Kloster Amelungsborn in der deutschen Literaturgeschichte,* 1970.

Nicolaus Heutger, *Loccum.* Hildesheim, 1971.

THE USE OF BERNARD OF CLAIRVAUX IN REFORMATION PREACHING

William O. Paulsell

BERNARD OF CLAIRVAUX was one of the fathers who has often been quoted by Protestant preachers. While criticisms of the Catholic Church may have abounded in the Protestant pulpits, the Abbot of Clairvaux was used as a source of support by the Reformers. Luther, Calvin, and John Donne are three excellent examples of Protestants who found a friend in Bernard and who often used him against his own tradition.

William O. Paulsell

MARTIN LUTHER

Martin Luther had a great fondness for Bernard of Clairvaux. In a sermonic exposition on *John* 16:23 he called Bernard "a fine man, one who had Christian thoughts."[1] Elsewhere he said: "I regard him as the most pious of all the monks and prefer him to all the others, even to St Dominic."[2] He put Bernard in good company: "I believe that SS Ambrose, Jerome, and Bernard were holy and godly men."[3]

Why did he have so much affection for Bernard? It was because, in Luther's mind, Bernard was devoted to Christ as the source of our salvation. In an oft quoted statement, Luther wrote: "I love St Bernard as the one who, among all writers, preached Christ most charmingly. I follow him wherever he preached Christ, and I pray to Christ in the faith in which he prayed to Christ." He was not, however, taken with Bernard's monastic vocation. "I will not consent to wearing his cowl, his hair shirt, or his monkish garb; for by doing so I would be condemning all other Christians, as if their stations were not as good, honorable, and dignified as that of the monk Bernard. A father, mother, or child, a hired man or a maid, may believe exactly what St Bernard believed. They share his baptism and his faith.... This put them on a level with St Bernard."[4] For Luther, Bernard did not seek salvation in his monastic vocation, but in the cross of Christ.

Luther repeatedly told three erroneous stories about Bernard. One of these concerned Bernard's asceticism. In a sermon on the *Gospel of John*, Luther said: "St Bernard is reputed to have abstained from eating and drinking so long that his lungs began to rot and his breath stank so much that he was excluded from the choir and from association with his brethren."[5] The story was repeated in a later *John* sermon[6] and was mentioned at least twice in his commentary on *Genesis*.[7] The reason for his unpleasant behavior, said Luther, was that Bernard was trying to overcome lust.[8] In another context Luther wrote about forced versus voluntary chastity. "I am speaking about men," he said, "who, like Bernard and Bonaventure, were continent and fought against lust. Although they were saintly and good men in other respects, yet they could not be free from the itch."[9]

The *Vita Prima* has given us a slightly different version of that story. We are told that Bernard frequently vomited up undigested food to the annoyance of his brothers, but, for a long time, would not leave the "assemblies of the community." To deal with this problem he had a basin "sunk into the floor next to his place in choir." However, his symptoms eventually became so disgusting that he absented himself from community exercises and lived alone. Luther should have known that the *Vita Prima* editorialized: "His illness may well have been part of God's wise plan to abash the great and powerful things of this world."[10]

A second amazing belief which appeared frequently in Luther's writings was that Bernard gave up the monastic life for the sake of Christ. In one of the sermons on *John*, Luther said: "St Bernard dropped out of the monastic role, forsook cowl and tonsure and rules, and turned to Christ: for he knew that Christ conquered death, not for Himself but for us men that all who believe in the Son should not perish but have eternal life. And so St Bernard was saved."[11]

This renunciation allegedly occurred on his deathbed. Speaking of the saints, Luther said: "If they desired to be saved, they, too, had to entrust themselves to none but Christ, the only Savior, on their deathbeds. St Bernard did that."[12] In a sermon on the Sermon on the Mount, Luther related a little dialogue with Bernard. Bernard said: "Oh, I have lived damnably and passed my life shamefully!" Luther replied: "How so, dear St Bernard? Have you not been a pious monk all your life? Are not chastity, obedience, preaching, fasting, and praying something valuable?" "No," replied Bernard, "it is all lost and belongs to the devil." Luther concluded: "He would have had to be damned eternally by his own judgment if he had not come to his senses through his loss, turned around, walked away from monkery, taken hold of a different foundation, clinging to Christ, and being preserved in the Creed that the children pray."[13]

The story of the deathbed conversion was told again in another of the sermons on *John.* Luther told of his own fears that he might be damned if he had made a mistake in any part of the Mass, and complained of those who thought their salvation depended on monastic rules. But with the Reformation, he said, some people came to their senses. "Many discarded cowl and other tomfollery in the hour of death and would have none of it. St Bernard was one of these. He hung his cowl on the wall. O St Bernard, that was a timely return!"[14]

A third item which appears in Luther's writings with some frequency was his citing of Bernard as the source of the story that Lucifer fell from heaven because he did not like the idea that God would take on humanity. For example, it is found in the lectures on *Genesis* at least twice as well as in at least one of the sermons on *John.*[15] In fact, Luther believed Bernard had invented the story, "as the poets do."[16] Bernard, said Luther, while commenting on the Jacob's ladder story, "thinks that when Satan was a good angel in the sight of God, he saw that one day the divinity would descend and take upon itself this wretched mortal flesh and would not take upon itself the nature of angels. Moved by that indignity and envy, thinks Bernard, the devil raged against God, with the result that he was thrown out of heaven. These thoughts of Bernard are not unprofitable," said Luther, "for they flow from admiration for the boundless love and mercy of God."[17]

In a sermon on "The Word became flesh," Luther referred to the jealousy of the elder brother in the prodigal son story and compared his feelings with those of Lucifer. Here Luther told his hearers that Bernard had said that the good angels rejoiced at Lucifer's exit and remained in heaven to recognize Christ as their Lord and God. This, said Luther, did not constitute an article of faith, but the story was plausible. "Thus," wrote Luther, "St Bernard's heart and mind gave free play to his reflections on the words of our text ["And the Word became flesh"], and his meditations betoken his wondering delight over them. That is also what he wants to convey to and impress on us."[18]

JOHN CALVIN

A perusal of Calvin's *Institutes* reveals a broad knowledge of the writings of Bernard. The index of the Ford Lewis Battles edition lists twenty references to the *Sermons on the Canticle*, eight from *De Consideratione*, six from *On Grace and Free Will*, and eleven references to other works by Bernard. It would appear that Calvin used Bernard in two ways: first, to support his theology and, second, to support his criticism of the Church.

Calvin found Bernard to be a theological soul brother. Calvin's theology was grounded on the belief that the Christian's hope is not in accumulating merit, but in the mercy of God which freely forgives sin. In Book III of the *Institutes* Calvin quoted from Bernard's sermon "On the Feast of the Annunciation of the Blessed Virgin" to the effect that one cannot have forgiveness apart from God's mercy, that one has no good works at all unless God gives them, and that one cannot merit eternal life by works unless they are given by God.[19]

In Chapter 21 of Book Three of the *Institutes*, which is titled "Eternal Election by Which God Has Predestined Some to Salvation, Others to Destruction," Calvin cited a statement by Bernard in *Sermon 78* of the *Canticle* series in support of his belief that God saves according to God's own good pleasure. "As Bernard rightly teaches," wrote Calvin, "'it could not be otherwise found or recognized among creatures, since it lies marvelously hidden . . . both within the bosom of a blessed predestination and within the mass of a miserable condemnation?'"[20] But earlier in the *Institutes* Calvin stated that "Bernard rightly teaches that the door of salvation is opened to us when we receive the gospel today with our ears, even as death was then admitted by those same windows when they were open to Satan."[21].

Critical to Calvin's theology is his doctrine of human nature. In a section of the *Institutes* called "Man sins of necessity, but without compulsion," Calvin quoted from Bernard's eighty-first *Canticle* sermon to say that the human will, but not nature, has been done violence by sin, so that the necessity to sin is voluntary. He used a rather ambiguous statement by Bernard that said: "In some base and strange way the will itself, changed for the worse by sin, makes a necessity for itself. Hence, neither does necessity, althougth it is of the will, avail to excuse the will, nor does the will, although it is led astray, avail to exclude necessity. For this necessity is as it were voluntary."[22]

Although Calvinism has often been described by its detractors as a dark and somber faith in which one lives in despair over sins, Calvin saw it as a positive and hopeful theology. He did not want people to carry around a heavy burden of guilt, but to rejoice in the Gospel. He quoted from Bernard's eleventh *Canticle* sermon: "Sorrow for sins is necessary if it be not unremitting. I beg you to turn your steps back sometimes from troubled and anxious remembering of your ways, and to go forth to the tableland of serene remembrance of God's benefits. Let us mingle honey with wormwood that its wholesome bitterness may bring health when it is drunk tempered with sweetness. If you take thought upon yourself in your humility, take thought likewise upon the Lord in his goodness."[23]

Calvin used the twenty-third *Canticle* sermon to support the comforting nature of predestination. Bernard had spoken of God's purposes of peace for those who fear God, "overlooking their evil and rewarding their good actions." Later, Calvin added more words from that sermon of Bernard's: "That vision does not terrify but soothes; it does not arouse a restless curiosity but allays it; and it does not weary but calms the senses. Here true rest is felt. The God of peace renders all things peaceful, and to behold him at rest is to be at rest."[24]

One of the major issues in Reformation theology was the question of merit. There is much discussion of this in Book III of the *Institutes*. Calvin, of course, opposed any idea of salvation based upon human merit. Whatever merit we may have is a gift from

God. "To the extent that a man rests satisfied with himself," said Calvin, "he impedes the beneficence of God."[25]

Bernard had used the term *merit* with some frequency. Calvin, however, excused this as "the custom of the time," and claimed that Bernard's only intention had been to "strike fear in hypocrites."[26] A few sections later in the *Institutes* he complained: "I wish that Christian writers had always exercised such restraint as not to take it into their heads needlessly to use terms foreign to Scripture that would produce great offense and very little fruit. Why, I ask, was there need to drag in the term 'merit' when the value of good works could without offense have been meaningfully explained by another term? How much offense this term contains is clear from the great damage it has done the world. Surely, as it is a most prideful term, it can do nothing but obscure God's favor and imbue men with perverse haughtiness."[27]

He then insisted that Bernard had known the true meaning of the term, that merits are given by God. Calvin quoted a line in *Sermon 68 on the Canticle*: "For merit, it suffices to know that merits do not suffice."[28]

Finally, how did Calvin use Bernard to support his criticism of the Church? No doubt mindful of the indulgence controversy, Calvin presented a question from Bernard: "Why should the church be concerned about merit, since it has in God's purpose a surer reason for glorying?" There is no need for merit because we rest in the Savior's wounds. "The mightier he is to save, the more securely I dwell there."[29]

Book IV, Chapter VII, Section 18 of the *Institutes* is titled "The decay of the church until the time of Bernard of Clairvaux." Calvin attributed the problems of the Church to incompetent and greedy bishops, and says that Bernard "complains that there converge upon Rome from the whole earth the ambitious, the greedy, the simoniacs, the sacrilegious, the keepers of concubines, the incestuous, and all such monsters, to obtain or retain churchly honors by apostolic authority, and that fraud, deception, and violence have prevailed."[30] He quoted from *De consideratione*: "I voice the murmur and common complaint of the churches. They cry out that they are mangled and dismembered. There are either none or few churches that do not lament or fear these cruel blows. You ask what blows? Abbots are pulled away from their bishops; bishops

from their archbishops, etc. Strange, indeed if this can be excused!
By behaving this way you prove that you have fullness of power,
but not of righteousness."[31]

Later, in Section 11 of the same chapter, Calvin complained
about the temporal power of the papacy and its claims to Empire.
He quoted from *De consideratione*: "Peter could not give what he
did not have; but he gave to his successors what he had, the care of
the churches." Calvin was happy to note that Bernard had said to
Pope Eugenius: "Let us remember that a ministry has been laid
upon us, not a lordship given. Learn that you need a hoe, not a
scepter, to do the prophet's work. Lordship is forbidden; ministry
is bidden."[32]

JOHN DONNE

John Donne may best be known today as a poet, but he was
without doubt one of the most remarkable preachers of the seventeenth century. A royal chaplain, a Dean of St Paul's, and a meta-
physical poet, Donne's preaching attracted large audiences. His
sermons are heavy with patristic quotations, and Augustine was
clearly his favorite. However, he was also fond of quoting Bernard
of Clairvaux, and the index to Simpson and Potter's ten volume
edition of Donne's sermons list 132 references to Bernard.[33]

Donne used Bernard in three ways: (1) to support his own ideas,
(2) as a source of images used in his sermons, and (3) as a source of
outlines for sermons or sections within sermons.

Many examples could be cited of Donne using Bernard to support his own ideas. In a sermon preached on April 21, 1616, on
the text, "Because sentence against an evil deed is not executed
speedily, the heart of the sons of men is fully set to do evil" (*Ecclesiastes* 8:11), Donne quoted both Augustine and Gregory on human inclination to sin. The lascivious and lustful heart, said
Donne, moves from riotous feasting to blasphemous gaming and
on to malicious consultation and never considers God. He pointed
out that Bernard, in *De consideratione*, had the same fear for Pope
Eugenius, that his involvement in the business of the papal court
might draw him away from God.[34]

Donne called for Bernard's support in a sermon on the text, "You
were sold for nothing, and you shall be redeemed without money"

(*Isaiah* 52:3), preached on April 30, 1615. When we sin, said Donne, we mingle sin with the image of God within us. "We draw the image of God into all our incontinencies, into all our oppressions, into all our extortions, and supplantations; we carry his image, into all foul places . . . yea we carry his image down with us, to eternal condemnation." He quoted Bernard as saying that even in Hell, "uri potest, non exuri Imago Dei," the image of God can be burned, but not consumed. The same phrase was quoted in an April 18, 1619, sermon on *Ecclesiastes* 12:1, "Remember also your creator in the days of your youth." Here Donne returned to the theme that we will suffer torment in Hell because the image of God within us can never be destroyed. "The image of a Lord, the image of a Counsailor, the image of a Bishop, shall all burn in Hell, and never but out; not only these men, but these offices are not to return to nothing; but as their being from God, so their being from Man shall have an everlasting being, to the aggravating of their condemnation." To this Donne reminded his listeners: "As St Bernard sayes of the Image of God in mans soul, *uri potest in gehenna, non exuri*," it can be burned in Hell but not consumed.[35]

At Lincolns Inne Donne once preached on *John* 8:15, "I judge no one." In an exhortation on slander and calumny he referred to Bernard again, obviously to his *Steps of Humility and Pride*, where Bernard had spoken of monks gossiping about their brothers. "Take in some of Saint Bernard's examples of these rules, that it is such a calumny to say, *Doleo vehementer*, I am sorry at the heart for such a man because I love him, but I could never draw him from such and such a vice, or to say, *per me nunquam innotuisset*, I would never have spoken of it, yet since all the world talkes of it, the truth must not be disguised, and so take occasion to discover a fault which nobody knew before. This being the rule, and this the example, who amongst us is free from the passive calumny."[36]

And in a sermon on the vanity of riches Donne wrote: "Let Saint Bernard do it: *vanun est, quod nec confert plenitudienem continenti*; for whom amongst you hath not room for another bagg, or amongst us for another benefice; *nec fulicimentum innitenti*, for who stands fast upon that, which is not fast itself? and the world passeth, and the lust thereof; *Nec fructum labornati*, for you have sowen much, and bring in little, yee eat, but have not enough, yee drink but are not filled, yee are cloth'd, but wax not warm, and he that earneth wages, puts it into a bagg with holes, midsummer runs out at Michaelmas, and at years end he hath nothing."[37]

While preaching on *I Corinthians* 15:50, "Flesh and blood cannot inherit the Kingdom of God," Donne interpreted the words of Bernard, "Preadestinati non possunt peccare," the elect cannot sin, to mean that when the elect face judgment their sins are regarded by God as no sins "because," as Bernard had said, "the blood of Jesus covering them, they are none in the eyes of God."[38]

Second, Donne found Bernard to be a rich source of images. For example, he quoted Bernard on the threefold nature of the soul. "So we have in our soul, a threefold impression of that image, and, as Saint Bernard calls it, A trinity from the Trinity, in those three faculties of the soul, the Understanding, the Will, and the Memory."[39] In another sermon Donne quotes Bernard on the memory as the *stomachus animae*, the stomach of the soul: "It receives and digests, and turn into good blood, all the benefits formerly exhibited to us in particular, and exhibited to the whole Church of God."[40]

In addition to using Bernard to support the trinitarian nature of the soul, Donne used him to explain a trinitarian character of sin which is suggestion, consent, and delight in sin. But after sin God infuses another Trinity in us: faith, hope, and love. "For so far," Donne concluded, "that Father of Meditation, St Bernard, carries his consideration of the Trinity."[41]

Donne made use of Bernard in explaining the familiar images of tears when preaching on *John* 11:35, "Jesus wept." In his introduction he noted that Bernard had called his hearers to listen to Christ who seeks "not to make you praise with them that praise, but to make you weepe with them that weepe."[42] Donne noted that Jesus told the women not to weep for Lazarus because there was no sin for which to weep, and quoted Bernard with an additional comment: "*Ordinem flendi docuit*, saies S. Bernard, Christ did not absolutely forbid tears, but regulate and order their teares, that they might weepe in the right place; first for sin." The first tears that we shed must be for sin and, according to Donne, "our most pretious devotions receive an addition, a multiplication by holy tears. S. Bernard means all that they all meane in that, *Cor lachrymas nesciens durum, impurum*, A hard heart is a foule heart."[43]

A particularly unpleasant image was drawn from St Bernard by Donne in a sermon preached in 1618 at the churching of Lady Doncaster. The text was from the *Song of Solomon* 5:3, "I had bathed my feet, how could I soil them?" It was, of course, a sermon on baptism and the need for baptismal washing. If any thought themselves pure, but were not washed from sin, they deceived themselves. Donne proclaimed, "*Erubesce vas stercorum*, says good Saint Bernard. If it be a vessell of gold, it is but a vessell of excrements, if it be a bed of curious plants, it is but a bed of dung; as their tombes hereafter shall be but glorious covers of rotten carcasses, so their bodies are now, but pampered covers of rotten soules: *Erubescat vas stercorum*, let that vessell of uncleannesse, that barrell of dung, confesse a necessity of washing."[44]

And in a later sermon on the baptism of Christ, Donne drew another baptismal image from Bernard. He quoted Bernard as calling baptism "*Investitura Christianismi*, The investing of Christianity, as St Bernard cals it, There we put on Christ Jesus. . . ."[45]

Finally, Donne drew upon Bernard for images of Christ. In a St Paul's Christmas sermon of 1624 Donne said: "A minute will serve to repeat that which St Bernard saies, and a day, a life will not serve to comprehend it . . . . *Immanuel est verbum infans*, saies the Father; He is the ancient of daies, and yet in minority; he is the Word it selfe, and yet speechless; he that is All, that all the Prophets spoke of, cannot speake: He addes more, He is *Puer sapiens*,, but a child, and yet wiser then the elders, wiser in the Cradle, then they were in the Chaire: Hee is more, *Deus lactens*, God at whose breasts all creatures suck, sucking at his Mothers breast, and such a Mother, as is a maid. Immanuel is God with us; it is not we with God: God seeks us, comes to us, before wee to him."[46]

Third, Donne looked to Bernard as a source of simple outlines of ideas. In a sermon on *Psalm* 6, the first penitential psalm, Donne recounted four steps by which Bernard had said one might come to God. First was *ad supplicationes* whereby one fearing judgment seeks God's mercy. The second was *ad orationes*, by prayer. The third was *ad intercessiones*, "that he durst put himselfe betwixt God and other men, as Abraham in the behalfe of Sodome." The fourth was *ad gratiarum actiones*, which meant that one felt no need to ask for anything but simply offered thanksgiving to God for the mercies received.[47]

In a 1624 Christmas sermon at St Paul's on *Isaiah* 7:14, the sign of the virgin, Donne drew upon Bernard's analysis of the four conjunctions that occurred on Christmas Day. First was the conjunction of God and Man. Second, was the conjunction of Maid and Mother. Third, was the conjunction of faith and reason. Fourth, was the conjunction of God's anger and mercy which caused the giving of a sign.[48]

And on Whitsunday, probably in 1625, Donne noted that Bernard had seen three ways of knowing God: "first, understanding which relies upon reason; faith, which relies upon supreme Authority; and opinion, which relies upon probability."[49]

In another sermon on *Psalm* 6 Donne mentioned four ways in which the individual can speak of God. He spoke of Bernard's "patheticall and usefull meditation to this purpose." Bernard had said that first, one can say "Creator meus es tu," you are my creator. Second, one can say "Pastor meus est tu," you are my shepherd. Third, one can say "Redemptor meus es tu", you are my redeemer. Fourth, one can say "Susceptor meus es tu", you are my protector.[50]

The Abbot of Clairvaux would have opposed Luther, Calvin, and Donne ecclesially and theologically, but they found him to be a rich source of support. They cited him frequently, often misusing him, but even in this, his contribution to the Reformation was significant.

Lexington Theological Seminary

NOTES

1. *Sermons on the Gospel of John*, Luther's Works, 24, ed. Jaroslav Pelikan (Saint Louis, 1961), p. 395.
2. *Sermons on the Gospel of St John*, Luther's Works, 22, p. 388.
3. *Ibid.*, p. 264.
4. *Luther's Works*, 22, p. 268.
5. *Luther's Works*, 22, p. 335.
6. *Luther's Works*, 22, p. 360.
7. *Luther's Works*, 4, p. 273 and 5, p. 71.

8. *Luther's Works*, 4, p. 273.
9. *Luther's Works*, 5, p. 323.
10. *St Bernard of Clairvaux*, trans. Geoffrey Webb and Adrian Walker, (Westminster, Maryland, 1959), p. 64.
11. *Luther's Works*, 22, p. 360.
12. *Luther's Works*, 22, p. 269.
13. *Luther's Works*, 21, p. 283.
14. *Luther's Works*, 22, p. 387.
15. *Luther's Works*, 5, p. 221; 4, p. 256; 22, p. 103.
16. *Luther's Works*, 4, p. 256.
17. *Luther's Works*, 5, p. 221.
18. *Luther's Works*, 22, p. 104.
19. John Calvin, *The Institutes of the Christian Religion* (Philadelphia, 1960), 3:2:41, p. 589.
20. *Institutes*, 3:21:1, p. 922. See *Sermon 78*, 4 in Bernard of Clairvaux, *On the Song of Songs IV* (Kalamazoo, 1980), p. 132.
21. *Institutes*, 2:1:4, p. 246.
22. *Institutes*, 2:3:5, p. 296. See *Sermon 81*, 7 in Bernard of Clairvaux, *On the Song of Songs IV*, p. 70.
23. *Institutes*, 3:3:5, p. 609.
24. *Institutes*, 3:24:4, p. 970.
25. *Institutes*, 3:12:8, p. 762.
26. *Institutes*, 3:12:3, p. 757.
27. *Institutes*, 3:15:2, p. 789.
28. *Institutes*, 3:15:2, p. 790. See *Sermon 68* in Bernard of Clairvaux, *On the Song of Songs IV*, p. 23.
29. *Institutes*, 3:12:3, p. 757.
30. *Institutes*, 4:7:18, p. 1137.
31. *Ibid.*
32. *Institutes*, 4:11:11, pp. 1223–24.
33. Evelyn M. Simpson and George R. Potter, *The Sermons of John Donne* (Berkeley: University of California Press, 1962), X, 346–48, 352.
34. *Sermons*, I:2, p. 180.
35. *Sermons*, II:11, p. 247.
36. *Sermons*, II:16, p. 329.
37. *Sermons*, III:1, p. 48.
38. *Sermons*, III:4, p. 128.
39. *Sermons*, II:2, pp. 72–73.
40. *Sermons*, II:11, p. 236.
41. *Sermons*, III:5, pp. 144–45.
42. *Sermons*, IV:13, p. 324.
43. *Sermons*, IV:13, p. 341–42.
44. *Sermons*, V:8, p. 172.
45. *Sermons*, VI:6, p. 137.
46. *Sermons*, VI:8, p. 184.
47. *Sermons*, V:17, p. 341.
48. *Sermons*, VI:8, p. 1168.
49. *Sermons*, VI:16, p. 317.
50. *Sermons*, V:16, pp. 325–26.

A NUN AT MONTIVILLIERS

Beatrice Hibbard Beech

B ECAUSE OF THEIR WEALTH religious houses oftentimes suffered a great many adversities such as being sacked, pillaged, and assaulted. Monasteries in Normandy were especially vulnerable because of their geographic location. From maurading Vikings to Allied Armies in the twentieth century, this province, with its long coastline, was an ideal route for invading armies to conquer France and pick up booty from defenseless abbeys. Montivilliers near Le Havre in Normandy was no exception. In its long history from its founding in 682 by St Philibert until its dissolution, the abbey was destroyed by Vikings, ravaged by the English in the Hundred Years War, and sacked by Protestants in the Wars of Religion in the sixteenth century.[1] Historians often concentrate on the material aspects of the monastic life such as the construction and embellishment of the church and other buildings, and eventually their destruction, but we often forget that there were people involved with these institutions who suffered and whose lives were in danger and disrupted. I should like to shed a little light on one nun of Montivilliers and show how the Wars of Religion in the sixteenth century affected her life.

The Kingdom of France had become more and more divided by the religious question. Civil war erupted in May of 1562. Normandy with its strategic coastal position, easy access to foreign influences, and a large middle class already converted to Protestantism, quickly became a battle field in the war.[2] Huguenots took control of the major cities of Rouen, Le Havre, and Dieppe and other small fortified places along the Seine River Valley such as Tancarville.[3] Montivilliers, due to its location within the triangle of these three major Norman cities, was immediately engulfed in the violence. The Huguenots sacked parish churches, burned archives and destroyed images in the local churches. The abbey was also attacked, and the Abbess Guillemette de la Platiére escaped to her brother's Chateau d'Éspoisses, in the diocese of Langres, where she remained for more than a year.[4] Some of the inhabitants of Montivilliers, both Catholic and Protestant, took refuge in Le Havre.[5] Between May and the end of October, towns along the Seine River would be taken, sacked, and then retaken by both sides as they struggled for control of the valley, the vital link between Rouen and Le Havre for the Protestants and ultimately the route to Paris.[6]

The protestant leaders, hard pressed for ammunition and gold, signed the treaty of Hampton Court with the English, the terms of which surrendered Le Havre to the English for the much needed supplies and cash. The English took possession of the city in early October.

To better observe the Huguenots and English in Le Havre, Montivilliers became the headquarters for the German mercenary troops of Philip Rhinegrave, count of Salm, whose forces consisted of 6,000 men and 800 horses.[7] Their purpose was to secure the area around Le Havre and prepare for the seige of the town. The German Reiters, as they were called, were hated and feared by the Protestants,[8] but they were not necessarily considered protectors by the Catholics. In 1574, when Rouen was chosen by the King to be the headquarters for the feared Reiters, the city immediately dispatched an embassy to the King to plead with him to send the troops elsewhere.[9]

On October 26, after a bloody seige the Royal troops retook Rouen in the presence of Charles IX and Catherine de Medici. The city was pillaged for eight days before order was restored.[10]

On November 2, 1562, the English attacked the town of Montivilliers but were repulsed.[11] Orders from the German commander show that the countryside was being depleted of provisions by the army as well as by the refugees streaming into the village.[12] The dirth was compounded because the English in Le Havre expelled all Catholics from the city,[13] forcing them to take refuge in Montivilliers and other small towns. Huguenots, however, were not spared either; on January 1563, the English, preparing for a long seige, expelled all civilians from Le Havre. A fragile peace returned to Normandy in March when the Huguenots were accorded the right to practice their religion in non-fortified towns. Violence and assasination continued between the two sides, but they put aside most of their animosities to fight the English and retake Le Havre in July of 1563.

For over a year, from May 1562 until July 1563, the city of Montivilliers and the surrounding countryside was the battle ground for a civil war as well as occupation by English forces. The abbey was closed, but what had happened to the nuns? We know that the abbess escaped to the chateau of her brother, but what of the nuns who did not have this refuge?

I have the answer for at least one nun. In France in the sixteenth century contracts officially passed before a public notary; the notary was required to preserve a copy of the contract for future reference. The thrifty French *notariales*, who never threw anything away, preserved these copies until the twentieth century when they were deposited in the National Archives in Paris. These contracts constitute a little used treasure trove of information about ordinary people in France. While systematically searching through these contracts for the sixteenth century, I discovered a contract for a nun from the abbey of Montivilliers.

On October 29, 1562, three days after Rouen had been liberated by the royal troops, in fact, while it was still being pillaged and sacked by the troops, and three days before the English attacked Montivilliers, a contract was passed before a Parisian notary by one Pierre Brunier "procurateur en cour laic de parlement" and his wife Jehanne Morreau living in Nôtre Dames des Champs. In the contract[14] Jehanne the daughter is identified as having been a religious in the abbey and monastery of Nôtre Dame de Montivilliers in the country of Caux in Normandy. From internal evidence we know that Jehanne has been a professed nun for more than thirty years, so she must have been in her middle to late forties, or perhaps as old as fifty. Her parents must have been in their late sixties or early seventies; the father might have been even older. She must have entered the monastery before 1532 or during the abbacy of Quitére de Navarre, abbess from 1528 until 1536.[15] Ironically this abbess was a member of the royal house of Navarre, one of the strongest supporters of Protestantism.

From May to whenever Jehanne arrived in Paris sometime before October 29, the Norman countryside around Montivilliers
and the whole Seine River basin was the battleground of two opposing armies subject to the daily violence of a civil war animated
by religious convictions—perhaps one of the most unmerciful
kinds of war. Montivilliers is approximately 211 kilometers from
Paris. In peace time the easiest route for Jehanne to take from
Montivilliers to Paris would have been by boat on the Seine river.
This very river was, in fact, the center of fierce fighting because of
its strategic importance. Consequently, it is very doubtful that
Jehanne took the normal route to Paris. She probably took an
overland route, a far more dangerous and slow way to travel. But
however she got there or how long it took her, she was in Paris,
on October 29, 1562, before the notary.

The contract says that the daughter, having been professed more
than thirty years had always lived there (at the monastery of Montivilliers), and hoped to live and finish her days there.

> A short while before, the Huguenots and heretics and their
> accomplices and allies by force and violence had taken the
> land of Normandy and Caux, which is well known, and en
> tered by force of arms the said city of Montivilliers where
> the abbey is situated. In which they [the Huguenots] have
> broken and demolished all the images and crucifixes and
> saints which were there and totally profaned and ruined the
> church of the said abbey. They took all the ornaments, chal
> ices, and similar things that were there. Similarly the abbess
> and the religious have been constrained to leave and abandon
> the said monastery and to withdraw with their relatives and
> friends to avoid the forces and violence of the said Hugue
> nots and heretics because they were afraid.
>
> The said Jehanne Brunier by the aid and special grace of
> God and the great diligence and cost and expense of her said
> mother and father had come to the house of her mother and
> father to save her life and honor, disguised, badly dressed,
> and almost naked, having left all her things in the said abbey
> for the reasons and considerations mentioned.
>
> As they said, even though it is said that the said Jehanne
> Brunier their daughter had been constrained to abandon the
> said abbey and to leave everything she had there to save her
> life and honor to avoid the furor of the said Huguenots and

heretics such that if her said mother and father died before
her she would be constrained to beg for her maintenance
and life.[16]

Contracts are normally written in legal formulaic language which
allows us only occasionally to glimpse the human beings involved.
But here, I think, we can be moved by the story of a victim of a
long past war who had lived all her adult life in a monastery and
who now found herself, in her forties, destitute, terrified, and
forced to flee her home and way of life. She has somehow made
her way to Paris through warring armies and hostile people to arrive at the home of her aging parents.

With hindsight we know that the monastery would reopen a year
or two later, but one of the reasons I sketched briefly the progress of
the war around Montivilliers was to try and reproduce the at-
mosphere of uncertainty at the time the contract was written.

The parents came to the notary because of their concern for the
precarious position of their daughter. To alleviate her situation
they made a donation or gift to her: "donation entre vifs" is the
legal term.[17] Jehanne could obviously live with them until their
death, why did they not just leave her something in their will in
the event she had not returned to the abbey? Inheritance for non-
nobles was strictly controlled by the Paris customary law. Without going into all the complexities and nuances of the inheritance
laws, it can be said that the Parisian law operated under the principle that "you can not advantage one child over another," that is,
all children must inherit equally. The corrollary of that principle is
that parents are not free to leave their wealth to whomever and in
the amount that they pleased. They can only leave it equally to all
their children.[18] Once Jehanne was professed she could not inherit
anything more because whatever dowry she received on her entrance into the monastery was her inheritance.[19] She had had to
abandon that dowry when she fled the monastery. It was probably
stolen or destroyed by the Huguenots when they sacked the monastery. To support her now her parents must give her outright a
gift of money before they die, otherwise she cannot receive anything and she would be destitute.

This gift that the parents made to her to circumvent the inheritance laws of Paris would be Jehanne's to do with as she wished at

the time of the donation—if the parents did not put any conditions on the gift in the contract. So there were two things occurring in this contract. The parents were circumventing the inheritance laws of Paris, but they were also controlling the money.

First of all, what did they give Jehanne? They gave her sixty pounds annually of "rentes" or annuities on the Hotel de Ville, which she cannot give, alienate, or mortgage without the consent of her parents. I have found only four other contracts involving such gifts of annuities to nuns, and, of the four, three were for twenty-five pounds and the third was for fifty pounds.[20] On the basis of such a small number of contracts for this type of living it is impossible to know whether Jehanne's annuity was small, adequate, or lavish for nuns at that time. However, the contracts for salaries of teachers in colleges, that is, secondary schools, for about the same period of time range from forty to 100 pounds. This situates the value of the *rente* as far as a standard of living is concerned.[21]

Jehanne's parents gave her a measure of wheat every year from a farm they owned in the commune of Rungy. After their death she would have the right to occupy one room of her choice in their house for the duration of her life. For this room they gave her outright one bed, one smaller bed, covered with sheets and blankets. She also would receive a trestle table and chairs, two pillows, twelve sheets, twelve table cloths, two dozen napkins, a half dozen pillow cases, a dozen plates, a half dozen cuvettes, half a dozen pewter plates, a lead pot, three choppines (a type of measure), half a dozen candlesticks, and a tapestry decorated with their coat of arms. There is no mention of gold or silver or jewelry. We know that nuns at Montivilliers did in fact have silver at a slightly later period, because that is one of the things they agreed to give up under the reforming abbess Louise l'Hospital, abbess from 1596 until 1643.[22] They also agreed to have all their property in common, so presumably before then the sisters had had personal property which they could dispose of as they wished. Therefore the mere fact that her parents equipped a room for her in their house does not exclude the possibility that they would refurnish a room in the monastery for her if it should reopen. If that is the case, we have an idea of how nuns in the second half of the sixteenth century lived. Jehanne would not live in luxury, but she would be comfortable and with money to spend, since most of her physical needs were taken care of.

The contract ends with a very curious provision. "If the said Jehanne Brunier their said daughter dies without heirs, issue, and procreation of her in loyal and legitimate marriage where because afterwards she has found an honest husband by dispensation of her superior, that she was married, and the said dispensation had been well and properly made, as said in this case, if she has no children the measure of wheat and sixty pounds will belong to their other daughter Françoise Brunier and to the children of said Françoise and to nobody else. But if she has children, which come from a marriage as said before these children can inherit."

Legal contracts are drawn up by people to solve certain problems. The parties to the contract know what the problem is so that they do not have to state explicitly what the problem was in the contract. They only state what the solution was. In interpreting the contract we can only deduce what the problem was from the solution. The exact nature of the problem may not always be obvious.

It seems strange that parents of a nun professed for more than thirty years should provide for her children, albeit only if the children are legitimate and she has married with the consent of her superior. But if it is in the contract then we have to assume that there was a possibility that Jehanne would never return to the monastery and she might even marry. We could assume that she might not wish to return to the monastery because life was more pleasant outside the abbey or she had become a Protestant. But here, I think, we have to accept what the contract says. It specifically states that "she had always lived there [in the monastery] and hoped to live and finish her days there." So I do not think that Jehanne might refuse to return to the monastery. Parenthetically, I might add Catholic Paris was a strange place for a crypto-Protestant or renegade nun to take refuge.

Another contingency, which might have entered into their calculations, was that there was no guarantee that the abbey would reopen. Thirty years before, during the lifetime of the Brunier's, monasteries had been dissolved in England and Germany as well as other countries. If this should happen in France Jehanne would be taken care of.

Another possibility is that the monastery might not reopen whether France was Catholic or Protestant. Not only had the abbey been pillaged and suffered damage but its financial situation had been declining even before the war. The inflation of the sixteenth century was taking a severe toll on the revenues of the abbey, and its real as well as actual revenues were diminishing. If the abbey reopened it would need large amounts of capital to repair damage and replace stolen goods—all of this on inadequate revenues. If there was no increase in the abbey's revenues, it might not be able to reopen.[23]

The abbey followed the Benedictine *Rule* but it was not affiliated with any congregation, so no other monastery would be obligated to take Jehanne if Montivilliers did not reopen after the war.[24] So I think the problem the Bruniers were facing was that, if the abbey did not reopen, Jehanne needed support. In this case, unless she had legitimate children, she could only leave her money to her sister or the children of her sister. The possibility that she would have legitimate children as heirs is slight because of her age and the difficulty of getting dispensations. This effectively blocked Jehanne from willing her money to anyone outside the family.

There is a third possibility, however, which seems to me most likely. If she should go back to the monastery after the troubles are over, she would have furniture and an income to support her for the rest of her life. But the monastery will not permanently benefit from that money; when Jehanne should die it would revert back to the family.

This legal contract involved money and cannot tell us anything about the personality or the spirituality of Jehanne Brunier, although I think it does give us a glimpse of the hardships and suffering inflicted on religious in the civil wars. It also tells us something of the values of the French family in the sixteenth century: how they tried to take care of each member of the family, and how they tried to cope with external events that affected the family. The primary duty of the family was to see that each child was taken care of financially to the best of their ability according to their rank and station in life.

The Brunier family, bourgeoisie of Paris, had thought they had taken care of Jehanne, but the religious wars upset their calculations for her. But parental love and care still governed them, and she was not abandoned to live in distress or poverty after their death. They had taken care of her whether the monastery should reopen or not. But as good french bourgeoisie they were not letting that money leave the family and be alienated to a religious house or anybody else. Wars and heresies can come and go, but the proper Parisian bourgeoisie family would protect both the family and the family patrimony.

Western Michigan University

NOTES

1. Cottineau, Dom L-H., *Répertoire topo-bibliographique des abbayes et prieurés* (Mâcon, 1937–38), cols. 1958–60. Ernest Dumont, *L'Abbaye de Montivilliers* (Havre, 1876), p.20.

2. Borély, A.-E., *Histoire de la Ville du Havre et de son Ancien gouvernement* (Le Havre, 2 vols., 1880–1881), II, 21.

3. Amphoux, Henri, *Essai sur l'histoire du Protestantisme au Havre et dans ses environs* (Havre, 1894), p. 44; Achille Deville, *Histoire du Chateau et des sires de Tancarville* (Rouen, 1834, rprt. St Pierre-de-Salerne), (1980), p. 291

4. Dumont, Ernest, and Alphonse Martin, *Histoire de la ville de Montivilliers* (Fécamp, 1886), p. 219.

5. Borély, p. 63.

6. Borély, pp. 47–50; Deville, pp. 260–65.

7. Béze, Théodore de, *Histoire ecclésiastique des églises réformées au Royaume de France* (Paris, 3 vols., 1883–1889), VII, 882.

8. Borély, p. 74.

9. Benedict, Philip, *Rouen During the Wars of Religion* (Cambridge, 1981), p. 37.

10. Léonard, Émile, *Histoire de la Normandie* (4th ed., Paris, 1972) p. 91.

11. Dumont, *Histoire*, p. 220.

12. Deville, pp. 274–75.

13. Dumont, *Histoire*, p. 222.

14. M.C. LXXIII-27, October 29, 1562.

15. Dumont, *L'Abbaye*, p. 22.

16. M.C. LXXIII-27, October 29, 1562.

17. Richebourg, Charles A. Bourdot de, "Les Coutumes generales de la prevosté et vicomté de Paris, . . ." in *Nouveau Coutumier general, ou corps des Coutumes generales et particulieres de France, et des provinces connues sous le nom des Gaules* . . . (Paris, 1724), Tome III, pt. I, pp. 1–87. Chapitre VII, XCVII of the 1510 *coutumier* says: "Il est loisible à toute personne franche aagée & usant de ses droits, de donner & disposer par donation & disposition faite entre vifs, de ses heritages propres, ou conquests, à personne capable" (p. 8). The 1580 *coutumier* which incorporates the 1539 law says: "Il est loisible a toute personne aagée de vingt cinq ans accomplis et saine d'entendement, donner & disposer par donation et disposition faite entre vifs de tous ses meubles & heritages propres, acquests & conquests à personne capable" (p. 49).

18. Yver, Jean, *Egalité entre héritiers et exclusion des enfants dotés, essai de géographie coutumière* (Paris 1966). Emmanuel LeRoy Ladurie, "Système de la coutume" in *Le territoire de l'historien* I (Paris 1973), pp. 222–51, 224–27.

19. *Nouveau Coutumier general*, T. III, pt. I, CLII: "Religieux et religieuses profès ne succedent point à leurs parens, ne le monastere pour eux" (p. 11).

20. M.C. LXXIII–78, April 22, 1572; M.C. LXXIII–61, April 27, 1567; M.C. LXXIII–30, July 11, 1564; M.C. VIII–445, June 16, 1556 (for twenty-five £. but the girl also received 100 pounds for her clothes).

21. M.C. LXXIII–25, July 30, 1560 was for 200 pounds, but a second contract which follows it was for forty pounds for the same school. M.C. XLIX–55, May 30, 1556 was for 100 pounds, and M.C. XLIX–55, June 5, 1556 was for twenty-five escus de soleil dor.

22. Décultot, Gilbert, *L'Abbatiat de Louise de L'Hospital, 1596–1643: Montivilliers son prestigieux passé* (Rolleville, 1975), p. 19.

23. Bottin, Jacques, "Le temporel des abbayes de Montivilliers et de Saint-Ouen, 1550–1650," in *Les Abbayes de Normandie*, Actes du XIIIᵉ Congrès des Sociétés Historiques et Archéologiques de Normandie, Caudebec-en-Caux 1978, (Rouen, 1979), pp. 197–203. "La conjoncture, envisagée du point de vue de la seigneurie ecclésiastique (mais seulement elle?), est marquée par la succession de deux évolutions contradictoires: la premiére voit l'affaiblissement de l'institution, particulièrement sensible entre 1562 et 1595, elle est suivie d'une période de 'récupération' engagée dès la fin du XVIᵉ siècle à Montivilliers, quelques dizaines d'années plus tard a Saint-Ouen" (p. 200). "Ainsi entre 1555 et 1570 les dîmes perçues par l'abbaye de Montivilliers ont-elles perdu 25% de leur valeur nominale, c'est-à-dire bien davantage en réalité" (p. 201).

24. Priem, Georges, *Abbaye royale de Montivilliers* (Rouen, 1979), p. 7.

TABLE OF ABBREVIATIONS

General Abbreviations

AHDL	*Archives d'histoire doctrinale et litteraire du moyen-âge.* Paris, 1926–.
ASOC	*Analecta Sacri Ordinis Cisterciensis; Analecta Cisterciensia.* Rome 1945–.
CC	*Corpus Christianorum* series. Turnhout, Belgium, 1953–.
CCCM	*Corpus Christianorum, continuatio medievalis* series. Turnhout, Belgium, 1953–.
CCSL	*Corpus Christianorum, series latina.* Turnhout, Belgium, 1953–.
CF	*Cistercian Fathers* series. Spencer, Massachusetts; Washington, D.C.; Kalamazoo, Michigan, 1969–.
Cîteaux	*Cîteaux in de Nederlanden; Cîteaux: Commentarii cistercienses.* Westmalle, Belgium, 1950–.
Coll.	*Collectanea O.C.R.; Collectania cisterciensia.* Rome; Scourmont, Belgium, 1934–.
CS	*Cistercian Studies* series. Spencer, Massachusetts; Washington, D.C.; Kalamazoo, Michigan, 1969–.
CSEL	*Corpus scriptorum ecclesiasticorum latinorum* series. Vienna, 1866–.
CSt	*Cistercian Studies* (periodical). Chimay, Belgium, 1961–.
DHGE	*Dictionnaire d'histoire et de géographie ecclésiastique.* Paris, 1912–.
DSp	*Dictionnaire de Spiritualité.* Paris, 1932–.
MGH	*Monumenta Germaniae historica.*
MS	*Mediaeval Studies.* Toronto, 1939–.
PG	J.-P. Migne (ed.), *Patrologia graeca.* Paris, 1857–1866.

PL	J.-P. Migne (ed.), *Patrologia latina*. Paris, 1844– 1864.
PO	*Patrologia orientalis*. Paris, 1906–1976.
RAM	*Revue d'Ascétique et de Mystique*. Toulouse, 1920–.
RB	*Regula monachorum sancti Benedicti; Rule* of St Benedict.
R Ben.	*Revue Bénédictine*. Maredsous, Belgium, 1884–.
RHE	*Revue d'histoire ecclésiastique*. Louvain, Belgium, 1900–.
RTAM	*Recherches de théologie ancienne et médiévale*. Louvain, Belgium, 1929–.
SCh	*Sources chrétiennes* series. Paris, 1942–.
Trad.	*Traditio*. New York, 1943–.

The Works of the Cistercian Fathers: General

Ep	*Epistola;* Letter
Epp	*Epistolae;* Letters
Hom.	*Homilia*, Homily
S	*Sermo;* Sermon

The Works of Bernard of Clairvaux

SBOp	Jean Leclercq *et al.* (edd.), *Sancti Bernardi opera*. Rome: Editiones Cisterciensis, 8 vols. in 9, 1957– 1977.
Apo	*Apologia ad Guillelmum abbatem*
Csi	*De consideratione*
Ded	*Sermo in dedicatione ecclesiae*
Dil	*De diligendo Deo*
Div	*Sermones de diversis*
Hum	*De gradibus humilitatis et superbiae*
JB	*Sermo in nativitate sancti Ioannis Baptistae*
Miss	*Homilia super "missus est" in laudibus Virginis Matris*
SC	*Sermo in Cantica Canticorum*

The Works of William of St Thierry

Cant	*Expositio super Cantica Canticorum*
Contemp	*De contemplando Deo*
Ep frat	*Epistola (aurea) ad fratres de Monte Dei*
Med	*Meditativae orationes*
Nat am	*De natura et dignitate amoris*
Orat	*Oratio domni Willelmi*
Spec fid	*De sacramento altaris*

The Works of Aelred of Rievaulx

Gen Angl	*Genealogia regum Anglorum*
Iesu	*De Iesu puero duodenni*
Inst incl	*De institutione inclusarum*
Oner	*Sermones de oneribus*
Spec car	*Speculum caritatis*
Spir amic	*De spirituali amicitia*

The Works of Baldwin of Ford

Cf	*De commendatione fidei*
Sa	*De sacramento altaris*
Td	*Tractatus diversi*

Biblical Abbreviations

Am	*Amos*
Co	*Corinthians*
Dt	*Deuteronomy*
Ep	*Ephesians*
Ex	*Exodus*
Ezk	*Ezekiel*
Ezr	*Ezra*
Ga	*Galatians*
Gn	*Genesis*
Heb	*Hebrews*
Is	Isaiah

Jb	*Job*
Jl	*Joel*
Jn	*John*
Jr	*Jeremiah*
Lk	*Luke*
Mk	*Mark*
Mt	*Matthew*
P	*Peter*
Pr	*Proverbs*
Ps	*Psalms*
Qo	*Ecclesiastes*
Rm	*Romans*
Rv	*Revelation*
S	*Samuel*
Sg	*Song of Songs*
Si	*Ecclesiasticus*
Tb	*Tobit*
Th	*Thessalonians*
Tt	*Titus*

CISTERCIAN PUBLICATIONS INC.

Kalamazoo, Michigan

TITLES LISTING

THE CISTERCIAN FATHERS SERIES

Texts and Studies
in the
Monastic Tradition

Temporarily out of print   † *Forthcoming*

THE CISTERCIAN STUDIES SERIES

T 69995